A Sacred Thread

A Sacred Thread

Modern Transmission of Hindu Traditions in India and Abroad

Raymond Brady Williams, Editor

ANIMA
Publications

The cover photograph by photographer W. Richard Waghorne captures a scene at the Cultural Festival of India sponsored by the Bochasanwasi Swaminarayan Sanstha at Edison, New Jersey, in August of 1991. Asian-Indian immigrants thread their way around a replica of the Statue of Liberty constructed in India by Bengali artisans from bamboo strips and then reassembled in the United States. The scene illustrates three generations of immigrant families and modern adaptation of traditions. Mr. Waghorne is involved in a project to preserve photographic records of Hindu rituals and festivals in India and abroad.

Some material from Mark Juergensmeyer's book *Radhasoami Reality: Transmission of a Modern Faith* is used in his chapter in this book with the kind permission of Princeton University Press.

Cover design consultant, Vasant Nayak

Library of Congress Cataloging-in-Publication Data

A sacred thread: modern transmission of Hindu traditions in India and abroad/ Raymond Brady Williams, editor.
  p. cm.
  Includes bibliographical references and index.
  ISBN 0-89012-065-X
  1. Hinduism–History–20th century. 2. Hindu sects–History–20th century. 3. Hinduism–Missions–History–20th century.
  I. Williams, Raymond Brady.
  BL1151.5.S33 1992
  294.5–dc20   92-5733
                                                                         CIP

Printed in USA

Contents

II

Authors

Brahmviharidas Swami is a young sadhu of the Akshar Purushottam Swaminarayan Hindu movement. He was educated at Leicester, England, and gained admission to Oxford before he took vows as a sadhu in 1981. He has studied in India since then in the sect's School of Philosophy in Amdavad and is now associated with the newly-established Akshardham Center for Applied Research, Gandhinagar, India.

Douglas Brear taught in the Religion Department of the University of Leicester in Great Britain until recently. He conducted extensive research on Hindu immigrants in Great Britain, especially on the Swaminarayan Hindus. He is currently an independent scholar living in Finland.

John B. Carman is Parkman Professor of Divinity and Professor of Comparative Religion at Harvard University and sometime Director of the Center for the Study of World Religions. His early education was in India, and his Ph.D. is from Yale University. He is a specialist on Srivaisnavism and the thought of Ramanuja, and his book on *The Theology of Ramanuja* was published by Yale University Press. He was one of the directors of the Harvard, Chicago, Berkeley Seminars on the study of religion and the liberal arts.

William Cenkner is Dean of the School of Religious Studies at The Catholic University of America in Washington, D.C. He received the Ph.D. degree from Fordham University in 1969 and has written extensively on Hinduism and education. He is the author of a seminal work on the Sankaracaryas, *A Tradition of Teachers: Sankara and the Jagadgurus Today* (Motilal Banarsidass, 1983).

Fred W. Clothey was born in Madras, India, and received his higher education in the United States, including the Ph.D. from the University of Chicago. He is Professor and Chair of Religious Studies at the University of Pittsburgh. He is the recipient of several grants for research on Hinduism, including Fulbright Fellowships in 1978 and 1982. He has published and edited several books on Hinduism, including *Rhythm and Intent: Ritual Studies from South India*, and is the founding editor of *The Journal of Ritual Studies*. In 1990-91 he studied the religions of South Indian emigres in Bombay, Malaysia, and Singapore, to add to his extensive knowledge of Asian Indians in Pittsburgh.

John Y. Fenton was educated at Davidson College and Princeton University (Ph.D., 1962) and now teaches at Emory University. His recent research is on the Asian Indians in the United States, which is the topic of his book from Praeger Press, *Transplanting Religious Traditions: Asian Indians in America* (1988).

Dennis Hudson is Professor of Religion at Smith College. He was an undergraduate at Oberlin College and received the Ph.D. from Claremont Graduate School. He is a specialist on religion in Tamil Nadu, both on Hindu-Christian relations in the nineteenth century and on the Minaksi temple in Madurai, the latter the topic of his current research and forthcoming book.

Brian Hutchinson is a Methodist pastor in Randburg, South Africa. His Ph.D. dissertation at the University of South Africa was "The guru-devotee relationship in the Akshar-Purushotttam Swaminarayan Sampradaya" (1988).

Mark Juergensmeyer recently moved from the Graduate Theological Union in Berkeley to become Dean of the School of Hawaiian, Asian and Pacific Studies at the University of Hawaii. He has published widely in comparative religion and society in South Asia, including works on the Sikhs. His most recent book on the Radhasoami is published by Princeton University Press. An earlier translation of *Songs of the Saints of India* with John Stratton Hawley was published by Oxford University Press in 1988.

Vasudha Narayanan teaches in the Department of Religion at the University of Florida in Gainesville. Her degrees are from the Universities of Madras and Bombay in India, and she received the Ph.D. from Harvard University. She has published several works on Srivaisnavism and Tamil literature, including *The Way and the Goal: Expressions of Devotion in the Early Sri Vaisnava Tradition*. She is the recipient of a Guggenheim Fellowship for 1991-92.

K.K.A. Venkatachari is the Founding Director and Professor of the Ananthacharya Indological Research Institute in Bombay, India. He received a classical Sanskrit education in Tamil Nadu and later received the Ph.D. at Utrecht University. He has been the advisor and teacher of several American scholars in both Madras and Bombay in addition to the Ph.D. students in his institute. He has written and lectured extensively on Srivaisnava texts and philosophy.

Vivekjivandas Swami was born in Kenya and raised in London by immigrant parents. He received his religious education in the Akshar Purushottam Swaminarayan Temple in London as a youth and then joined the corps of sadhus. He has been studying and writing in the sect's School of Philosophy in Amdavad, and is now associated with the newly-established Akshardham Center for Applied Research, Gandhinagar, India.

Raymond Brady Williams is the Charles D. and Elizabeth S. LaFollette Distinguished Professor in the Humanities and Chair of the Department of Philosophy and Religion at Wabash College, where he began to teach in 1965 after completing the Ph.D. at the University of Chicago. He is the author of *A new face of Hinduism: the Swaminarayan religion* (1984) and *Religions of immigrants from India and Pakistan: new threads in the American tapestry* (1988), both published by Cambridge University Press, and several articles on modern Hinduism and the religions of immigrants from India. He serves on the Board of Directors of the American Academy of Religion.

Glenn Yocum is the Milo Connick Professor of Religion at Whittier College. He studied at Franklin and Marshall, Oxford, and Union Theological Seminary and received the Ph.D. from the University of Pennsylvania. He is the author of *Hymns to the Dancing Siva*, and editor of *Religious Festivals in South India and Sri Lanka* and *Structural Approaches to South Indian Studies*. He is Managing Editor of *Religious Studies Review*.

A Sacred Thread: Introduction

Raymond Brady Williams

A Hindu parent carefully places a sacred thread over the head and across the shoulder of the son in a ceremony of initiation. Then the boy dresses in the traditional garb of a student, symbolically ready to leave home for a period of wandering to study ancient wisdom in the "school of spiritual vagrancy." Now most often as part of the ritual, an uncle restrains the youth from leaving and urges him to remain at home and to study modern subjects in the local schools. Nevertheless, the sacred thread remains a symbol of the transmission of religious tradition through the stream of generations. Possession of a sacred thread admits the young person to the storehouse of ancient wisdom through the study of sacred texts, participation in rituals of home and temple, and acquaintance with learned saints and teachers. Thus, it is thought, a boy becomes a man with a solid identity, a clear focus on a definite tradition, and a secure place in a community.

Hindu tradition itself can be viewed as a variegated sacred thread made up of many strands woven in constantly evolving configurations by the work of centuries. A still snapshot catches only a small portion of the thread from a particular angle, and much of the rest is lost in the mists of the past, recovered only by observing the texture and colors of what remains at hand. Traditions of even the simplest of societies are amazingly complex, so it is no surprise that the traditions constituting what we call "Hinduism" are of bewildering complexity, resulting from the heterogeneity of the society in which they emerge and coalesce. Any person experiences directly only a small portion of a tradition, just as individuals in conversation use only a small fraction of the potential of their native language. The entire structure of a language is essential, however, for a single sentence to be spoken and understood. Transmission of tradition is essential to existence of humans as symbol creating and bearing creatures, but the shape of the tradition is as fragile as gossamer blown by the winds of time. Hence, the unending work of preserving, shaping, and transmitting tradition, especially religious tradition, is one of the most difficult and demanding tasks of any community or generation.

Chapters in this book focus on the four primary media for transmission of Hindu traditions: temples, rituals, texts, and exemplary persons. Societies transmit messages to themselves and to those outside through symbols shaped in elements of the material culture (temples), a gesture language organized in ceremonies of rituals understood as the communicative aspect of customary behavior (rituals), written and oral texts (sacred scripture), and persons who are thought to embody society's values (gurus). Hindu temples form messages in stone that enable devotees to read the sacred world and history at the same time they experience the sacred. Rituals are systems of communication made all the more powerful because they involve the whole person in actions that reinforce identity and commitment. Texts and their interpretations arrive as voices out of the past to shape the present and direct the future. All of this is orchestrated by persons who are invested by the tradition itself with authority as exemplars, interpreters and proponents of the tradition — by necessity both its conservers and its transformers.

Modernity is marked by rapid mobility and mass communication that greatly complicate the transmission of traditions. The resulting heterogeneity of society and the juxtaposition of a multiplicity of traditions, which is characterized as modern pluralism, require transformation of traditions to facilitate adaptation to modern circumstances. The process of change is rapid, and it is especially pronounced among immigrants, who face the double task of remembering the traditions from far away and increasingly long ago, renewing them in the new land of residence, and creating new traditions for themselves and their children.

The chapters that follow deal with the transmission of Hindu traditions in the modern period in India and abroad. Social change is rapid in India, so that emigrants returning for visits do not enter the same society that they left, and the wrenching change is even more dramatic in countries of Indian immigration, making the transmission of Hindu traditions there a more difficult process. Both the content of the tradition and the process of its transmission constitute the subject of this book. Themes prominent in these studies of the transmission of tradition are transformation of traditional religious institutions in the modern period in India and abroad, adaptations of educational programs of temples, monastic institutions, and schools, the importance of religious leaders and heads of sects in transforming traditions to meet modern demands, and changes in the process of disseminating and interpreting religious texts. Establishment of Hindu temples, schools, and institutes in Southeast Asia, Africa, Great Britain, and the United States represent valiant attempts of immigrants to preserve their identity and that of their children. Controversies accompany attempts to adapt traditional rituals and programs in new contexts. Religious leaders, both in India and in the United States, take up the difficult tasks of holding together the past with the future, the generations, and Hindus in India with those abroad, and incorporating new media of communication along with new interpretations.

All but two of the chapters in this collection were first presented and discussed in an academic conference on these challenges, "The Transmission of Religious Traditions in Times of Rapid Social Change," held in conjunction with a Cultural Festival of India, August 1991, at Middlesex County College in Edison, New Jersey. The authors are grateful for the opportunity provided by the Cultural Festival of India, sponsored by the Bochasanwasi Swaminarayan Sanstha and the Akshardham Center for Applied Research, to

discuss these chapters in the context of the Festival and to share
them with a wider audience in book form. The context of the
Cultural Festival is the reason that several of the chapters deal
explicitly with transmission of tradition in Swaminarayan Hinduism.

The Cultural Festival of India presented a vivid confirmation that
transmission of Hindu traditions is now an international phenomenon, stretching from India to Malaysia, Singapore, Africa,
Britain and the United States, as these chapters document. The
sacred thread stretches across seas as well as across generations, and
even though it is on occasion almost "bent out of shape" or
"stretched to the breaking point," it demonstrates a remarkable
strength and elasticity. Religious leaders and institutions adjust to
new demands, temples take new shapes and enshrine new, revised
symbolic worlds, rituals are recast, and sacred texts are interpreted as
the truth for new generations, who live lives that could not be
conceived by their spiritual ancestors.

In homes, temples, mathas, and schools in India and abroad new
generations of Hindus participate in investing others with the sacred
thread of Hindu traditions in a process that John Carman in his
keynote paper calls "handing down and reaching across." The
chapters that follow focus attention on that process of initiation into
the sacred thread of tradition.

As a result of the process of international transmission of tradition
and "reaching across," many Indian words have become regular parts
of English vocabulary; others remain for a time quite foreign. The
result is that any decision about the use of italics and diacritical
marks in the text seems arbitrary. The practice in this work is to
italicize the first appearance of words from Indian languages about
which some question may arise. Each such word then appears in the
glossary with diacritical marks and a brief definition or description.
Some variation in spelling results from transliteration from several
languages. Indian words, especially those closely associated with the
cultural tradition, will become increasingly common in the United
States and other places of continued Asian-Indian emigration.

1

Handing Down and Reaching Across Stability and Movement in Indian Religious Traditions

John B. Carman

Introduction: Tradition and Transmission

> The rich
> will make temples for Siva.
> What shall I,
> a poor man,
> do?
>
> My legs are pillars,
> the body the shrine,
> the head a cupola
> of gold.
>
> Listen, O lord of the meeting rivers,
> things standing shall fall,
> but the moving ever shall stay.[1]

Professor A. K. Ramanujan begins the introduction to his translation from Kannada of selected Virasaiva *vacanas* ("utterances" in blank verse) with this poem by the community's controversial founder, Basavanna. In some ways the sentiment here is not at all typical of the Hindu tradition as a whole, a tradition in which temples have been important for at least two thousand years, and, indeed, continue to be important to Hindus emigrating from India to various parts of the world, including North America.

The Virasaiva tradition has in fact come to include temple building and temple worship, but it has not forgotten the critique by its founder, a critique of a pious donation that only the wealthy could afford, and an alternative vision of the human body not only as the symbolic model for a temple, but as itself a worthy shrine for Lord Siva, the very god who disrupted the stable order of the old Vedic deities at its central point, the performance of the Vedic sacrifice. Both Basavanna's poem and the religious establishment that it criticizes are integral parts of Indian religious traditions, but I think the poem's last lines may shed light on a paradoxical juxtaposition in many of these traditions: *Sthavara* means standing, and we can hear its connection with such related words in English as status, static, stability, and establishment. *Jangama,* in contrast, comes from the verb "to go"; it signifies the homeless ascetic who walks from village to village, the disciple of Siva who also represents the Lord to his human worshipers; as their guru, he is to be regarded as Siva himself.[2] "Standing firm" and "moving about" are not only two sides of Indian religion; they are two sides of almost every religious tradition, traditions that so often claim to be permanent but that can go on living only by continuing to change.

The English word "tradition" is a noun; both its religious and its cultural use frequently suggest a deposit from the past. That noun comes, however, from the Latin verb *tradere,* which means both to "give away" and to "transmit." Transmit in Latin literally means "send across." I suggest that we might paraphrase both tradition and transmission with two verbal nouns: "handing down" and "reaching across." Transmission from one generation to the next can be positively or negatively regarded. "Hand-me-downs" are (or used to be) clothes passed on from older to younger children. They're not very welcome if you really want new clothes, but sometimes there is a special hand-me-down, a wedding dress that is worn one or even two generations later with pleasure and pride.

"Reaching across" might suggest a relay race, or the rapid transfer of the mail from one pony express rider to the next. The runners or riders change, but what they hand over stays the same. We can focus on that object changing hands, but we can also look at the process: at the effort and coordination needed to assure that the baton is not dropped, the mail not lost. Sometimes, however, the message itself must be translated because it is no longer intelligible or because it is being shared with people speaking a different language.

Glenn Yocum has with good reason used the word "coronation" to describe the installation of the new Sankaracarya at Sringeri. As he says, there is a crown adorned with real gold and real jewels. More importantly, a great deal of royal symbolism has become attached to this ruler of one branch of Sankara's order. We recall the European saying when a king dies: "The king is dead. Long live the king!" The funeral and the installation taken together affirm the continuity of the office and the inward identity of the old and new pontiff; only the external human form has changed. A coronation is transmission in the conservative sense of "handing down," yet it is also the authorization for a new reign.

Translation, on the other hand, is a risky "reaching across," one in which there is a real danger that continuity will be lost. Hindus have been much less willing than Buddhists and Jains to translate their scriptures or their ritual chants, not only because it is so difficult to translate verse or aphoristic puns, but also because Hindus doubt that the power in the sound of a word can be conveyed by a different sound in a different language. They have, however, retold their stories and sung new songs, and they have composed many commentaries on texts, which in a sense "translate" them for later generations.

We should look at both sides of religious traditions, the standing still and the moving along, when we consider the transmission of these traditions, especially in times of rapid social change. We also need to be aware of our differing perceptions of stability and movement, which often depend on whether we are looking at a par-

ticular tradition from the inside or the outside. Looking at this transmission of traditions as scholars does not mean we approach this
subject with total detachment. Indeed, we are all involved, though in
many different ways. We need to understand others' perceptions in
order better to understand our own, and vice versa, we need to
understand ourselves, including our own use of words, if our scholarly
conversation is to be more than talking to ourselves, if it is to
become a lens as well as a mirror, a means of reaching out to other
people's experience in a common world.

Combining the Multiple Strands in Indian Traditions

Many modern treatments of Indian religious history divide this
history into stages named for major scriptures like the Upanishads,
for major movements like *bhakti*, or the times of particular dynasties.
I think that the very Indian metaphor of the strands of a rope is more
interesting and more accurate. We can distinguish between these
strands for the sake of analysis, but the actual functioning traditions
have usually combined several of them, though, as in the case of the
Samkhya philosophy's analysis of material bodies, in each body one
strand may predominate.

There are many basic elements in Indian religion: forms of
religious practice that are undertaken with a fairly clear sense of the
intended result. Most of them can be followed in the context of one
of the major paths to final liberation: meritorious action (*karma*),
transcendent insight (*jnana*), or loving devotion (*bhakti*). I can do no
more than list these basic forms here:

  1) Sacrifices to local deities or guardian spirits of village, clan, and
tribe, often at times of danger or crisis;
  2) Vedic sacrifice to the gods and to the ancestors, both to insure
the regular rhythms of life and to celebrate grand new undertakings;
  3) Special journeys to special places such as a river crossing (*tirtha*),
which also symbolize spiritual "crossings";
  4) Ceremonial bathing to cleanse the soul's subtle body and ritual
purification through heat (*tapas*). Both can be undertaken literally in
external actions and at the same time interpreted as a spiritual transformation;

5) *Puja*: the worship of a divine image with offerings of fruits and flowers in order to secure the blessed vision (*darsana*) of the deity;

6) Singing the Lord's names with devotion, often to particular divine images in temples or home shrines, but also to an image in the devotee's mind, or even to God conceived without bodily form or personal qualities;

7) Ascetic practices, which include many forms of self-denial and bodily discipline;

8) Meditation, usually involving techniques of posture, breathing, and mental concentration and frequently part of a secret tradition, open only to a few qualified initiates.

Each of the major organized Hindu groups, and some other religious communities as well, combine a number of these basic forms or elements in distinctive ways, sometimes with considerable difference between one part of India and another. Animal sacrifices to local goddesses have their own low-caste priests in South India, and Brahmins stay as far away from such ceremonies as possible, while in Bengal, Brahmin priests perform animal sacrifices: they officiate at the goat sacrifices to Kali. Vedic ritual has for centuries been combined with puja in all parts of the country, but in different ways in the worship of Visnu and the worship of Siva. While the authority of the Vedas is accepted in theory even by many Hindus whose lives are hardly touched by Vedic ritual, it has been rejected, not only by Jains and Buddhists, but also by one important community of Siva-devotees in South India, the Virasaivas, and by such North Indian devotees of the formless God as Kabir and Nanak, the first of the Sikh gurus.

One particular group may be worth noting because they have been so influential in modern India: the Smarta Brahmins. Their name may indicate that they were once considered innovaters by more conservative Brahmins, for *smarta* comes from *smrti*, the secondary category of sacred texts, outside the Vedas, that includes the great epics and the manual of sacred law. In accepting other scripture as authoritative and in worshiping in image form five major Hindu deities, the Smartas have gone beyond the Vedas and Vedic. Any one of these five deities may be chosen by a Smarta individual or family as the focus of devotion: the personal form of the ultimate reality, Brahman.

For at least the past thousand years, however, the Smarta community has been a bastion of Vedic orthodoxy. In South India and some other regions, Smartas also have close ties with the Hindu monastic tradition and the philosophical school of Sankara. Smarta Brahmins have taken the lead in presenting a modernized form of Sankara's philosophy as the basic and most important statement of Hindu belief, one that defines "Hinduism" for most Westerners and English-speaking Hindus. Perhaps because Smarta Brahmins so often think of themselves as the leaders of Hinduism they have thus far written little about themselves as one distinct Hindu community. This makes it more difficult to recognize the importance of Smartas among Hindu immigrants in North America. Their distinctive social customs and religious practices are obscured by their claim to represent all Hindu practice and to expound the most profound Hindu philosophy.

The relation between different elements of the tradition has changed over the centuries. While renunciation continues its symbolic suggestion of a ritual death, a radical breach with ordinary lay society, some features of ascetic practice have become part of the religious life of many lay people, either on a regular basis or during special rituals or pilgrimage journeys. The "renouncers," moreover, often have an important leadership role with respect to lay Hindus, providing direct instruction and examples, and sometimes ritual leadership as well. One important example of this are the heads of the various monasteries who trace their lineage back to the "original" Sankara. They serve as spiritual consultants to large sections of the Smarta community as well as to other Hindus.

Some of the changes in Indian religious tradition may owe something to contact with Islam, especially in the medieval period, and with Christianity, especially in the modern period. Such influences are hard to demonstrate; they may have been exaggerated by some modern Christian and Muslim scholars, and they are often difficult to acknowledge by those within the Hindu communities. Such influences are most likely to occur in one of two situations: either contact at the point of greatest similarity, as in the meditation or devotion of particular groups, or borrowing from one's opponents in the process of defending oneself intellectually from "outside" influences.

There was also influence from Hindus on other religions, a fact that has been obscured by the conservatism of orthodox Hinduism in recent centuries and especially by the practice of "outcasting" those who had "crossed the seas." The Buddhist expansion into Southeast and East Asia is well known; there was also an extension of Hindu traditions to Southeast Asia, as far as Bali and Cambodia, both by the immigration of Hindu rulers and merchants and by the conversion of local inhabitants.

In many of these changes, both those developing internally and those stimulated by external factors, Brahmin leadership has been important. Although in some respects Brahmanical tradition became more rigid through the centuries, particularly with respect to certain regulations to insure ritual purity, in general Brahmins have shown remarkable flexibility in incorporating all the Indian religious elements mentioned above within a particular framework. Even so, their authority has not gone unchallenged by many Indian rulers, merchants, and artisans, in addition to the outright rejections of the Vedic tradition. Whether and in what way Brahmin leadership continues outside India is important for future developments among Hindu immigrants.

Some Factors in the Modern Transmission of Tradition

Many of the important mechanisms for the transmission of Indian religious traditions to other countries were developed in India in the nineteenth century. Some were quite consciously borrowed from Christian missionaries in the process of reacting to them. Dennis Hudson discusses the importance of printing books and establishing modern schools where such books could be studied. Arumuga Navalar, about whom he writes, was also involved in another characteristic activity of Protestant missionaries: translation. Two generations earlier the Serampore Baptist missionaries translated both the Christian scriptures and Hindu scriptures into Bengali and other languages, though for very different reasons, and printed all these books at the Serampore Press. Other missionaries, under the leadership of Alexander Duff, wanted to Christianize high-caste

Hindus gradually through an education in the English language that would expose them, not only to the Bible, in what was regarded as its most beautiful translation (the "King James" or Authorized Version), but to all English literature as well as to works of science and philosophy imbued with the value of European Christian civilization. Although Brahmanical objection to translating scriptures from Sanskrit to any other language remained, a growing number of Hindus read their own scriptures as well as the Bible in English translation. It became easier and easier, moreover, for European scholars to gain access to Vedic texts and their commentators, and some of this Western scholarly work, notably that of Paul Deussen in German and Max Müller in English, was studied by Hindus.

Dr. Venkatachari's paper takes up a question that is more difficult than first appears: "Can we pray in English?" Both the appropriateness of translating existing prayers and the difficulty of translating poetry need to be discussed. With the Protestant tradition of free prayer that has influenced Hindus in India as well as in English-speaking countries, it might seem that if you can speak in English you can pray in English. In fact, however, Christians composing "free prayers" try to use appropriate words, most of them coming originally from the Psalms in the Bible and from various post-biblical liturgical traditions. What difference does it make if Hindus express themselves in prayer with the vocabulary of Christian English? This situation mirrors that of Indian Christians praying with words that are often taken from Hindu *bhakti*. Christians in India have struggled with the question of making their religious language genuinely Indian, and they continue to differ as to whether they become in the process "Hindu-Christians." Does the use of English for Hindu prayers subtly produce a "Christian-Hindu" mindset for Hindu immigrants? If so, is this to be welcomed or deplored? Perhaps modern English, like the rest of Western culture, is so secularized that this question does not arise, but if this is the case, there may be an even bigger problem: adjusting to a world that is assumed to be devoid of any divine powers. In what direction should one pray in such a "brave new world"?

There are, to be sure, some more novel developments for Hindus, Jains, and Sikhs in North America. One is the adapting of the ritual calendar to new times and places. The other is the concentration in one building, or at least on one piece of land, of rituals and communal gatherings that in India would occur in quite separate places. There are similar developments in Singapore and in Kuala Lumpur, as Fred Clothey reports. What are brought together are not only temple rituals and domestic rites, but also, at least in some cases, rituals that are in India conducted in different temples consecrated to different deities and having different priests. This leads to our next point.

Some Problems in Transmitting Indian Tradition to North America

First of all, a small immigrant community does not have the luxury of building many different temples for different groups. Moreover, Indians have followed the example of other immigrants, who often view their ritual center as an appropriate place for domestic rituals and for social gatherings. Far away from India, various caste and regional differences often seem less important. Whether there is any problem in this change in the function of a temple is again a matter for discussion. There is also an important difference between the homeland and the "New World" that makes it more difficult to find the appropriate sacred space. Hindus are coming to a new land that is devoid of Hindu stories of previous appearances of Hindu deities. I grew up in Hyderabad State in a town named for "Hanuman's hill." I could easily imagine that typical Deccan hill of bare rock as a giant stone that Hanuman had dropped as he flew overhead, going south to Lanka. Where are there such places in North America, to say nothing of temple sites where a divine image has been discovered in the mud or beneath the surface of a pond? And where are the places where the Lord has mysteriously appeared and commanded that a temple be built? Land in the vicinity of American cities is expensive. Indian immigrants often have to buy whatever property is available and then concentrate their ritual efforts on making these places sacred.

Perhaps what will be a more serious problem is the new pressure for different sectarian groups to compromise in the interests of a larger harmony. The problem is precisely that those groups who are most dedicated and most willing to undertake the financial sacrifices necessary to build a temple are least inclined to give up their distinctive beliefs and practices in order to merge into a "least common denominator" form of "generic Hinduism." This does not mean that all these groups see themselves as intolerant or excluding those of inferior social status, but each may have a distinctive way of defining an inclusive religious community. Mark Juergensmeyer has described the effort of the Radhasoamis to create a community that is intellectually as well as socially accessible to people of different national backgrounds and yet quite distinctive.

Vasudha Narayanan has pointed to a very old difference between two Hindu interpretations of the icon or divine image. The prevalent interpretation in modern Hindu or neo-Vedantic teaching, perhaps in response to Islamic and Christian attacks on Hindu "idols," is that these images are symbols of Ultimate Reality, that Reality which not only has no bodily form but even transcends our mental conception of a personality. Many of the Hindu traditions, especially the Vaisnava tradition, that have motivated the construction of temples in North America and supervise their ritual performances, have, however, the very different conception of arcavatara, incarnation as a consecrated image that really contains the presence of the Lord. Dr. Narayanan rightly raises a question about a program of teaching for lay adherents that propounds the symbolic interpretation of images while the temple priests and their orthodox disciples continue to hold a very different view. Is this a theological dispute that should be brought out into the open, or would such debate reopen old wounds between Smartas and "sectarian" Hindus?

Another question, sometimes a sensitive question, needs to be mentioned. What are the relations between Indian immigrants and American converts to a variety of Eastern "new religions" or "cults"? So far it is only a few of the converts who have been subject to harassment or persecution. Immigrants sometimes find it hard to recognize these converts as "Hindus" and may be reluctant to make common cause with them, especially if that would endanger their fragile position in American society.

Finally, most Indian religious traditions share with many other religions the belief in some pronounced sacred hierarchy. All such views clash with the egalitarian ideology of American society. It is not that all Americans are actually treated as equals, but there is a strong conviction that they ought to be, and this conviction has made it possible to appeal to the general public, and to religious people in particular, to remove inequalities. Even those Indian religious groups that reject caste inequalities affirm elements of spiritual hierarchy. Will it be difficult for those of Indian background, especially after two or three generations in the United States, to accept the superior religious status of traditional religious leaders? This remains a question for each group in the next generation.

Scholarly Transmission of Indian Traditions

At the end of December 1989, a conference on Srivaisnava studies was held at the Ananthacharya Research Institute in Bombay, under the leadership of Dr. K. K. A. Venkatachari. At the last conference session, in the presence of many of us who were not Srivaisnavas, the scholars within the community voiced their serious concern about the future of the Srivaisnava tradition. Few sons of *acaryas* are now acquiring the traditional education in Sanskrit and Tamil, and fewer still are willing to spend their lives dependent on uncertain contributions from the remaining faithful disciples in the family's network of parishoners. Potential scholars and priests who have turned to secular employment often do not have the time to fulfill their ritual obligations or to continue their studies of traditional texts. Those students who do get the traditional education miss not only the economic advantages but also the cultural broadening of the alternative "modern" education. Why not, then, send all students first to modern schools? First, they would miss the years spent memorizing texts, which is so crucial to traditional scholarship. Second, even if they made the economic sacrifice of not getting a Bachelor of Science, the B.A. course in most colleges would give them only a brief exposure to Sanskrit and Tamil literature and to Indian philosophy.

There was general agreement that some drastic steps were called for, that what was at stake was the spiritual as well as the intellectual leadership of the community, but there was no agreement as to what should be done, apart from a call for a massive scholarship program to encourage boys and young men to take up traditional studies. I noted myself one new and hopeful development: the number of Srivaisnava women who have done doctoral studies with Dr. Venkatachari at the Institute. Some of the scholars present, moveover, had managed to combine traditional and modern education in a way that others might follow.

It was a privilege to be permitted to be present for this frank discussion, but by mentioning it I do not want to suggest that religious scholarship here in North America is in a much better state. Christian theological studies suffer from a similar bifurcation between the narrowness of more traditional training and the shallow treatment of past traditions by more modern approaches. Western studies of Asian cultures have recently been criticized for the faults of so-called "Orientalism." On the one hand, our supposedly impartial scientific approach has often masked involvement in both grosser and subtler dimensions of Western colonialism. On the other hand, those Western scholars who really do manage to stick to "pure scholarship" are accused of lack of concern with the "real issues" confronting the cultures and the religious communities they are studying.

We are all involved. While to a considerable extent we continue to be either insiders or outsiders to a tradition, we now live, not only in the same world, but often in the same city. John Fenton reminds us that within the last ten years, the number of South Asian students taking courses in religion in the United States has drastically increased, and both he and Fred Clothey emphasize that the academic study of religion could be important for the future development of all Indian religious communities in North America, not only in students' acquaintance with their own heritage, but also in their learning something about other religious communities as well, notably the various Christian communities.

Traditional Indian scholarship now has to be imported to North America, and most of the modern Indian scholars teaching here were trained in Indian universities and sometimes also in *pathasalas* (traditional religious schools). Do we expect that as the Indian community increases in size, such traditional schools will be started here, or do we expect that the scholarship of American Hindus will develop through their study in our religion departments? If it is the latter, then we really have to ask whether American "Religious Studies" can adequately prepare Hindu scholars in their own religious traditions.

One of the related questions is the one with which I began this paper: the relative importance of the standing and the moving in a religious tradition. Basavanna is an exception, and even in his own tradition, *jangama* came to be the standard name for a Virasaiva priest, who may be more mobile than other Hindu priests when he travels from village to village to visit his "parishoners" but who is also part of a religious "establishment." Moveover, when one views a tradition from the inside, no matter how dynamically it is conceived, there is always some constant. For each of the Virasaiva saints that constant is Lord Siva, addressed in each poem by the same favorite name. For Basavanna this name was "Lord of the Meeting Rivers," a reference to a particular shrine at a particular place.

There are some American scholars who can affirm that they are insiders to a particular Indian religious tradition, but they, too, are outsiders with regard to other Indian traditions. I hope that those of us who are outsiders can be so with respect and courtesy. The strength of all Western scholarship, going back to the Greek geographers and philosophers, is confidence in the intelligibility of all human experience, from whatever culture. Without believing in universals, at least in commonalities between cultures, we would not even inquire about other cultures. Sometimes, however, we get too confident about our Western definition of the supposed universal category and we insist, not only on translating, but on substituting our translation for the original. May we be preserved from such arrogance in our scholarship, even if — perhaps especially if — we have found a way to universalize some facet of Indian experience and share it with the world.

We need not be immobilized by past sins of Western orientalists, even if we cannot entirely avoid repeating them. It is one mark of the hospitality of India that some of these orientalists continue to be honored among the teachers of modern India. There is nothing inherently wrong, moreover, with any Western universalizing language, whether of depth psychology, sociology, or Christian theology, provided we can advance it with due caution and respect as a "tentative translation." There are, after all, universalizing discourses in Indian thought to which precisely the same cautions apply. As scholars in the modern world, we all need to translate; we cannot simply describe something in its own terms if we are to share significant meaning. It is such sharing of meaning in which we are engaged as scholars of Indian religions, both in South Asia and elsewhere. All of us face a new situation of "reaching across."

In Michelangelo's great painting of creation on the curved ceiling of the Sistine Chapel in Rome, it is God the Creator who reaches across the heavens towards the first human being in order to convey the gift of life. Genuine tradition, as the Hindu notion of the succession of Gurus affirms, goes back to a Divine beginning. We are neither at the beginning nor at the end but on the way, so for us "standing still" can be no more than a pause; the "reaching across" must continue, for "things standing shall fall, the moving ever shall stay."

PART I

2

Winning Souls for Siva
Arumuga Navalar's Transmission
of the Saiva Religion

Dennis Hudson

If a religious tradition is to move from one culture to another, its
transmitters must think about at least three questions. What defines
the tradition as a specific "religion" that can be transmitted? What
means may be used to communicate it to others? What is the rational
basis for extending it to people outside the culture of its origins? The
career of Arumuga Navalar of Jaffna (1822-1879) allows us to
glimpse the way a formulator of an important Hindu religion dealt
with those questions as he responded to challenges posed by colonial
British rule and aggressive Protestant missions. Yet in answering
those questions, he carried into modernity methods of transmission
more than a thousand years old. And he illustrates a pattern that
other Hindu religions would later follow as they moved throughout
the world.

Arumuga Navalar's primary concern was the salvation of souls
already born to the Saiva community, which acknowledges Siva as
the God of gods. Yet because of his work, others have taken the
religion to non-Saivas in the countries of Southeast Asia and
elsewhere. He worked to clarify "Saiva Orthodoxy" (*Saiva Siddhanta*)

as a religion distinct from others among the Tamils and he developed modern means to communicate it through the printed book, the modern school, and preachers. Although he never sought to convert non-Saivas to Siva, he did suggest a theology that provided others with a rational basis for transmitting it to anyone anywhere. One of its more influential expressions in North America today is the publication called *Hinduism Today*, an international journal addressing Hindus of all sorts from a monastery in Hawaii and a church in California, both founded by a man of European descent from Oakland, California. His newspaper seeks to unite Hindus around the world into an ecumenical community, but explicitly advocates "Saiva Orthodoxy."[1]

Arumuga Navalar's Life

Arumuga Navalar was born in 1822 in Nallur, a village in Jaffna, the Tamil-speaking northern peninsula of Sri Lanka across the Palk Strait from Tamil-speaking India. Since I have discussed the origins of his career elsewhere, I will summarize it briefly here.[2]

His name at birth was Nallur Arumuga Pillai and he was born to a literary Saiva family. At home he learned traditional Tamil literature and Saiva belief and practice, while in a Christian mission school he learned English. Eventually he was hired to teach Tamil and English at the Wesleyan Mission School in Jaffna. More importantly, from the age of nineteen he served as a Tamil scholar to Peter Percival, the missionary principal of the school. He assisted Percival in writing and editing Tamil treatises and hymns and in translating the prayerbook and the Bible. That career lasted eight years, a period during which, in a highly charged context of Protestant scholarship and Protestant campaigns against Saivism, Arumuga Pillai came to understand himself as Siva's devotee.

While working with Percival, Arumuga Pillai turned his considerable intellect to the *Saiva Agama* in its various Tamil modes and learned Sanskrit to read other Agama texts. Agama, Saivas believe, is a practice that Siva taught specifically for the degenerate Kali Yuga in which we live and has been handed down in unbroken continuity to this day. Agama acknowledges the authority of Veda, but modifies it by making its all-encompassing way of life called Dharma open to everyone through purifying initiations (diksa). He also applied his growing knowledge to the Christians and Saivas around him. He began to criticize Protestant thought and action anonymously through letters to the Christian periodical *Morning Star* (*Utaya Tarakai*). He participated in unsuccessful local efforts to establish a Veda-and-Agama school and then at age twenty-four began his own classes in the Saiva religion. At the same time he criticized the faulty worship of Siva. In 1846 during a festival of the Kandaswami Temple in Nallur, he antagonized certain factions among the Saivas when he advised the Temple's trustees that their rites violated Agama: The temple was irregularly constructed, it inappropriately housed a spear as the primary icon for Murugan, and the officiating Brahmins had not received the required Agama initiations.

In his twenty-sixth year Navalar adapted the methods of the Methodists to his own purposes. In December of 1847 he and a Smarta Brahmin friend began to preach on Friday nights at the Vaidisvara Temple in Vannarpannai. They openly criticized both the Christians and the Saiva trustees of Nallur's Kandaswamy Temple while they preached to men and women on how to be properly Saiva. Eventually those preaching sessions turned into a Methodist-like circuit that moved from village to village. Eight months later he opened his own school, called the "Saiva Splendor School" (*Saivaprakasa Vidyasala*), which met before and after his work with Percival in a house opposite the Vaidisvara Temple. A month later he left Percival's employment to devote full time to the school, which subsequently met in the temple's monastery (*matha*).

During the following year, 1849, Arumuga Pillai left the school in the hands of former pupils who were now teachers and, with a student and colleague named Sadasiva Pillai, left for Madras to purchase a printing press funded by local patrons. Sadasiva Pillai proved to be his indispensable co-worker throughout his career. On the way to Madras Arumuga Pillai was invited to the Saiva scholastic and monastic center of the time, the Tiruvavatuturai Atinam near Kumbhakonam (discussed briefly by Glenn Yocum elsewhere in this volume). The presiding monastic head knew of his work in Jaffna and to acknowledge his scholarship conferred on Arumuga Pillai the title, "The Learned" (Navalar). Thenceforth he was known as Arumuga Navalar.[3]

Arumuga Navalar and Sadasiva Pillai obtained a printing press in Madras which they took to Jaffna. Late in 1849 they established "The Preservation of Knowledge Press" (Vittiyanupalana Yantiram) near their Saiva school and from then on divided their efforts between publication and education. In 1858 Navalar returned to Madras to establish a second press that continues there to this day. In 1864 he established a "Saiva Splendor School" at Cidambaram near the temple that serves as the religion's cultic heart, which also continues to this day. Arumuga Navalar left India for good in 1870 and continued his vigorous publishing, teaching, and preaching activities in Sri Lanka until his death in 1879.

At his death Arumuga Navalar had published approximately seventy-four works, including twenty-three of his own. Notable among the latter are a three-part "Children's Primer" in prose for use in his Saiva school;[4] "The Way to Worship in a Siva Temple" for the instruction of Saivas in the fundamentals of puja;[5] "The Periya Puranam Rendered in Prose" that made Cekkilar's twelfth-century canonical lives of the saints available to the devout;[6] "The Abolition of the Abuse of Saivism," a lengthy guide for Saivas to use in refuting the attacks on Saivism by Protestant preachers;[7] and a "Saiva Catechism" of four hundred and eighteen questions and answers.[8] Due to works such as these, Arumuga Navalar is now regarded as the "father" of modern Tamil prose.[9]

Saivism as a Religion

Arumuga Navalar's career presents a clear example within South Asian history of the self-conscious articulation of a "religion." He referred to it in differing contexts as "Saivism" (Saivam), as "Saiva Observance" (Saiva Samayam), as "Saiva Orthodoxy" (Saiva Siddhanta), and as the "Dharma of Siva" (Siva Dharma).

His use of the word "samaya" to describe Saivism as "observance" comes close to thirteenth century English meanings of the word "religion": both share the primary sense of people voluntarily binding themselves to certain kinds of behavior because of their beliefs.[10] In the Saiva Samayam, the agreement to observe the rites and conduct appropriate to a devotee of Siva is made first through a series of initiations (*diksa*). The first is the initiation into observance, the Samaya-diksa, in which one receives the five-syllable mantra, "Sivaya-namah," for meditation and rites. The mode of life (*sadhana*) it requires carries obligations such as abstinence from liquor and meat in order to keep the bodily vessel containing the mantra pure. One may increase the degree of observance and one's understanding of its esoteric meanings by receiving the two other diksas in sequence, the Visesa-diksa and the Nirvana-diksa. One may even receive the Acarya-diksa that qualifies one to initiate others. Depending on personal piety, that sequence could lead to a "monk-like" state of discipline that Arumuga Navalar and Sadasiva Pillai themselves exemplified, that of a *naistika brahmacarin*, a permanently celibate scholar.

Initiation implies acceptance of the doctrines of the three eternal realities taught by "Saiva Orthodoxy": the Lord Siva (*pati*), the individual soul (*pasu*), and matter (*pasa*). It also requires devotion to one's teachers expressed through the rites of Guru Puja, to the linga or iconic "body" of Siva expressed through temple and domestic rites, and to the assembly of ascetics, saints, and devotees expressed through gifts (*dana*) and rites of feeding called Mahesvarar Puja. Those doctrines, objects of devotion, and rites come to the initiate through an unbroken tradition of persons and institutions that appeared in Bharata (South Asia), it is believed, at the beginning of the Kali Yuga from Siva himself and have been transmitted as Agama.

The Saiva Samaya is a religion that in the South Asian context can be distinguished clearly from the samayas of the Protestants, Catholics, Muslims, Buddhists, Jains, Vaisnavas, Smartas, Vaidikas, and more recent traditions such as the Samarasa Sanmarga taught by Ramalinga Swami. In that complex religious environment slowly being transformed by the colonial situation, Arumuga Navalar was concerned that the boundaries of the Saiva religion be clearly delineated in order that it be reformed, revived, and transmitted accurately.

Some members of South Asia's colonizing cultures aggressively demeaned all of Bharata's indigenous religions as "heathen." Navalar denied that status for Saivism by arguing its claim as the religion of "true being," by distinguishing it from classical and popular cults of animal sacrifice, and by insisting that its temple liturgies, doctrinal beliefs, and priestly leadership be reformed according to the coherent system of faith and practice that Siva had intended. It is hard not to see Protestant and Roman Catholic models interacting in his mind with the traditional heritage (parampara) of Saiva Orthodoxy. Let us briefly examine the three boundaries he drew for Saivism as a distinct religion, with attention to the theme of transmission.

Saivism as the Religion of "True Being"

Regarding Saivism's claim to be the religion that imparts "true being" (satsamayam), Arumuga Navalar addressed himself for the most part to Saivas rather than to missionaries. He did not argue points of theology so much as explain to people who considered themselves to be Saivas what Saiva theology and practice are. He taught the largely Velala and Brahmin upper classes how to view their own heritage and identity in ways that defused the accusation of "heathenism" lobbed by Christian Westerners and their converts. His exacting publications showed them that they had a scriptural heritage to rival the Bible and that their scriptural narratives written in poetry could be transformed accurately into an accessible prose Tamil in the same manner as the Protestants had translated the Bible into Tamil. Moreover, his educational efforts articulated a coherent Saiva monotheism that had its own standard by which to judge "heathenism."

In an 1878 writing, for example, Navalar explained that anything that is born and dies is a soul (pasu), which includes the three hundred and thirty million gods (deva) down to the smallest forms of life.[11] Whatever is not born and does not die is the master (pati), he explained. That master is singular and is the Lord Siva, for whom all souls are slaves (atimaikal). Any religion (samayam) that says others are supreme is not the Saiva religion and the belief that anyone is higher than or equal to Siva is blasphemy (droha). Many stupid people, he observed, say that the Saiva religion is the path that worships all the three hundred and thirty million devas as supreme, but since devas whirl in birth and death just like people, that is a complete blasphemy of the Saiva religion.

Siva's auspicious grace (*tiruvarul*), he continued, is not different from the Lord himself. It is the potency of Siva (*sivasakti*) known as Parvati. To show grace toward souls, Siva's potency emanates four male forms (*murti*) that are transcendent beings (*katavul*) rather than devas: Vinayaka, the elephant-headed ruler of obstacles; Subraminya, the ever-youthful warrior; Bhairava, the fearsomely radical ascetic; and Virabhadra, the terrifying manifestation of anger. In contrast to the worship of devas, the worship of any of those four is worship designated for the singular Lord Siva because they are forms of him. Of course from the Christian point of view, he noted, Saivas are heathens (*ajjnani*) because they do not know the true God, Jehovah; yet from the Saiva point of view the Christians are the heathens because they do not know the true God, Siva.

The Prohibition of Animal Sacrifice

In that same document Arumuga Navalar turned to the issue of animal sacrifice. Saiva Agama prohibits the killing of any living being in its rites despite the teaching of Veda to the contrary. Twenty-seven years earlier Navalar had published a traditional text against killing in the vedic sacrifices, the "Prohibition of Killing," which argued against animal slaughter practiced by those Brahmins who claimed to follow only Veda and not Agama (called Vaidika Brahmins).[12]

In this 1878 writing, however, Navalar rejected animal sacrifice as practiced according to local custom. He criticized the "stupid people" (*mutarkal*) who thought of themselves as belonging to the Saiva religion but offered victims to "wicked devas" (*tustadeva*).[13] In India, he then noted, many stupid people worship (*cevi*) at the entrances of Muslim mosques (*palli*) and in Lanka many donate to the Roman Catholic churches of Mary. All of them blaspheme against Siva, he said, and are "heathens" just like the Christians.

Navalar also observed in passing that ignorant people think that Saivism is the "Tamil religion" and that the temple of Siva is the "Tamil temple." But, he said, Tamil is the name of a language, not a religion. Such ignorance, he insisted, was the fault of Saiva leaders themselves because Saiva gurus wandered around claiming the privileges of their status without preaching the religion.

In Navalar's mind the Saiva Observance should be perceived by Saivas as a distinctly different religion from others indigenous to Bharata with which it nevertheless has much in common. On the one hand, Agama superseded Veda in authority so that the goat of the *agnistoma* sacrifice, for example, would have to be replaced by a non-animal substance if it were performed by Vaidika Brahmins who had received Agama initiation. On the other hand, the local devas who received offerings of goat, buffalo, and chicken at their shrines were not denied their reality, but assigned a "wicked" status and forced to be vegetarian, at least when fed by worshipers of Siva who knew what they were doing.

Now whether he intended it or not, Navalar's opposition to animal sacrifice helped Saivas to remain "true" while at the same time aligning themselves to modern sensibility. Having completely secularized the slaughter of animals, modern Western civilization had removed blood sacrifice from sacred acts other than war, except in the symbolic form of wine. Agama's prohibition of animal sacrifice, therefore, could be viewed by colonial Westerners as a sensibly "civilized" religious act even though done by "heathens."

Saivism as a Coherent System of Faith and Practice

Regarding Navalar's efforts to reform Saivism into a coherent system of faith and practice, it is here, I think, that we see his uniqueness. He did not fit the obvious traditional categories of Saiva religious leadership. He was a not a monk (*tampiran*), nor a priest, nor an acarya, nor a guru. He was a monk-like celibate scholar (*naistika brahmacarin*). He had received the third of the initiations, the Nirvana-diksa, and was committed to the daily liturgy it pre-scribed, but he held no official position within traditional Saiva insti-tutions. He was not a poet and he was attached to no matha and to no court.

What then was he? He was a scholar, devotee, and preacher who was vowed to celibate purity. He may in fact have represented a category of religious leader in South Asian history about which we know little, the "lay" celibate teacher committed to a discipline (*sadhana*) more ascetic than the householder but not yet the asceticism of the renunciant. Such figures do exist among the Buddhists and the Jains, and Arumuga Navalar may have exemplified that same position among the Saivas.[14] If so, then he assumed that role in order to be a "missionary" to Saivas and one not unlike the Protestant missionaries from Britain that he knew, although few if any of them would have thought of themselves as monk-like. The title of "The Learned" bestowed upon him by the religion's most esteemed scholar-monk of the day was the closest symbol of a Saiva ordination to his self-generated mission that he possessed.

Navalar's sense of mission appears to have emerged entirely through his personal intellectual, emotional, and moral response as a Jaffna youth to the denigration of Siva and Saivism that he experienced. Once generated, that sense of mission developed into maturity while he worked with Peter Percival in translating the Bible into Tamil. The coherent view of Saiva faith and practice that he had gained he later expounded in his influential pamphlet of 1858, "The Abolition of the Abuse of Saivism."

That pamphlet is interesting for the way it compares the coherent faith and practice of the Saivas with the coherent faith and practice of the Bible, mostly of the Israelites. On the one hand, by demonstrating the detailed similarities between the temple worship of Siva and the temple worship of Jehovah in the Bible, Navalar proved to Saivas that their own worship of the Siva linga in temples was, so to speak, "biblical." The missionaries could not rationally use their own sacred scripture to argue against Saiva worship, he maintained, because comparatively speaking they were too similar, they had too much in common. (Significantly, however, he did not attack the biblical practice of animal sacrifice; that omission helped him sustain his argument for similarity and its implied correlate that Saiva worship was "biblical.")

On the other hand, by demonstrating that the Protestant missionaries were themselves disobdient to Jehovah because they had forsaken the temple worship that he had commanded for all times in their own scriptures, he questioned their validity as accurate expounders of their own religion. He taught Saivas how to question the missionaries' interpretations of the Bible on the basis of the Bible itself, a rather effective way to diffuse Protestant preaching against Saivism. The clever Saiva who knew the pamphlet well, for example, could entangle the Protestant who was preaching in public against Saivism in the task of explaining on the spot the entire rationale of the Protestant Reformation.

Apart from presenting the Saiva religion as a coherent system that would withstand the assaults of the missionaries, Navalar also tried to make temple liturgies conform to Agama's doctrine and practice. He struggled with Vaidika Brahmins in Jaffna and in Cidambaram over that matter.

The Cidambaram temple illustrated the problem: The Diksitar priests of that cultic heart of Saivism viewed themselves as following liturgies of the Veda, not of the Agamas. Navalar believed that thousands of years earlier the original priests had been initiated Saivas and followed the Agamas. He insisted, therefore, that the Diksitars conform to Agama practice, which they of course refused. The issue was symbolized by goat-sacrifice, which Navalar successfully opposed, and by the shrine of the Sudra poet and saint, Cekkilar, which Navalar unsuccessfully tried to place within the Cidambaram temple for worship.

Aside from the issue of caste status in the religion (which we shall address below), the issue raises the complex fact of differing and overlapping liturgical schools in Saiva temples. Over the centuries, liturgical schools have been removed from some Siva temples and replaced by others (the Diksitars may have been imported to replace an earlier liturgy), and some liturgies have been subordinated to others within the same temple complex (the Vaikhanasa Agama addressed to Visnu has been subordinated to Diksitar rites addressed to Siva at Cidambaram). The process of liturgical change and variation is difficult to discern and requires study; it probably has to do with royal patronage of the same temple at differing times.

A complex liturgical history has complex theological implications. Being Vaidika, the Diksitar priests at Cidambaram, for example, could follow the theology of Sankara's Advaita Vedanta and believe that the Lord (*pati*) and the soul (*pasu*) are ultimately the same. At the same time, Saiva initiates could worship with the services of the

Diksitars at Cidambaram according to their own belief that the Lord and the soul are eternally distinguished in the joyous relation of slave to master. No doubt other theologies could be expressed there too.

Now in Western religious history, doctrine has tended to express itself through liturgy, so that doctrinal changes also give rise to liturgical changes. The Protestants and the Roman Catholics, with their differing approaches to the Eucharist, exemplified that fact in Sri Lanka and India. But a similar close connection of doctrine to liturgy does not appear to exist in South Asian temples. As Vasudha Narayanan points out in her chapter in this volume, the Pancaratra Agama (which is the Agama among Vaisnavas most like the Saiva Agama) is followed at the Venkatesvara Temple in Pittsburgh, yet the theology of the temple's publications tends to be neo-Vedanta and not Sri Vaisnava as traditionally understood.

Yet Arumuga Navalar, driven by his sense of mission, tried to make crystal clear what had to be transmitted liturgically. He tried to make temple liturgies, diksa, sadhana, and theology consistent with one another in a way that had not been customary at various Saiva temples for centuries, including the most important one at Cidambaram. That concern for coherence and consistency suggests not only Protestant and Roman Catholic models in his mind, but also the logic of transmission. Any effort consciously to conceive of a religion as a coherent whole and transmit the whole of it inevitably will run into the inconsistencies that history produces and memory then labels as "custom." The question then arises whether those customary inconsistencies have their own authority by virtue of their status as traditional practice (*valakkam*); if so, scriptural norms need not be applied literally or consistently everywhere. Navalar's answer to that question, however, was no: customary practice is completely subservient to the written authorities that express Siva's Agama.[15] In terms of the history of Christianity, we might say, he was more Protestant than Catholic, and more Tridentine than Byzantine.

Opposition to Ramalingaswami

A similar concern to define the Saiva religion as a coherent system engaged Arumuga Navalar in a dispute with the saintly siddha poet Ramalinga Pillai (now known as Ramalingaswami) that some Saivas today believe reflects negatively on the reformer.[16] The issue was connected to Navalar's conflict with the Diksitars who controlled the Cidambaram temple because some of the Diksitars venerated the advaitin Sankara and his "Mayavada" that Saiva Siddhanta found offensive and opposed Navalar's efforts on behalf of Agama, yet also took Ramalinga Pillai's teachings and siddha claims seriously. Explicitly, however, the issue for Navalar had to do with the canonical status of poems claimed to be "poems of grace" (arutpa), the technical term for Saiva Orthodoxy's revealed Tamil scripture. The controversy reveals a problem any religion faces that seeks to sustain a received standard of "orthodoxy" in the midst of religious creativity. It also reveals a "severe" quality in Arumuga Navalar's devotion to Saivism not unlike the "severe bhakti" (tivra bhakti) of Nayanars he admired.[17]

Just one year younger than Navalar, Ramalinga Pillai (1823-1874) had been born near Cidambaram, but after his father died he was raised in Madras by his mother and eldest brother. He showed unusual intellectual and devotional qualities as a child and received diksa from a Sivacarya. He developed special devotion to Murugan and to the Nayanar known as Tirujnanasambandar, whom he believed was Murugan's reincarnation.[18] At the age of nine, when he saw Murugan directly in a vision, he began to compose poems. By about the age of twelve he had written fifty two poems for Murugan and had given a public talk on Tirujnanasambandar at a private house in Madras.[19] From about age twelve Ramalinga Pillai wandered outside the city, spent much time in solitude, and devoted himself increasingly to the dancing Siva for whom he also composed poems. Followers gathered around him and often accompanied him for his daily temple worship and sought his guidance.

At the age of twenty-seven a marriage was arranged for him, but his wife died some months later (though Arumuga Navalar later repeated hearsay that said he had left her and that she was living at the time with a foreigner in Madras).[20] Prompted by increasing devotion to the dancing Siva, Ramalinga Pillai moved to Cidambaram in 1855, traveled around the south lecturing, and six years later settled in nearby Karunkuli. His experiences increasingly moved in the direction of the Tamil Siddhas. He claimed occult powers (*siddi*) such as alchemy in his poems, and his disciples spread word of his miracles. Navalar wrote that in June-July (Ani) of 1866, Ramalinga Pillai had promised Diksitars in the Cidambaram temple that he would give them two hundred thousand rupees from the wealth he had accumulated from alchemy for the purification of the Temple's Citsabha (perhaps another case of hearsay).[21]

In the meantime, Ramalinga Pillai's poems increasingly were being used for worship in temples and homes and by itinerant singers, and in some temples they replaced the sacred scripture of Saiva Orthodoxy, the "Tevaram."[22] The poet corresponded with followers in Madras, lectured in temple towns, worshiped in Cidambaram, and composed beautiful poems replete with esoteric meanings. His practice of compassion for the poor and ascetics in Karunkuli led him to write an essay on compassion as the essence of Dharma, two poetic appeals for charity from "the son of God," and essays on compassionate service.[23] (Like Arumuga Navalar, Ramalinga Pillai also shaped the development of Tamil prose.)[24]

By 1867 Ramalinga Pillai had formulated teachings called the "Samarasa Suddha Sanmarga" that he believed had been taught first by Tirujnanasambandar and he founded a guild to embody them.[25] In that same year he established the Satya Dharma Sala in a village he called Vadalur where everyday the poor were fed regardless of caste, gender, or religion and where he went to live.

The point of controversy for Arumuga Navalar did not arise out of those acts of compassionate service, but out of claims made regarding the divinely revealed nature of Ramalinga Pillai's poems that placed them on the level of the "Tevaram." Out of his own ecstatic experience Ramalinga Pillai taught a path in which he used the word "Sivam" to refer to the Ultimate. He experienced Sivam as Light and as the sound of the five-syllable mantra expressed as Siva's dance. Consistant as that was with Saiva Orthodoxy, he went beyond Agama to claim that it and Veda were equal means to an end (*Sivam*) that transcends both and that he had experienced that end directly. Having passed through all the levels of sadhana (*carya, kriya, yoga, jnana*) by means of the Light-that-is-grace (*aruljyoti*), he had gone beyond them and now embodied deathlessness.[26]

Believing that Ramalinga Pillai's poems were created out of a direct experience of *aruljyoti* and were thus "poems of grace" (*arutpa*) like those of the Nayanars, his disciples called him the "Boundless Giver of the Splendor of Divine Grace" (*Tiruvarut-prakasa-vallalar*) and his songs the "Auspicious Poems of Grace" (*Tirvarutpa*). Accordingly, in 1867 they published four collections of his poems under the title "Poems of Grace" (*arutpa*), a title that Arumuga Navalar and other Saivas found offensive because it implied equality to the Saiva Siddhanta canon called "Arutpa." Later, during an important day of worship, Diksitar supporters of Ramalinga Pillai held a meeting within the Great Hall (*Perambalam*) of the Cidambaram temple to hear him explain the doctrines of his "Path of True Being" (*Sanmarga*).[27] That meeting prompted Arumuga Navalar to hold a meeting elsewhere in the town to refute Ramalinga Pillai's path and his Diksitar supporters. As various public disputations followed, two lawsuits emerged.[28]

Arumuga Navalar sued first. He claimed Ramalinga Pillai had slandered him while teaching in the Cidambaram temple. Even though Ramalinga Pillai testified that the words of slander were not his, Navalar nevertheless pressed the suit. Yet in the course of the proceedings, when Ramalinga Pillai entered the court dressed simply in two pieces of cloth, people stood to honor him and Arumuga Navalar stood as well. When the judge asked why he stood up when it was he who had brought the suit, Navalar replied that it was customary to stand for a great man (*periyavar*). The judge dismissed the suit. The slanderous words, it appears, were those of some men around Ramalinga Pillai who intentionally wanted to stir up the angry and impatient Navalar, which they had nicely succeeded in doing.[29]

The second suit was brought by some of Ramalinga Pillai's Diksitar supporters. They brought criminal charges against Navalar that Navalar in fact thought would succeed against him. His "severe love" for Saivism then revealed itself in a scene that shows the degree to which his sense of identity was inseparable from his career as evangelistic reformer. On the day he was to be examined in court, we are told, he gave the crystal linga that he used for worship according to his Nirvana-diksa to Sadasiva Pillai; he said that if he lost the case that day he would kill himself and that Sadasiva Pillai should immerse the linga in the Ganges. Instead, the judge exonerated Navalar and fined the Diksitars fifty rupees.[30] In the meantime, Arumuga Navalar attacked the authority claimed for Ramalinga Pillai through a tract that appeared in November-December (Karttikai) of 1869 entitled "Refutation of the Spurious Arutpa" (*Poliyarutpa maruppu*). He published it under a pseudonym, which he had done also for other works in other contexts.[31] Perhaps he hid his identity this time in order to speak freely without compromising his status in court.

Nearly a year before Navalar had written the pamphlet, heads of mathas and various scholars who met in Madurai had confirmed the invalidity of Ramalinga Pillai's use of "Arutpa" for his poems; Navalar included a letter reporting that fact at the end of the tract. He summarized his lengthy arguments as follows. He wrote the tract, he said, to show that the following were *not* true: that Ramalinga Pillai was learned in everything even though he had never studied; that he had had a direct vision of Siva; that he had received auspicious grace; that he dispensed that grace to others; that he was able to perform miracles; and that he knew alchemy. He also argued that it was ridiculous to give him the title "Boundless Giver of the Splendor of Divine Grace" and to call his songs "Auspicious Poems of Grace." They were all merely disguises that Ramalinga Pillai and his students wore, he said, to deceive people and to become falsely famous in order to fill their stomachs.[32]

That rather severe, though not unreasonable, attack on Ramalinga Pillai somehow has to be reconciled with the story of his standing in court out of deference to the poet as a "great man" (*periyavar*). Was Navalar insincere in his courtroom gesture? Was it a clever ploy in a legal game? More likely I think it was his genuine response in a charged public context to the charisma of an ascetic and compassionate poet whose exceptional devotion to Siva he respected but whom, in his own zealous bhakti, he genuinely regarded as a threat to the integrity of Saiva Orthodoxy.

Transmission Through the Printed Book

One of Arumuga Navalar's earliest acts was to establish his own printing press adjacent to his school in Jaffna. To understand the sig-

nificance of that act in 1849, we need to consider the nature of the
traditional palmleaf book and the colonial context of the press in
India for nearly three hundred years.

The traditional transmission of Tamil literature had been a simple
though relatively costly matter for the elite from earliest times.[33]
Written literature was primarily poetry not understood by most
people and no commonly understood style of prose had been used.
Poets were sponsored by the wealthy and usually functioned within
the framework of a worldview based on Dharma. Composed
mentally, poems and their prose glosses and commentaries were
written with a stylus onto single palmleaves that were then tied with
strings into a book. Authors and patrons kept those costly books in
private libraries, either at home or in monasteries (*matha*), and they
survived only if succeeding generations neither ignored nor destroyed
them, but instead oiled the leaves and transcribed them when
necessary.

In contrast, the art of printing with its potential for relatively
inexpensive mass distribution of literature had arrived from Europe
in 1556 at Goa on the southwest coast. The first book printed in
India in an Indian language was a Tamil book printed in Quilon
twenty-two years later. From there printing and type cutting traveled
southward along the coast to Cochin, around the peninsular tip, and
northward up the east coast to Tranquebar where, in 1714, the Four
Gospels and Acts appeared from a Tamil press.

Neverthless, printing remained in the hands of the colonial elite.
Indians were not allowed to license printing presses from the
European colonizers until 1835.[34] European scholars, who depended
heavily on the Indian scholars they supervised, were the first to
authorize the printing of traditional Tamil texts. They did so out of
cultural and historical interests born from their role as rulers. They
studied and printed Tamil literature as Christians or as humanists
who were spreading modernity through their government, not as
Saivas or Vaisnavas or Muslims attempting to preserve and nurture
their traditions while being modernized.

Once printing presses were licensed, however, Tamils indigenized
them quickly. In 1865 — sixteen years after Navalar had established
the "Preservation of Knowledge Press" in Jaffna and seven years after

he went to Madras to establish its companion press — John Murdoch estimated that there were at least a dozen Tamil presses in Madras, three or four of iron, the rest of wood. Usually, he said, families owned a press in common and divided the labor between printing and sales, paying the Madras Presidency fifty rupees annually for a license. Tamil books were sold in the bazaars of every town in the country. Local missionaries identified two hundred and ninety-six titles for sale in Kumbhakonam, four hundred and thirty in Tanjore, and one hundred eighty-four in Tinnevelly, few if any by Christians, but no doubt including Navalar's products. Book-hawkers walked the towns in the early part of the day and resorted to the bazaars in the afternoon and evening, where (referring probably to Madras) Murdoch noted that twenty-five hawkers could be seen sitting behind their piles of books. Book-hawkers also visited neighbourhood temples on festival days.[35] Tamil literature had moved into the marketplace of modernity.

That transmission from inscribed palmleaves to printed paper had its influence on the way Tamil religious cultures developed and transmitted themselves — a subject that needs more study. Printed books implied new contexts for old texts (Navalar's school and his curriculum for example) and those new contexts in turn shaped interpretations of those texts and of the traditions that produced them, and new developments in the means to transmit them. Catechisms for beliefs, manuals for worship, essays about the religious life, religious journalism, new religious organizations, and concepts such as "Hinduism" spring to mind as some of the consequences. The process is visible in our own North American experience in the temples Hindus build, in their study of themselves through traditional texts subjected to historical criticism in modern universities, and in the ideas about Hindu identity spread worldwide by international organizations and publications like *Hinduism Today*.

Arumuga Navalar is acknowledged as the originating force among Hindus of the recovery and transmission of traditional Tamil literature through the printed book free of European control. In 1944, V. K. Kalyanasundara Mudaliyar described his role through the metaphor of building a temple for Siva, linking Navalar with his most distinguished heirs. Arumuga Navalar, he said, laid the foundation for publishing the literature, Damodharam Pillai raised its walls, and Swaminatha Aiyar capped it with a sloping roof and became that temple's servant.[36] As it turns out, Navalar built a small temple in Cidambaram that extends that metaphor by enshrining the literary "ground" on which he had laid his foundation. In turn, his followers have used it to venerate his career as the modern continuation of that ancient literary dynamic within Saivism.

In February of 1984 I went to Cidambaram to gather material about Arumuga Navalar. In 1864 he had established a Saiva school there like the one in Jaffna called the "Saiva Splendor School" (*Saivaprakasa Vidyasala*), which continues today as a government high school following a secular curriculum. The Sri Arumuga Navalar Saivaprakasa Vidyasala Trust, whose headquarters are in Jaffna, has its office in the house Navalar once occupied, shared with a branch of the Parasakti Society of Madras.[37] Mr. K. Swaminathan, retired principal of the school and a member of the Trust, was a gracious and generous source of information about Arumuga Navalar's career in Cidambaram.

Mr. Swaminathan took me to a pond or tank built by an ascetic named Jnanaprakasa Muni, an ancestor of Navalar who had lived in the mid-seventeenth century. Jnanaprakasa Muni is interesting in his own right, but especially so as Navalar's ancestor, because he was an ancestral model of Saiva piety and moral conviction, of learning, and of independence that Navalar appears to have followed.[38] The story about him portrays a devout Saiva caught between the cattle-eating barbarism of Europeans to the south and Brahmin orthoprax disdain for Sudras to the north, a situation that Arumuga Navalar addressed in his own way two hundred year later. His innate intellect and Agama Saivism at Cidambaram resolved his dilemma and allowed him to express his devotion to Siva creatively and effectively — an apt model for his Navalar descendant.

Arumuga Navalar and Jnanaprakasa Muni belonged to the Karkatta Velala class (*varna*), a class that Dharmasastra classified for ritual purposes as Sudra.[39] According to traditional memory, they descended in the linage of Pandimalavar who had long ago gone to Jaffna from the Pandya country and was instrumental in the founding of Nallur, the town of Navalar's birth.[40]

According to the story about Jnanaprakasa Muni, after the Portuguese annexed the kingdom of Jaffna in 1619, each house in Jaffna was required to supply a sleek cow to feed the resident Portuguese official.[41] When Jnanaprakasa Muni's turn came, he feared that the sin of giving a cow to be killed for food would fall on his head and fled during the night. He left Sri Lanka and went to the great temple of Siva in Cidambaram. There he bathed in the temple's Siva Ganga Tank and for forty-five days ate pepper and pure water and worshiped "The Mother Beloved of Siva" (*Sivakami Ammai*) at the garbhagrha.

Once he had received Sivakami's Ammai's grace, the story continued, Jnanaprakasa Muni left Cidambaram and went north to Gauda (Bengal). There he encountered a Brahmin sannyasi who daily taught logic, grammar, Mimamsa, and other subjects to a few boys and instructed them in chanting Veda. Jnanaprakasa Muni went there regularly, stood at a distance, and memorized what he heard. Yet because it was forbidden for a Brahmin sannyasi to talk with a Sudra, the sannyasi never once spoke to him.

One day the sannyasi examined his pupils, but they only stood silently, unable to answer any of his questions. The sannyasi then thought of the young man who had listened so attentively to his lessons and wondered if he remembered them. So he summoned Jnanaprakasa Muni and told him, "Repeat everything you have heard since the first day you came here." To everyone's astonishment he immediately repeated it all. The Brahmin sannyasi then told him (a Sudra), "You alone are a Brahmin," and subsequently taught him logic, grammar and other texts in sequence. He then instructed him to return to the Tamil country to work.

Accordingly, Jnanaprakasa Muni returned to the south and received the ochre robe (*kavi*) at the scholarly monastery (*atinam*) in Tiruvannamalai, where he studied Siddhanta texts thoroughly. He then moved to Cidambaram. There he wrote commentaries on Sanskrit texts in Sanskrit, translated Tamil texts into Sanskrit, and wrote a Tamil gloss on *Civajnanacittiyar*, all of which he handed over to the Tiruvannamalai Atinam.[42] He also built the tank now named after him in Cidambaram where he later died.

Mr. Swaminathan then took me to a small temple standing

adjacent to that Jnanaprakasar tank that Arumuga Navalar had built before his own death. The primary icon (*mulamurti*) in its garbhagrha is of Cekkilar, the twelfth-century Velala author of the *Periya Puranam*, a long sequence of poems that relates the lives of the Saiva saints known as Nayanars.[43] According to Mr. Swaminathan, Navalar erected the temple only after his attempts to have an icon of Cekkilar enshrined within the authoritative Cidambaram Siva temple had failed. The Cidambaram Diksitars, who are the temple's Vaidika priests, opposed Cekkilar's icon, he said, because Cekkilar was not a Brahmin. Like Arumuga Navalar and his ancestor Jnanaprakasa Muni, Cekkilar too was classified for ritual purposes as Sudra. Unlike Agama, the liturgy of the Cidambaram Siva temple did not incorporate Sudra saints for worship.[44]

Mr. Swaminathan took me inside the Cekkilar temple, and two Saiva Brahmins who conduct rites according to the Saiva Agama appeared. Over the doorway of the garbhagrha was written *Siva Cekkilar* in Tamil script. On the outer wall flanking the garbhagrha, to the mulamurti's right, was a sculpture of Jnanaprakasa Muni. Inside the garbhagrha the immoveable Cekkilar icon was flanked by three moveable festival images (*utsavamurti*). To Cekkilar's right was an image of him and below it a small image of Kacciyappa Sivacaryar, the fourteenth-century Siva Brahmin who wrote the Tamil *Kanda Puranam*.[45] To the mulamurti's left, much to my surprise, was an image of Arumuga Navalar himself.

Instructed by Mr. Swaminathan, the attending priests brought the Navalar image to the doorway of the garbhagrha to give me a better view. The image is made of the traditional five metals, Mr. Swaminathan said, and was commissioned about fifteen years earlier from contributions made by the teachers in Navalar's school and by others. That was around the same time that the government replaced Navalar's curriculum with its secular curriculum (as if his iconic embodiment compensated for his curricular dis-embodiment). Every year on Navalar's death day, Mr. Swaminathan said, students and teachers process his image around Cidambaram in an act of guru puja. They do so to gain Navalar's blessings because they believe he now resides in Siva's realm and can bestow blessings in the way that any servant of the Lord can, such as a Nayanar. The worship of

Arumuga Navalar as a saint may in fact have been going on for many decades; at least since 1910 his anniversary has been celebrated in Jaffna along with those of the Nayanars.[46]

The handsome image of Navalar is barechested and carved with rudraksa beads around the head and neck. Its lower body sits in a crosslegged seated posture appropriate for instruction, but at the time it was wrapped in a cloth garment. Navalar is sculpted holding an

Movable image of Arumuga Navalar at the Cekkilar Temple near the Jnanaprakasar Tank in Cidambaram, Tamilnadu. Photo by Dennis Hudson, 1984, courtesy of K. Swaminathan of the Arumuga Navalar Trust.

open printed book with both hands and the details of its spinal binding are depicted faithfully. His open-eyed gaze is directed straight forward, as if he has just looked up from the book whose contents he is expounding. That book symbolizes all the approximately seventy-four writings he had published during his life, but in this context it symbolizes most notably his impressive and influential prose renderings of Cekkilar's *Periya Puranam* (1852) and of an initial portion of Kacciyappa Sivacaryar's *Kanda Puranam* (1861).

The Rational Basis for Transmitting Saivism

That icon of Arumuga Navalar holding a book is a telling statement about the Saiva Samayam and Navalar's role in transmitting it. Placed in the *garbhagrha* housing a Sudra saint and served by Agama Brahmins, it also signifies a crucial difference between the classical vedic view of dharma and the agamic view, a difference that in principle allows the Saiva Samayam to take root in the lands of the "barbarians" (*mlecca*), as in Hawaii and California today, and in Cambodia, Thailand, Java, and Bali in centuries past.

Like the Pancaratra Agama of the Vaisnavas, the Saiva Agama significantly revises the steretyped class and caste relations of Dharmasastra. That image of a Sudra, after all, was cast for worship according to Agama, and is used for worship that is led by Siva Brahmins in a temple where the mulamurti is also of a Sudra. Moreover, the *Periya Puranam* by the Sudra Cekkilar celebrates Siva's revelation of himself through men and women of all classes, and in the vernacular rather than in Sanskrit. Furthermore, the *Kanda Puranam* is a Siva Brahmin's vernacular rewriting of a portion of a Sanskrit Purana that makes esoteric mysteries accessible to the Tamil literati. And of course the works by Jnanaprakasa Muni, also enshrined by the temple, include translations of Tamil Siddhanta texts into a Sanskrit that he, as a Sudra, had learned from a Brahmin sannyasi in Bengal despite his ritual status and by virtue of his brilliant intellect, texts that he then taught to Brahmins and Sudras, to priests and monks.[47] Agama appears to turn Veda's hierarchical order topsy-turvy.

Nevertheless, although Agama does alter the ritual distinctions and rankings of Dharma, it does not erase them nor its hierarchical order — it does not advocate the modern idea of social equality. Navalar explained Agama's approach to ritual hierarchy in an essay entitled "Varna" in his "Children's Primer."[48] Sudras, he wrote, are qualified to recite Itihasa, Purana, and other smrti texts, to hear the meaning of Veda, and to perform all of the "five great sacrifices" (*panca-maha-yajna*) except for the recitation of Veda: tarpana offerings to the ancestors, homa offerings to the devas, bali offerings to the bhutas, and offerings of food to human guests.[49] They are also qualified to give the ritual gifts called "dana." Sudras, he explained, fall into two types, the "Sudra of true being" (sat-sudra) and the "Sudra of untrue being" (asat-sudra). Those who do not consume liquor and meat and keep the religious conduct prescribed by the texts are the "Sudras of true being" and are equal in ritual status to Vaisyas.

Sudras, he then said, may also be "twice-born." They receive the sacred thread (upanayana) during Agama's diksa at any appropriate age, while the other three varnas receive it only at stipulated ages. Prior to thread investiture, a Brahmin is a Sudra, and if after receiving the thread he does not recite Veda, he is disqualified for any vedic rite and becomes a Sudra again.

Moreover, those among all four varnas who become twice-born by means of diksa have the authority to recite Agama. Indeed, males among all four varnas (save the "Sudras of untrue being") may become acaryas.[50] If Brahmins, Ksatriyas, and Vaisyas receive diksa they must practice both vedic and agamic rites, but if they do not receive diksa, they must practice only vedic rites. Sudras and females of all four varnas, if they have received diksa, must practice agamic rites; and there is no benefit from diksa for anyone if agamic rites are not practiced. Those Sudras who have not received diksa may perform rites for others, but with hymns to the devas containing reverential homage and without Om.

Navalar then noted an interesting inversion in the ritual hierarchy. Initiated Sudras who practice the way of life appropriate to them are deemed "Brahmins," while initiated Brahmins who do not practice the way of life appropriate to them are deemed "Sudras." In fact, in each of the four varnas there are equivalents to the Brahmins, Ksatriyas, Vaisya, and Sudras, depending on their conduct. Conduct that is appropriate to one's varna and one's agamic status determines one's ranking, so that in a given context, a "Sudra" Brahmin presumably would be deemed inferior in status to a "Brahmin" Sudra.

Moreover, there is a place in Saivism for the "fifth varna." Members of castes (jati) not innately pure enough for the diksas prescribed in Agama for the four classes (varna), Navalar said, may nevertheless go to an acarya, receive the "sacred glance" (tirunokkam) and other diksas suitable to their status, learn of God's qualities, visualize him, praise him, and worship him by circumambulating (though not entering) his temple. They too will attain the supreme end (*paragati*) and be saved.[51] Agama, then, does have a means for incorporating "unclean" peoples wherever they may be and a rational basis for transmitting and establishing itself anywhere in the world.

Interestingly, evidence for that Agama modification of Dharmasastra appears from about 200 B.C.E., the influence, I think, of the Saiva and Pancaratra Agamas that had been spreading throughout the subcontinent from before that period.[52] Arumuga Navalar brought that ancient Agama heritage as it had developed in the Tamil south into the modern context through the printed book held so dramatically in the hands of his icon. The printed volume is Navalar's iconic *laksana*, his distinguishing sign. That murti, commissioned by teachers from the high school Navalar had founded at the cultic center of Saiva Orthodoxy, represents the Saiva curriculum that he had composed, printed, and taught in that school but that had now been abandoned under a secular government. By Siva's grace working through Arumuga Navalar's printed books, the murti says, word of Siva continues to be heard despite secularizing modernity. And that word is now read and heard outside Bharata.

Saiva "Evangelicalism"

Arumuga Navalar, I think, can be described as an "evangelical" Saiva similar in signifcant ways to the "evangelical" Protestants who ran the missions in Jaffna and India. George M. Marsden has defined "evangelicanism" as a largely Protestant movement that emphasises the Bible as authoritative and reliable, eternal salvation as possible only by personal regeneration, and a spiritually transformed life that is expressed through moral conduct, personal devotion such as Bible reading and prayer, and zeal for evangelism and missions.[53] Following that definition, Navalar appears to have been an "evangelical" Saiva, though given that he worked only among Saivas, a contemporary parallel may be found less among Protestants than among Jews, in the Lubavitcher "evangelicalism" that Hasidic Jews address to other Jews urging greater observance of Torah.

Arumuga Navalar relied exclusively on the scriptures of the Saiva Samaya as authoritative and described the canon repeatedly in his writings. He assumed that the canon is unquestionably reliable as a source of history, just as the nineteenth century missionaries did regarding their canon. Over and over he reiterated the belief that individual devotion to Siva would be born from the knowledge of scripture and that devotion would lead to individual salvation (mutti).

As he repeatedly wrote, his purpose was to allow Saivas to attain the salvation that they had available to them by virtue of being born in a Saiva culture, itself the product of merit generated through countless previous lives no longer remembered. In contrast to the goals attained through any other religion, which are subject to birth and death, he said, Saivism grants participation in the penultimate stages of emancipation in which the soul resides in Siva's realm (salokam), or near Siva (samipam), or with Siva's form (sarupyam), and then the final and complete emancipation in which the soul unites with Siva (sayujyam). Simply because they had been born in Bharata among Saivas, individuals already stood at the doorway that would end all further births, and they should seize the opportunity. He taught that personal regeneration brought about through devotion expressed itself through a devout life of strict ritual and moral observance, which he described in detail. His criticism of the immoral behaviour of the Saiva upper class (prabhu) according to Agama's norms was equal to anything the Methodists said about them according to the Bible's norms.[54]

Given those similarities, how did Arumuga Navalar fit in terms of zeal for world-wide evangelism and missions? He was deeply concerned for evangelism among the Saivas in Tamil-speaking Sri Lanka and India; that was the entire purpose of his career of printing, teaching, and preaching. Yet, so far as I know, he never wrote about missions to non-Saivas. He did not write about converting the Buddhists of Sri Lanka or the Vaisnavas or the Christian missionaries. Whatever the reason, he did not see the whole of Bharata as his mission field and he was not out to win non-Saiva souls to Siva. In that respect he was like Martin Luther in sixteenth century Europe, who addressed himself only to Christians and Jews; the colonizing context that stimulated the later British and American evangelicals and their missions had not yet developed. Similarly, in the nineteenth century the economic and social involvement of South Asians in Europe and North America through education and emigration had not yet developed.

That did not mean, however, that in Navalar's mind Saivism had no personal relevance to non-Saivas and could not be transmitted to them for their personal salvation by others. He made that point in 1872 in an essay entitled "Jaffna's Religious Situation."[55] Let me conclude by describing the theology his few remarks suggested.

A Theology of Transmission

Navalar noted that a few Protestant missionaries had lived in Jaffna for a long time and had frequently debated Saiva Siddhanta scholars. Through those debates they had learned of Saiva Siddhanta truth and had become Saivas inwardly. That fact, he said, was known at the time by insightful men who had socialized and talked with those missionaries in private. Even while they thought they were preaching Christian doctrine to us, he observed, they had spent their time as they did now and would do in the future, like the "Buddhist" saint named Sakya Nayanar in the *Periya Puranam*.

We will understand Navalar's theological point if we look at the story of Sakya Nayanar. He was Velala who had became distressed about birth and death and went to Kanchipuram and became a Buddhist.[56] That is why he bears the name "Sakya." Yet while wearing the garb of a bhiksu and studying Buddhist treatises, he realized that Buddhism is not the true religion. By the grace of Siva he realized instead that Saivism is true. He learned of souls comprised of a consciousness that knows another but not themselves; he learned of material karmas called merits and sins generated by those souls; he learned of pleasure and pain as fruits bestowed by those karmas; and he learned of the Lord comprised of a self-knowing consciousness who is the giver of those fruits. He learned that those realities are taught in the treatises of the Saiva Samayam and he learned that the Lord who taught those treatises is the Supreme Siva himself. Sakya Nayanar believed that essentially one was never to forget the auspicious feet of the Supreme Siva no matter where one was or what one wore, so he did not renounce his Buddhist dress even though he went on visualizing the Supreme Siva continuously with great love.

Now Sakya Nayanar knew the greatness of Siva's embodiment as the piller-like linga and so he decided that each day he would eat only after he had worshiped it. He then saw a linga in a nearby open space and overwhelming bhakti arose within him. Without knowing what he was doing, he picked up a burnt brick lying nearby and smashed the linga with it. That pleased the Supreme Siva, just as careless acts of little children please their fathers.

The next day while returning to fulfill his religious duty, Sakya Nayanar thought about his motivation when he had smashed the linga with a stone the day before. He concluded that the idea had come from the grace of the Supreme Siva himself; and since it was therefore auspicious service, he would do it that way everyday. He knew, after all, that all doings are Siva's doings. Each day he performed that rite of smashing the linga with brick lovingly and without fail and thereby fulfilled a highly outstanding and auspicious service to the Supreme Siva who permeates all souls and observes all things.

One day, however, Siva's auspicious grace caused the Nayanar to forget. When he began to eat he suddenly remembered, "I completely forgot to smash my Lord today." With overwhelming desire he dashed out, approached Siva's linga, picked up a brick, and while he was smashing the linga the Supreme Siva, who gets caught in the net of bhakti, appeared in the sky seated on the Bull with the Mother, Umadevi, and took him to his auspicious feet.

That story encodes a theology for the transmission of the Saiva religion to "barbarians" (*mlecca*). To the outside observer the Nayanar looked like a Buddhist because of his dress and he acted like a Buddhist who was antagonistic toward Saivism because each day he smashed the linga with a brick. The contemporaneous parallel for Navalar was the missionary who dressed like a European and preached Christian doctrine to "smash" Saivism. To the inside observer, however, the smashing of the linga by the "Buddhist" had actually been prompted by Siva, it expressed pure love for Siva, and it gave Siva pleasure. What was crucial, then, was not external appearance and behavior, but internal motivation and intention.

Analogously, the missionary who in his innermost being was a Saiva was prompted by Siva to preach Christian doctrine that "smashed" Saivism as a way to express his love for Siva, and it gave Siva pleasure. All doings, whether the smashing of the linga with a stone or blasphemous talk of Siva are the doings of the Supreme Siva who distributes the fruits of karmas generated by souls. In other words, "Siva bashing" by the Protestants in Sri Lanka and India, even when they did not know it, was actually the doings of the Supreme Siva for his own purposes.

The crucial question, then, was whether the missionary knew the meaning of the linga he "smashed" in the way that Sakya Nayanar did. As Arumuga Navalar lamented, "Other heathen missionaries do not know the wind that wafts fragrance from those who know Saiva Siddhanta and what will they do? It is too bad, too bad."[57] He lamented their fate because they intentionally blasphemed against Siva and would go to purgatory, whereas the "Saivas" in the guise of missionaries only appeared to blaspheme against Siva and like Sakya Nayanar might attain Siva's feet. Only Siva truly knows the motivation behind one's deeds and he distributes their fruits.

Siva mixes himself with all souls everywhere. That is why it is possible for even a mlecca Protestant missionary inwardly to be "Saiva" if he has learned accurately of Saiva Orthodoxy. And the accurate knowledge of Saivism was Navalar's overriding concern. How can anyone among the Saivas, much less among its opponents, know the Saiva religion if it is not defined accurately, is not expounded clearly, and is not made easily available even to dispute? How can it be made easily available except by printing its scriptures and by teaching them? How can one begin to print them and to teach them without a printing press and without a school and without a curriculum? Arumuga Navalar's answer to those questions was his life's work. With it, in V. K. Kalyanasundara Mudaliyar's metaphor, he laid the foundation for a clearly defined and well proportioned Siva temple constructed from Tamil literature. Later scholars built an elegant structure upon that foundation, creating a Siva temple that now could be transmitted to anyone anywhere in the world. And wherever it was taken it could be received truly, because Siva's grace permeates all souls and operates everywhere.

Arumuga Navalar died in 1879. That was fourteen years before Swami Vivekananda made his public appearance in Chicago to expound the wisdom of Veda. It was sixty years before Siva Yogaswami in Jaffna gave diksa to a twenty-two year old dancer from Oakland, California, whom he gave the name Subramuniya. That Western initiate later spread Saivism as Sivaya Subramuniyaswami, the founder of the Saiva Siddhanta Church, head of the Kauai Aadhinam (*Atinam*) in Hawaii, and the publisher of *Hinduism Today*.

3

The Sankaracarya of Kanchi and the Kamaksi Temple as Ritual Center

William Cenkner

Sri Vedantadesika (b. 1268 C.E.) sings of the excellence of Kanchi (Kacci) as one of the seven sacred cities of India:

> Like a crow that flies in every direction and falls exhausted, I being unable to obtain the Lord through devotion, etc., have sought as refuge the grace of the Lord Hastigiri of Kacci which is the most important of the seven cities that give salvation.[1]

Kanchi served as a religious site for both Hindus and Buddhists. Old Tamil Sangam literature acknowledged such uniqueness: "The city of Kacci is an ancient one (mudur) in the world whose excellence is enhanced by festivals celebrated by followers of various faiths."[2] Naccinarikiniyar commenting on the text above attests to the celebration of various faiths in Kanchi.[3] From classical times, moreover, arose the notion of Siva-Kanchi and Visnu-Kanchi. It was not only a site of pilgrimage and devotion, but Appar refers to Kanchi as a place of boundless learning. Classical literature also has Kanchi as a center of ascetical practices.[4]

Kanchi in Sanskrit (*oddiyanam*) is a belt worn as an ornament around the waist of a woman. The ornament surrounds the navel.

Kanchi is the navel of the world in the *Kancimahatmyam* and the *Kamaksivilasam*.[5] Sivajnana Munivar refers to Kanchi as the navel-region of the Goddess Earth.[6] The navel of the earth is a mythic symbol of the center of the world, the *axis mundi*. It is at the center, the navel, observes Mircea Eliade, that a breakthrough occurs in communicating with the gods and heaven.[7]

There are many temples dedicated to Siva and Visnu in Kanchi but the goddess Kamaksi temple holds central importance in so far as the deities of other temples when taken in procession always circumambulate through the main streets around the temple of Kamaksi. All the temples, moreover, have their main *gopurams* facing the Kamaksi temple. The centrality of Kamaksi is also evident from the fact that no other Saiva temple in Kanchi has a sanctuary for the goddess whereas throughout Tamilnadu most Saiva temples have the goddess enthroned.

Some of the major works dealing with the life of Adi Sankara refer to his establishing a temple for Kamaksi at Kanchi and consecrating the *sricakra* there.[8] Tradition also credits him with placing his close disciple, Suresvara, as the *acarya* of his lineage in Kanchi.[9] A similar pattern appears in the other major centers attributed to Sankara at Sringeri, Dwarka, Puri, and Badrinath: namely, the presence of a temple, the centrality of the goddess, a major disciple as the first acarya, and the creation of a seat of learning, asceticism, and devotion. What distinguishes these major Sankara institutions is that they are from the beginning known as *vidyapiths*, seats of learning. They are neither merely mathas for ascetics nor temple sites for devotion and pilgrimage. The religious centers, attributed to Sankara, are not in imitation of the Buddhist monastic *sangha* but are a transformation of the Brahmanic *gotra* and household *sampradayas* and as such are dominated by the Sankara lineage. They are distinguished as vidyapiths where wisdom, both traditional and popular knowledge, is sought within an ascetical, devotional, and a hierarchical context dominated by an acarya, and in the case of the major mathas, by a *jagadguru*.

It is important, I believe, to place an analysis of the Kanchi Vidyapith of the reigning Sankaracarya within the context of the Kamaksi temple and the socio-anthropological integration taking place within pilgrimage, temple life, and piety. What happens in temple life is a key in understanding the role and function of a living Sankaracarya.

The Vidyapith of Kanchi Today

The Vidyapith of Kanchi today is a formidable institution extending not only throughout South India but further into Orissa, Karnataka, Maharashtra, and even Delhi itself. Although each vidyapith is a complex of temple, matha, library, educational center, and guest house, Kanchi has extended these configurations.[10] The Kamaksi temple of Kanchi has undergone restoration in the past years. Yet, the Kamakoti matha remains quite modest, with a place for public worship, offices, and a simple residential quarter for the guru and his immediate attendants. The educational center has not been present in Kanchi for several generations. The Kanchi matha supports a few young students in Sanskrit studies at New Kanchi. The major school at Kumbakonam, which was the seat of the Kanchi Sankaracarya in the not too distant past, usually has twenty to thirty students and three or four *pandits* as principal teachers. The junior acarya of Kanchi, who is now the reigning Sankaracarya, was educated within these traditional schools, following Vedic and Sanskrit educational models, under the supervision of the Sankaracarya but drawing freely upon experts in various areas of Sanskrit study. The education is highly traditional with emphasis on Vedic recitation and understanding, and, as the years advance, a broader and deeper understanding of the Vedanta tradition.

The Kanchi institution has educational centers elsewhere with one highly successful center in Puri, the seat of another major Sankaracarya. Likewise, secondary mathas exist which are governed by the Kanchi institution and which may be used by the acarya when out of Kanchi or used by the elderly retired acarya, such as his past residences in Maharashtra or Karnataka. The junior acarya, moreover, consecrated an enormous temple in March 1986, in Allahabad, Uttar Pradesh, that depicts the supreme god of the Saiva, Vaisnava, and Sakta sects.[11] This major temple of Hindu unitarianism, begun in 1969, reflects how the vitality and centrality of

Kanchi has been diffused somewhat widely. In fact, I conclude from the above that a principle of diffusion is operative in this Sankara institution in terms of its religious center, in this case the Kamaksi temple of Kanchi.[12]

The Living Acaryas of Kanchi

The senior acarya of Kanchi was born in 1894 as Svaminathan Sastri in Viluppuran, a village south of Madras.[13] At the age of thirteen in 1907, the youth became Sri Candrasekharendra Sarasvati, the 68th Jagadguru of the Kamakoti Pitha. The child-guru studied Sanskrit and the Vedanta with learned teachers of the matha until 1919, while still a young man, when he began his public ministry that continued vigorously for half a century. Like all the major Sankaracaryas, he became a peripatetic guru travelling the length and breadth of India. On tour the acarya was not only a preceptor, giving practical advice on *dharma* issues, but also a leader of *puja*, exemplifying to the people the need to fulfill daily ritual. The acarya spent most of his life on tour: from 1919 to 1938, mostly on foot which ended with six months of silence, and from 1943 to 1950 in South India with long periods in and around Madras. One detects the distinctive mark of this teacher, namely an itinerant figure who seldom taught within the site of the matha or temple itself. It has been said that what a deity is to the temple, the guru is to the matha.[14] This is clearly evident in Kanchi where the reverence and worship given in the Kamaksi temple is not in the least mitigated in the matha or wherever the acarya may be when reverence and worship is given to him.

In 1954, Sri Candrasekharendra selected his successor, a youth of nineteen who remained his personal disciple for the next twenty-five years. The junior swamiji, as he was then called, became the reigning acarya in 1970 and is known as Sri Jayendra Sarasvati. By 1972, he made a "tour of victory" on foot to Varanasi, Delhi, and throughout North India, and he continued to travel throughout ensuing years, especially in South India. The same itinerant teaching pattern emerges. The ceremonial activity on public tour demonstrates the unity of the Hindu community, for it brings together people from all sectors of society, rich and poor, high caste and low caste, literate and illiterate, Saiva and Vaisnava. Just as the Kamaksi temple and the Kamakoti Vidyapith are sites of religious and social diffusion, so too a principle of diffusion is operative as the acarya fulfills the task of the itinerant figure.

His Holiness Jagadguru Sri Sankaracarya Chandrasekharendra Sarasvati of the Kanchi Vidyapitha. Born in 1894, he lives in silence and retirement as the senior acharya of Kanchi, along with the reigning acharya, Sri Jayendra Sarasvati.

I have written elsewhere that the acarya is both the bearer of an institutionalism and an institution unto himself.[15] He carries with him the centuries of the Sankara lineage in terms of teaching, worship, and life; but he is also an institution because a guru is to the matha what a deity is to the temple. Just as the Kamaksi temple is a living institution as well as the bearer of an institutionalism, so too the guru is a living institution due to charisma, personal wisdom and piety, while bearing an institutionalism of traditional wisdom and the Sankara lineage. The principle of social and personal diffusion seen operative in temple life is also operative most explicitly in the life of this itinerant teacher.

The Socio-religious Context

It requires a closer look at the various levels of contextualization in order to further specify the particular character of the Kamaksi temple of Kanchi. Kanchi remains an important pilgrimage site with its temples open both to those who have come to worship their *ista-devata* and to those who seek *darsana* from the deities. There is a "mixing" of the deities in Kanchi, especially in pilgrimage experiences. As a local or subregional pilgrimage center, one or another temple in Kanchi may have preference, but as a regional or supraregional center the devotee is far less discrete. Since Kanchi has been closely associated with the life of Adi Sankara and the Sankara tradition, there is also evidence of the "mixing" or diffusion of this particular tradition in the temples of Kanchi and the environs. There is evidence, for example, that sculptures of a *samnyasi* with an *eka-danda* adorning many of the sectarian temples of Kanchi are identified with Adi Sankara.[16] One wonders why a sculpture relating to *advaita-siddhanta* appears in a temple under control of the followers of Ramanuja. One may conclude that the craftsmen in and around Kanchi were familiar with and devoted to the tradition of Adi Sankara to such a degree that they sculptured his figure in the prominent temples of Kanchi without regard to the deity to whom they were dedicated or the sect to which the temple itself was consecrated.[17] A type of social "mixing" takes place in a temple city and even within a particular pilgrimage site. Goddess temples have consistently attracted the scheduled castes and the Kamaksi temple evidences this. The Kamaksi temple is not merely a center for Smarta Brahmins but there is a "mixing" of social classes and a crossing of sectarian lines.

It has troubled scholars of Advaita Vedanta in reconciling both ritual and devotion as integral to the teaching and practice of the Sankaracaryas. It must be maintained, however, that the Advaita philosophical lineage is but one part of the Sankara tradition, the latter is far more comprehensive than a philosophical school. A matha is a place for teaching and puja. Worship in both temple and matha draws devotees and pilgrims. The popular and eclectic worship found in all the Sankara Vidyapiths, including Kanchi, is based upon the tradition that Adi Sankara instituted six alternate ways of worship: Saiva, Sakta, Vaisnava, Saura, Ganapati, and Isvara. Puja in the Vidyapith consists of both Vedic and Agamic elements, freely drawing upon tantra. With the Kanchi acaryas, especially when on tour, this mixed-puja is carried out by attendant Brahmins in the morning and the evening, and by the Sankaracarya at noonday worship. I have heard on occasion the guru greeted by both Vedic recitation and *bhajan* at one and the same time. Cow-puja serves as an introductory rite. The acarya presides over the puja itself which is performed by Brahmins, but he at times may carry out his own worship behind a drawn curtain, hidden from the devotees, especially if prostration before a deity takes place. As there is a "mixing" of deities and social classes, there is also a "mixing" of worship and devotional forms both in Kanchi and as it is diffused when the acarya is on tour.

Indian anthropologist Surinder Mohan Bhardwaj offers an interpretive tool in understanding pilgrimage, applicable here in terms of Kanchi and its more comprehensive phenomenon, namely the itinerant Sankaracarya of Kanchi. He maintains that religion, especially in pilgrimage, generates a circulatory mechanism in which all the social strata of the Hindu traditions participate. The sacred place, in this case the Kamaksi temple, creates a space in which cultural diversity becomes mitigated. A circulatory mechanism brings about a manageable heterogeneity and in some cases even contributes to homogeneity in religious life.[18] This seems to be the case with Kanchi as a pilgrim center when it draws upon regional and supraregional socio-religious diversity. The religious site generates a circulatory mechanism which functions to integrate social strata, ritual diversity, and the world of the gods.

Bhardwaj's insight, when coupled with Mircea Eliade's work on the center of the world, the *axis mundi*, offers one articulation of Hindu socio-religious unity in diversity. For Eliade the center of the world, whether imaged as sacred tree, mountain, pillar, temple, royal city, or palace, is a mythico-symbolic hierophany. It may be any space filled with spiritual presence and manifestation.[19] It is that center of communication where heaven and earth, the divine and human orders meet. According to Eliade, only at the center can a breakthrough occur wherein a passing from one cosmic level to another takes place. As the creation of the world establishes a sacred center, the recreation of the world and humanity does the same. The heterogeneity of the created order is homologized at the *axis mundi*. The verticality of the center, temple or matha, is rooted horizontally in the earth, world, and the amassing of pilgrims and devotees.

But the Kamaksi temple is neither the *axis mundi* nor the navel of the world for the Kamakoti matha. The guru is the sacred center of the matha, and he is the place wherein cultural diversity is diminished. Just as the act of pilgrimage or the temple or matha lend themselves to a circulatory mechanism of diffusion, creating an integrative function, so in this instance the itinerant guru performs the same function in the socio-religious process.

A Socio-political Reality

Although the pattern of ritual center may not be a universal symbol, it holds interpretive value in this case. Yet, recent work of Jonathan Z. Smith convincingly argues that the language of the center is primarily political and only secondarily a cosmological structure decoding myth and ritual.[20] Kanchi as a political center is well established since it served as the capital city for the kings of the Chola period, especially the Pallava and Chalukya dynasties. The kings not only took refuge within the walls of Kanchi but they also built temples and had their victories inscribed in the temples. Likewise, the Sankaracaryas throughout history were regally enthroned and drew freely upon royal symbols. As chief administrators of the temple and matha with vast land holdings and ownership, their civil role was significant. The network of secondary mathas, temples, schools, regional discipleship, and caste leadership established their socio-political role.

The public status over the centuries of the Kamaksi temple, the

Kamakoti Vidyapith, and reigning Sankaracaryas has been formidable. In replacing Eliade's notion of ritual center with that of
socio-political "place," Smith intends place "not simply in the sense
of environmental generation, but also in the sense of social location,
of genealogy, kinship, authority, superordination, and
subordination."[21] It is readily granted that such functions of place
have operated in the histories of the Sankaracaryas of Kanchi. The
point of this study, however, will indicate the different configurations
of place in modern times. Just as in the past place was a social
position within a hierarchical system, so too modifications of place in
the present are appearing in the lives of the Sankaracaryas of Kanchi
and the Kamakoti matha.[22]

Moreover, there is significant correlation between socio-religious
diffusion, as previously understood, and socio-political place. Social
diffusion is a political reality.

The Many Publics of the Guru

A major factor bringing popularity and reverence to the two
Sankaracaryas of Kanchi is their capacity to teach. They are sought
out by devotees, pandits, university professors, ascetics, and their
Brahmin attendants for their intellectual leadership. Yet, the public
discourses of Sri Jayendra Sarasvati are marked by simplicity and
practicality, with talks on orthopraxis more than orthodoxy. At the
same time, he lectures ascetics on the *Upanishads*, discusses the
Brahma Sutras with university professors, and gives pandits solutions
to knotty problems from the *sastras*. The public discourses on
dharma, however, is the principal medium and message for the
majority of the people. Sri Jayendra spoke to large audiences in Delhi
on the worship of popular deities, the Indian epics, puranas, and
Dharma Sastras. Themes included, for instance, the elimination of
dowry, early age of initiation for the twice-born ritual, the dangers of
eating cow meat, the benefit of religious prostrations, and the
meaning of sacred ash.[23]

When Sri Jayendra Sarasvati speaks publicly to householders, he
stresses obligatory duties, worship, and devotion. Devotion is the
broad context for public instruction. His teaching resonates with the

karma yoga and bhakti yoga of the *Gita*. Sri Jayendra reserves mental
worship to the ripened mind, and recommends the worship of images
and the use of *mantra* and japa for the wavering mind, the lot of the
majority.[24] The majority of devotees perceive the most significant
teaching of Sri Jayendra as an exhortation to bhakti. Evoking bhakti
through teaching, puja, and *darsana* is considered a principal
function of his public life. Moreover, devotion is the most visible and
accessible quality of his personality and ministry. Although Sri
Jayendra follows the path of *jnana* in his personal spirituality and is
recognized as doing so, most of his followers are *bhaktas*.

Devotion is selected as the principal *sadhana* at this moment of
history because it is easy to cultivate; yet it is not the final goal in the
teaching of Sri Jayendra. Bhakti is a discipline preliminary to and
leading to knowledge.[25] It seems that bhakti and ritual and household
duties are taught within a loose Advaita context. Sri Jayendra intel-
lectualizes devotion and views it as the context for higher
knowledge. In public discourse Advaita may be dealt with only infrequently and obliquely but it remains the highest idea and goal.[26]
When engaged with pandits, ascetics, and their personal attendants,
the acarya directly and decisively articulates Advaita themes.
Certainly when instructing a *sisya* who stands in line of succession,
Advaita may be the principal subject of exposition. Nevertheless, a
diffusion of ideas and teaching takes place with the wider publics of
the acarya.

Adi Sankara is extolled by the public of devotees primarily as a
religious personality and founder who reinstituted Vedic religion,
dharma, reformed ways of worship (*sanmata*) and only secondarily as
the major exponent of Advaita Vedanta. The sage of Kanchi, as Sri
Candrasekharendra is referred, has called Adi Sankara the expounder
of bhakti and jnana from which no school of thought is excluded.[27]
The acaryas are recognized devotees of Adi Sankara, and it is not
uncommon for their own devotees to install Sankara images in their
homes and make the master Advaitin a part of their daily devotional
life. The acaryas embody not merely the Advaita tradition but more
universally the Sankara tradition. The former is the framework for a
scholastic articulation, while the latter actualizes the tradition in the
present life of people. Evident again is the diffusion of religious ideas

and the knitting together of seemingly diverse positions and teachings as the greater publics are encountered.

The acaryas of Kanchi are explicitly conscious of their integrative role in Indian society. This was evident in March 1986, previously mentioned, when Sri Jayendra consecrated a major temple in Allahabad depicting architecturally the social and theological principle implied here. The temple houses separately the Supreme God of the major Hindu sects — Saiva, Vaisnava, and Sakta. The first tier of the three-tiered edifice houses Sri Kamakshidevi (Sakti); the second tier enshrines Tirupati Venkatachalapthi (Visnu) surrounded by 108 *saligramas*; and the third tier contains a thirteen foot Saiva lingam weighing one and a half tons and is surrounded with representations of hundreds of holy sites and mathas. The temple was conceived by Sri Candrasekharendra over twenty years ago and was a clear departure from temple architecture based upon the *agamas*. Sri Jayendra consecrated the deities with water and sand collected from all parts of India, and on the occasion said that he hoped the temple would bring about national unity as the teaching of Adi Sankara "brought about religious unity."[28] This illustrates the socio-political role and intention of the acarya.

Sri Jayendra Sarasvati abdicated the vidyapith in late 1987 for a short period during which time his sisya, Sri Sankara Vijayendra, an eighteen year old youth, initiated in 1983, took over leadership of the matha.[29] Upon Sri Jayendra's return to leadership a few months later, a radical transformation began to take place in the work of the acarya and the outreach of the matha. The Kamakoti vidyapith, previously a bastion of South Indian Brahmins, opened its doors to scheduled castes and tribals. Nadars and Gounders are frequently seen with Sri Jayendra, while a South Indian Muslim is one of his ardent devotees. Most visible are the social programs initiated by the matha, some exclusively for Harijans, such as training courses in handicrafts for school drop-outs, brief programs in moral training for youths, three month training courses in radio and television repair, and tailoring are open to all communities. The Kanchi matha also organized a blood-bank for wounded soldiers from Sri Lanka. Sri Jayendra intentionally now reaches out to all communities and castes. He observes: "The reason for our social work is to sincerely do service to the people. Another motive is to spread the feeling of humanitarianism. The third, most important reason is to dispel the impression that only other religions do missionary and social work."[30]

Thus, a paradigm shift has clearly been orchestrated whereby the verticality of the sacred center, matha and guru, in the past socially and religiously hierarchical, is now actively diffused on the horizontal plane of human life. This further illustrates that social diffusion is a political activity and reality.

Transformation and Kinship Relations

Early research on Indian asceticism attributed to Adi Sankara and his successors the establishment of a non-biological *sampradaya* (teaching lineage) carried forward by renunciants and attesting to a particular doctrine, to an autonomous ascetical life, and to particular ways of worship. This may be true in the private life of an ascetic but it is not true in his public life or teaching. What has been said above demonstrates this conclusion in the public life of the current Kanchi acarya. Also significant is the transformation Adi Sankara brought to the Brahmanic hereditary gotra system.[31] In this case he changed the biological hereditary lineage system into one of fictive kinship relationships. The Kanchi acarya by moving beyond the Brahmanic gotra system has universalized further the fictive kinship relationships.

Sri Jayendra distinguished on one occasion three levels of encounter between teacher and student. The first, he said, takes place with the teacher who gives a mantra to a youth, initiates him into a religious world, and serves as a guide in his development. The second level is between the traditional pandit and the youth whom he educates in both secular and religious knowledge. The third level of encounter is between the acarya and the particular student he selects to continue a specific lineage and institution in religious wisdom.

I can identify three sets of such fictive kinship relations drawn from the framework given by Sri Jayendra.[32] The broadest based relationship is between the acarya and his vast following of devotionalists which is regional and supraregional in scope. It is this level of relationship that in recent years explicitly transcends caste and religious parameters. A second type of relationship exists between the acarya and his attendants, namely, those residing in the matha, those dedicated to his service, and those who tour with him. Many of the pandits and other intellectuals associated with him or the mathas are included in this group. In the past, this group had either begun the discipline of jnana yoga or were in readiness to do so. As more and more of the Kanchi acaryas' intimates enter into social reconstruction, it is improbable that jnana yoga will remain as a primary concern. The third type is the classical guru-sisya relationship and among the Kanchi acaryas this is found only between the Sankaracarya and his chosen successor. Although these three sets of relations are socially hierarchical, they are ontologically and theologically egalitarian in the Sankara lineage since "All is Brahman." Several Sankaracaryas have confirmed for me that spiritual equality is desirable and attainable in the classical guru-sisya relationship. When an acarya turns a matha over to his successor, as was the case when the senior acarya of Kanchi relinquished the matha to Sri Jayendra Sarasvati, the implication is that equality, spiritual and ontological, had been achieved.[33]

Each set of relations sketched above, however, is brought about through different configurations of Bhardwaj's notion of a circulatory mechanism. The threefold set of relations is not necessarily exclusive, and one may pass through several levels of relationship with the same teacher, indicating that the acarya may operate in diverse roles with the same individual.

The western savant, Paul Brunton, many years ago went to Sri Candrasekharendra in search of a personal guru who in turn sent him to Sri Ramana Maharsi with the words: "I am at the head of a public institution, a man whose time no longer belongs to himself. My activities demand almost all my time....How can I take personal pupils? You must find a master who devotes his time to them."[34] Even with this caution both Sri Candrasekharendra and Sri Jayendra have instructed personally, in both devotion and knowledge, a significant discipleship, including pandits, brahmacaryis, university professors, and even several western seekers.[35] Nonetheless, this more intimate form of discipleship in the past was usually local or subregional and somewhat limited to the environs of Madras and consisted basically of Smarta Brahmins. With the shift in focus introduced by Sri Jayendra in 1988, the discipleship has expanded far beyond these parameters. Bhardwaj observes that ascetics exert an immediate, continuing, and unifying influence due to their charismatic and normative roles.[36] Such an influence and role have been exercised by the Kanchi acaryas upon an ever expanding group of religious seekers whereby they now constitute a distinctive coterie of discipleship. The third set of relationships embraces the wider public and the acaryas. The Sankaracaryas function here most visibly in the diffusion and circulation of religious ideas and practices which are again based upon fictive kinship between them and their devotees. It is at this level of socialization that the acaryas have their most universal appeal and impact. On several occasions in the last ten years, Sri Jayendra called an Indian conference on Hindu dharma which crossed over social lines. Following the custom of his predecessor, he does not hesitate to meet with other Saiva and Vaisnava ascetics from a variety of sampradayas. He has taken a keen interest in the restoration of South Indian temples and frequently preforms consecration rituals. At these times, especially, he exemplifies extraordinary charisma to a wider devotional public and teaching audience. When the acarya is in Madras, he moves his camp from neighborhood to neighborhood every four of five days. I have seen three to four hundred people gather under tents for the noonday worship and teaching of the acarya. Various sectors of Madras society are represented at these times and are touched by his charisma, devotion, and teaching. He is still distinctive as a Saiva ascetic and usually is surrounded by Smarta Brahmin attendants. Yet even as he is acclaimed as a Sankaracarya, he brings together divers social, cultural, and religious groups at significant integrative levels.

Recent Assessments

In March, 1983, Sri Jayendra called a World Hindu Conference that met in Madras with foreign and regional representatives attempting to achieve a sense of corporate unity and cultural solidarity. Heads of mathas and a variety of scholars reflecting different sampradayas lectured the representatives on the broad cultural and religious heritage of India. Special attention was given to those Hindus living outside India and the transmission of Hinduism to their new countries. Likewise, Sri Jayendra attended a World Hindu Conference in Kathmandu in 1988, along with the three heads of the Madhva Udipi mathas and other acaryas representing a spectrum of sampradayas. These events reveal the new role the Kanchi acarya has taken. On the one hand he represents a conservative position in attempting to transmit traditional ritual and religious customs, and on the other hand he is in the forefront with a modern social vision as he meets with other religious leaders.[37]

The elder acarya, Sri Candrasekharendra, recently criticized the wide-spread construction of temples in the United States. It is reported that his rationale involved three factors: the claim that *homa* rites are more fundamental than temple worship; the fear that these temples would fall into disuse if Hindus left their new country; and the growing problem of staffing these temples with qualified priests.[38] The last point was considered the most pressing. The negative criticism of these positions from Hindus of other sampradayas was swift, since they saw them as eclectic positions of liberal Smarta Hinduism.

In a study completed in 1984 on the ascetics and lay Smartas of the Sringeri Vidyapith, Yoshitsugu Swami concluded to a gap between religious ideal and practice, a gap he sees as dynamic.[39] A convergence of paths is evident in the life and practice of the Sringeri Smartas. The same universalistic tendencies, which may appear ambivalent or eclectic to the outside observer, are present in both the Kanchi and Sringeri Vidyapiths.

Drawing upon the suggestions of Milton Singer and S. M. Bhardwaj, I have attempted to focus the role of the ascetic-acarya within the context of pilgrimage in order to allay the ambiguities that are present.[40] As the temple is the *axis mundi* for the religious pilgrim, the ascetic-acarya is the *axis mundi* of the matha. This is a fact of significant magnitude when the acarya is an itinerant preceptor because the *axis mundi* exists wherever the acarya fulfills his role. Just as the pilgrimage temple integrates diverse populations socially, culturally, and religiously, the ascetic-acarya creates the diffusion and integration of diverse religious ideas and practices based on fictive kinship relationships. The significance of a pilgrimage site is measured by its capacity to generate and maintain a system of religious circulation. I argue that the acaryas of Kanchi have created a massive system of religious circulation exhibiting vitality, resilience, and a mixing of socio-religious ideas and customs. The circulatory mechanism, evident in both pilgrimage site and the ascetic-acarya, gives to the Hindu tradition another syncretic capacity and another principle of coherence. This mechanism is sustained in the verticality of the center — temple, matha, or guru — and vitalized horizontally by the circulation of socio-religious classes, ideas and, customs.

Following Jonathan Z. Smith's insight into the political nature of the ritual place elicits further understandings. It appears that power explains the sacred site more easily than the sacred site explains power.[41] Kanchi was the power-site of kings; the Sankaracaryas of Kanchi were powerful for their place in the Sankara lineage and the increasing socio-political influence of the matha. The acaryas today exert extraordinary power through the force of their personalities along with their position in the Sankara tradition. Power, so to speak, has specified place as the ritual center. The ritual center, in this case the acarya himself, has become more an ideological distinction than a spatial distinction.[42]

The Coronation of a Guru: Charisma, Politics, and Philosophy in Contemporary India

Glenn Yocum

"Transmission," "tradition," "transformation," "transition" — good categories for describing the processes at work a few years ago in a monastic coronation ceremony (*pattabhisheka*) at one of India's premier religious institutions.[1] That this monastic transition occurred at a politically charged time, only a month before an important Indian national election, influenced both what occurred as well as some of the interpretations I put on these events. My observation of and reflection on this ceremony reinforce a methodological point, namely, that the information one collects — or, is confronted by — selects the theory one uses to an extent at least equal to the extent that theory selects the data. In a political season political meanings will be apparent.

Description of the Coronation

The Shri Sharada Pitha, one of the four mathas said to have been founded by Adi Sankara, is located in the small town of Sringeri in the Western Ghats of Chikmagalur District of Karnataka. The

Sringeri matha claims its gurus stand in an unbroken disciplic lineage (*acaryaparampara*) traceable to Adi Sankara's foremost disciple Suresvara, whom Sankara named as the first head of the matha.[2] Counting Adi Sankara and Suresvara as the first and second gurus, Shri Bharati Tirtha, the newly installed pontiff of the Sringeri matha, is the thirty-sixth in succession. The matha is noted for its emphasis on traditional Sanskrit learning, especially in its *pathashalas*, and for its association with Advaita Vedanta philosophy.

On September 21, 1989, Shri Abhinava Vidyatirtha, since 1954 the reigning guru of the Sringeri *pitha*, died in Sringeri of a heart attack. His funeral was a major national event and drew then Prime Minister of India Rajiv Gandhi to Sringeri. Abhinava Vidyatirtha's *samadhi*, now covered by a temporary shed, is situated next to those of the thirty-third and thirty-fourth Sringeri Sankaracaryas in a grove called Narasimhavana on the right bank (i.e., here south bank) of the Tunga River.

On October 19, 1989 the pattabhisheka of Shri Bharati Tirtha was celebrated in the Sharada Temple of the matha. Again, nationally prominent political leaders were present, most conspicuously the then Governor of Karnataka P. Venkatasubbiah and the Union Minister of Steel M.L. Fotedar. Other leading Congress-I dignitaries, including the President and Vice-President of India, had planned to attend the coronation but called off the trip at the last minute since parliamentary elections were unexpectedly announced two days before the ceremony.[3] Here I shall describe some of the rituals connected with the pattabhisheka, at least to the extent that I was able to observe and reconstruct them in interviews with devotees.

Some background information on the new swami will set the stage. Bharati Tirtha was born on April 11, 1951 to Telugu Smarta Brahmin parents in Andhra Pradesh. (All recent pontiffs of the Sringeri matha have been Telugu Brahmins.) According to a matha pamphlet,[4] before the future Bharati Tirtha's own birth, four daughters had been born to his parents. They laid their plight at the feet of Lord Bhavani Sankara, a local form of Siva, petitioning him to grant them a son. When they gained the object of their petition, they named the boy Sitarama Anjaneyulu, as they had also performed pujas to Rama. Sitarama's father was a *purohit* knowledgeable in Sanskrit and had his son begin formal Sanskrit instruction when he was five years old. When Sitarama was seven, his *upanayana* was celebrated. The boy learned quickly and was celebrated as a local prodigy, acquiring prizes in Andhra Pradesh for his proficiency in Sanskrit.

Sitarama's first encounter with Abhinava Vidyatirtha came when the Sringeri pontiff was on tour at Vijayawada in Andhra Pradesh. Asked to give a talk in Sanskrit before the swami, Sitarama received a special prize from the Sankaracarya. This initial meeting, according to Bharati Tirtha's own report, was crucial: "At the time it struck me that His Holiness was my teacher and my savior. His beaming smile I felt was giving me a message. I thought I got what I wanted. From that day onwards his benevolent looks remained in my mind. A bright planet had descended from heaven to give me light. It was more pleasant than the affection of my parents. I decided then that he was to be my guru."[5]

Upon finishing high school at age fifteen, Sitarama sought out Abhinava Vidyatirtha, who was observing *caturmasya* at Ujjain in north India. Sitarama met the swami one morning as he was returning from his bath in the river Sipra. Sitarama prostrated himself before the Sankaracarya and sought acceptance as the guru's disciple. Thereupon Abhinava Vidyatirtha began teaching him the very next day. Sitarama never returned to his parents in Andhra but remained with the Sringeri guru as a *brahmacari*. Nine years later in 1974 Abhinava Vidyatirtha initiated Sitarama into sannyasa and designated him his heir, assigning him the name Bharati Tirtha.

Official matha publications highlight Bharati Tirtha's erudition in the *sastras* and his extraordinary linguistic abilities, especially in Sanskrit, but also in Telugu, Kannada, Tamil, and Hindi.[6] Above all, it is Sanskrit learning that distinguishes Bharati Tirtha in official accounts, facility in Sanskrit being an important attribute of guruship in this tradition. Given that the temple to Sharada, a local form of Sarasvati, centers the Sringeri's matha's precincts north of the river Tunga, the emphasis on Bharati Tirtha's erudition in Sanskrit is not surprising.

Sri Sannidhanam's love of Sanskrit is inborn. At a very early age he composed poetry on everything he saw. It was indeed all a sort of the dance of Goddess Saraswati. Even at games he would talk in verse. Rules of prosody were never violated. Rhyme, rhythm, irony, suggestion: every poetic beauty came naturally to him. Even ordinary things of life found expression in his poetry. Even today His Holiness' love for Sanskrit continues unabated. But the extensive poetic composition has lessened, if not completely stopped. A sense of seriousness has entered because of the study under his guru.[7]

To supplement information about Bharati Tirtha gleaned from matha publications, I want to summarize a story recounted to me by a prominent lay devotee of the matha. My informant was a man who enjoyed a close relationship with Abhinava Vidyatirtha and who claimed to be intimately familiar with the process by which Sitarama came to be Abhinava Vidyatirtha's heir.[8]

Abhinava Vidyatirtha had two boys under his tutelage whom he considered as potential heir designates. One was Sitarama, the other a Telugu Brahmin boy from a village near Udipi on the Karnataka coast. Both were extensively trained in Veda, the sastras, and Vedanta. The Udipi boy was very quick to grasp things, whereas Sitarama was a slower learner, though he had an extraordinary memory and devoted himself to the study of Sanskrit texts even in his spare time.

During the time that these boys were being trained an auto accident claimed the life of Abhinava Vidyatirtha's private secretary, who had served the guru for twenty years. The loss of his private secretary greatly saddened the Sringeri pontiff, for my informant said the swami confided in him: "I'm a sannyasi. I'm supposed to be detached. But why should this happen? I don't understand." Thus, this particular jagadguru, despite official matha pronouncements about the sterling *vairagya* of its heads,[9] was not immune to grief and the kind of questioning prompted by the untimely death of a loved one. My informant, i.e., a lay disciple of the *jagadguru*, suggested that Abhinava Vidyatirtha appoint a "junior" (i.e., an heir designate) and turn over administrative matters to him. This would allow Abhinava Vidyatirtha to retire to the solace of a life of meditation, as, in fact, his own teacher and predecessor (Shri Candrashekhara Bharati

[1892-1954]) had himself done. But the swami responded that he didn't know which boy to appoint.

Shortly after this conversation, however, the Udipi boy disappeared; he simply left the matha one day and did not return. Still Abhinava Vidyatirtha did not act. But at the next Navaratri,[10] in 1974, an extraordinary event occurred. At every Navaratri the jagadguru performs a lengthy puja that is completed by noon. He does this in the Sringeri matha's Sharada Temple with the doors of the sanctum closed. During the 1974 Navaratri festival the swami went into the temple sanctum to do the puja but did not come out at noon. Even at 2:00 pm he had not appeared. People were very concerned. Finally at about quarter past two the doors were pulled open. The jagadguru was revealed sitting in the temple sanctum in the "jnana posture." Just then a flower fell from the icon of Sharada. Immediately Abhinava Vidyatirtha got up, left the sanctum, and announced that his successor would be Sitarama. Sharada had given the jagadguru an answer to his questions regarding the appointment of a junior. In November 1974, not long after the Navaratri incident, Bharati Tirtha was initiated into sannyasa and named the pontiff's heir apparent.

My informant was furthermore quite willing to talk about the differences in personal style between the senior swami and his junior. Abhinava Vidyatirtha was "flexible," "practical," "could see alternatives," and "gave disciples what they wanted." Bharati Tirtha, in contrast, is "bookish," "cut and dried," and "goes by the book." Clearly my informant hoped that the new pontiff would develop some of the practicality and flexibility that characterized his predecessor.

The principal rituals surrounding Bharati Tirtha's installation were spread over two days, culminating in the coronation itself just after noon on the second day. On the morning before the pattabhisheka an elaborate *homa* lasting over two hours was performed in the south corridor of the inner *prakara* of the Sharada Temple. Ten to twelve priests were involved in chanting and making oblations. At times flames leapt five to six feet into the air. The inner precincts of the Sharada Temple were filled with eye-searing smoke. At about noon Bharati Tirtha came to the temple in procession. Inside the temple he sat on a low silver throne in the company of other sannyasis of the order. Bharati Tirtha and the other sannyasis sat just to the east of where the homa had only minutes before concluded. Various pujas were performed in front of Bharati Tirtha, but the crush of the crowd was such that I could not follow what was being done. The guru then made a *pradakshina* of the Sharada shrine, pausing for *diparadana* at various ancillary shrines before he stopped at the Sharada sanctum for a longer puja. On leaving the temple through its north entrance, Bharati Tirtha made what appeared to be an inspection tour of the choultry buildings north of the temple. Some in the crowd prostrated themselves and touched his feet as he passed. Thereafter lunch was served. Brahmin lay devotees who were properly attired (i.e., men in veshtis and without shirts, women in saris) were served inside the choultry. The general public was served outside underneath some coconut palms in a courtyard-like area surrounded on three sides by matha buildings.

Later that afternoon Bharati Tirtha held a press conference. This took place in a large upstairs room located in one of the matha buildings near the Sharada Temple. About twenty-five to thirty members of the press attended. This session lasted approximately forty-five minutes. Though the swami responded to questions mainly in Kannada (I don't know Kannada), I was able to reconstruct some of his responses from conversations with reporters, from accounts in the next day's English newspapers, and also from some of the questions. (One rather tenacious reporter asked all his questions in English, and the guru responded to a few Tamil questions in Tamil.)

My sense of the reporters' attitude toward the swami was that most of them showed respect but not devotion. Several reporters persisted in asking follow-up questions when they were not satisfied with Bharati Tirtha's replies. In fact, a couple of times the press conference seemed to resemble a debate. Bharati Tirtha is an animated speaker, of forceful voice, rocking back and forth as he talks, and given to frequent vigorous gestures to emphasize his points. His whole demeanor could not be more different from one western stereotype of swamis as gentle, heavy-lidded, and a little sappy.

At the end of the press conference reporters lined up before the jagadguru, and he dropped an apple into the outstreched hands of each one. Most of the media representatives bent over and touched the floor immediately in front of Bharati Tirtha's low simple throne before each announced his/her press affiliation and was then given an apple. After all the members of the press had been received, several devotees of the swami were allowed to approach him.

A number of statements made at the press conference are important to interpretations I will advance below. Reporters' questions were mainly focused on issues of considerable current interest in India, political issues strongly tinged with religion: the Ramajanmabhumi-Babri Masjid controversy, Shila Pujas, communal tensions, religious conversions, the status of Harijans, etc. In general Bharati Tirtha's responses stressed tradition, especially tradition based on the sastras. He asserted that social-religious harmony would ensue if only these traditions would be faithfully followed.

On Ramajanmabhumi the swami said that the site was incontrovertibly the birthplace of Rama but that all parties concerned should accept the court decision as final.[11] Thus the swami supported Hindu claims to the site but refused to align himself with the Vishva Hindu Parishad and other Hindu "fundamentalists."

Asked if he would support the admission of Harijan boys to the Sringeri pathashala, Bharati Tirtha recommended that they study the Puranas instead and noted, "The Shastras stipulate that Upanayana is a pre-requisite for study of the Vedas by anyone. We cannot violate the Shastras."[12]

Bharati Tirtha stressed the need for heads of mathas to work for harmony among Hindus. He called for love and harmony among all sections of society. When asked about religious conversions, the jagadguru said that they were not due to evils in Hindu society and that there was no need for conversion given government concessions to the underpriviledged. Moreover, he added that conversions from the Hindu faith to other religions were induced mainly by money, and "We can bring them back into our fold by offering them more money."[13] According to a newspaper report, this last remark prompted a protest on the part of the Bangalore unit of the Karnataka Dalit Sangharsha Samiti. While the Bangalore association found the swami's remarks about Harijans generally insulting, the notion that Harijans could be retained for the Hindu religion by paying them more money than others who would convert them was labeled "an affront to the self-respect of the Dalits."[14] The above-mentioned Dalit association planned a protest in Bangalore's Cubbon Park at which the swami was burned in effigy and his remarks condemned.[15]

The pattabhisheka itself was celebrated in the Sharada Temple's south *prakara* close to the site of the previous day's homa. Only a very select group of devotees, "V.V.I.P.s," representatives of other mathas, and the press were permitted inside the Sharada Temple for the pattabhisheka. Everyone else watched the ceremony on closed circuit television, sitting under a large shamiana outside the temple but still on the matha grounds. (Thanks to the efforts of acquaintances in Mysore, I was given a press pass.)

Shortly after 11:00 am the swami left his residence, the Satchidananda Vilasa, in the Narasimhavana on the right bank of the Tunga. He crossed the river on the footbridge and stopped for worship in the Vidyasankara Temple at the top of the ghat that ascends from the river. Meanwhile the matha's chief purohit prepared the ritual implements in the Sharada Temple. The following people were seated on the platform running along the exterior wall of the south prakara where the throne had been placed: to the left (west) of the throne, the purohit and his assistants, sannyasi disciples and heads of other mathas, Bharati Tirtha's parents, and, on the throne's right, the two V.V.I.P.s with their guests and bodyguards. A great flower arch had been erected behind the throne, and garlands extensively decorated the temple pillars and hallways.

Shortly before the jagadguru arrived, a curtain inscribed with the word "shri" was held in front of the throne. Behind the curtain a ritual called *mangalashtaka* was performed. Soon thereafter Bharati Tirtha arrived, and between noon and 12:05 pm he ascended the throne to shouts and applause from those inside the temple. This was the climactic moment of the ceremony, whose timing was astrologically very auspicious. A number of rituals followed, all performed by the matha's purohit. In the program distributed to the press these rituals are identified as follows: *guru manasa puja*; puja to the *kalasha* and then to the *paduka*; *prokashana* of holy water while mantras were chanted including *abhisheka, suvarna, suvarna puspa,* and *navaratna.*

The abhisheka proper consisted of the priest sprinkling the swami with water by means of bundles of grass that were dipped into small metal pots. While the purohit performed this sprinkling, all of which lasted about fifteen minutes, mantras were intoned, not only by the purohit but also by the sannyasis and anyone else present who knew them. Several times during the pattabhisheka, from the moment Bharati Tirtha ascended the throne, he interrupted the purohit to give the priest instructions and to tell him to remove items used in the ritual from his left side to his right. Quite unlike the self-presentation of the swami at Guru Pujas of the Thiruvavaduthurai Adheenam that I have attended,[16] during his coronation the Sringeri pontiff was anything but a mute icon.

After the abhisheka proper a silk, sari-like cloth was held in front of the swami for a period of about twenty minutes. When this cloth was removed, the guru was wearing his gold and gem-encrusted crown as well as other jewels and a splendiferous gold-thread and silk shawl. These regalia he continued to wear for the remainder of the ceremony. When the curtain opened to display the resplendent jagadguru, the sannyasi to his left showered him with flowers. Then followed a brief *arati* in front of the swami, including a lamp waved by his mother. After the arati Bharati Tirtha got down from the throne. According to the festival program he went outside the Sharada Temple in a palanquin having received blessings from one of the matha's elephants. He also again visited the Vidyasankara Temple and various *adhistanam-s* (i.e. samadhis) before returning to the Sharada Temple after being outside for about half an hour.

As Bharati Tirtha re-entered the temple, the crowd responded to a litany-like series of cries praising the guru with shouts of *"jai."* The swami proceeded directly to the Sharada sanctum where *mangalarati* to the goddess was performed. Then the swami, again facing north, sat on his silver throne in the *mandapa* immediately in front of the Sharada sanctum. Here a durbar-like scene was enacted. Bharati Tirtha was presented gifts by the V.V.I.P.s as well as their statements felicitating him. A message "just received" from the President of India was read. After all the formal well-wishing, Bharati Tirtha presented shawls to visiting *mathadhipatis* and, I think, to some of his own sannyasi disciples, and finally to the two politicians. Thereafter, in a chaotic scene, devotees from among those granted admission to the temple were allowed individually to approach the pontiff in order to present gifts and to receive his blessing.

When Bharati Tirtha left the temple, it was raining heavily, and after his departure rain-soaked devotees streamed into the temple from the outside. The swami himself, according to the festival program, visited shrines to Sankaracarya and Ganapati on his way to take his daily *anhika*.

On the evening of his coronation the swami addressed his assembled devotees. According to newspaper accounts, he called upon people to help and not to harm each other, and he said that "if only one did [one's] duty without expecting any reward he would receive God's blessing."[17] On this occasion Bharati Tirtha also resolved to continue the traditions of the Sringeri matha in the path set by his predecessor and guru Abhinava Vidyatirtha.

At about 10:00 pm the pontiff left the matha in a palanquin to go in procession through Sringeri's streets. This public display beyond the matha's walls had a carnival-like atmosphere — a flame twirler, elephants, several floats, saxophone players and drummers, *utsavamurti* of Sharada in a small car, the swami in his palanquin followed by the generator used to power the tube lights carried next to the palanquin. One informant told me that at the conclusion of the pontiff's street procession, identical to what occurs at the end of Navaratri, Bharati Tirtha would hold a durbar in the Sharada Temple. I did not observe this myself.

Finally, a comment regarding the swami's jewelry, specifically about what he wore during the night procession, this observation from another devotee I met in Sringeri: My informant and her husband had presented Abhinava Vidyatirtha, on the occasion of his sixtieth birthday, with a gold necklace containing sixty gold bilva leaves. She had designed the *mala* herself so that it symbolically expressed several Advaita Vedanta philosophical meanings. From other conversations I had with this couple, it seems fair to say that she and her husband had not yet really warmed to the new pontiff. She noted with great satisfaction, however, that during the night procession on the very evening of his coronation day Bharati Tirtha was wearing the mala that she and her husband had presented to his predecessor.

Comments and Reflections

Many meanings could be put on what I have just described. And were my data more complete, say, due to extended observation at Sringeri or through textual study and historical research, other meanings would doubtless suggest themselves. To reiterate a point made above: What we pay attention to, i.e., the individual scholar's selectivity, along with what we are physically able to observe combine to play a major role in what meanings we construct. Here I want to select three varying sets of data from the above, each for view from a different theoretical perspective.

Symbolic Geography at Sringeri

The Sringeri matha demonstrates a rather neat spatial division marked by the Tunga River. Given the location of a "forest" on one side of the river and a town with its matha and *agraharam* on the other, one immediately thinks of binary oppositions, structuralism, and Louis Dumont.[18] Indeed, the spatial map of Sringeri reflects a cognitive universe that seems intent on stressing an opposition between householder and sannyasi, man-in-the-world and renouncer, dharma and moksha, temporality and its transcendence. The matha, of course, is located on both sides of the river and, therefore, mediates these oppositions.

It is quite clear to anyone who walks across the footbridge on the Tunga that the south side of the bridge is a very different environment from what lies north of the river. The pilgrim enters the matha from the north, having almost undoubtedly come up Sringeri's single main street, at one time apparently an agraharam, now largely a business district. The matha entrance stands at the south end of this street. Once through the gate one encounters matha offices and choultries in an outer courtyard area. A much larger courtyard further south encompasses the Sharada and Vidyasankara Temples, a bathing ghat on the north (left) bank of the river, the *pathashala*, another building containing a large hall that can be used for serving meals, and the residences of the principal matha administrators. There are very modest samadhis of several previous gurus in the area near the two temples, these being the one symbolically dissonant element on the matha's north bank. The open spaces in this area are almost completely covered by a paved stone courtyard. The entire matha complex on the Tunga's left bank sits on a bluff above the river down which the long steps of the bathing ghat spill.

At the west end of the ghat a low modern footbridge spans the river. In October 1989 a new arched concrete bridge was under construction to the east of the bathing ghat. The south bank of the Tunga is low, the inside of a large meander in the river. It is covered with grasses and, further back from the river, with trees, mainly arecanut and coconut palms. A sign warns to "Beware of Snakes." A few hundred yards back from the river the grove opens to reveal a cluster of buildings: the office of the pontiff's "Private Secretary"; a large double-domed building that encloses the samadhis of the thirty-third and thirty-fourth pontiffs; next to it, on the west side, a small shed-like structure that marks the samadhi of Abhinava Vidyatirtha (though I was told that the double-domed structure will be extended to cover his grave as well); and a large two-story building, the residence of the pontiff and of his sannyasi disciples.

The atmosphere on the two banks contrasts markedly, given the differing terrain and vegetation as well as the significantly greater density of buildings on the north bank. But clearly the buildings on the two banks have quite different functions too. Although the public is not excluded from the south bank, not everyone by any means who enters the matha to worship at the Sharada Temple or perhaps to conduct some business matter at the matha offices crosses the river to the Narasimhavana. Crossing the river leads to a different order of spiritual questing — to meet the sannyasi pontiff or to pay respects at the tombs of his predecessors. The south bank bespeaks a concern with transcendence, renunciation, moksha.

Quite distinct from mathas in Tamilnadu in the Saiva Siddhanta tradition with which I am familiar, the Sringeri matha is decidedly world-affirmative on its north bank. What anchors the sacred complex there is a goddess temple. And Sharada-Sarasvati is definitely a deity concerned with this world, a world of Brahmin learning, education, and prosperity.[19] Indeed, she seems a goddess well-suited to the this-worldly concerns of modern-day urban Smarta Brahmins as well as highly traditional ones. In his dharmic functions the pontiff of the matha stands as a virtual incarnation of Sharada.[20] His coronation is celebrated in her temple. His annual public ritual activities culminate in the Sharada Temple on Navaratri, the quintessential Sanskritic goddess festival. Furthermore, women, who in the Hindu tradition are typically linked with this-worldly welfare and auspiciousness, are hardly excluded or discouraged from entering the matha. Many of the jagadguru's devotees are householder couples, and women are clearly welcome at the matha. The Sringeri matha has one foot firmly planted in the world.

The binary opposition between dharma and moksha, this world and its transcendence, is symbolically, spatially, and conceptually present at Sringeri, but the matha and its head exist on both sides of this spiritual divide, so beautifully and appropriately demarcated by the river Tunga. The matha marks a *tirtha*, a literal crossing of a river and a spiritual transformation. Indeed, the Sringeri pitha's two most recent pontiffs have themselves been named tirthas.[21] The matha at Sringeri is thus very much a Brahmanical institution, a center whose geography and ritual performances give vivid expression to a holistic Brahmanical universe in which this world and the beyond, dharma and moksha, are simultaneously separate, opposite, and yet linked by the crossing of a river, a tirtha.

The Charisma of the Guru

Sitarama Anjaneyulu was not the only person taken by Abhinava Vidyatirtha's beaming smile and affection. I interviewed several devotees of the elder pontiff both in Sringeri and in Madras who also described their initial encounters with Abhinava Vidyatirtha in terms of the jagadguru's arresting smile. They typically understood this smile as an expresssion of the guru's "greatness," "love," and "utter lack of self-interest." Abhinava Vidyatirtha clearly had a gift for making some people feel loved, especially the urban, English-educated, professional, male Brahmins whom I interviewed. More than one devotee referred to the swami's remarkable memory, in particular his ability to remember faces and individuals. Several devotees with whom I talked mentioned *rudraksha malas* given to them by the former pontiff of Sringeri, beads that had remarkable powers to alleviate illnesses from which they suffered.

Two of Abhinava Vidyatirtha's devotees whom I interviewed emphasized that Bharati Tirtha, who they agreed is very learned, would now have to "build his own following." I had the strong sense that the devotion for the old guru was not automatically transferable to the new one. In fact, three of my informants came from Tamil Smarta Brahmin families whose traditional religious allegiance was to the Sankaracarya at Kanchi, whose claim to unbroken disciplic lineage stretching back to Adi Sankara is rejected by the Sringeri matha. Personal encounters with Abhinava Vidyatirtha, however, led each of these Tamil Smartas to become the Sringeri guru's disciple. Hence, in contemporary India at least the Sankaracarya's charisma seems to rest on personal magnetism rather than being a

Bharati Tirtha directing the priest at his coronation

quality ascribed to the swami by virtue of his office. A coronation invests the new pontiff with symbols of authoriy, but the charisma of his own guru does not thereby automatically devolve on the new head of the matha. The acaryaparampara at Sringeri is — or has become — a lineage of teaching authority rather than of personal charisma. Even among south Indian Smarta Brahmins, widely considered to be upholders of Hindu tradition, spiritual charisma appears to be a somewhat free floating commodity not necessarily tied to one particular institution.

The extent to which Abhinava Vidyatirtha's love was a key factor in his power to attract disciples raises interesting questions about the kind of religious charisma that appeals to contemporary, urban Hindus, particularly to highly-educated Brahmins. None of the devotees I met who mentioned his experience of being the object of the elder guru's radiant love seemed to lead an especially traditional Brahmin life. Certainly all were vegetarians and maintained some kind of home worship area. But none was learned in Sanskrit, nor were any of them very knowledgeable about Brahmanical texts or about Advaita Vedanta philosophy. All referred to the new jagadguru's erudition, but one sensed that they did so mainly as a polite way of saying something about him that could be positively interpreted. No one mentioned the warmth, radiance, or love that had been so appealing in Abhinava Vidyatirtha. In fact, when I recently showed photographs of Bharati Tirtha's coronation to a group of south Indian Brahmins residing in the United States, several spontaneously commented, simply from seeing the pictures, that the new Sankaracarya does not possess his predecessor's magnetic radiance. "He doesn't have the look, the smile," someone said. I began to suspect that wealthy, urban Brahmins whether in India or in the United States, who are less traditional than their typically small-town parents had been, harbor deep-seated needs to be accepted, loved, affirmed — needs the old guru clearly met but ones that Bharati Tirtha has not yet shown himself capable of filling.

Devotees of the Sringeri Sankaracarya show great respect to the jagadguru, typically in the form of pranams (prostrations) and kanikais (offerings, gifts). Nonetheless, some lay disciples evince an extraordinary degree of familiarity, indeed intimacy, with the Sringeri

pontiff, especially with Abhinava Vidyatirtha, and the old guru
seemed to go to considerable lengths to be accessible to his devotees.
Again the contrast with the Saiva Siddhanta mathas is noteworthy.
It is almost as if the old Sringeri pontiff was collectively owned by his
lay disciples. Parallels with being the senior minister or rabbi of a
large, wealthy American Protestant or Jewish congregation come to
mind. Does he "give them what they want"? Charisma needs a
receptive audience to manifest itself. To emphasize again, while

Bharati Tirtha in full coronation regalia

Bharati Tirtha now wears the crown of the Sringeri matha and has
been invested with the emblems of its office, there was no obvious
transmission of charisma at his coronation.

Reflecting further on the nature of charisma among Hindus in
contemporary India, it is quite striking the degree to which disciples'
reports of their relationship with Abhinava Vidyatirtha overlap the
interactions described in three neo-Hindu movements that are the
subject of a recent book by anthropologist Lawrence Alan Babb.[22]
Babb's study focuses on the Radhasoamis of Soami Bagh, the Brahma

Kumaris, and the cult of Sathya Sai Baba. His interpretation of guru-disciple interactions (especially true of the sant satgurus of Soami Bagh and Sathya Sai Baba) applies remarkably well at many points to what I heard devotees say about their relationships with the late Sringeri Sankaracarya. This is true despite the fact that the Sringeri matha is generally — and correctly I believe — perceived to be a bastion of Hindu traditionalism in contemporary India, whereas the groups studied by Babb see themselves — and/or are viewed by more mainstream Hindus — as being on the margins of the tradition.

In the groups studied by Babb, devotees describe their interactions with the guru in ways that emphasize the guru's compassionate look (*drishti*) as well as the love and trust they experience in the guru's presence. What devotees of the sant satgurus and Sathya Sai Baba seem most to want — and to succeed in getting — is an experience of what Babb aptly calls "hierarchical intimacy."[23] Such intimacy with an exalted religious authority figure is characterized by the devotees' experience of extraordinary love bestowed on them by the guru. At the same time, the guru functions for his devotees as a kind of mirror in which they are able to recognize their own higher selves, their own truer identities. One is reminded of Max Weber's well-known notion of exemplary charisma; the guru's exemplary presence enables his disciples to discover their own true identity. Or to speak, as Babb sometimes does, in terms of transactions, so important to many interactions in Hindu society, the devotee gives his utmost respect to the guru while at the same time surrendering his old con-stricted sense of self. In exchange for this respect and self-surrender the disciple receives the guru's love and an enlarged sense of who he really is.

Hierarchical intimacy and exchange characterize very well the relationships lay disciples of Abhinava Vidyatirtha described to me. Moreover, it could also be said that self-recognition and a heightened sense of who one really is are exactly what the Advaita Vedanta phi-losophy espoused by the Sringeri gurus is all about.

With regard to the Sankaracarya's charisma a final anecdote: Three close friends of mine from Madras all reacted nearly identically when I told each one about my visit to Sringeri. Upon hearing that I had been to Sringeri for the jagadguru's pattabhisheka, virtually the first question from each was "Did you meet the swami?" My reply that I had joined the press queue and received an apple from him was not really what they'd hoped I'd experienced. Of primary significance for each of my friends was a one-on-one audience with the guru, and I could detect disappointment when each learned that I had not had such a meeting. I mention this reaction as a cautionary prelude to my next set of reflections on the Sringeri matha and its guru. Some may find the following social and political comments unsympathetic and at odds with the matha's own self-understanding. Had I met the guru privately and experienced a smile from him, my data would have been enlarged and who knows then what other interpretations I might now be putting on the Sringeri matha and its coronation ceremony.

A Discourse That Maintains Brahmin Privilege

To put my thesis bluntly, the Sringeri matha, its pontiff, its inter-pretation of Advaita Vedanta philosophy and Brahmanical tra-ditions, and its pattabhisheka festival constitute a symbolic ensemble, a system of discourse, that legitimates and perpetuates a set of power relations in which Brahmins are superordinate and the non-Brahamin rest are subordinate. So as not to be mistaken, this is not a Dumontian argument where Brahmins are correlated with purity and the king with power. In modern India, I am referring to Brahmins who wield power directly, who flock to Sringeri for its pattabhisheka, hear pronouncements from its guru, learn something of its phi-losophy, and are confirmed thereby in their sense of superiority and deserved privilege. I am not claiming that this is *all* or *really* what the Sringeri matha is about, but I do want to suggest that this is one of the meanings that can legitimately be ascribed to the set of phenomena clustered at the Sharada Pitha. I have already argued that the Sringeri matha is open to the world and is a bridge between householders and renouncers. The world to which the Sringeri matha is open and the householders to whom it most builds bridges, in contrast to the wider audience of the contemporary Kamakoti Pitha at Kanchi described by William Cenkner, are those of upper-middle-class urban India and its well-to-do Brahmin professionals and entrepreneurs.

My interpretation of the social meanings of Sringeri's discourse can be supported at several levels. Most obvious are the statements of Bharati Tirtha himself at his press conference and at the talk on the evening of his coronation. To recognize why Harijans in Bangalore took offense at his remarks about religious conversion requires little imagination. Bharati Tirtha's taking refuge in sastric precedent when the issue is whether Harijans should study the Veda at the matha pathashala is slightly more complex, if for no other reason than that it evinces a selective use of tradition in the matha's discourse. Passages from the *Dharma Sastras* that require Brahmin austerity or ritual punctiliousness or thoroughgoing female subordination to males are unlikely to appear in matha pronouncements. Emphasis on such norms would no doubt be out of step with much of the matha's current lay clientele.

Furthermore, it is quite evident that Bharati Tirtha's calls for harmony and love, and the recommendation that each person do his/her duty, are pleas for unity based on social hierarchy and Brahmin privilege.[24] To observe that social and economic inequality is widespread in contemporary India and that communal tensions constantly threaten to erupt into violence is an understatement. Under these circumstances for the Sringeri swami, or anyone else, to suggest that all would be well if only people did their duty and loved each other seems rather naive. Such a response is from one per-spective plainly not to address the problem. When the swami's Brahmin devotees hear such remarks, they do not experience dis-comfort nor are their consciences piqued. The harmony being rec-ommended is founded on patterns of extensive and continuing inequality. I suspect that the frustration demonstrated by some of the reporters at Bharati Tirtha's press conference was prompted by the swami's refusal to face the very issues, the "real" issues some would say, that they wanted him to address.

To see that Bharati Tirtha's socially conservative pronouncements are not deviant in recent Sringeri tradition, one need only consider an event much celebrated in the matha's publications. In 1979, for the first time in 125 years, the pontiffs of all four *amnaya* mathas said to have been established by Adi Sankara met in Sringeri. The four Sankaracaryas issued a joint message in which they advised that "everyone should follow his dharma handed down to him through the ages and this was the only way to realize welfare and progress."[25]

The effect of the Sringeri matha's moral pronouncements came into sharp focus for me during a conversation I had in south Madras with a man who had been a long-standing devotee of Abhinava Vidyatirtha. This elderly retired gentleman had enjoyed an illustrious career in the Indian foreign service. He lived on a street of finely appointed houses, where one of his daughters, herself alienated from Brahmin piety, told me with biting sarcasm that when the Sringeri Sankaracarya visits Madras, he must visit every house on their street. In the course of my conversation with her father I mentioned my previous work on a non-Brahmin matha in the Cauvery delta. My informant was skeptical about the morality of the pontiffs of the Tamil Saiva Siddhanta mathas, a response I have encountered before among urban Tamil Brahmins.[26] Stories about corruption, ignorance, and sexual misconduct in non-Brahmin monastic foundations are, I'm convinced, part of the discourse that legitimates Tamil Brahmin moral authority and superiority. When I mildly protested the charge of corruption in the Saiva Siddhanta mathas, my informant replied that the only question he had for such institutions was "Do they do some good?" I told him what I thought they did. I'm not sure he thought it was "good," for he then recounted to me his feelings of repugnance on having seen the matted locks, which he claimed were thirty feet long, of one of the *tampirans* (ascetics) of the very Saiva Siddhanta matha I knew well from first-hand experience.

While the old man's affection for Abhinava Vidyatirtha was obvious and his grief at his guru's passing still quite evident over a month after the swami's death, my informant expressed the hope that Bharati Tirtha would follow in his predecessor's mold, doing things that were "pure," "non-controversial," and "good." I think Sringeri's moral message for its lay Brahmin followers can be summed up in words I heard both from the guru and from lay devotees: "goodness," "love," "harmony," "duty," "purity," and "non-controversiality" — a moral discourse well suited to a privileged elite.

Two related observations: The Congress-I political establishment obviously wanted to be associated with this rhetoric, politically useful to its interests.[27] I would guess that a high percentage of the matha's lay devotees have sided with the Congress-I in recent elections given the tendency of south Indian Brahmins to be Congress-I supporters. Second, in newspaper reports of the pattabhisheka in the English-language press, The *Times of India* and *The Hindu* were most extensive in their coverage. *The Hindu* especially demonstrated its Brahmin orientation in the ready and sympathetic coverage it gave to the Sringeri matha. Only the *Deccan Herald* reported the Dalit protest in Bangalore.

Another level at which one could detect the discourse of power relations at Sringeri was in how human bodies were carried, dressed, cared for, and fed. The body served as a boundary for expressing social segregation and superordination. Lay Brahmin devotees were fed separately from the *hoi polloi*. The ritual purity of high-ranking matha officials could be maintained only by their avoiding direct physical contact with those deemed ritually impure. And the manner in which many lay male disciples presented themselves in public expressed, more subtly perhaps, similar messages. Here a stereotypical image, which obviously does not fit all cases, will have to suffice. It is that of a middle-aged to older Brahmin male in a silk veshti, shirtless with silk shawl, frequently with a gold chain around his neck containing one or more rudraksha beads. He carries himself with a certain degree of aloof confidence, head slightly tilted back.

The Sringeri jagadguru's ritual attire expresses lordship, temporal authority. The crown, which is a matha treasure, resembles the crowns worn by kings in the recent Doordarshan Mahabharata series, except in the Sringeri case the gold and diamonds are real. I have observed a number of temple and matha festivals in Tamilnadu over the past ten years but have never seen jewels and gold as lavish as those used during the pattabhisheka in the Sharada Temple and the subsequent evening procession, both those adorning the jagadguru as well as those used to decorate the icon of Sharada in the temple sanctum. The Sringeri pitha was closely associated with Hindu dynasties in the Deccan, particularly Vijayanagar and the Wodeyar rajas in Mysore. The royal trappings of the coronation, particularly the use of the crown, are no doubt attributable to the Sringeri matha's long-standing connections with worldly power. Indeed, the Sharada Pitha is sometimes said to be a raja pitha, a "royal seat," which entitles its gurus to use palanquins and automobiles rather than to go on foot like the Sankaracarya of Kanchi.[28]

The Sringeri matha's physical arrangement with the worldly, dharmic complex on the north bank of the Tunga occupying the high ground, having the goddess at its ritual heart, bespeaks a concern with worldly influence, with power. Though the guru's residence in the Narasimhavana is a co-ordinate symbolic center of the matha, the Sharada Temple is undoubtedly the Sringeri matha's ritual focal point. It is there that the Sringeri matha's heads are crowned and where, sometimes at least, matters of succession are decided. The body of the goddess expresses the matha's temporal authority.

Finally, I want to advance a hypothesis for further research and reflection. Prompted largely by the contrast in ethos between the monastic establishments at Sringeri and at Thiruvavaduthurai, I think these two mathas' differing styles, differing devotional emphases, and differing degrees of openness to the lay world are not unrelated to the differing philosophies they espouse. The strong Tamil Saiva bhakti tradition at Thiruvavaduthurai engenders an emphasis on humility, on servitude before God and the guru who manifests Siva. (Indeed this is a convenient ideology for legitimating servitude before kings, which may be why the Cholas were such generous patrons of the Saiva devotional cult.) Ritually, in the Saiva Siddhanta mathas, devotion is expressed in careful attention to elaborate ritual performances in the presence of icons that are embodiments of the deity. While the Thiruvavaduthurai Adheenam acknowledges a teaching function, expressed mainly in its many publications of Tamil Saiva classics and its support of lay propagandists, and while it supports some "good works" in the form of schools and provision of room and board for poor children, the Thiruvavaduthurai matha is an institution far more closed to the outside world than its counterpart in Sringeri.

Advaita Vedanta, on the other hand, relativizes devotion, subordinates it to a higher truth of universal non-duality, of the identity of the human being's innermost self with the universal Brahman. Advaita Vedanta thus seems a philosophy well designed to divest social, economic, and political relations of any fundamental significance. It typically does not to seek to transform these relations but to argue that traditional ideal relations be left alone. This is so even when the argument for traditional ideal relations, as in recent Sringeri prouncements, seems mainly to support the distinctly modern class interests of urban Brahmin professionals. On the other hand, William Cenkner's chapter in this volume clearly demonstrates how at the Kanchi matha in recent times quite non-traditional social values have been espoused.

Kanchi notwithstanding, one might still hypothesize, particularly so in view of the Sringeri matha's social ideology, that Advaita philosophy sits comfortably with notions of separate but hierarchically ranked ideas, deities, and social groups, all the while claiming that at a higher level everything is encompassed in a fundamental, overarching unity. Gerald Larson has recently characterized Sankara's Vedanta as follows: "It...cleverly tinker[s] with concepts that deny everything on one level while allowing everything to remain just as it is on another level."[29] What Advaita does with concepts, its interpreters can also do with social organization, relativizing social formations at one level, but allowing everything to remain the same at another.

While I want to acknowledge that Advaita Vedanta may be true in some cosmic sense (indeed, its metaphysical cogency and grand vision are in some respects quite compelling), the configuration of the socio-moral universe that it has legitimated and for which some of its spokesmen continue to apologize is also part of its "truth," perhaps a truth deserving more attention from scholars of Indian religion, culture, and society than it has heretofore received.

Concluding Remarks

The transition that took place at the Shri Sharada Pitha in late 1989, while in important ways unique to that institution, offers a window for viewing some of the larger issues confronting the transmission of religious tradition in contemporary India. Certainly tensions present in the wider society and its religious heritage were visible at Sringeri in October 1989. Sringeri's geography as well as the names of its recent jagadgurus may condense in a single, richly multi-faceted Sanskrit term (*tirtha*) meanings of the various English words "transmission," "transition," "transformation," and "tradition," but the current Indian context in which these "crossings" take place renders transmission of religious tradition problematic. This applies especially in present circumstances to an institution espousing sastric socio-ritual values and Advaita Vedanta philosophy, accustomed as well to religious authority closely linked to royal power.

Electoral politics and the rise of an urban middle class pose challenges for traditional Hindu institutions. These social, political, and economic processes have created a new class of prosperous and powerful Brahmins at the same time they have undermined the traditional, ritual foundations of Brahmanical authority and superiority. Institutions such as the Sringeri matha are good lenses for focusing these changes and challenges. But the choices made at Sringeri are not automatic. Again, one need only call to mind the quite different recent history of the Kamakoti Pitha at Kanchi to realize that institutions in the Sankaracarya tradition closely identified with south Indian Smarta Brahmins are capable of adopting quite varied postures vis-à-vis socio-religious change and Harijan aspirations.

A final musing: The issues facing Indian society and the Brahmanical tradition are not totally new, for they are not unlike some of the tensions present in the more than millennium-long South Asian encounter with Islam. From one perspective, contemporary conflicts besetting Indian society appear to revolve around incommensurable world views — on the one side, a traditional Hindu *Weltanschauung* that is simultaneously polycentric, monistic, hierarchical, and organic and, on the other, a web of values and aspirations that are egalitarian, socially atomistic, and utilitarian, all connected with a powerful modern state. While these tensions may not be completely new, the pace of change, fuelled by burgeoning population and globalization of the world economy, and the consequent push and pull of social forces in India sometimes seem truly daunting for the integrity of institutions and values both "traditional" and "modern." These conflicts are not only or even primarily between competing institutions but play themselves out in the minds and decisions of innumerable Hindus in India, among them certainly the Sringeri pontiff and his devotees.

The Divine-Human Figure in the Transmission of Religious Tradition

Brian Hutchinson

> Like other things religious, guruship is not simply an object to be examined and dissected with the various academic tools at our disposal. A guru has to be experienced and this experience may reduce all our learning and scholarship to pretentious chatter.[1]

This statement from C.D. McMullen is particularly apt for the guru-devotee experience discussed in this chapter. The sentiments could also be applied to the experience of Christ outlined in E. Stanley Jones's work and even to the work of C.G. Jung where his observations of a very broad spectrum of psychic experience are here reduced to a few "dry" concepts. It needs to be kept in mind that it is the experience itself which is the phenomenon and that descriptions are only inadequate attempts to articulate it.

Whilst there are wide differences in the religious context of the divine-human figure in the case of the guru of the Akshar-Purushottam Swaminarayan movement and that of Jesus Christ in the Christian religion, both focus upon a historical person who is understood to be a vital link between the worshiper and the ultimate God. Further, relationship to this human figure is regarded by both traditions as essential to liberation/salvation and, in both cases, being in right relationship to this divine-human figure is regarded as synonymous with being in right relationship with God.

In the the Akshar-Purushottam Swaminarayan movement (where the term "movement" is used in the rest of this chapter it refers to the Akshar-Purushottam Swaminarayan sampradaya or tradition) the Guru is considered to manifest Lord Swaminarayan (1781-1830 C.E.), who is understood to be the incarnation of the ultimate God, *Purushottam*, whilst retaining a difference in identity. The Guru incarnates the second-order entity of *Akshar* which is understood as the "abode" of Purushottam. This effectively means that the Guru performs a dual role, first as intermediary between the devotee and God, and secondly as a focal point himself for adoration and worship; a position strikingly similar to that of Jesus Christ for the Christian disciple. (The term "disciple" is used in this chapter to indicate a devotee of the divine-human figure of Jesus Christ. This is not necessarily synonymous with the term "Christian" as persons within that faith vary in their orientation towards the divine figures. Or, in Jungian terms, in some persons belonging to the Christian faith a different archetype may predominate).

Both Guru and Christ, in addition to their divine attributes, are considered by their followers to be ultimate examples of the highest human moral and spiritual values. Whatever else may exist of common psychic experience, this moral and spiritual value characteristic provides common ground for both faiths and incidentally can also do so for persons who adhere to secular humanistic values. The Guru is portrayed as concerned with the uplift of spiritual values throughout the world, somewhat in the style of the avatar whose task is to restore dharma, (right order in society), when righteousness is seriously threatened. Pramukh Swami, the present guru, has himself affirmed this common focus in his contact with the Anglican Archbishop Robert Runcie and Pope John Paul. A publication of the movement asserts of the Guru that "Unswervingly his purpose remains to preserve, protect and promote moral, cultural and spiritual ideals; to create an addiction-free society and to crown it with world peace."[2]

Whilst Guru and Christ emerge from widely differing doctrinal traditions, their followers appear to share a psychic core of similarity in their devotion to their respective divine-human figure. Partly this can be seen as the shared natural tendency to admire and even to love the person in whom the values one holds are clearly manifested. However, over and above this there is with both devotee of the Guru and disciple of Christ a somewhat similar psychic image and an orientation towards the divine-human figure within which goes beyond this natural admiration. The external focus of this psychic orientation is the divine-human figure of the Guru or of Christ in external historical reality form. However, for the devotee and disciple this external image is clothed with the idealized figure existing in the psyche of devotee and disciple. This internal idealized figure of Guru or Christ could be described as the result of an extrapolation of the external historical form of the divine-human figure which has now moved into the realm of mystical experience. It appears in both cases that the psyche of the devotee or disciple has added something to the historical form to create this internal idealised image. It follows that when the devotee speaks of the Guru or the disciple of Christ that the description contains both external historical elements and internal impressions. The extravagant language of devotion and worship used for both figures is a collective expression of that combination, as is the mode of proclamation to the world of both figures by their respective faiths. This needs to be borne strongly in mind by the person who is neither devotee nor disciple in any attempt to grasp the nature of the Guru-devotee and Christ-disciple relationship. In this regard Jung with respect to the person of Christ says, "It is not Christ; it is his parallel in the subjective realm, which dogma calls Christ."[3] This appears also to be true for the devotee of the Guru in whom, in the developed stage of the relationship, the Guru becomes the Guru within and it is this Guru of the subjective realm who is the center of the movement's proclamation. In terms of Jung's work discussed later in this chapter it is suggested that this Christ or Guru within is only partly created by either figure, and that both Guru and Christ evoke the psychic tendency or archetype which already exists universally in the human psyche. It appears to the present writer that the divine-human figure, and the psychic response to him, can provide an area of understanding for devotees of the Guru and for disciples of Christ. That is, both in the portrayal of the nature and function of the divine-human figure, and in the reported experiences undergone by both devotee and disciple in relation to Guru or Christ. This seemingly common ground of the divine-human image and related experiences has significance for the transmission of religious tradition. The present writer as a Christian can attest from personal experience with the devotees of the movement over the past ten years that there appears to be a natural spiritual empathy between those of psychic orientation to the divine human figures of either Guru and Christ; that a kind of transference can occur in the devotee or disciple from the one object of adoration to the other. This affinity of psychic orientation appears to be present despite all doctrinal and world-view differences which exist between the Hindu and Christian traditions. Where people so inclined can meet others across the doctrinal barrier, and not merely rely on second-hand descriptions, this area of understanding could develop further.

This chapter approaches this phenomenon of devotion to divine-human figures by first examinining an attempt at the transmission of the Christ figure into a Hindu context as it appears in the record given by E. Stanley Jones of his own missionary work in his book *The Christ of the Indian Road*. Reading the book after contact with the devotees of the movement it struck me forcibly that there was first a great similarity between the experience described by Jones and descriptions of the Guru-experience related in interviews I had had with devotees in the movement, and secondly in the conception of the divine-human figure in both cases. In respect of Jones's communication attempt it is suggested that he has emptied the traditional understanding of the Christ figure of those aspects which would be more immediately incongruent with the Hindu context and is in fact unknowingly working within what Jung suggests is the universal psychic orientation towards the divine-human figure. It would seem that Jones mistakenly assumes that this psychic orientation/liberation is exclusively tied to the Christ figure, and that his hearer's acceptance of this reduced divine-human figure is synonymous with acceptance of the "true" Christ of history. Secondly, in the case of the Akshar-Purushottam movement's Guru, it will be shown, based on reported experiences of devotees, that acceptance of the movement's belief is synonymous with acceptance of the divine-human figure of the Guru. As a sadhu said, "The Guru is the message." Transmission of the religious tradition is therefore here ultimately dependent upon acceptance of the Guru; to receive the message is to enter relationship with the Guru as a devotee. There is much to indicate that in this case again the core of the acceptance is the universal psychic orientation towards, (or projection upon), a divine-human figure.

The movement presents the Guru largely to people of Indian Hindu background in the context of an awakened sense of the richness of their culture. Exhibitions such as the recent cultural festivals in London and New Jersey first attempt to induce or restore respect for Indian history and culture. The knowledge and respect for this, especially by those who have been born and brought up outside of India, is in danger of being lost. It appears for many immigrant families that interest in the movement first comes in its representing for them their background Hindu Indian culture and that it is within the context of respect for their culture that they then become members of the movement and devotees of the Guru. This progression from culture to Guru was given tangible form in the arrangement at the New Jersey exhibition where the halls depicting Indian culture preceded those presenting the Guru and the movement. A sadhu remarked to the writer after the exhibition that the visitors book had shown that many had been impressed by the displays of Indian history and culture and that some had written, "Now I am proud to be Indian."

In the reverse direction of what is suggested for Jones, when the movement attempts presentation to Western non-Hindu hearers then it tends to empty the Guru of those specifically Hindu beliefs which would hinder acceptance, and to stress generally recognised aspects of spiritual and moral values which are common to both Hindu and Christian cultures. The Guru is then presented as functioning within universal spiritual principles and, as with Jones with the Christ figure, the doctrines which would create barriers in the hearer's context remain unmentioned. The writer's suggestion to the Guru Pramukh Swami that the unity in purpose, which he referred to in contact with the Anglican Archbishop and with Pope John

Paul on the subject of moral and spiritual regeneration, seemed to ignore important doctrinal differences, received the following reply: "Final means of emancipation differ, but moral and spiritual principles are in common. They [different faiths] can co-operate there. [It is] at least an inital stage, perhaps more later." In this context the Guru often refers inquirers back to the practice of their own faith in their search for spiritual enlightenment, advising Christians to imbibe the message of Jesus Christ and Muslims to perform their prescribed five daily prayers.

The present writer's understanding of the Guru-devotee experience is based on responses of devotees, especially of sadhus, given during interviews.[4] Whilst sadhus represent the inner ring of devotees and therefore as a group are more intensively involved with the Guru, they nevertheless by common consent among devotees, exhibit the experience of the orientation towards the person of the Guru which is true in varying degrees for all members of the movement. It is not suggested that all devotees go through the radical changes in inner dynamics described by those at the center, anymore than this would be true for all disciples of Christ, but in both the intense form of devotion to the divine-human figure is considered to be the desired authentic response.

The third section of the chapter considers this response which is apparently common to both devotee and disciple in terms of the work of C.G. Jung and relates it to Jung's concept of individuation. It may be that oneness with Akshar, oneness with Christ, and oneness with the self is the same human psychic experience articulated according to the differing religious or philosophical context to which the individual belongs. That is, the same experience may be described in terms of Christian doctrine, in Swaminarayan philosophy, or by Jungian psychology. However, it needs to be borne in mind that the mystical phenomenon itself is prior to, and superior to, any attempt to describe or define it.

The Christ of the Indian Road

E. Stanley Jones was a Christian missionary to India in the early part of this century at a time shortly following what may be called the triumphalist period of Christian missionary endeavor. In that period it was considered that the other religions would shortly disappear and be replaced by Christianity as the superior religion. Whilst Jones appears to have had considerable respect for his hearers this assumption appears to underlie his approach and whilst he selectively quotes the actual words of Hindus he encountered there is little in the book which could be called objective dialogue with Hindu belief.

Jones's basic conviction was that the figure of Jesus Christ would become predominant in the Indian religious scene. At the time of his writing (1925) his perception was that the process by which this will happen was already underway. He says, "We believe that India will fall intensely in love with the Christ of the Indian Road, that love will turn to glad submission to him, that out of that loving submission to him will come a new radiant expression of him in thought and life."[5] Whilst this profound belief in his cause is a tribute to a remarkable man with a great missionary zeal the years since he made that prediction have proved him to be wrong. There has been no such movement in India.

Jones was a deeply committed Christian, and when he speaks of Christ he does so out of his own devotion towards him. The result is that the figure of Christ which he speaks of in such glowing terms is partly based upon the Jesus of the Gospels and the affirmations of Jesus' nature and work recorded in the New Testament, but largely based upon the liberation in himself which Jones has experienced and for which the name Christ appears to be a symbol. The Christ which he attempts to convey is not so much the Christ of the Indian (or Palestine) Road, but the Christ of his own inner road of experience. That is to say, his own subjective impression of Christ predominates over the proclamation of the historical person of Jesus himself. In this he may well be exhibiting what is a common feature in proclamation of the Gospel, for example the preaching of St. Paul where the Jesus of history and the Jesus of experience are inextricably combined in that attempt at communication. However, Jones appears to exaggerate the subjective aspect to the point where the objective content of the person of Jesus as appearing in the New Testament and in more orthodox Christianity is emptied in his attempt at communication. Consequently, in his communication attempt at least, if not for his own personal faith, Christ loses its moorings in the historical person of Jesus Christ and in the context of the Bible. The divine-human figure, now bereft of exclusive attachment to the Christ of orthodox Christianity, he finds has a more universal appeal. In his book he labels anything which does not fit neatly to this reduced Christ as accretions to the pure form which have been added through time particularly by Western culture. A clear example of this general tendency is the following, "Christianity must be defined as Christ, not the Old Testament, not Western civilization, not even the system built around him in the West, but Christ himself and to be a Christian is to follow him."[6] However, the precise content of "Christ himself" having been removed from the context of these elements, remains vague and seemingly consists in Jones's own numinous experience of Jesus Christ. Further, speaking of the person of India, Jones says, "He is making an amazing and remarkable discovery, namely that Christianity and Jesus are not the same — that they may have Jesus without the system that has built up around him in the West."[7] It seems clear that Jones's understanding here goes further than the stripping of Western culture and ecclesiastical systems: it extends also to doctrines which decidedly had their origin not in the West but in the (Middle) East.

This removal of the Christ symbol, freeing it from the restrictive confines of orthodox Christian doctrine, is further illustrated by Jones when he quotes a Hindu with approval as saying that they [Hindus] have been unwilling to "receive Christ into our hearts because up to now...missionaries have held out a Christ completely covered by their Christianity...their special effort has been to defeat our religious doctrines and therefore we have been prepared to fight in order to self-defence [sic]."[8]

This attempt which Jones makes to wrest Christ free from its usual context did not go unchallenged. A Jain lawyer, who after Jones has declared his definition of Christianity being Christ in much the same way as mentioned above, asked him who gave him the authority to make this distinction: what church council gave him this authority? Jones's reply that it was "his own Master" who gave it to him reduces to the fact that it is on Jones's own psychic conviction.[9]

The guru-like figure of Mahatma Gandhi seems to have provided a transitional concept for Jones in the communication especially of the human aspects of the divine-human image which he held of Jesus Christ. He has a chapter headed "Jesus comes through irregular channels — Mahatma Gandhi's part."[10] Here, for example, he admits to the observation made by a Hindu that "Mahatma Gandhi was responsible for a great deal of new interest in Jesus." Earlier another Hindu has asked him why he preaches on the second coming of Christ when "he is here — Gandhi." Jones's comment on this is illuminating, he says: "Blasphemy? That is not the point — the point is that Gandhi is their ideal, and they are identifying that ideal with Jesus. It is the gripping of the mind by the Jesus ideal."[11] In the third section of this chapter it will be suggested that this "ideal" is inherent in the human psyche and is capable of being focused upon, or evoked, by more than one divine-human image. For example this could be Gandhi, the Guru, the Christ of orthodox Christianity or the reduced version of the Christ which Jones was proclaiming.

Some Hindus of his time apparently responded positively to Jones's preaching of this Christ divested of doctrinal accretions. However, Jones fails to recognize or make clear the distinction between the acceptance of this ideal Christ figure and the acceptance of the Christ of orthodox Christianity. His book is of a devotional nature and was well accepted by many Christians as supporting their belief in the superiority of Jesus Christ. It not surprising that they were undiscriminating in their assumption that the Hindus acceptance of Jones's Christ meant also acceptance of the essentials of the Christian faith. However, nowhere in the book does it appear from quoted words of Hindus that this was really so. The present writer can readily affirm the high respect in which Jesus Christ is held by many Hindus, for example by the devotees of the Akshar-Purushottam Swaminarayan movement. However, it is clear that for them, and similarly tolerantly disposed Hindus, Jesus and Christlikeness serve as symbols for the generally accepted image of the divine-human saint. They see Jesus in this respect in a similar way to their own Guru, as incarnating the highest spiritual principles. In addition, perhaps by the process of transference mentioned above, the name of Jesus Christ is a kind of symbol which evokes feelings related to their own Guru. However, those in the movement who see the figure of Jesus in this way, and who inci-dentally often use the words of Jesus to illustrate the Guru's rela-tionship to God (quoting Jesus' "he who has seen me has see the father" from John 14:9b), in no sense include other central beliefs of Christianity. For example, they do not include that of the suffering of God in the person of Christ and of its central part in the Christian understanding in the scheme of salvation. The present writer's attempt to relate the suffering of Jesus to the suffering of the Guru, (here regarded as Akshar, the choicest devotee of God and the second principle to God [Purushottam]), fell on polite but stony ground. It is not that the concept of the suffering of God for the sins of mankind has been considered and rejected but that it clearly has no place in the system to which they belong. Neither is there any evidence in Jones's book that it was accepted by those Hindus who responded positively to his message. When Jones speaks of the ideal of Jesus or Christ receiving wide acceptance it is again clearly on the basis of Jesus' symbolizing saintliness and in no sense on the orthodox understanding of the place of Jesus in the Christian faith. Jones fails to make this clear and for example falls prey to his own metaphorical use of the term "saviour," failing to distinguish between this and the more specific meaning of Jesus Christ dying for the sins of the world.

However, whilst the quoted words of the Hindus who responded positively to his message give no indication of the acceptance of basic Christian doctrine, Jones's use of Biblical texts relative to their comments gives rise to the unfounded assumption that they did. For example he asserts that he had found that "I [Jones] could take my stand at Christ and before that non-Christian world refuse to know anything save Jesus Christ and him crucified."[12] "And him crucified" comes from the statement of St. Paul (1 Cor. 2:2) and is central to the New Testament understanding of Jesus Christ in the whole plan of salvation. In the responses quoted there is no indication of his respondents' acceptance of this aspect of his message. Another example is where Jones states that the Christ to be presented "must not be a Christ bound with the grave-clothes of long-buried doctrinal controversy...but a Christ as fresh and living...as the one that greeted Mark at the empty tomb."[13] The implication of this statement and its context in Jones's book associates the acceptance of Jones's "preached Christ" with a belief in Jesus' resurrection, whereas there is no evidence of this in the recorded responses.

A statement which is tempting to regard as a classic example of the psyche actually producing the divine-human figure occurs when, speculating on the universal recognition of the highest as existing in the person of Jesus Christ, says, "If the finest spirits of the human race should sit down and think out the kind of God they would like to see in the universe, his moral and spiritual likeness would gradually form like unto the Son of Man."[14] ("Son of Man" is a term sometimes used of Jesus Christ in the New Testament.) On the face of it this observation could be reduced to universal wish fulfilment but it could also be seen as the externalization of an inner archetypal tendency. It may be described in Jungian terms as an impression originating in the collective unconscious and focusing upon a man of heroic proportions, be it Guru or Jesus or other divine-human incarnate images. It seems to the present writer that unknown to himself Jones was operating within the area of the Godman to which Jesus, Gandhi, and Jones's more abstract entity Christlikeness, could be said to belong. Clearly this divine-human image has some universal psychic currency but Jones's error would seem to lie in his seeking to limit it to his understanding of Jesus Christ. When he states that the great lack in Hinduism is that they have no Christ, he surprisingly fails to recognise that an acceptance of a divine-human image already exists in his hearers in their approach to Krishna, in the attitude to Gandhi, or in the guru-devotee institution which is basic to Hinduism.

In short, by Jones's emptying of the term Christ, it becomes a symbol of the divine-human image acceptable to those of his Hindu listeners who responded to his preaching. However, its content for them does not include the beliefs which are associated with it in Jones's understanding. His Christ-message is accepted only where it is divested of large areas of Christian theological content. What he and his hearers do appear to share is on the unconscious level: a similar psychic orientation towards the divine-human figure. In all this in no sense is it suggested by the present writer that Jones was anything but entirely sincere in this his attempt at transmission of religious tradition.

The Akshar-Purushottam Movement's Guru-devotee Experience

The Akshar-Purushottam Swaminarayan movement is a Guru-centred tradition which believes that the final avatar (identified by devotees as Lord Swaminarayan, Purushottam, and God) appeared on earth 1781-1830 C.E.. The Guru-devotee relationship is elevated to divine status in that the Gurus of the movement since that time are understood to incarnate the "choicest devotee" of Purushottam, that of the entity of Akshar. Akshar is related to Purushottam as devotee is to Guru. The way to liberation (Akshardham) is by being at one with the Guru through bhakti (love) and submission to him. Essentially the way to God is through one's relationship to the human form of God, that is with Lord Swaminarayan through his manifestation in the present Guru. Images (murtis) still function as objects of worship in the movement but as secondary to the Guru's manifestation of God. In fact the murtis are seen by most devotees as mediators between themselves and the Guru rather than as direct means of access to God. The grace of the Guru is understood to operate in the devotee thereby assisting the devotee towards the attainment of spiritual heights which will result in this present birth being his last and in his translation to Akshardham at the end of this life. (Another branch of the Swaminarayan movement focuses upon the person of Swaminarayan but denies the doctrine of Akshar's becoming incarnate. With them the Guru institution still functions but Gurus are regarded as no more than elevated human teachers.)

Jones, in his summing up of the reasons why he and other Christian missionaries were in India says: "We are there because Christlike character is the highest that we know, because he [Christ] makes the offer of a complete moral and spiritual change, he gives men a free, full life, and most important of all, he gives them God. And we do not know of anyone else who does do these things except Christ...."[15] If for the Akshar-Purushottam movement the name "Christ" was replaced here with that of their Guru, then the description would reflect their view of him and how they present him for acceptance. Space here prevents a more adequate description of how the Guru of the movement is experienced and transmitted by the movement in its handing down to the new generation in its followers and its reaching across to others. What follows is a description under headings suggested by Jones's above summary where the term Christ is replaced by that of the Guru.

"The Guru's Character Is the Highest That We Know"

Whilst in Bombay in 1983 I was invited to speak at the celebration of Guru Pramukh Swami's 63rd birthday. I said, (and this before reading Jones's book which is replete with this type of comparison), that as a Christian the highest thing I could say of a person would be that they were Christlike. That it seemed to me that the whole character of Lord Swaminarayan in his desire to uplift the spiritual state of the people, in his concern for the poor and for the people of his day in general, that he appeared to me to be a very Christlike character. The spontaneous applause from the audience of some twenty thousand people which greeted that observation left an impact upon me that I have never forgotten. To me it showed the openness to other faiths which is characteristic of the movement and, more to the point here, the general acceptance of the term "Christlike" as indicating the highest value. However, as already observed, the term serves as a symbol for the highest in the realms of the human (with its intimations of the divine), of the divine-human revered figure readily identifiable with the saint, that is, the person who actualizes the highest spiritual principles. It does not indicate acceptance of the Judaeo-Christian world view or the doctrinal beliefs about Jesus Christ which are central to the Christian faith.

The Guru is understood to concern himself with the good of his devotees; he is the man for others. One young man having just been initiated into the first stage of sadhuhood said, "Just seeing his behaviour, character and personality...his love for others, made me become one of his sadhus...." Membership of the movement is ultimately relationship to the Guru; each devotee feels that he is known intimately by the Guru even though he may never personally have met him. This feeling of being uniquely regarded is partly based on the personal interest in and knowledge of the devotee exhibited by his Guru.

Humble service of his devotees is a highly revered aspect of the

Guru's character. It was said of this Guru's predecessor, Yogigi Maharaj, that he never had to cut his finger nails, they had been worn down by cleaning his devotees' cooking pots. One sadhu expressed great admiration that on one of the world tours, Pramukh Swami wanted to help to carry luggage into the hotel lift. This humility is not mere outer show, it is seen to belong to the real character of the Guru. A sadhu of the Amdavad temple spoke of Yogigi: "He was so much one of us, so normal. He never used to feel he was superior to us, although he was superior in all respects...full of renunciation, full of devotion, full of all virtues, but at the same time we felt he was one of us...." In his relationship to devotees the Guru is not as one said "high and mighty", but he adjusts himself to the characteristics and mood of the devotee who consults him. To the question of what human relationship was nearest to the devotees' relationship to the Guru, an answer typifying the feelings of other devotees was: "You are on one wavelength...he is not above you. Talks to you as if you are the same age. He can also be a friend to an eight-year old and an eighty year old...and a teenager...."

The selfless love of the Guru was his most frequently and enthusiastically reported characteristic that had influenced persons to become devotees and sadhus. A sadhu whose family had not been members of this movement articulated the general response to the question of what had attracted him to the movement. He said, "It was Swamiji's pure love, his magnetic personality which attracted me." Another, on reasons for his becoming a sadhu said, "The love he used to offer us, share with us, that was the main thing that attracted me to become a sadhu." This experience of love is felt in inner experience and also outwardly in the Guru's expressed human concern for the devotee's worldly existence. It is reciprocated in adoration and devotion on the devotee's inner level, and the outward response of the devotee to the Guru includes seeking to please him by devoted service. All service undertaken for the movement is considered service of the Guru; it is therefore accepted as a privilege and as part of one's love relationship with the Guru. The readiness of so many to devote so much time and energy to the recent festivals is one instance of this characteristic.

The Guru Makes the Offer of a Complete Moral and Spiritual Change

Moral uplift and the implementation of values in personal and social life have a very high profile in the message of the movement for which the character of the Guru and, to a lesser but important extent, the character of the sadhus provide examples. The moral and spiritual standards exemplified by the Guru appear to represent a structured way of life for his immigrant devotees; a symbol of stability in the anomie often experienced by persons in immigrant communities in their new alien cultural environment. Discussion with devotees during the New Jersey festival suggested that the first concern for immigrants has been to attain economic viability, a concern which has absorbed a great deal of their time and energy. Once this had been achieved they have, as one devotee said, "Looked around for something more." There was an expressed concern for the preservation of their family life and for their children, who as second generation immigrants could be left without a sound cultural and moral background and vulnerable to what their parents regard as negative traits in Western society. The movement's high moral standards based upon the 212 commandments found in the *Shiksapatri*, declared by Lord Swaminarayan himself and linked with the personal example of the Guru, have been strong initial attractions for many entering and remaining within the movement.

However, whilst these high moral standards are attractive in themselves and in the stability of life which they offer, motivation to aspire to that high standard comes from the devotees' relationship with the Guru. A sadhu explained how a person who had been smoking for forty years had given up at Pramukh Swami's request: "He left it because there is a relationship of love, and a person will always act according to the person whom he loves...Swamiji works through his love." It is generally accepted that his devotion to the Guru brings about moral change in the devotee. Partly this is considered to be the result of the devotee's personal effort to please the Guru and to attain the self discipline which being his devotee demands. One devotee explained the need for moral improvement in the words of Jesus; he said it is a case of "If you love me, keep my commandments." Mainly, however, it is considered that a devotee's moral improvement is by means of the grace of the Guru; that is the Guru's working within him and his granting of blessings to the devotee. Devotees readily attribute their overcoming specific moral deficiencies to the grace of the Guru. For example sadhus who had wondered if they would ever be able to attain the complete celibacy required of them assert that this would not have been possible without the grace of the Guru. In fact even to have the urge to aspire to such moral and spiritual heights is also considered as the grace of the Guru. However, grace does not replace individual effort but is given by the Guru as something over and above the effort supplied by the devotee himself. This personal effort is essential if the Guru's grace is to be received and retained. The image often used for this required effort is that of preparing your vessel in order to receive and hold the grace which the Guru in his love pours out.

Whilst the Guru himself displays the highest moral excellence the effect of this is to motivate the devotee to higher endeavor rather than to demoralise him with the realisation of how far he falls short of that ideal. A sadhu described how he is influenced by the Guru: "Yes everything he does is divine...watching as he eats...when he is sleeping I am just sitting for two hours...I feel very happy...you feel like repenting of whatever you have done...You think from today I don't want to do this bad thing...I'll try my best to please him...sometimes tears in your eyes...thinking...I'll be perfect." However, failure to attain certain ideals does seriously impact upon the devotee's feelings, and in this regard the Guru acts as father-confessor for devotees and particularly for sadhus. A sadhu explained that whenever the Guru comes to the temple they are each given time with him: "He tells no one [it is confidential]....We tell him I am like this, feel this...He will say okay you do one fast...Five minutes later you forget it and laugh with him." When the Guru is not present or available the mental worship (*mansie puja*) of the devotee serves as a kind of personal interview with the Guru. It is believed that this mental activity involves actual contact with the Guru and is more than mere imaginative contemplation. In the absence of the Guru a devotee may approach the murtis; the idols in this regard are understood by most as mediators between themselves and the Guru.

The radical improvement of moral character is seen as a central feature of the Guru's work. Whilst miracles of the more sensational variety are understood to be within his power they are regarded as low in importance relative to the radical moral improvement of those who enter relationship with him. Instances are cited where even the appearance of the Guru has brought about such a change in persons who have come into close contact with him. According to the "great saints" of the movement the Guru's real miracles are where persons of previously low character have undergone complete moral and spiritual change through the work of the Guru. "The miraculous thing about him is that he promises no miracles yet works one with your life."[16]

The Guru Gives Men a Full Free Life

Doctrinally Askar is able to grant liberation from samsara and to translate the devotee to Akshardham. It is believed by members of the movement that this liberation can be achieved during this present lifetime through the grace of the Guru. Grace here operates as described above in the sense of assisting in the development of a high moral and spiritual nature rather than in the sense of granting forgiveness and accepting the devotee in spite of his not having yet reached that state (as grace is often seen to operate in the Christian sense). There is no vicarious function of the Guru on behalf of the devotee in his relationship to God except perhaps in the sense that the Guru is the devotee's spiritual link between himself and God. In this regard being in right relationship with the Guru is more directly necessary than approaching God himself, as the individual would be ill-equipped to cope in that context due to his limited spiritual development. Being so spiritually undeveloped the devotee would receive little, whereas approaching the Guru who knows God intimately, and who can relate to the devotee on a human level, can bring about the needed spiritual development and ultimately true knowledge of God.

On the face of it, submission to the external authority of the Guru seems to represent the direct opposite of freedom. However, it is the experience of devotees who surrender to the Guru that submission to him and living in obedience to him has resulted in their greater freedom; in an expansion rather than a restriction of their own personality. This submission of one's own will to that of the Guru has occured to various degrees with different devotees but its complete form is presented as a goal to which devotees should aspire. Various terms are used to describe the submission, but the general explanation is of losing one's ego and being at least in the process of adopting the will of the Guru over and above one's own. This is synonymous with the doctrine of becoming one with Akshar as the devotee becomes one with the Guru in seeking to lose his own will in that of the Guru's and being joined to him in a loving (bhakti) relationship. Doctrine and experience are therefore united in this Guru-devotee relationship. Dr. Swami, one of the highly respected sadhus, explained: "Yes he orders that we eradicate our ego...by following his instructions ego is lost. Individuality remains...he becomes one with Pramukh Swam...imbibes all his qualities by following him. Even though he [the devotee] remains a disciple he is uplifted so high. He remains an individual...he has got his own will...but his will is guided by him [the Guru] also."

The human experiential component of this doctrinal liberation is that of the bliss experience. Devotees report a heightened psychic state of peace, elevation, liberation which they descibe as "bliss." The English edition of the movement's monthly magazine goes under the title of *Swaminarayan Bliss*. Bliss is the overall state devotees experience relative to their pre-guru condition in general. In addition to this from time to time they experience sublime elevated moments which are understood to be glimpses of the ultimate bliss; these may arise simply out of a gesture, a glance or a touch of the Guru with no suggestion that this was his intended purpose. Atmaswarup, a sadhu lecturer at Amdavad training school, explained how he had been holding Pramukh Swami's headgear: "Just how he took it and placed it on his head conveyed so many things to me. A feeling of joy in my heart that again was just lovely. Whenever I feel low I remember these incidents...anytime I remember this incident it happens, joy...peace...bliss...words fail...no language can convey it. A fountain of joy spurts through your heart....It is the experience of many people and maybe a glance of his conveyed it."

Most Important — The Guru Gives Them God

The sadhu librarian at Bombay temple articulated what is believed in general about the Guru and of contact with God. Speaking of God he said: "He is manifested throughout in equal intensity...we all accept this...but we cannot have much to do with anything in that state. Specially in the space dimensions he should be locatable and then [subsequently] in the form of powers spread through the universe. Human form...that attracted me...that he is manifest now in the form of the Guru...."

The Akshar-Purushottam belief about the Guru takes form within the traditional Hindu belief regarding the Guru institution. Here truth is seen to come to the devotee through the "realized truth" existing in the Guru himself. The Guru is thus able to dispel darkness, which is the meaning of the term "guru." Such enlightenment or truth can be experienced only in devoted relationship to the one in whom it has become incarnate. The Guru-devotee relationship is thus seen as an essential channel for the spiritual uplift and enlightenment of the devotee. The Guru functions in this context of belief and in addition is regarded by the movement as a *sadguru* who, being beyond maya — the cosmic ignorance which pervades the minds of lesser beings — is understood to have the power to grant liberation to his devotees.

The mental image of God held by devotees of the movement in general is that of the physical form of the Guru. Worship is thus conducted with this image in mind. In mental worship lavish gifts may be brought by the devotee and adulation of God takes the form of adulation of the Guru. The present writer's suggestion to the sadhus that it seemed to be the Guru's form rather than that of Lord Swaminarayan — Purushottam or God — which was central to the vision of devotees in worship evoked the following replies: "Pramukh Swami is the physical form, but all the devotees they think that Lord Swaminarayan is walking through him, seeing through him, speaking through him." "Idol is a fixed form of the Lord; our Guru is moving form of the Lord. So to remember him is equal to remembering the Lord. Some people say Lord is in heaven, say he is no more here, but we don't have that, Lord is here and now; he manifests through the Guru." Ramesh Dave reports the belief: "Limb by limb, every tissue of his body radiates the presence of God.....His striking humility, fathomless wisdom and graceful simplicity have been instrumental in introducing God into the lives of hundreds of thousands who worship him as Spriritual Guru."[17] Commenting on the misunderstanding which can sometimes occur with the uninformed observer where some are inclined to say that the Guru is "making himself out to be God," a sadhu explained: "...but he's a priest between you and Shreeji Maharaj [the Lord]...showing the ideal you should become. As jivas we are not capable of offering devotion as it should be offered to God. We are material...immersed so much in maya that we do not know how to worship God."

Persons who come for darshan — to see and be in the presence of the Guru — retain their mental images of the Guru and even trivial actions may be retained for mental worship later. This fascination with the physical form of the Guru would seem to create problems on the demise of a particular Guru and the need to transfer to the next. However, the concept that each Guru is the same entity of Akshar assists in this transfer. Respondents declared that the love is the same regardless of the personality and physical form of the Guru of the time. Further the previous Gurus are not allowed to die in the minds of devotees in that festivals commemorate significant events in their Gurus' lives. For example the previous Guru to Pramukh Swami, Yogiji Maharaj, is remembered with great affection by many present members of the movement and it seems that for some he is still their mental image of the divine in their devotions. A sadhu said: "When you see Lord in Pramukh Swami...when you see Lord in him with all powers and everything....Then you forget he is Pramukh Swami, he is Lord himself. When you have achieved that state, then you are his devotee and he is your Lord." It follows that all who see the Guru's physical form will not have reached the stage where his true nature is appreciated. Many will see the Guru's physical form but to have reached the state of realizing the human form of God in him is considered an advanced stage of spiritual development; a stage to which moral and spiritual achievement in previous lives, including reactions to gurus met in those lives, is understood to contribute.

Whilst this association of Guru and God operates in the thought and feeling of devotees and operates in their daily puja and mental worship, the association is resisted externally by the Guru and the teaching of the movement. The Guru reinforces what he considers the essential understanding by his genuine humble bearing, by his way of asserting that he is nothing and that all that is done is God working through him. He insists that garlands presented to him are first offered to the small image of the Lord which he carries with him. He identifies with his devotees in prostrating daily before the temple murtis of the Lord. In his dress he is identical to other sadhus, and it is remarkable that when seated up high on the gadi (a kind of bench from which a guru teaches) before his devotees he is able to retain a decided air of humility which is evident even to the outsider. In keeping with the attitude his devotees have towards himself, the Guru ascribes his own spiritual development to the excellence of his own Guru. In the chanting of the succession of names of the Gurus (*guru paramampara*) he joins with devotees up to the name of his own Guru (Yogiji Maharaj), whilst his devotees continue with his own name (Pramukh Swami). However, in all this he is not understood to be denying the divine aspects of his person but that he is expressing outwardly the nature of his divine role as Akshar, the perfect devotee of the Lord. Therefore, for his devotees the Guru's human worship exemplifies perfect devotion and externalizes his doctrinal identity as Akshar. By this externalizing — here including his own perfect devotion to the memory of his own Guru, that is the one prior to himself in the guru paramapara — the Guru-devotee relationship is also itself being reverently observed as something more than the merely human. An extrapolation of the human Guru-devotee relationship extends to that of Purushottam and Akshar. It is a manifestation of the *bhakta-Bhagwan* (loving devotee and loving God) relationship, which incidentally members also see in the Krishna-Radha, Rama-Sita relationship, images of which are also to be found in temples of the movement in addition to the central murtis demonstrating the Askshar-Purushottam relationship.

The Guru has the authority, as representing all the previous Guru's and manifesting Lord Swaminaryan himself, to make changes in the movement's belief and practice. A sadhu explained, "Pramukh Swami is interpreting Swaminarayan's will for this present age...there is no change [in essential meaning] only interpretation."

However, such changes so far have been minimal and are those which relate to the changes in society, for example the changes which have occured in the caste system in India in recent times. Such changes are thought anyway to have been in the mind of Lord Swaminarayan and only delayed as he considered the state of society of the time not being suitable for such innovation.

Devotees in general state that God has become real to them in their association with the Guru. They have experienced radical changes for the better in their psychic and religious life. Morally they declare they have overcome previous defects and vices through the grace of the Guru. These factors are for them their own personal evidence of the authenticity and excellence of their Guru. The Guru is thus far more to devotees than a religious functionary, he is the one whom they admire and love and whose love they experience as the foremost influence in their lives. Their human relationship with the Guru phases into the divine relationship; it is their experience that he "gives them God."

The Experience of the Divine-Human Figure Understood in Terms of the Work of C. G. Jung

It needs to be emphasised firstly that the object here is not to attempt to explain or explain away the above experiences, nor to reduce the phenomenon of the Guru-devotee or Christ-disciple relationship to psychology. The aim is to consider those aspects of each of both relationships which appear to lend themselves to discussion in terms of Jung's model of psychic functioning.

In his psychological work Jung focused upon the empirically observable effects of religion within the psyche, and maintained that he could have nothing to say on metaphysical issues.[18] However, whilst as a psychologist he can say nothing about the absolute existence of God, he was able to demonstrate the existence in the psyche of a "totality supraordinate to consciousness."[19] He leaves open the question of how that situation comes about and concerns himself with the reality of the universal God-image in the psyche, and with the experiences which cluster around it. Jung's observations lead him to postulate the existence of a collective unconscious which he understands as containing all the contents of the psychic experience of mankind.[20] Each individual is thus understood to enter the world, not only bearing evidence of the physical characteristics of earlier man, but with his psyche also bearing the imprint of its own heritage. It is this collection of common characteristics which is central to Jung's psychological work.[21]

Jung maintains that the collective unconscious operates in an autonomous manner producing its effect on the ego, which is the seat of the intellectual faculty and which is, prior to the occurence of the individuation experience, also the experienced center of consciousness. When contents of the collective unconscious enter the conscious area of the psyche they are felt to have a numinous quality. They do not appear in the form of logical concepts but as symbols, which are the natural language of the collective unconscious.[22] When they enter consciousness they are said to fascinate and grasp the conscious mind and subjectively to appear as the result of something entering from outside.

Archetypes is the term given to the contents of the collective unconscious.[23] They operate in the psyche in a similar way to instincts in the physical realm,[24] providing the psyche with an inherited tendency to function in a particular way.[25] Archetypes are not images in themselves but dispositions to the formation of images. They produce typical images and are responsible for the creation of myths, the themes of which are common to all mankind.[26] Archetypes appear in different symbols, dreams, and myths, but they have the same underlying pattern, they produce symbols and myths with the same ground plan.[27] Forms the archetypes take change according to culture and particular individuals, but the same underlying psychic pattern supports them.

Being contained within the collective unconscious, the archetype is therefore not directly encountered, it appears in its indirect form in the symbol, dream, or the myth.[28] In this form the archetype takes upon itself the quality of the numinous and appears as an energizing experience of fundamental importance.[29] For the experiencing subject, the effect is of an encounter with a "wholly other" reality which engages his whole attention. The images produced by archetypes are more powerful in the psyche's dynamics than are concepts which are created by consciousness, they behave as powerful centers of energy with a life of their own.[30]

There are many archetypes. Amongst them are those with seemingly particular relevance to the experience of the Guru, these are, the spiritual father, the old wise man, the divine-human figure (Godman), and the central archetype, expressing wholeness, that of the self. These do not necessarily operate as discrete entities, for example the divine-human figure archetype may carry that of the self. According to Jung, "Anything that a man postulated as being a greater totality than himself can become a symbol of the self."[31] It appears that the divine-human figure is particularly suited to act as a greater totality, appearing, according to the particular religious culture, in such figures as Rama, Krishna, the Christ, the Buddha, Gurus, and to a lesser degree, holy men or women in general. The modern day holy man in Hinduism, according to C.S.J. White, is a composite figure, "belonging to the traditions of guru, ascetic, avatar and saint...in fact a blending of all,"[32] which suggests that the Guru, where he is central to belief as in the case of the Akshar-Purushottam movement is particularly suited to be the recipient of a number of related archetypes, amongst them being that of the self. The same would seem also to apply to the Christ image in those instances in the Christian faith where the person of Jesus is central to experience.

Jung maintained that: "under certain conditions the unconscious spontaneously brings forth an archetypal symbol of wholeness. From this we must conclude that some such archetype occurs universally and is endowed with a certain numinosity."[33] The frequency of the appearance of the divine-human figure in religions is suggestive of the universality of this particular symbol of the self. The archetype may lie dormant in the psyche until aroused by an external image.[34] In the case of Christian experience, and the pattern of the Western psyche, according to Jung, it may never be perceived at all "until a consciousness illuminated by conversion recognizes it in the figure of Christ."[35] And, although Jung did not specifically make the suggestion, it appears to the present writer that this awakening could also serve to describe the effect of the guru in the Eastern psyche.

The archetype of the self is of central importance to Jung's understanding of religion, for him it is indistinguishable in subjective experience from that of the God-image.[36] This is not necessarily to reduce the origin of God to being a mere product of the psyche, but to say that within the psyche both self and God-image function in a similar manner and evoke a similar experience.[37] Comments from members of the Akshar-Purushottam movement, and from other Guru-oriented persons, give the decided impression that experience associated with the Guru and the experience of the self are at least strongly associated if not synonymous. In their submission to the Guru devotees experience an expansion of their own individuality. Jung says, "They submit to him [the divine-human symbol] as a person — believing him to be an objective reality — because he is in fact simply the most precious part of themselves."[38] Abhishiktananda says, "the mystery of the guru is the mystery of the depth of the heart….[the] experience of being face to face with the guru…[is] that of being face to face with oneself."[39] Response to Jesus seems to be similarly placed in the psyche of the disciple one example being given by St. Paul in Galatians 2:20, "I have been crucified with Christ: it is no longer I who live, but Christ who lives in me."

The divine-human figure acts as a symbol which is the form the archetype takes when it becomes conscious. Such symbols appear regularly in dreams, visions, and fantasies, and always possess the quality of a *fascinosum*.[40] In other words the symbol makes the archetype, which is a concentrated form of energy, discernible; it is the "essence and image of psychic energy."[41] Symbols perform a mediating role between the conscious and unconscious; bringing signals from the unconscious into consciousness.[42] They have the capacity to evoke massive response.[43] Acting as channels through which psychic energy is made available to the conscious, the experience of the arrival of this energy in the conscious area of the psyche is apparently synonymous with the experience of the holy (numinous).[44]

Jung's model of the psyche is based upon the idea that the conscious and the unconscious parts belong to a greater totality which he terms the "self."[45] The self constitutes the whole of the individual's psychic existence, it is the "essence of psychic wholeness, i.e., the totality of conscious and unconscious."[46] But for Jung the self refers also to that particular consciousness of the whole, which is located in a center other than that of the ego;[47] self includes ego as a "supraordinate concept."[48] The self is also described as the midpoint of personality, which is experienced, when once realized, as a new center existing midway between the conscious and the unconscious. The self is the center of the total personality, just as the ego is the center of the conscious aspects of personality. In the process of individuation, the term used by Jung to describe this realization of the self,[49] the individual ceases to identify the ego as the center of his personality and now identifies with this new mid-point, that of the self. The ego now feels small as it experiences itself in the presence of a greater whole, as appearing before the wider expanse and numinous quality of the consciousness of the self. An experience which, from the subjective view, is at least similar to the reported experience of being in the presence of God.[50]

For Jung the quest for individuation is in effect the attempt to shift, "...the center of gravity from the ego to the self...."[51] He understands the pursuit of this end to be a life-long activity which gives meaning to life.[52] Individuation as the realization of a new center of the personality, that of the self in place of the ego, accords well with descriptions of mystical experience where there is a sense of expanded consciousness or oneness with something greater. The experience of submission to Guru or Christ could be described in these terms as abdication of the ego in favor of the greater power of the self.[53] It is more than the result of an intellectual process; it is brought about at a level deeper than consciousness and in the presence of symbols of wholeness, one important form of which appears in the symbol of the divine-human figure which again can represent the central symbol of the self. Jung understands individuation to be the goal of what he refers to as Eastern religious practice, and of the mysticism of the West. The realization of the self he sees as the goal to which all psychic life aspires.

Both Guru and Christ are understood by their respective traditions to be divine-human figures and are presented as such for acceptance. As the sadhu explained: "The Guru is the message." That is, over and above all else, it is the figure of the Guru who is the center of the movement's message to the world, this is also true for the Christian faith in their presentation of Jesus Christ. That some persons respond appropriately whilst others do not is variously explained; for example with the Guru, that previous lives have not yet developed the spiritual perception of the human form of God, or in the case of Jesus Christ that the devil has blinded the eyes of those who would otherwise see. Described in Jungian terms it could be that individuals have not yet made the projection of their self onto the symbol of the proclaimed figure and at least in this way have not undergone the process of individuation. (Jung does not suggest that individuation is necessarily dependent upon traditional religious symbols).

According to Jung, projection is the unconscious process which attributes a subjective but unconscious element to an object in such a way that the element in question seems to be part of it.[54] That is, an image or idea is placed on an object which is then treated as if it conforms to that image or possesses that idea.[55] Taken into the realm of worship this projection phenomenon means that the devotee is held in awe by something that is, unknown to him, a projected numinous element from his own psyche. For example, in relation to the Guru, the symbol of the divine-human figure becomes the "screen" onto which the symbol of the self is projected. The person and form of the Guru then acquires a numinous quality in the experience of the devotee and is worshiped as such. A similar process could be said to occur with the disciple in the case of the person of Jesus. Although the revered object itself, which is the focus of the projection, is not in reality the possessor of the highly valued attributes which emanate from the devotee's projection, the pro-jection is only made onto an object which has some likeness to the image to be projected. Jung says, "…the carrier of a projection is not just any object but is always one that proves adequate to the nature of the content projected."[56] Whitmont uses the term "hooks" to indicate that the object upon which the projection is made must have some intrinsic correspondence but that, "…the intensity of the projection does not depend so much upon the magnitude of the hook, the degree of likeness, but rather upon the intensity or charge of the projected content."[57] This would mean that the Guru's human attributes must coincide sufficiently well with the conception of the divine-human figure, but that the projection thus made is on the strength of the psyche of the devotee. In other words, the Guru's humanly existing form should prove an adequate screen upon which the projection can be made. Afterwards the interaction is between the person who has made the projection himself and the image he has projected. The same would take place in the case of Christ.

This explanation of projection is supported by the observation made by Brent, that a relationship with a flawed Guru can still effect positive change in the devotee.[58] Seemingly the flaws do not interfere with the process up to a certain point. When they do interfere, the projection is withdrawn and this guru is then seen for what he is in reality without the rose colored spectacles of the subjective archetypal element. Again, this appears to support the idea that the relationship is not primarily between an object who actually possesses these numinous attributes, but, once the projection has occured, between the devotee and that which he projects onto the Guru.[59]

By this process the projected father or mother figure, Godman, magician, old wise man, or whatever symbol is projected, becomes the other party with whom the devotee unconsciously interacts. Jung sees the symbol of an overpowering, all embracing, complete or perfect being as represented amongst other things by a man of heroic proportions which again he regards as a reflection of the individual's wholeness, i.e., of the self which is present in him as an unconscious image. Referring to the person of Jesus he appears to be saying that the historical figure of Jesus was the object upon which the archetypal image already existing in the psyche of his followers was projected. "At a very early stage, therefore, the real Christ vanished behind the emotions and projections which swarmed about him....He becomes the collective figure whom the unconscious of his contemporaries expected to appear....It was this archetype of the self in the soul of every man that responded to the Christian message, with the result that the concrete Rabbi Jesus was rapidly assimilated by the constellated archetype."[60]

However, whilst in the movement the present-day actual human form of the Guru is the screen upon which the projection is made, it is elaborated by the socially constructed reality of the Guru, which exists in the tradition of the movement. The potential devotee is encountered not only by the human form of the Guru but also by this further reality contained in the descriptions of the nature of the Guru conveyed by the body of devotees in their adulation of him, by the movement's ritual, by its literature and by the general atmosphere of its beliefs. The screen thus presented is thus not only the lauded attributes of this particular Guru, but also by those of all the previous Gurus of the guru parampara, including the culturally accepted attributes of the guru from wider Hindu tradition. The result is that, although the carrier of the archetype is humanly present, he is already clothed with archetypal dress and is the screen onto which his psyche is invited to project the symbol of the self. That is, he projects onto an abstract socially constructed image rather than simply onto a specific person; onto this image which is already the possessor of the projected numinious contents of the movement's tradition. Again, this can also be applied to the disciple and the figure of Christ.

Experiences described in worship, and particularly the fascination with the form of the Guru, seem to provide evidence of this projection taking place.[61] The Guru is different, all he does is sacred, his walk, the way he eats, smiles, takes medicine, the whole rapt fascination with the physical form of the Guru seem to support the idea that he is the bearer of the numinous contents of the devotee's psyche. Something similar could be said to be taking place with the fascination with the personal form of Jesus in the incident referred to as the transfiguration (Matthew 17:1-8) and also in Jones's adoration of the person of Christ.

Again, in both the case of the Guru's devotee and of the Christian disciple, this projection does not originate with the individual of today. For example, in the case of Jesus in the Gospel accounts,[62] and particularly in the letters of Paul,[63] he is already the bearer of projected archetypes. So that "the real Christ is the preached Christ," and the historical image presented to the potential believer is that image which has been "worked over by the community of faith in the light of their faith."[64] The same in turn seems to have occured with the Guru who, in addition to all that is lavished upon him in the present, is considered to be the bearer of the qualities and person of the Gurus of the movement's guru parampara, and also the form which manifests Lord Swaminarayan himself. However, whilst this dynamic may remain true for the general case, there are still instances where the projection in the case of the Guru has seemingly been of a more spontaneous nature and independent of the communication of the extravagant feelings of others about the Guru. These reported experiences perhaps provide more radical illustrations of the unconscious nature of projection, and accord well with Jung's description of the encounter with the holy man: "Holiness is…revelatory: it is the illuminative power emanating from an archetypal figure....He does not perceive holiness, it takes him captive and overwhelms him...."[65]

It needs to be borne in mind that, whilst the projection of the Godman archetype appears at least to be one important element in the Guru-devotee relationship, the attachment which appears in this relationship is not fully accounted for by reference to the unconscious psychic sphere. With the Guru, in addition to any projection to which the devotee is relating, there is also the quality of the conscious human relationship in the here-and-now with a loved person. To the writer this seems to create a very significant difference in the response to the living Guru relative to the response to the divine-human figure who has gone beyond normal human interaction, for example the relationship to the Christ image or to the image of Lord Swaminarayan (1781-1830 C.E.). Relationship with the presently existing Guru involves interaction in the concrete world, and includes receiving tangible signals of response to the love which the devotee exhibits towards the Guru. Through this the devotee's relationship to the Guru also rests upon these outward manifestations; it is not solely dependent on the archetypal projection.

For the movement it is considered essential, in order to attain the highest spiritual state, for its members to be able to recognize the human form of God — does this mean, to have made the archetypal projection? This appears in the doctrine of the movement, in the form that it is only by attending to the personal form of Akshar (the Guru), that Purushottam (God) can be experienced. Reported experience supports this doctrinal belief in that devotees affirm that by association with the Guru, they have been spiritually uplifted to the state of seeing God in all things, and to the experience of the highest bliss. Translating this into terms of the Christian faith, a somewhat similar situation seems to exist. For example, it is affirmed in the reported words of Jesus that, "...no man cometh to the Father but by me" (John 14:6). This could be interpreted such that the human form of God is being presented by the early Church as the essential means whereby a person may come into true awareness of God; that recognition of the human form of God (making the archetypal projection) is the essential means to what is considered to be true encounter with God, or in Jungian terms, to realization of the self. As there is no evidence of Christian influence in the formation of the doctrine of Akshar and Purushottam, or of the reverse, it would seem that, assuming the psychic basis of doctrine, that the same psychic dynamic is responsible for the incarnational doctrine in both cases. If, as suggested by Jung, doctrine originates in psychic experience, then it follows that the Christian doctrine of Christ — as the means by which God may be known and through whom right-relatedness to God may be achieved — has its origin or basic region of response, in the collective unconscious. A similar situation could be said to exist in the Akshar-Purushottam movement with its doctrine of Akshar, of which the Guru is the manifest form, being essential to attainment of Purushottam (God). That is, in both traditions the divine-human figure is believed to function as the mediating entity between man and God. In Jungian terms, the divine-human figure operates as a symbol onto which the individual projects his self and to which he then submits resulting in the experience of individuation. To focus upon the divine-human figure is effectively to evoke the archetype which leads to the experience of God.

It was the reported experience of devotees of the Guru that their individuality was not in any way restricted by their submission to the Guru, and rather, that as a result of their submission to him, they experienced a general enhancement of their own personality. This observation was also made by Brent, after contact with a number of Gurus and their devotees, including those of the Akshar-Purushottam movement.[66] Feelings of security, confidence, peace, and bliss were reportedly experienced as a result of the relationship.

Jung's state of wholeness,[67] experienced by the person who has undergone the process of individuation appears similar to these reported experiences, and Jung himself believed that the individuation experience was common to the religious experience of mankind "the world over and throughout history."[68]

Jung's concept of individuation as a developing state may also provide a useful model with which to explain the developing experience of the devotee. The varying stages of submission, obedience, sense of oneness and love for the Guru, being understood as varying stages of the attainment of the self (individuation). Bearing in mind that, whilst the process of individuation includes sudden revelations of a numinous quality, it is also understood by Jung as a progressive state which lasts throughout one's lifetime, and that the goal of individuation, the full realization of the self, is never completely attained.[69] Nevertheless, the pursuit of the goal of full individuation, the attainment of the self, is said to give life its meaning, and it "appears as a task of the highest order."[70] This allows for the possibility that the varying stages of experience reported by devotees could be considered in terms of a continuum of the individuation process. The numinous experience gained in this process could well be that which respondents describe as bliss, and which is understood by devotees to be a progressive state dependent on the extent of their achieved degree of submission to the Guru.

Whilst the experiences which occur in the devotee are beyond the capacity of his own will-power to produce unaided, there is a still a conscious element involved. It is only after conscious acceptance of, and submission to, the outer person of the Guru that such inner changes are experienced. This submission may be externally expressed in the outward signs of acceptance of the Guru, and especially in submitting to his commands rather than one's own will in performance of the ordinary duties of the devotee. Service, highly valued in the movement, is always service to the Guru whatever form it should take; even sweeping the floor and other similar tasks are service to the Guru. Humble service can then be seen as the natural external expression of the situation which exists in the psyche, and such service would in turn be helping to strengthen and confirm the inner submission; this accords with the reported experience of devotees interviewed. Service is seen in the movement as a privilege afforded to devotees. By this service they are able to further their own spiritual development, whilst expressing their love and devotion to the Guru.

Comments from respondents show that, even with devotees who are considered to be advanced, some resistance to complete submission remains. Striving towards the deepening of the Guru-devotee experience, and the pursuit of individuation, could be seen to coincide in this evident longing for greater submission; greater submission to the Guru reflecting greater submission of ego to self. This is more than a desire to escape from one's self into a dependency relationship, although that element is not absent in some devotees, but a longing to be at one with something greater than the ego center. Not a longing for extinction and elimination of consciousness, but a longing to be united with something greater, to be at one with a higher consciousness (that of the self or God?).

Whilst Jung claimed that a difference exists between the psyches of individuals in the East and West,[71] the description he gives of the functioning of the symbol of Christ in the Christian's experience appears to the present writer to be readily applicable to that of the Guru as he has appeared in experiences reported by members of the Akshar-Purushottam movement.[72] The psychic response to the divine-human figure, and the reported experiential change resulting from it, both seem to suggest that this symbol functions in the psyche in a similar fashion in both East and West. For example, the disciple's experience of response to Jesus and the Akshar-Purushottam devotee's response to Swaminarayan or the Guru who manifests him appear strikingly similar.

PART II

6

Ritual and Reinterpretation: South Indians in Southeast Asia

Fred W. Clothey

A number of strategies have been used by South Indians settling outside their ancestral home by which they are negotiating their identities and transmitting their heritage in not always hospitable cities. Responding to globalization, the traumas of urbanization and the exigencies of raising children in multi-cultural contexts, communities of Tamils, Telugus and Malayalis have experimented with a variety of ways to be who they are and enable their children to claim some sense of that heritage. In this context I wish to explore only two strategies that most South Indians (and especially Tamils) are wont to use and to illustrate these strategies from the context of Singapore.

Pragmatic Ritualism

Even the casual observer cannot but notice the proliferation of ritual events in the temples of overseas South Indians. Everywhere *kumbabhisekas* are being held as temples are built in North America or renovated in Southeast Asia. These temples are becoming the venues for more elaborate rituals as the sponsoring communities become more affluent. Recently, for example, the *sahasrakalas-abhisekam* (libations with 1008 pots) was held in North America for the first time (Pittsburgh, 1987) and in Malaysia for the first time (Kuala Lumpur, December, 1990). In Malaysia, the Ceylonese Tamils sponsored the same ritual in April 1991 as if to demonstrate how it should really be done. The same ritual was done in Singapore for the first time within the last five years at a temple administered by the Hindu Endowment Board. Libation with shells (*cankabhisekam*), whether 108 or 1008, are done almost routinely now in Southeast Asia but only for the first time with 1008 shells in Singapore some seven years ago at the Mariyamman temple (another HEB - administered board). Patrons are signed up months in advance for the privilege of sponsoring cankhabhisekam held daily at the Pillaiyar temple in Pudu, Kuala Lumpur. *Homam* of various kinds have become commonplace. Not least elaborate are those done for the goddess, for example, during Navarattiri in Bombay's Chembur temple and the South Indian Samajam in Matunga, for the Astalakshmi puja in Pittsburgh (1988), or periodically for Vadapathira Kaliyamman in her temple in Singapore. In these sacrifices, a number of offerings deemed specially pleasing to the goddess are offered by means of fire — often including jewelry and silk garments. At one level, to be sure, these kinds of rituals are sponsored by temples seeking to demonstrate they are large and wealthy enough to warrant the support of devotees. Often they are explicitly intended to raise funds from the faithful.

But these events are part of a larger strategy by which temples become "cultural spaces" and the venues for a "pragmatic ritualism." There are a number of reasons why ritual is so visible in the mushrooming temples of South Indian Hindus living outside their ancestral homes — visible even when participants themselves are unable to express the meanings of specific ritual events. Not least significantly, ritual expresses and purveys the essence of Hindu identity. For most South Indians (and probably for most Indians) religion is expressed primordially as performance. Ritual is pre-discursive, supra-textual, experiential, visceral. In ritual one hears, albeit not propositionally, but also senses, sees, even smells, the tradition. In theory at least, it invites the engagement of the entire person.[1]

Ritual acts out aesthetically and dramatically that which the tradition is. It links one to one's community and to one's lineage symbolically. It affords in its expressiveness the opportunity to reflect on its meanings, in so far as one wishes to do so. This ritualism is pragmatic in other respects, however. People engage in it to seek redress for the very mundane concerns with which they are engaged in their urban lives: academic hurdles, financial crunches, domestic uncertainties, loss of a sense of community or personhood. It is no accident that ritual is the recourse for persons at all those stages of life which are boundaries — transitions to adolescence, parenthood, retirement — and at those geographic and societal interstices in which people live. The practice of Hinduism in the contemporary world is hardly "other-worldly" (if indeed it ever was). It is very much the product and result of mundane pragmatic concerns.

More specifically, ritual is used to maintain and restate historical identities at the same time that it is expected to ease transitions into new and more satisfying situations.[2] It re-presents one's image of India even as it acts out the reciprocities and social landscape of one's new home. Contemporary South Indian Hindu temple rituals overseas (and Singapore is no exception) are increasingly expressions of perceived "agamization." The term "agamization" is used advisedly here, for it does not connote a matter of locating ritual texts and following them to the letter. In fact, many of the priests conducting these rituals overseas neither have access to the texts nor can they read them (at least not in Sanskrit). For that matter, Smarta Brahmins (even Tamil ones, for example, in Bombay) denigrate the "agamas" and evoke the authenticating arche of Sankara, Sankaracarya, and the presumed "Vedic" character of Sanskritic utterances.

Rather, "agamization" is more a matter of inviting Brahmanic priests, tutored in the performative traditions of their forefathers, to preside over the ritual life of the temple. It is no accident that such priests are usually drawn from those geographic and sectarian centers that most characterize one's sense of "ancestral home." Tamils and Telugus seem most concerned for such "authenticated" ritual technicians and the rituals they perform — after all, many of the agamic texts were largely a post facto description of rituals done by priests in

Tamil and Telugu areas. Virtually all the Brahmin priests in Singapore are on work permits; these are almost always from Tamilnadu, suggesting the Tamil domination of the Singaporean Hindu temple landscape. (Of some thirty two or so temples in Singapore, some thirty are primarily Tamil in character with various accommodations made to other groups in specific icons or ritual events. The major exception to this pattern in Singapore is that of the Ceylon Tamils who bring their priests from Sri Lanka). Pittsburgh's Sri Venkatesvara Temple, on the other hand, has installed a priest representing each of three southern regions in an attempt at political compromise, satisfying the sense of geographic, ethnic authenticity of its major devotees. This relative "agamization" serves to upgrade the ritual life, link it to the performative tradition's perceived ancestral roots, and lend it greater status. At the same time, it is believed to enhance the power of the ritual to achieve its intended aims.

This process thus symptomizes a return to orthopraxy on the part of many emigre South Indians. It is an orthopraxy not uncommon for those who feel a sense of enclavement, marginality or distancing from one's roots. It is not uncommon for those whose very uniqueness is perceived to be at stake in the face of majority cultures, migration and change.

At the same time these ritual events act out the alliances and reciprocities that have become part of the social landscape of the emigre community. In Singapore, Telugus may negotiate with a Tamil priest to perform a marriage in a Telugu Naidu way. Icons to Sri Visalatci or Krishna in forms generally associated with Uttar Pradeshis or Bengalis, may appear in primarily "Tamil temples" and include ritual sequences especially compelling to those North Indians. Malayalis have incorporated a shrine to Ayyappan in a Munisvaran temple, while Telugu Vaisnavas have added a coterie of Vaisnava shrines in the Vadapathira Kaliyamman Temple where Vaikhanasa priests do the honors in an otherwise Saiva shrine maintained by Saiva *gurukkals* (in which shrines to Madurai Viran and Periyachi are tended by *pantaram* or non-brahmin priests). Muniandi becomes Siva by way of Munisvaran. Kaliyamman and Mariamman have become the mother of Vinayakar and Murukan. In Bombay, similarly, Tamil

Brahmins, in alliance with "Malayali" Brahmins, (usually, descendants of Tamil Brahmins who had migrated to Kerala) maintain temples wherein the Aryankavu (married) form of Ayyappan is enshrined with Murukan (at Chembur); Rama is coupled with Rajarajesvari (in the South Indian Bhajana Samajam in Matunga); the Sabarimala Ayyappan and Guruvayur appear in shrines with various Saiva deities (in the Ashtika Samajam of Matunga). These iconic and ritual compromises suggest the kinds of alliances, horizontal and vertical, that are enacted in the temple life of contemporary South Indian Hindus.

As a result, one can find in the temple and ritual life of a city like Singapore an acting out of the economic, social, even political landscape of the South Indian communities. Relatively affluent and elite patrons and their families have assumed ownership of entire temples (e.g., The Vadapathira Kaliyamman Temple) and along with trade guilds have assumed responsibility over the years for patronizing certain ritual events during festival occasions. In exchange for these acts of patronage they receive *mariyathi* (or honor) from temple authorities who thereby affirm the status and authority of the patron. Such patrons (*upayam*) are also able to assume the role of "watchdogs of orthopraxy."[3]

Less affluent middle class groups by purchasing tickets for the ritual occasion are believed to accrue benefits from the ritual in their own behalf and concomitantly gain stature and affirmation of place in the social hierarchy. Lower class persons who wish to similarly "purchase in" are able to receive the accrued benefits, gain stature and a sense of vertical mobility through alliance with the patronizing *periyavar* ("big shot"). The ritual alliances thereby enact the kinds of interdependencies and alliances that characterize the social landscape.

One moment in a ritual enactment will illustrate something of those patterns and people's various perceptions of them. The occasion was the *Pankuni Pirumamam Urcavam* (*Pankuni Brahmovatsam*) at the Sri Srinivasa Perumal Temple on Serangoon Road, Singapore. The temple had been founded in the 1860s as the Narasimha Perumal temple, named after the family deity of the founding patron, Mr. Narasimhan Perumal, a Telugu Naidu. In 1906 in the face of financial disarray the temple and its endowments came under the management of the Hindu Endowment Board (HEB), then known as the Muhammedan and Hindu Endowments Board. In 1971 the temple was the focus of some controversy as the Endowment Board renovated and upgraded it and at the behest of the Telugus on the board, installed largely Tamil Vaikanasa Vaisnava priests in place of the Saiva gurukkals and Pancaratra priests who had shared the ritual chores earlier.[4] While some Telugus were unhappy with the change, most devotees were unaware of its significance and continued to patronize it, particularly (but not exclusively) Vaisnavas.

The festival now celebrated is one of the biggest of the year in this temple. On Pankuni Uttiram, the marriage of Andal to Perumal had been re-enacted. Two days later, the Brahmotsavam started. This day, the ninth of the Brahmotsavam (Tuesday, April 9, 1991) is the highlight of the festival. This morning, on the day said to be Visnu's birthday, the deity and his consort have been paraded around the temple pavilion in the silver chariot. They are dabbed with the water which had been sacralized during the week with homams and *abhisekam*. Following *darsan*, the deities in the main shrine are offered extended abhisekam (libations of water, sandal, milk, honey, etc.) and *aratanai* (ornamentation and showing of the lights and insignia of kingship). Around noon the people who have been in attendance are fed a vegetarian feast. There is time for conversation.

A priest whose major chores for the morning are completed chats with a Western observer. He seems nostalgic for his home. He had been affiliated with a small Vaisnava shrine dedicated to Alakar near the bus stand in Madurai, Tamilnadu. He is in Singapore without his family on a work permit provided by the government for a period generally not to exceed two years. He is earning a better salary in Singapore than he was back home and is able to send a significant portion of it to his family. He maintains the priests are doing the rituals in Singapore just as they would back home, except for the compromises and modifications they are asked to make by temple authorities and patrons. "We do whatever the *yajamana* wants us to do," he says; "he is like the king used to be, you know; we do his bidding." This day is a happy occasion for him, even though he is busy, as it is "Visnu's birthday" and the power of the *naksatra* overrides the fact that it is the dark side of the fortnight. The priest in many ways reflects the attitudes of many of Singapore's early Indian sojourners — they came temporarily and without families. The temple serves as home away from home, the lifeline to the heritage and roots still missed.

The yajamana, or patron of the day, is a wealthy Telugu Naidu, S.L.P. Mohan, grandson of "Govindasamy Chettiar," a philan-thropist, given that honorary name because he had been generous in the support of temples during his lifetime. The family had assumed ownership in the 1920s of the Vadapathira Kaliyamman temple (just up Serangoon Road from the Perumal temple) when it had floundered financially, had assumed the patronage of festival events and helped in the building of *gopurams* in several temples. Mr. Mohan's father, S.L. Perumal, had been largely responsible for ren-ovating the Perumal Temple for the 1971 *kumbabhisekam*, for changing its name to the Sri Srinivasan Perumal Temple and for installing the Vaikanasa priests (because they were perceived at the time to be more popular than Pancaratra priests). Mr. Mohan himself, when he took over after his father's death in 1982, installed a coterie of Rama shrines in the Vadapathira Kaliyamman Temple and installed Vaikanasa priests to officiate at those shrines.

Mr. Mohan is anxious to maintain his family's obligations in Singapore's temple life. He and his family provide patronage for at least four ritual events per year at the Perumal temple along with their other obligations because "it is our duty" and because he understands himself to be a "religious man" — "I get freedom from stress when I come to the temple in the midst of this pressure-packed city." He wants to make the rituals as much as possible like those to be found in India, which he visits often, there to consult with "various gurus," especially the Kanchi Sankaracarya. He apologizes to the Western observer that this particular ritual is somewhat more modest than it would have been in India — "Here the government won't let us hold processions whenever we want and we don't have access to much water so we have to settle for this small well in which to bathe the god." He estimates that his sponsorship of temples and rituals in the city costs him about S$ 200,000 (U.S. $120,000) annually, excluding the amount devotees help to defray.

Mr. Mohan is less concerned about the meanings of the rituals than with the fact that they are done "right" and without regard to expense. In exchange he gets "peace of mind," a sense of family obligation fulfilled, the honor and status accorded one who is performing these rites for the "good of devotees," and the privilege of being a guardian of orthopraxy. He is given *mariyathi* and the first *prasadam* on this occasion.

A devotee, standing nearby, finds this to be an occasion in which he can express his identity as a Telugu. I paraphrase his comments:

> We really are a minority in Singapore, perhaps 500 families of us [actually 8% of the total Indian population as compared to 75% Tamils, according to the 1980 census]. We often come to the Perumal temple, as most of us are Vaisnavas — we come on this occasion, but especially for Ugadhi, [i.e., New Year], which falls on the new moon of Pankuni (March 17, 1991).
>
> I consider myself a religious person, just like my mother was (though my father wasn't). Whenever I go to India, I spend a lot of time on pilgrimage, so much so my family makes fun of me.
>
> Many of our [Telugu] forefathers came to work as stevedores in the harbor; in fact, I work in hoisting container cargo on and off ships.
>
> Occasions like this bring a number of Telugus out and we've gotten to the point we mix well without much consciousness of caste backgrounds. Of course, we still have a sort of "class system", made up of about four economic levels. Our parents were more serious about caste observance than we are, but we still tend to observe these class levels when it comes to marriage — intermarriage may take place now between levels 1 and 2 or between 2 and 3, but not between levels 1 and 4.

Finally, a teenage girl standing on the fringes of the ritual event throughout, talks with the foreign stranger. She understands but a little of what's happening ritually: "I was told today they would put the deity in water and we believe that water is auspicious once the deity has touched it, so we like to touch ourselves with that water." Within minutes she is romping about the temple precincts with a number of teenage boys, who are squirting each other with water and trying to dump each other into the small temple tank.[5]

This girl and her colleagues speak for some of Singapore's marginalized Indians, who don't quite understand or feel comfortable in the ritual system. For others, however, the system provides an opportunity to experience the enactment of their heritage, linking them with their lineage and the authenticating sources of their identity even as it expresses the alliances and reciprocities of their Singaporean socio-cultural landscape.

For all these reasons enumerated and illustrated above and more, the ritual life of South Indian emigres is a pragmatic and important part of the expression of ethnicity. In this respect, ritual is indeed a form of "cultural performance," to use the term Milton Singer coined two decades ago.[6]

It is performance which presents within set times and places something of how a people envision themselves and wish to be presented to others — their own young, a majority culture, even the tourist.

Reinterpretation

And yet this pragmatic ritualism is not without its critics — even if these are silent ones who express themselves by not participating. Among those who fall between the cracks in these patterns of ritualization are those who don't quite feel a part of the system. Often these are the less affluent who can't afford to purchase darsan or the young who don't understand the significance of certain rituals and hence may be seen on the fringes (or not at all) at temples during ritual events. More seriously, there are those young who feel marginalized in a society like Singapore's because they are in the city with temporary work permits or have trouble competing in the high pressure school system (some 25 percent of Indian children of school age in Singapore have dropped out of school).[7]

Ironically, these young people may also express themselves ritually — by taking vows and undergoing self-flagellation in the Thai Pucam procession (or even by dancing frivolously on the fringes of the procession); by gravitating toward "anti-establishment" forms of religion, such as toward mediums who purport to induce trance and predict the future — figures who are generally dismissed as "charlatans" by the "establishment." The sense of alienation is exacerbated among some of the working classes by the fact Singapore's government in its concern for modernization and maximal use of space has eliminated most of the temporary shrines to which workers might otherwise have been going — shrines, that is, to Muniandi, Manmatha, and others. Further, some temple authorities are increasingly concerned to exclude from ritual events those who do not participate with the decorum expected.

There are also some Indians (including some South Indians) who raise questions about this form of ritualized Hinduism. A number of them agree that it is a form of religion that is more emulative than innovative, more pietistic than ethically explicit; more the product of an era of kingship than of a "democratic" society, more ethnic than global. Such persons are often inclined to challenge traditional ritual patterns — to wonder, for example, whether it is necessary to spend more money to buy a silver chariot or a gold leaf rajagopuram. Indeed, experiments have been tried in Singapore's ritual life — in 1987, for example, at two of the HEB temples, including the Sri Srinivasan Perumal Temple, an attempt was made to replace the traditional betel leaves, nuts and *kumkum* used in puja with the offering of raisins and cubes of cane sugar and vermillion wrapped in plastic. The experiment was abandoned within months at the insistence of more traditional devotees, despite the fact the "newer" combination was deemed easier to clean up.[8]

Many of these kinds of persons are in the forefront of a different kind of expression of South Indian Hinduism which is less dependent on temple — perhaps is even spawned inversely in contradistinction to temple-oriented religion, though it certainly does not tend to replace it. It is the more discursive, reflective style of Hinduism, generally oriented by the tradition of the guru-diksa or teacher-student. Simply put, this movement is a quest for understanding of what it is to be Hindu; for self-conscious legitimation (or "rationalization," to use Weber's term); for finding a viable Hindu *nomos* for the boundary situations in which they live. This is not peculiar to expatriated Hindus, but is particularly problematic for Hindus (as well as for overseas Chinese) inasmuch as, unlike most Muslims and Christians, there are no centrally coordinated agencies, hierarchies and educational programs to interpret the tradition for people on the religious frontiers. There is, as a result, a scramble everywhere where one finds expatriated Indians to redefine who they are, to be informed as to what they are supposed to do, even what they are supposed to think. This becomes, even more crucial, I have come to believe, in the second and third generations of life in societies outside India (and more for the third than the second), as, for this generation, there is less likelihood of memory. They have received the tradition selectively and in refracted terms, if at all. The question of identity becomes much more self-conscious in pluralistic settings, as being a minority in a multicultural setting has a way of forcing very fundamental questions upon one.

The Quest for Gurus

The responses to this perceived need are abundant — so much so it is difficult to summarize and discern patterns. But there are a few which might be identified. Quite striking, for example, is the quest for gurus. The term "guru" can be loosely defined. Anyone who is perceived to know more than oneself may be recognized as an ad hoc guru. More significantly, the "guru" or senior savant is perceived to combine several qualities at once: authentic humanhood and/or charisma; wisdom beyond the seeker's own; representation of that portion of the tradition most central to the follower's own sense of identity; and others; the relationship is often geographically remote — a few hours or days in the presence of one such person (sometimes even a single lecture) becomes the beginning of a long term following — attending lectures when that person is in town, being in his presence when possible, as if in the entourage of a *periyavar* ("big shot"); reading whatever he may have written. The most effective method of communication is more likely to be oral than textual, however, and often more exemplary than discursive. The guru's aura will usually be purveyed through a network of followers. As a result, in places like Singapore and Malaysia, very few South Indians will fail to have someone to whom they have looked as exemplar and interpreter of the tradition.

These gurus are numerous. One person's salvation is another's charlatan. There is very little quality control, though those groups that deem themselves the guardians of orthopraxy will have their own criteria as to which voice says the right things. Smarta Brahmins in Bombay, for example, are divided as to whether the Sringeri or Kanchi Sankaracarya is the most appropriate "leader." The choice can be based on several things: sometimes it is a function of geographical or ethnic background — whether one comes from Eastern Tamilnadu or from Western Tamilnadu, Kerala or Karnataka; it may result from a relation or friend's having brought one into the orbit of said leader; occasionally, one believes the finding of such a leader was the result of a series of divinely-initiated events. Ceylon Tamils in Southeast Asia, on the other hand, will take most seriously those who are perceived to most accurately represent Saiva Siddhanta (and these are most likely to have had some connection with Sri Lanka). Those Tamils emerging into self-conscious Hinduism from the estates and urban working class in Southeast Asia, and who are less likely to know English, look to those who can speak mellifluous Tamil and can make the forgotten (or never known) Tamil classics come alive and seem relevant (however selectively these classics are re-presented). So there will be pockets of persons learning to sing (and occasionally discuss) small portions of the *Tirukkural* or the *Tevaram*, even with people whose credentials may be suspect to the more orthodox.

English-educated persons, for their part, look to Anglicized and globe-trotting leadership. For these folk English has become the legitimating language, so the tradition is most credible when interpreted and refracted in Anglicized form. Scientific or quasi-scientific language is used to legitimate the message. Here again, the content of the message heard will often reflect the follower's self-understanding — middle to upper class Tamils want to have their Tamil identities legitimated by hearing Saiva Siddhanta straight from the saints by way of the "West." Some de-Sanskritized Tamil Brahmins and urban alienates, on the other hand, are more likely to want their Hinduism to have a pan-Hindu, presumably more modern, cast, so Vedantism and various forms of neo-Hindu hybridizations are likely to strike a chord. That theology often matches self-perception is a hypothesis that seems to have some credibility in this quest for re-definition on the boundaries.

Persons may look to more than one "guru" for affirmation. Any number of self-proclaimed teachers have arisen on these boundaries who offer their services as occasional preachers and teachers. In Malaysia over forty organizations and in Singapore over fifteen have emerged purporting to cater to the educational or social needs of the Indian community. Some of these groups are sect or caste-based; others have arisen around strong personalities seeking self-expression. There is virtually no co-ordination or quality control of these agencies, save as they retain (in Malaysia) membership in the "umbrella" Malaysian Hindu Sangham.

Orality in Community

In addition to the following of a guru, another way in which the perceived tradition is transmitted is through various uses of oral communication, most commonly done in groups. Orality conveys an electricity of its own, for in the spoken word several long-standing Indian assumptions are evoked: the cosmogonic power of sound; the sense that "teaching" is done orally and by recitation (the word for teaching in Tamil is *collikkotu* — literally, "giving by saying"), the charisma of the orator and rhetorician, and the power of Tamil (and other vernaculars) as spoken (more than a written) language. That these oral expressions are done in congregational settings increases their significance as purveyors of tradition, as in the act of sitting, listening and reciting together the sense of community and the common sharing of identities are enhanced. Accordingly, groups meet with considerable frequency at prescribed hours of the week (the most popular time in Islamized Kuala Lumpur, for example, is Friday noon). Together, groups attend classes, meditate, hear homilies, give bhajans, and recite memorized portions of classical texts. Often the groups are organized in terms of sub-ethnic configurations: college students, government workers, workers on a particular estate or in a particular town, Ceylon Tamils, English-speaking young Telugus, etc. Young persons attend camps organized by various coalitions of organizations. Temples often become the venues for such meetings, but various other meeting halls can be pressed into service. These "oralized communities" become paradigms of Hindu, vernacular and/or sub-ethnic identities and serve to heighten the sense of appreciation for and commitment to one's heritage.

The Written "Word"

Quite apart from the attempts at oral communication, including camps, conferences, classes, sermons, and contests in singing *Tevaram* or reciting the classics, there is a groping for the written word, both Tamil and English. The patterns are much the same as in oral communication. There is seldom quality control, save as one group or person distributes that which he or she perceives to represent one's own sense of tradition, truth, and identity. Simplified pamphlets purport to offer the "correct" understanding of virtually everything: how to do home pujas (prepared by the head of the Malayalam sangam in Singapore because "our people don't know the basics of doing puja"); why it is inappropriate to skewer yourself during Tai Pucam (written by the guru of an anglicized Telugu group, The Rudra Deva Sangham, who sets up a "truth booth" annually during the Tai Pucam festival at Batu Caves, near Kuala Lumpur); why the *gayatri* mantra is so important to do and how to do it (first appearing in *Omkara*, produced by the Hindu Centre in Singapore, and now distributed in xeroxed form amongst Brahmins in Kuala Lumpur because "we have lost the meanings of essential things"); a classic comic production of the *Tirukkural* (produced and distributed by the Ceylonese Tamil proprietor of the EVS Bookshop in Singapore because "those arrogant Brahmins who put out those classic comics in Bombay don't appreciate Tamil culture"); why the Hawaii swami is wrong when he claims that God is always creating new souls (distributed by the Ceylon Tamils in Kuala Lumpur, self-appointed guardians of Saiva Siddhanta orthodoxy). Blessed be he who can read English as such a one can read the truth as crafted by the wise. Of course, those who can read it in Tamil (or some other vernacular tongue) will get their nectar straight from the gods.

Similarly, the written materials tend either to appeal to the Tamil (or vernacular) side of one's identity by discussing (and usually praising uncritically) those aspects of the tradition mediated in Tamil (e.g., the Saiva poets, etc.) or to the "Indian" and pan-Hindu side of one's identity — by purporting to discuss the Sanskritic traditions and the neo-Hindu interpreters thereof. Anglicized elites often alienated or under-educated as to the ritual and intellectual traditions of South India are those Tamils most likely to look toward the latter kind of literature, along with Malayalis, Telugus or Tamil Brahmins and other "elites" wanting to distance themselves from mainstream Tamils, still known all to well as "klings" (dirty people) in the Malay peninsula.

Translation of Texts

The translation of texts, when it is done (and that is rather infrequently in the Southeast Asian setting) is still another marker of changing identity patterns of upper class South Indians. To convey the Tamil classics, for example, in English, the new international *lingua franca*, is to legitimate them, make them competitive in the international market place of ideas and accessible to generations for whom the vernacular is fading — this despite the fact that many of the ad hoc translations attempted of Tamil classical poetry are terrible. (Incidentally, I have encountered precious few "expatriated Indians" in Southeast Asia who work with Sanskrit well enough to attempt any kind of translation at all). Such translations as are done in Southeast Asia even from vernacular literature are usually piecemeal — selected portions of larger texts which serve as someone's "favorite"; these often become parts of anthologies of hymns and classical stanzas. Nonetheless, there is a long-standing tradition in India itself of translating whole poets and texts into other languages, a tradition which is increasingly common amongst South Indians in North America. Such translations usually reflect the values and self-perceptions of the translators. In another essay, for example, I have documented the metamorphosis of the work of Arunakiri from a relatively obscure fifteenth century Tamil mystic-poet into a paradigm of Tamil sainthood and poetics for the contemporary world. V. Chengalvaraya Pillai, a Murukan bhakta, more than anyone else, resurrected Arunakiri for the 20th century Tamil world by collating his works into twelve volumes, editing and commenting on them. In the process of textualizing a poetry first intended for performance and dance, Chengalvaraya Pillai (an MA in English literature) depicts Arunakiri as the equal of any of the Saiva Bhaktas and great Tamil poets. Arunakiri is further legitimated and upgraded by various other attempts at translation — most particularly as a saint *par excellence* in K. Kartikeyan's rendition

(Kartikeyan was a member of The Divine Life Society) and as a philosophical giant in V.A. Devasenapati's effort. No translations, of course, have been able as yet to do justice to Arunakiri as a poet with skills commensurate with those of any internationally renowned poet. The point simply is that classical figures are often re-cast during the textualization process in the image of the translator — no less so by translators bridging more than one cultural world.[9]

A Singaporean Illustration

Some interesting experiments in groping toward a contemporary reinterpretation or restatement of the Hindu "essence" have been attempted in Singapore. There the Hindu Centre, for example, an organization founded in the late 1970s primarily by Professor A.N. Rao, a Kannada Brahmin and a professor of biology at Singapore National University and by his "friend," Dr. Pillai, publishes a periodic newsletter, Omkara, and hosts lectures attempting to educate the less than religiously sophisticated as to the essence of Hinduism. In fact, however, a number of concerns were first raised in a pair of seminars held in 1969 and 1970. The first of these, held on May 23-25, 1969, was attended by representatives of 23 temples and religious organizations of Hindu Singapore. The group, after considerable discussion, published a series of recommendations to the effect that temples should pay more attention to education and social service. A great many concerns were raised as to how temples could more adequately address the needs of the Hindu community. Among the recommendations most relevant to our present discussion were the following:

> Temples have been too self-centered and have been merely places of worship. They should also be places of social service to the community.
> Temples/organizations should make provision for library and reading room facilities and the distribution of pamphlets on religious topics to propagate religion.
> Youth committees should be attached to temples/organizations to assist the management committees in providing social service.
> Management committees should give priority to religious

education of youth and children. A crash programme should be initiated by the Secretariat to assist temples/organizations to start religious classes. Parents should be encouraged to send their children to these sessions.[10]

Among the problems temples were asked to address were the following:

Lack of understanding of the basic principles of Hinduism as a whole and temple worship and ceremonies in particular. This has resulted in children not receiving religious education at home or in the temples/organizations the parents support.

The need to cut down time and money on ceremonies to suit present day conditions and to ensure that the ceremonies are understood by devotees.[11]

A year later, in June 1970, the seminar met again and set up five subcommittees for further implementation of concerns and to record a few signs of progress over the year: S$ 300 was donated to a home for the aged in Singapore's "little India"; a youth group had been started at one temple, with others preparing to follow; classes in Hinduism were being held by volunteers for young persons in some twelve different places. Of these three had been started during the year.[12]

One of the more interesting recommendations from the 1969 seminar with respect to the high priority that should be placed in religious instruction was that:

A common syllabus [should] be planned and the purpose made explicit to parents;

Modern methods should be adapted in the teaching of religion.

A teacher training Programme [should] be organized for this purpose;

Steps should be taken through the proper channels to foster religious studies, both elementary and secondary, by introducing Hindu religious knowledge as one of the open subjects for Public Academic Examinations.[13]

Lo and behold, some fifteen years later, by 1984, many of these things had happened when the Singapore government instituted a program in all the city's secondary schools in "religious studies." This was intended to follow up on courses in "moral education" offered in the primary schools and was to provide opportunity for each student to understand their own religion and value system. Accordingly, six sequential courses were set up for forms three and four, in Hindu Studies, Bible Studies, Islamic Religious Knowledge, Buddhist Studies, Sikh Studies, and Confucian Ethics. Each student was to opt for one of these sequences as a mandatory replacement for Civics. Curricular design, teacher and text book preparation were largely left to each group to implement.

In 1983 the editor of *Omkara* announced with no little pleasure that the program was about to start, that it was a "wonderful opportunity" to expose the younger generation (to say nothing of their parents) "thoroughly and extensively" to their tradition. Teachers (many of them apparently recruited from the ranks of Tamil-language teachers) had been "trained," a syllabus had been designed, and a text book prepared by one Dr. Manoj Das, Professor of English literature at the Sri Aurobindo International Centre of Education in Pondichery and Consultant for Hindu Studies in Singapore.[14]

Before long disillusion had set in. Children complained to parents that the classes were "boring." Some parents thought the text book was an "embarrassment." Some students were under-motivated in the program, in part because it had to compete with all the other core examination courses, in part because they often had to be bussed after school hours, when already tired, to their classes in "religious studies." (If there were fewer than fifteen Indian students in a school, they were bussed to a school where the class was being offered.) The Hindu community in Singapore was discovering what Christian congregations had known for almost a century: one of the most effective inoculations against religion is "Sunday School."

Some of the problems in the program were not peculiar to the class in "Hindu Studies." Various religious groups, especially Christians and Muslims, as well as Hindus, had trouble accepting what was being taught as "their religion." Which view of the Bible was to be presented and by whom exercised conservative Christians, for example. Tamils, for their part, were less than thrilled by their perception that the syllabus and curriculum (to say nothing of their planners) had a decidedly "Northern" slant and didn't do justice to the Tamil tradition. Indeed, Malayalis, Brahmins, and North Indians were particularly visible on the planning committees, and while Tamils were represented, they were not able to represent the teenagers of the lower to middle classes for whom the educational process was intended in the first place.[15]

As a result of the various complaints, the Singapore government had decided by 1990 to discontinue the experiment. In fact, it appears the government which seeks to socially engineer much of Singapore's life (from ethnicity to fertility), has washed its hands of trying to do anything further, for a while at least, in "the study of religion." It decided that was a matter to be done privately.

Epilogue

The problem of teaching one's religion and legitimizing one's self-understanding, in my view, is exacerbated by a lack on many of these frontiers of at least two things. The first of these is a self-critical or relatively objective lens with which to view and re-interpret one's own tradition in terms of its socio-cultural matrices and historical relativity. One of the reasons, I suspect, that a few of us teaching religions in the colleges and universities of North America are finding a growing trickle of second-generation Indian students in our classes on India is that they welcome the opportunity (even if in a class or two) to study their own heritage through the eyes of an outsider. It provides them the opportunity to think dispassionately about the tradition, to see it in terms of its historical developments and in contradistinction to other traditions, to read into it and experience it in an academically respectable way, then to make choices not necessarily based on the compulsions of familial expectations.

A second missing ingredient is an equally dispassionate way to explore and understand alternative religious traditions in the face of which re-definition must occur. Very few South Indians, for example, of any religious persuasion with whom I spoke this year had had the inclination or the opportunity to systematically study any tradition outside their own. To be sure, not a few Tamil Hindus, especially in Malaysia, now in active positions of leadership in Hindu organizations, had attended Christian schools. In retrospect, however, these incursions into Christendom were viewed negatively, particularly in light of vigorous attempts by contemporary Christian evangelicals to save the "benighted" Tamil Hindus of the peninsula. If anything, such Hindus have come away with perceptions of Christianity as Hindu-bashing, arrogant, and insensitive, and these perceptions have heightened their commitment to educate their own in their own tradition. Careful, sensitive comparison is absent and the self-propagation that emerges as a result becomes more ethnic, polemical, and propagandistic. The religion forged out of these kinds of insularity and confrontation are inevitably more orthodox than ecumenical, more insular than global.

In sum, there are precious few opportunities for dispassionate inquiry and the study of religion as an academic discipline between Europe and Japan. As a result, relatively few persons of the newer generation in the Indian communities living overseas are yet prepared for the task of investigative research and re-interpretation of the tradition in ways that meet the rigorous standards of comparative academic inquiry. Until the time such new interpreters appear, expatriated Hindu parents, like other parents in many religious traditions, continue to experiment with strategies, both traditional and contemporary, to keep their heritage alive.

7

Creating the South Indian "Hindu" Experience in the United States

Vasudha Narayanan

"Do not reside in a town where there is no temple."
Auvaiyar, a Tamil woman poet, circa 2nd cent. C.E.

In southern India, where the landscape is studded with temple towers and where deities are said to have manifested themselves spontaneously, it was hard to live in a town where there was no temple. When the early Saiva Brahmins crossed the seas in the fifth and sixth centuries C.E. to Cambodia and Indonesia, they carried on their temple building activity. We may never know if these early emigrants ever ruminated about leaving the land that Manu, the law-giver, describes as that "where the black antelope naturally roams." Manu urges members of the higher classes to dwell in the land which extends as far as the eastern and western oceans, for this is the land of the Aryas, the land that was "fit for the performance of sacrifice" (*Manu Smrti* 2: 22-24).

Manu notwithstanding, the process of emigration has continued for several centuries. In this chapter we shall see how some Hindu emigrants in the last quarter of the twentieth century are transforming the land where there are no obvious *svayam-vyakta* deities, (and where one is hard pressed to see the black antelope), into a sacred place where the lord graciously abides. I shall focus on the Srivaisnava temple at Penn Hills (near Pittsburgh) as a religious and cultural center of large South Indian Hindu urban professional immigrant population. We will see how this temple seeks to replicate the rituals and atmosphere of other Srivaisnava temples in general and the Sri Venkateswara temple in Tiru Venkatam (Tirupati), India, in particular; and more important, in what ways it is different from its parent. Specifically, we see how the Hindus near the Penn Hills temple adjust the sacred calendar to coincide more with long weekends in this country, but also affirm almost in mythic terms, the sacrality of the land where the lord dwells. We shall also see how dreams and visions sometimes precipitate the building of a temple or discovery of a Hindu deity in America; and finally we shall discuss a few specific methods of self-interpretation that some Hindus have adopted in order to explain their tradition(s) to themselves and their children.

My discussion is based on information obtained from several sources: years of observation and participation in Srivaisnava temples in India and in this country; interviews with the priests (*bhattars*) at Penn Hills and India; studying the pamphlets and bulletins from the Penn Hills temple over the last fifteen years, and just by being part of the larger South Indian/Tamil/Srivaisnava community in northern Florida, where two temples are to be constructed near Orlando and Tampa.

While a few places of worship had been built in the New York area, the first really ambitious south Indian temple which sought to reproduce the traditional architecture and recapture the flavor of a Vaisnava *divya desa* was the Sri Venkateswara temple built in Penn Hills, Pennsylvania in 1976. Right from the beginning, the community took pride in this being an "authentic" temple and stated it frequently in its bulletins and pamphlets:

> "Construction of an *authentic* Temple in Pittsburgh dedicated to Sri Venkateswara commenced on June 30, 1976 with the assistance of Tirumala Tirupathi Devasthanam."
> "Visitors from all over the U.S., Canada, and India have expressed their gratification at being able to pray in an *authentic* temple constructed on the North American soil." [Italics added.][1]

This temple has been successful in attracting large numbers of devotees from all over the eastern seaboard; until similar temples were built in other parts of the country, it attracted pilgrims from all over the United States and Canada. It is still seen as the trend-setting south Indian temple in its celebration of expensive, time consuming, and intricate rituals; many other younger temples want to be like the one in Penn Hills when they grow up. Its success story is overwhelming; in a recent annual report, the chairman of the board of trustees at the Penn Hills temple reported that "as an established religious organization...the temple has extended modest interest-free loans to temple's (sic) that are in embryonic stages..."[2]

The Penn Hills temple enshrines a manifestation of Vishnu in which he is called Venkateswara or lord (*Isvara*) of the hill known as "*Venkata*" in south India. Venkateswara temples are now seen in Penn Hills, PA; Malibu, CA; Aurora IL, and Atlanta, GA. The word "Venkata" is said to mean "[that] which can burn sins."[3] The American temple was built with the help, backing, and blessing of one of the most popular, richest, and oldest temples in India. The Indian "sponsor" was the Venkateswara Temple at Tiru Venkatam, better known as Tirumala or Tirupati. The Penn Hills temple bulletin specifically says that "Tirumala Tirupathi Devasthanam ... of India will be the main consulting institution on religious matters."[4] The deities were carved in India under the supervision of this temple, and officials from Tiru Venkatam attend the major rituals that the Penn Hills temple undertakes.

The lord of Tiru Venkatam is mentioned in fifth century Tamil literature; and in the later (seventh-ninth century) poems of the Tamil saints known as the *alvars*, the lord and the sacred hill were glorified thus:

The heavenly ones and their king,
carry the best flowers, water, flame and fragrance
and ascend sacred Venkatam to adore [the Lord].
That great hill will give heaven
to all of us, without distinction.

He who held aloft a mountain
to protect [cowherds] from the chilly rain,

the Lord who measured the earth, great one,
reaches and dwells on the high, sacred hill.
Let us just adore [the hill];
we shall be delivered from our sins.

Nammalvar's Tiruvaymoli, 3.3.7 and 3.3.8

While the temple at Tiru Venkatam has always been well known, and has enjoyed royal patronage in the last thousand years, it is only in the last hundred years that it has attracted exceedingly large numbers of pilgrims and revenues. The popularity of the temple is said to have increased phenomenally after the *maha santi samproksanam* in 1958. The wealth of the temple is also frequently reported and commented upon by the media; in 1989, it had assets worth 1.5 billion rupees (Rs. 150 crores), reserves of about a billion rupees (Rs. 102 crores) and an annual income —largely from the collection box or *hundi* — of about eight hundred million rupees (80 crores). Cars, diamonds, and approximately 20 kg. of gold (from various pieces of jewelry dropped in the hundi) are collected every month. The temple is located on 10.75 square miles of Tirumala Hills, and until 1965, when the government took them over, owned over 600 villages. Thus, the temple was in a unique position to offer help in tangible forms to the new shrine in Penn Hills.[5]

The temple at Penn Hills (like the one in India) can be called Hindu in that it is particular and sectarian; it is a Srivaisnava temple. The Srivaisnava community became important about the tenth century C.E; in fact, the first occurrence of the word "Srivaisnava" itself, as far as I have been able to trace the term, occurs in an inscription in the Tiru Venkatam temple in India, in the year 966. That year, a woman called Samavai endowed some money for the celebration of some festivals and for the consecration of the icon of Manavala perumal, ("The Lord-Bridegroom," also known as Bhoga Srinivasa), a silver replica of the main deity.[6] A record of her endowment is inscribed in stone and it concludes with the phrase "*Srivaisnava raksai*" (By the protection of the Srivaisnavas). We know from inscriptions that the devotees of Vishnu called themselves "*Emperuman atiyar*" (servants of the Lord) until the year 936; the community name "Srivaisnava" comes up only after 966, possibly after the time of Yamunacarya (Alavantar), a renowned teacher of the Srivaisnava community.[7] The community recognizes the validity of both Sanskrit and vernacular (Tamil) scripture and the philosophical vision of the vedantic teacher Ramanuja. Since the eleventh century, the community has instituted the recitation of particular Sanskrit texts and the Tamil works of the alvars in all their temples.

The entrance tower of the Sri Venkateswara Temple at Penn Hills, Pennsylvania.

The temple at Tiru Venkatam, India, is counted as one of the most important among the Srivaisnava temples in 108 sacred places (divya desas). In popular consciousness, the hill on which it is located defined the northern boundaries of the Tamil speaking area. The phrase "*venkatam mutal kumari varai*" ("From Venkatam to [Kanya]kumari") was used to define the region of the Tamil speaking peoples. However, Tiru Venkatam is now in the state of Andhra Pradesh, about 100 miles north of the Tamilnadu border. Although the Tiru Venkatam temple has attracted devotees from all over India, and has been a center of national pilgrimage, it has not compromised the particular, sectarian, Srivaisnava nature of its rituals conducted according the vaikhanasa scripture, and the recitation of both Sanskrit and Tamil scripture.

History of the Penn Hills Temple

The temple at Penn Hills carries with it some of the clout and the prestige associated with the Indian one on which it is modeled. The history of the Penn Hills temple can be traced back to 1972 when on January 14th (in connection with the festival of Pongal/Makara Sankaranti celebrated by Tamil and Telugu speaking people), a few residents of the area established a shrine in the basement of a shop; here they kept pictures of various deities. Later that summer, a "granite statue"[8] of Ganesha was sent by Mr. R. Balakrishna Naidu of Coimbatore to the Pittsburgh area devotees. Since Ganesha is the god worshiped before the commencement of any ritual or auspicious act, he was received by devotees as "a good omen to invoke blessings to a larger project." Local residents referred to him as the Hindu "trouble-shooter" in their pamphlets. Strictly speaking, however, in many Srivaisnava temples and rituals, Visvaksena, Visnu's "commander in chief" is propitiated before any important task is undertaken, and he is regarded as the "equivalent" of Ganesha for the Vaisnavas. "*Ganapati samana visvaksenam*," a phrase from a song called "*Ranga nayakam*" by Muthuswami Dikshitar (18th century) is repeated frequently by the Vaisnavas. However, Ganesha's popularity is overwhelming, and by the success of the Penn Hills temple, at any rate, his record seems to be unblemished. While Ganesha is worshiped, it must be noted that all important rituals in Penn Hills and the Malibu temple begin with "*Visvaksena aradhanam*" (worship to Visvaksena), and Srivaisnava theology is not compromised.

In 1972, with the assistance of the Hindu Temple Society of New York, negotiations were begun with the Tirumala-Tirupati board in

Priests performing ritual at the beginning of the dedication of the Sri Venkateswara Temple at Penn Hills, Pennsylvania

India. The Commissioner of Endowments as well as a traditional sculptor from India visited America, drew the architectural plans and selected the site because it reminded them of the "hilly terrain" in India where the original Sri Venkateswara Temple is located. The site was purchased on June 30, 1976, and construction began. Fifteen sculptors and one architect trained in traditional forms of temple construction arrived to make sure that the temple was built according to the very precise instructions in the agamic literature. Local American builders laid the foundations and also constructed a community activity area. It is important to see that this emphasis on community outreach is seen right from the beginning — a feature conspicuous by its absence in many Srivaisnava temples in India.

The first building enterprise associated with many temples in this country is the raising of a community hall; while the plans for the temple at Orlando are still not clear, there are efforts to build the community hall for language instruction and "cultural events" as soon as possible.

The "forms" of Sri Venkateswara and the consorts came to Penn Hills from India in 1976; the tower of the temple was constructed, and the deities were installed and consecrated in November 1976. Indian builders continued Phase 2 of the construction which involved the building of several towers and kept a delicate balance between scriptural specifications and city building code regulations. On June 8, 1977, the major consecration (*mahakumbhabhisekam*) of the whole temple took place. Further construction and improvements are going on as money continues to pour in from devotees all over the country. As the support of the Hindu community grows, increasingly ambitious ventures are undertaken: in 1986, a consecration with a 1000 pitchers (*sahasra kalasa abhiseka*) was undertaken; later, there was a project of getting special metallic coverings (kavaca) for the deities; in 1989, worship of the the "Eight Laksmis" (*asta Laksmi Puja*) was sponsored; in 1990, a larger marriage pavilion was built, wedding invitations for the marriage between the Lord and the Goddess were sent out, and the wedding celebrated over the Thanksgiving weekend. The major event for 1991 was the successful completion of cycles of recitation of the names of the Goddess Lakshmi; her thousand names were recited ten thousand times by priests imported for the event and the sponsors of the worship rituals were given little silver lamps.

The Penn Hills temples, like its parent temple, has Srivaisnava priests,[9] and in both daily and periodically recurring worship, there is ritual recitation of Tamil and Sanskrit scripture. The deities worshiped here are known by the local names as they are in Tiru Venkatam: Visnu is Venkateswara; his consorts are Sri Padmavathi and Sri Andal. The early brochures published by the temple made sure that the non-south Indian public recognized the deities by their pan-Indian, non-sectarian names:

> Initial batch of fifteen silpis arrived in August and returned in November 1976 after having completed the Garbhalayas acccording

to the silpa sastras for Sri Venkateswara (or Balaji, Visnu), Sri Padmavathi (Lakshmi), and Sri Andal (Bhoomadevi.)[10] The name "Sri Venkateswara" was invariably followed in the pamphlets by "Balaji" or "Visnu" in parenthesis, Padmavathi was identified as Lakshmi,[11] and Andal as Bhoomadevi.[12] Andal was a devotee born in South India about the eighth century C.E., and her Tamil songs in praise of the manifestations of Visnu are sung by Vaisnavas all over Tamilnadu and Andhra. Although Andal is a household name in these regions, she is not well known in other parts of India, and the Penn Hills temple, going along with one line of Srivaisnava theology, calls Andal by the generic name of "Bhoomadevi" or the Goddess Earth. This latter name, like Visnu or Lakshmi, is better recognized by devotees from all over India. The Penn Hills temple also has a shrine for Ganesha, but this is located on the way to the main shrines which are physically one level higher. There are no shrines here for Siva or Parvati in any of their regional manifestations; however, the Siva-Visnu temple at Washington D.C. and the Venkateswara temple at Malibu, California, do have shrines for Siva and Parvati. In India, most of the temples are devoted exclusively to a local manifestation of Siva, Visnu or Parvati; however, in Penn Hills and Malibu, while the temples are primarily dedicated to Venkateswara, manifestations of other deities are included within the complex to accomodate the spiritual needs of various communities.

Mythic Origins of Hindu Deities in the United States

The forms of Venkateswara and his consorts were carved in India, then brought to this country, and the processes of vivification and consecration were done at Penn Hills. While the establishment of the temple is somewhat of a miracle in itself, given the enormous bureaucracy and red tape involved in such a collaborative venture, the temple does not have an origin myth, as some other temples in this country do. By origin myth, I refer to a set of circumstances where someone has a dream or a vision, or discovers the form of the lord in natural formations such as mountains or caves. After looking at a few instances, it is my impression that these origin myths in this country are usually seen in connection with Saiva temples, especially if there is a strong connection with American devotees. Thus, the LOTUS ("Light of Truth Universal Shrine") temple at Yogaville, Virginia, became a reality after a vision seen by Swami Satchidananda, of the Divine Life Mission. Overlooking the temple is the Kailas mountain, and on March 27, 1991, the deities were consecrated. The Iraivan/Kadavul temple at Kauai, Hawaii, was built in 1970 by Swami Sivaya Subramuniyaswami who was born in America and initiated in Sri Lanka. In 1975, Siva appeared to him in three visions, seated and walking in the meadows near the Wailua River (which surely, in my opinion, is one of the most beautiful spots on earth!). Later, in 1987, a rare Siva *linga* (six sided quartz crystal) was said to have been discovered and brought to Kauai from Arkansas, and a stone temple which they believe will last for 1001 years is now being planned. The temple is being designed by Sri Ganapati Sthapati, the premier sculptor/architect of temples from India, who was also in charge of the Malibu temple.

Perhaps the most unusual temple with mythic origins is the one at Wahiawa, (Oahu), Hawaii, now completely run by Hindus from India. This temple is dedicated to Viswanatha (which they translate as lord of the universe"); and the organization that is in charge of it is called the Lord Of The Universe Society, or L.O.T.U.S. (no organizational connection with the Virginia LOTUS). The Siva-linga at the Wahiawa temple is said to be a "healing stone;" it is believed that this linga was the embodiment of the Hawaiian God "Lono," the priest-healer of ancient times. According to another myth, this stone represents two sisters from Kauai who were turned into rocks. Classic hierophany is seen from this statement issued by L.O.T.U.S.:

> The Sacred Healing Stone has been discovered and rediscovered. Several people have experienced healings, visions, dreams and profound feeling of peace and well-being after coming into contact with the Healing Stone and its powers.
>
> More recently, in March 1988, some Indians were taken to the Healing Stone by their friends and they were awe-stricken by the resemblance of the Sacred Healing Stone to Lord Siva in the form of a Siva Lingam.... In April 1988 a special Pooja was organized. It became apparent to those who attended the Pooja that this place was indeed special, sacred and holy.[13]

Regular Hindu worship at the open-air temple on the north shore of Oahu is conducted on the third Sunday of every month and a permanent temple is being planned. The Hawaiian deity has been taken over/discovered by the Hindus; or as one south Indian there told me, "Lord Siva has manifested himself here."

No such dream, vision, or discovery has been spoken of at the Penn Hills temple; rather, it shares the myth of origin with the Tiru Venkatam temple in India as is made apparent by the local names of the deities.

Recapturing the Tiru Venkatam Experience

Sacred Time, Rituals and Long Weekends

In the performance of rituals considered essential for the orthodox maintenance of the temple, the Srivaisnava tradition has a rigorous schedule. The daily rituals at Penn Hills, as in many Srivaisnava temples are done in a style called *pancaratra* and differs from the style of worship in Tiru Venkatam, India, where the style is *vaikhanasa*. The latter style can be used only when a high degree of orthopraxy can be assured; the *pancaratra* style which is adopted by the temple at Penn Hills is used when there is involvement by people other than the specially trained and initiated priests.

In both the daily and seasonal routines of prayers and services, the Penn Hills temple tries to remain faithful to the parent temple in Tiru Venkatam. The morning wake up prayer (*suprabhatam*), the offering of food to the lord, the daily round of worship (*arcana*), and the recitation of particular alvar verses during the day, are all followed correctly; however, unlike the Indian temple, here the commuity participation is seen primarily on the weekends. And so, the ritual bathing of the lord in Venkateswara temples (at Tiru Venkatam and a similar temple at Fanaswadi, Bombay) which normally takes place on Fridays in India, is done on Sunday mornings in Penn Hills; a large group recitation of the Suprabhatam is done in the weekends, and then at a much later time in the morning than in India. (Considering that the morning suprabhatam is recited anytime around 3.00 am, or earlier, in India, it is under-

standable why the Penn Hills temple has scheduled it to a more reasonable time like 9.00 am in the weekends). These may seem like
minor differences from the parent temple; but in a ritual schedule
where timing is important, the adjustment to the local devotee needs
may seem unacceptable to the orthoprax priests.

Some of the seasonal festivals like the springtime *Vasanthotsavam*,
and the *Brahmotsavam* (the most important annual festival) are celebrated by the Penn Hills temple. A popular feature of these rituals
in India is the procession of the Lord in various palanquins. The
Indian temple celebrates the fall ("Navarathri") brahmotsavam
festival with great pomp and eclat with crowds in the hundreds of
thousands attending each day. The Penn Hills temple is slowly
adding various palanquins to its collection, and has right now, a traditional chariot (*ratha*), a *Sesa vahana* (a palanquin in the shape of
Sesa, the serpent-servant of the lord) a *Garuda vahana* or eagle -
palanquin and a *Gaja vahana* (an elephant vehicle). Because of
limited financial and human resources (compared to the Indian
temple), these festivals are not celebrated in as grand a manner as
they are in Tiru Venkatam temple. In the past, several brahmotsavams were celebrated at Tiru Venkatam; by the year 1638,
eleven brahmotsavams were conducted there.[14] Queen Samavai, who
was also responsible for the consecration of the deity Manavala
perumal in the year 966, made provisions to conduct two brahmotsavams, the first during the month of Purattaci (Sept. 15 to Oct.
14), and the second during the month of Markali (Dec. 15 to Jan.
14).[15] Since then, the brahmotsavam of Purattaci has been very
important at Tiru Venkatam. The Penn Hills temple usually celebrates one, and occasionally two brahmotsavams a year. In 1987,
there was a "Big" ("Maha") brahmotsavam in July, and another one
in early September. Sometimes, the dates do not seem to correspond
with the dates of celebration in India. In 1988, the Penn Hills
temple had its brahmotsavam in September, and spread out its celebration in stages. Prior to the actual brahmotsavam, it had a "labor
day weekend" special to attract the touring pilgrims; this was a
darshan of the lord in a "*pushpa pallakhi*" or flower float, on Sept. 3rd.
The actual brahmotsavam was celebrated between Sept. 13th and
22nd and the lord was taken out in processions in the four vehicles.

This was a big celebration and during the following month, unlike the Indian temple, the American one celebrated the Navarathri festival and brahmotsavam in a subdued manner.[16] The Tiru Venkatam temple in India, on the other hand, celebrated the Navarathri brahmotsavam on a grand scale, with almost twenty different processions in various palanquins and floats.[17]

Despite the desire to remain faithful to the code and sequence of rituals, there are some compromises and innovations. While the Penn Hills temple chooses to celebrate a few seasonal festivals, it tries as far as is astrologically possible to plan big events around the holidays of the American secular calendar. Thus, the bulletin in 1988 announced:

> Maha Brahmotsavam was celebrated during the 4th of July weekend.
>
> Labor Day weekend celebration will be climaxed by a 'Pushpa Pallakhi,' a float decorated with flowers and lights. Other religious and cultural events planned for the Labor Day weekend are listed....[18]

The same bulletin also stated that restoration of the main tower (*rajagopuram*) was completed in time for the fourth of July weekend. In 1989, the "Temple News Briefs" in *Sapthagiri Vani* reported that for "Thanksgiving Weekend (1987) — All deities were decorated with silver kavachas. A special Poolangi Seva was performed to Lord Venkateswara."[19] In 1990, the inauguration of the special hall for weddings with the ritual celebration of the wedding of Venkateswara and the goddess Padmavathi was held during the Thanksgiving break, and in 1991, a special Satyanarayana Puja was held in conjunction with the Memorial Day weekend. Thus, the sacred-time orientation of the temple is made to coincide, as far as the ritual almanac will allow it, with the secular calendar of the land in which it is located. While the reasons for this time orientation are obvious — unlike the Indian temple, the festivals are organized by people working in other places, and long weekends are the time many families do long distance traveling — it is important to note the framework of the American secular calendar. The Penn Hills Temple is not the first one to emphasize secular holidays; some temples in India have organized special new-year day darshans and the Tiru Venkatam temple generally records the greatest monetary collections in the hundi on the first day of January.[20] The Penn Hills temple is consistently regular in weaving major events all around the American secular calendar, and in this, they are unique. However, while concessions are made in sacred time, and the ritual calendar is woven around the secular working calendar of the devotees in America, *the sacred land* on which the temple is located is extolled as being similar in many ways to the sacred land in which Tiru Venkatam is located. The importance of having a temple on American soil, the importance of having Venkateswara and Padmavathi dwelling on Penn Hills is celebrated in song and literature by the devotees.

The 109th Divya Desa? The Territorial Theology of the Devotees

The Srivaisnava community counts 108 sacred places (*divya desa*) as abodes of Visnu and Sri; they arrive at this number because the 12 alvars sang of these 108 places. In other words, a sacred place, however important it may have been, was not counted as a divya desa unless it was immortalized in the songs of the alvars. Places like Tirunarayana puram (Melukote, Karnataka), Sri Mushnam, and Raja Mannargudi (in the state of Tamilnadu) were important Vaisnava pilgrimage centers, but because the alvars did not sing about them, they remain *abhimana sthalas* ("esteemed places") and not divya desas.

In 1986, a cassette of popular devotional songs (bhajans) was issued by the Penn Hills temple. In it, the Pittsburgh area devotees praise Lord Venkateswara thus:

> *America vasa jaya govinda*
> *Penn Hills nilaya radhe govinda*
> *sri guru jaya guru, vithala govinda*

Glorifying the lord as abiding in a particular place is like the devotees' personal consecration of the deity in a temple and making him live within the person. While all temples go through formal ceremonies of vivification with pitchers of sanctified waters, the devotees' songs give life to the deity in the temple and in the heart. Srivaisnava devotees celebrate the lord's accessibility more than his supremacy; and to make himself accessible, he is said to abide in a local shrine, close to the devotee. In Srivaisnava theology, the lord's supremacy is seen in his containing, including, and yet transcending the entire universe, and by having it as his body; but his accessibility is seen through his incarnating himself on earth (*avatara*) as an *arca*, easy to approach and ready to be worshiped. Here, he is wholly, fully god; not a symbol, not an image, or a conduit to the supreme, but wholly, completely there. Thus, he is totally present in Tiru Venkatam, India, and this is important; but even more important is that this lord is now perceived as abiding in a local shrine at Penn Hills. The devotees in Pittsburgh, just as the alvars celebrated it, see the lord as being physically close to them, sanctifying the land they live in. Just as the earlier poet Auvaiyar wanted it, they now live in a town with a temple, a temple on a hill, just as it is in Tiru Venkatam. Tiru Venkatam in literature is hailed as a piece of heaven on earth,[21] and the temple at Penn Hills, a piece of Tiru Venkatam in America.

The concept of sacred land is not just abstract for the devotees of the American temple. They see the terrain where the lord dwells in Penn Hills as being physically very similar to the Tiru Venkatam hills. One of the earliest brochures of the community says:

> It is a beautiful wooded area located on a hill and offers a panoramic view of the surroundings. According to numerous visitors, the hill with lofty trees is reminiscent of Tirumala. A small stream flows along the path leading to the temple site.[22]

The Tiru Venkatam temple in India is reached after crossing seven hills; and the words "seven hills" is associated only with that particular temple. The Penn Hills temple calls its official bulletin *Saptagiri Vani*, "the voice of the seven hills." While the American temple is not located on seven hills, it is constructed on one verdant hill, and this similarity is close enough for the devotee. The brochure continues enthusiastically:

> Adjacent to the Temple is a property of about three acres with an eternal spring. We plan to acquire this and develop the spring into a Pushkarini in accordance with our Hindu tradition.

This land was acquired and around the spring was built the traditional "lotus pond" (*pushkarini*) and called "Swami Pushkarini," the name given to the lotus-pond in Tiru Venkatam, India.

Praise of Penn Hills is easy to understand if one looks at earlier Tamil literature and later manuals which extol the glories of a place (*sthala mahatmayam*). Traditional sthala mahatmayams of the various Vaisnava sacred places extolled the beauty, and frequently, the wealth of the land, and thereby paid tribute to the lord, the owner of the land. Nammalvar, one of the Tamil Vaisnava saints who sang in praise of the lord in 108 divya desas, praises lord Venkateswara thus:

> Lord of the immortal ones!
> Lord of the Sacred Venkatam,
> where the clear waterfalls crash,
> carrying the gems, gold and pearls!
> Lord of the Sacred Venkatam,
> where the glowing gems negate darkness
> and make night seem day!
> [Master] of the Sacred Venkatam,
> filled with crystal-clear mountain springs!
>
> Tiruvaymoli 6.10.3; 6.10.9; 3.3.3.

> Before your allotted time in this life
> is shortened by a just a day,
> before your body grows feeble,
> reach the sacred Venkatam, filled with groves,
> the mountain, covered with lakes and flowers,
> home of the Lord who reclines on the serpent-bed.
>
> Tiruvaymoli 3.3.10

In the rapture of the devotee, it is not just Penn Hills, it is the greater Pittsburgh area that seems to to be geographically similar to the sacred land of India. The excitement of the Penn Hills temple bhakta, drawing upon puranic lore and recalling the importance of Prayag, (the sacred place in India where the rivers Ganga, Yamuna, and the underground Sarasvati meet), and also the deity Sangamesvara, ("the lord of the meeting rivers") in Karnataka, is seen in this statement issued in 1986:

> Pittsburgh, endowed with hills and a multitude of trees as well as the *confluence of the three rivers, namely, the Allegheny, the Monongahela, and the sub-terranean river* (brought up via the 60 foot high fountain at downtown) to form the Ohio river is indeed a perfect choice for building the first and most authentic temple to house Lord Venkateswara. The evergrowing crowds that have been coming to the city with the thriveni Sangama of the three rivers to worship at the

Temple with the three vimanas reassure our belief that the venerable Gods chose this place and the emerald green hillock to reside in.[23]

The need that motivated the Hindus to build a temple in Pittsburgh, close to where they now live, and then to continue the process and build temples in the proximity of one's hometown in suburban America reflects a tendency within Hinduism that Kees Bolle calls "topographical religiosity." Bolle's comments in "Speaking of a Place" are particularly relevant:

> ...Naturally, some of the temples are more famous than others; one might say that they are more tangibly the real residence of God. But unless one understands the primacy of the place, the nature of the sacred in most of Hinduism remains incomprehensible, and the plurality and variety of gods continues to form an unsolvable puzzle. *God is universal because he is there.*[24]

In being there at Penn Hills, at Southern California, at Flint, Michigan, or Poughkeepsie, New York, this God becomes immediate; this land, holy. The gods are carved in India and brought here, the priests are imported and the rituals performed in America (although at more convenient times) as they are in India. The umbilical cord, the spiritual life line, tying the Hindus to the mother land is strengthened and reinforced with every temple built in this country.

It is interesting to note that the concept of "sacred land" is not confined to the Penn Hills devotee. Republicans from the Hindu community near the Ft. Worth-Dallas area understand the notion of "karma bhumi," the land where actions bear fruit, in a far more general manner than Manu and his compatriots had intended. The following quotation is from a document of a small group of Hindu Republicans who took an active interest in the 1984 elections and reinforces the importance many Hindus give to the sacrality of land. V.S. Naipaul, reporting on the Republican convention at Dallas, brought this passage to the attention of his readers. It deals with "the Hindu-Interpretation of Americanism and Republicanism" as given in the "Asian Indian caucus booklet:"

> Indians immigrated to the USA to pursue their "DREAM" to achieve fully their potentials in this land of "Opportunities." They came in pursuit of their dreams, visions, happiness and to achieve

excellence.... During the last few years most of the people have changed from "Green card holder" status to that of "U.S. CITIZENS," thus enabling themselves to be full participants in socio-economic and political processes. They have chosen, by their free will, the U.S.A. as the "KARMABHUMI"— the land of Karma or action.

V.S. Naipaul's comment on this was equally fascinating:

Texas as the theater of karma — what would Trammel Crow [Naipaul describes this gentleman as the "real-estate king" of Texas] have made of that? But it was, really, no more than a Hindu version of...fundamentalism, and in this Hindu version certain things could be seen fresh. To embrace one's economic opportunity and good fortune was more than a political act; it was also an act of religion...[25]

Texas and America interpreted as the *karmabhumi* — the place where actions could produce merit or demerit — is a new idea in the topography of Hinduism. According to Manu and other law-makers, the land of the aryas and the land where the black antelope freely roams was the only land that could be called karmabhumi. Some Hindus here — at least the Republicans near Ft. Worth-Dallas — interpret it as referring to the land with spacious skies and the land where the deer and the antelope play.

Articulation of a Faith: Symbolism, Syncretism, Self-Inquiry and Self-Perception

The devotees of the Pittsburgh area have expressed themselves eloquently on the matter of sacred space, and their sentiments seem congruent with traditional statements on the glory and sanctity of the land where a temple is located. However, the publications and activities of the temple sometimes reflect concerns that are not seen at other Srivaisnava temples in India. The publications have consistently offered articles (usually by well-known Hindu teachers such as Swami Chinmayananda or his followers) which symbolically interpret aspects of the Hindu tradition. The Penn Hills temple has included a *few* extra non-Srivaisnava rituals in regular worship cycle to accommodate other devotees. The volunteer committees sponsor various cultural programs and language classes, youth camps in summer, and workshops involving self analyses and self examination based on "Vedanthic principles of self-enquiry." It must be remembered that while the temple is sectarian in its mode of worship, in its following of pancaratra texts, and in its recitation of alvars' hymns, the devotees are drawn from many communities and many regions of India, and above all, many are learning about their religion anew. There seems to be a striking divergence between the philosophy of "symbolism" articulated through the temple bulletin and the sectarian pancaratric worship that is practised.

Symbols and Their Interpretation

Srivaisnava theology emphasizes the reality and tangibility of a temple, the deities enshrined in them, and the importance of serving the lord in the temple. However, many Hindus in this country, if one had to generalize, are wary of being known as "idolators"; early Western missionary terminology still rings in their ears.[26] By pursuing the publications of both the Malibu and Penn Hills temples, we see that the topic of "idolatory" concerns the writers most, and it seems to me that they are perhaps responding to 19th century criticisms by writing an *apologia* based on neo-advaita-vedanta. A writer (C.A.P. Iyer) from California, after quoting Dr. S. Radhakrishnan, the Sankaracharya of Kanchipuram, and Dr. Benjamin Rowland, says: "When a devotee worships an idol in a temple, the worship is paid to what the image stands for in philosophical interpretation. The worship is never paid to the idol per se."[27] The "visitor's guide," a pamphlet issued by the Penn Hills temple in 1979, emphatically explains, presumably to an American visitor: "Where the Hindu worships the idols in the shrines, he is aware that it is to God that he really offers his worship. It is wrong, therefore to characterize Hinduism as an idolatrous religion. The idols are symbols of the invisible spirit." The sentiments are repeated by a *brahmacharini* of the Chinmaya mission who wrote frequently for the Penn Hills bulletin; she states unequivocally that "[t]he ritual of worshipping God *represented* by an idol or *symbol* is replete with significance" and later adds, "the elaborate rituals of Tiru Aradhana are prescribed for propitiating the Lord *symbolized* in an idol [italics added]."[28] Words like "represent" and "symbols" give us the impression that what we are worshiping is only pointed to or signified by the "idol." These sentiments are at variance with traditional Srivaisnava acaryas who held that the deity in the temple is totally, completely God; the *arca* (literally, "that which is worshiped") has a non-material form composed of a non-earthly substance called suddha sattva, and this incarnation in the temple is as real as the incarnations as Rama or Krishna.[29] But several issues of the *Saptagiri Vani* have articles that emphasize the importance of this allegorical or "symbolic" interpretation, and insist that not to do so would make us think of Hindusim as "absurd":

> If one has to appreciate the real essence of Hinduism, one must learn to appreciate this science of symbolism. In absence of such an understanding the whole periphery of Hinduism will appear funny, unintelligent, and absurd. In the process of knowing this science of symbolism one discovers the deeper meaning of the real Hindu tradition which apparently appears to be superficial.

The article then gives the "symbolic meaning" of various rituals (when one burns camphor, the priest burns "all your past notions, beliefs, conclusions etc...the act of burning camphor stands for *Guru Upadesha*..."; breaking of a coconut symbolizes the breaking of the ego or ahamkara and so on).[30] It is my impression that many Hindus in this country accept the "symbolic" meaning as their heritage, and this generic neo-advaitin package seems to be entirely acceptable to them. They are almost relieved that their rituals have an esoteric meaning, that they now know the origin of words. For instance, there are categorical statements like this one on the origin of the word "Telugu": "Three lingas of the Siva temples... are located on the three borders of the State [Andhra Pradesh]. The language 'Telugu' comes from 'Tri-lingam'..."[31] While this may certainly be one etymology, the other possible explanations for this, or other matters in the Hindu tradition, are not generally acknowledged, and a more monolithic view of the tradition emerges from these articles. This is particularly significant for the symbolic interpretations, where the meaning given to any particular concept or ritual is strikingly at variance with the orthodox Tirumala-Tirupati (Srivaisnava) view point. For instance, in Srivaisnava theology, Garuda, a bird, and Sesa, a divine serpent, are the two eternal servants of the lord, ready to serve him every second. Sesa, the serpent, is the paradigmatic devotee and servant of Visnu, and this is clearly stated in the following verses:

> The Serpent is an umbrella [for the Lord] when he moves, a throne when he sits, sandals when he stands, and a bed in the large ocean. It is a brilliant lamp, a soft silk garment, a cushion for his hand...
>
> Poykai Alvar, (circa 8th Century) Mutal Tiruvantati, v. 53.

> ...the great serpent serves you in endless ways, assuming various forms; he is your dwelling, bed, seat, sandals, robes, pillow, and umbrella against rain and sun.
>
> Yamunacarya, (late 10th century) Stotra Ratna, v. 40

In mythology, Sesa is seen to have incarnated as Laksmana, the younger brother of Rama (in the epic *Ramayana*), and as Balarama (the older brother of Krishna) to be constantly with Visnu when he manifested himself on earth. More important, *in the mythology of the Tiru Venkatam temple, the hills on which the lord stands are said to be an embodiment of Sesa;* the hills are called "Sesachala" or "Sesadri." There is a tradition that out of *respect* for Sesa, some acaryas would not walk on the hills (that would be disrespectful), but would ascend the hills by crawling on their knees. Given this importance of Sesa, the interpretation in the following passage, which portrays Garuda, Sesa, and Gaja (an elephant) as the animal instincts of a human being is rather odd. The context for this passage was the description of various vahanas (palanquin-vehicles) for the Lord. The Penn Hills temple acquired three of them in 1986 and after describing them, the author goes on to say:

> The disciplining of one's undesirable qualities is symbolized in a subtle manner by the taming and conquering of an animal (instinct) and the servitude of the animal to the Master. Thus GARUDA (symbol of soaring AMBITION and DESIRES), GAJA (symbol of EGO that is usually found in the wealthy and powerful when the mind is not disciplined and virtues are lacking) and SESHA (symbol of ANGER and WRATH) each is enslaved and taken in a triumphant procession of the conquering Hero, symbol of VIRTUES, the Lord by assembled devotees. Total cost of each Vahana is $24,000.[32]

This interpretation certainly seems to owe more to some Western modes of analyses than to traditional Hindu exegesis. Topics interpreted as symbols include Ganesha (several times), Siva linga, Tiru *aradhana*, significance of Maha Sivaratri, the Temple (seen as a "tree of life") and finally, the details of an *arcana* (worship ritual) in "Symbolism in Indian Culture — Lord Ganesha."[33]

Many Hindus in India have been exposed to neo-vedantic interpretations of their religion and have some acquaintance with the publications of the Ramakrishna and Chinmaya missions. It is against this background that we can understand the preponderance of symbolic interpretations that have appeared in the temple's publications. Almost all articles until very recently have dealt with what is perceived to be the symbolic meaning. These inner or symbolic meanings are known in India, especially in the publications of several well-known religious missions; however, they are just not voiced in a Srivaisnava forum, like the Tirumala-Tirupathi (Tiru Venkatam) Devasthanam publications. It must be noted that the writers of these articles seem not to be Srivaisnavas. Recent issues of the bulletin (November 1990 vol. 15; and Feb, 1991, vol. 16) have added a disclaimer, "the views expressed in the articles published are those of the writers and do not necessarily reflect those of the S.V. Temple management." The *Saptagiri Vani*, despite listing the Srivaisnava festivals and almanac, and despite being a voice of a Srivaisnava temple is not necessarily a Srivaisnava bulletin; in the last two issues it has said that it is "the intention of [the] S.V. Temple management to provide through its publications, articles and other items that represent our rich cultural and religious traditions." In pursuance of this goal, recently, there have been occasional articles on rituals like Jirnoddharanam or Ashtothra Satha Kalasa Abhiseka which give the details of the celebrations according to the *samhitas*, short articles on Carnatic music, "origins of dance," and children's word games.

The influence of these articles in the bulletins should not be underestimated; unlike a person in India, where newspapers and regular television programming carry glimpses of varied rituals and synopses of religious discourses, these articles may be the only regular "religious education" the readers of the bulletin get. By appearing in this bulletin, the articles also seem authoritative. Thus we may have an entire generation of young Hindus growing up in this country, educated on the myths recounted by Amar chitra katha — where again, *one* story line is presented and is ratified as "true" unlike the oral tradition which may present alternative versions of a story — and on symbolic meanings of temples, deities and rituals. The effects of this controlled diet will have to be judged in future years.

Syncretism

The Penn Hills temple has included many small rituals as part of its repertoire, even though they are not traditionally part of Srivaisnava temples. The most important one is worship of Satyanarayana, especially on full moon days. While Satyanarayana is a form of Visnu, the worship is probably quite late in origin and is not part of traditional Srivaisnava lore. This puja, usually a domestic

Ritual at the Sri Venkateswara Temple at Penn Hills, Pennsylvania.

one in India, is popular in the Marathi, Kannada, and Telugu speaking regions, and in some communities in north India and in Tamilnadu. In India, the ritual is sometimes performed by family members, and sometimes, by a priest who is brought in for the occasion. Because there are very few priests to go around in this country, the *Satyanarayana puja*, a non-Srivaisnava rite, is conducted in this temple. Another largely domestic rite, (a non-Srivaisnava one, even though it is addressed to Lakshmi) the *Varalaksmi Vratham*, a ritual conducted by Smartha women is also held in this temple.

In this connection, *we must note that in Hinduism as it is practiced in this country, there is a blurring of lines between domestic, community, and temple rituals*. Domestic rituals like the pre-natal rites are conducted in the temple; family festivals like Deepavali are conducted by the whole community gathering together in a school gym, church auditorium or, if there is one nearby, a temple. It seems to me — and demonstrating this point would take us out of the realm of this chapter — that the celebration of rituals and festivals in suburban America is similar in many ways to their celebration in village India, where both domestic and temple rituals become community based celebrations. There are very few really private domestic functions in villages — they are invariably community-based celebrations, where one or two families are responsible for food and hospitality. Similarly, even temple utsavas in small Indian villages, especially where the temples have no fixed endowment, become the responsibility of a few "sponsoring" families and again community-based.

The Penn Hills temple, unlike other Venkateswara temples in this country, but more like other Srivaisnava temples, does not have other non-Vaisnava deities, (except for Ganesa). The Venkateswara temple at Malibu has a large shrine for Kannika Parameswari, a form of Devi; the Venkateswara temple at Aurora, Illinois temple has both Vaisnava and non-Vaisnava deities including Siva, Parvathi, Subramanya and his consorts Valli and Devasena, Satyanarayana, Hanuman, and Ganesa; and the new temple at Atlanta has a shrine for Durga. In India, most Srivaisnava temples have shrines only for local manifestations of Visnu, his consorts and his devotees, both celestial and human. Occasionally, some temples like the Kutal alakar temple at Madurai have the "Nine Planets" (*nava graha*) within its inner *prakaras*; more rare is to find Durga within the precincts, as is seen in the temple at Tirukkoilur, Tamilnadu.[34] While it is more common to see many deities of the Saiva pantheon having sub-shrines in the Venkateswara temples, at least in one instance, in Sri Meenakshi temple at Houston, a smaller shrine is seen for Venkateswara in an institution dedicated to a goddess who is perceived by many to be a form of Parvati.

The Penn Hills temple obviously is syncretic to a limited extent; it strikes a balance between the needs of its devotees and what is permissible by the written and practiced codes adopted by the Tiru Venkatam temple. Thus, while syncretism extends as far as some Telugu and Kannada practices, the temple has not actively sought to fulfill the needs of Hindus from many other regions. It appears from the cultural programs sponsored (Bharata natyam, Kuchipudi dances, and Carnatic music, with lavish celebration of the Thyagaraja *utsavam*[35]) and the language classes offered (Tamil, Telugu, and Kannada) by the Penn Hills temple that many of its devotees — like those of the Tiru Venkatam Temple in India — are from from the states of Tamilnadu, Andhra Pradesh and Karnataka. Just a few miles from Sri Venkateswara temple is another beautiful temple, known simply as the Hindu-Jain temple. The architecture, deities and rituals here are principally "north-Indian," and in tandem, the two temples serve the pan-Indian Hindu community.[36]

Self-Inquiry and Self-Perception

The Penn Hills temple sponsors several workshops and lectures based on connections between psychology and the Hindu tradition. The "Living In Freedom—an Enquiry" (LIFE) workshop lasted four days and was conducted by Swami Sukhabodhananda from Bangalore. According to the temple bulletin, "the workshop demonstrated how the Vedantic principles of self-enquiry can be used to resolve the day-to-day problems faced by individuals." It added that "material was drawn from the Bhagavath Geetha, the Upanishads, the Bible, the Koran, Tibetan Buddhism and Zen." The workshop examined "inhibitions that usually cloud the thinking process" and saw how special techniques like meditation, yoga, music and dancing "paved the way for unfolding the path to self-examination." It was billed as "a supreme stress management program spiritual workshop."[37] Similar language is seen in the interpretation of a *vratam*, a votary act usually observed by women; it is described as "human resource management."[38] This form of self-enquiry is also seen in the youth camps that the temple sponsors; they have been held since 1981, and in 1985, the theme was "positive thinking and living." The Chinmaya Mission West has sent volunteers to run the camp; Swami Sukhabodhananda who ran the LIFE workshop was sometimes in charge of it, and at other times, people from Bharatiya Vidya Bhavan have been responsible for the activities.

The emphasis on popular psychology is also evident from some of the lectures the temple has sponsored; they include: "Bhagavad Gita helps to reduce stress," "Molding modern children with ancient Indian culture," and "Value systems for positive thinking."[39]

It is always difficult to perceive oneself clearly and to articulate one's faith and tradition to oneself, the community and to one's children, especially if one has had no formal training or education in the field. But such is the predicament of a Hindu here; having grown up in India, soaking up the Hindu religious experience, does not make one a specialist in it. And yet, we are forced to articulate over and over again what it means to be a Hindu and an Indian to our friends and to our children, and one feels ill-equipped for the task. Frequently, all that one remembers of a festival in India is the food that was prepared for it; one was never called upon to explain Deepavali or Sankaranti, and least of all, "Hinduism." In India, one probably never thought much of Yoga; city folk had nothing more than a nodding acquaintance with the sacred cow, and certainly meditation was considered to be the province of specially chosen holy people. In this last section of this chapter, I will try to give some sense of how Hindus perceive themselves and how they portray their religion. In one sense, this is like Alice looking through the "looking glass;" I, a Hindu am looking at Hindus looking at themselves, or like Arjuna at the Viswarupa scene, looking at himself looking at himself.

We have already seen three major trends emphasized by the Penn Hills temple — a symbolic or psychological explanation of religious phenomena, a syncretic approach to the deities and rituals, and emphasis on the perceived connections between religion, western psychology, and stress management. I believe these are part of the larger picture; many educated Hindus, here and in India, hold some favorite views about themselves. I would like to call them "mythic structures" of the young urban professional Hindu; these are perceptions about their religion that seem extremely important to them and which condition their view of themselves and other religions. I will outline a few of these dominant structures that I have noted over several years; most of the following discussion is based on impressions gathered from being part of the Hindu community in this country, and some are reinforced by temple bulletins. I must emphasize that I am *not* stating that these positions or attitudes are necessarily incorrect; I am merely pointing out that these sentiments are repeated so many times that they have fashioned a "generic Hindu" outlook that is unique to this century.

1. "Hinduism is not a religion, it is a philosophy, a way of life." This is usually followed with "Hinduism is the oldest religion in the world." These sentences are probably most commonly heard in this country. Some of my American friends who teach religion here have told me how many of their second-generation Hindu students spout these lines at them. The "Visitor's Guide" to the Penn Hills temple tells us that "Hinduism might be better described as religious culture rather than a religion."

2. Hinduism is a tolerant religion. The "Visitor's Guide" has a statement that is typical of many others:

> The most significant feature of Hinduism is its belief in religious tolerance. The Vedas proclaim, "As the different streams having their sources in different places mingle their water in the sea, so the different paths which men take through different tendencies, various though they appear, all lead to the same one God."

Sentences like "Truth is one, Paths are many" are voiced even as India spins into crises expressed by communal rioting and separatist violence; perhaps it is time to go back, study and take seriously the truth one is ready to sacrifice one's life for.

3. The supreme being is seen as a trinity. Just about every educated Hindu seems to consider the "trinity" as the most important feature of the "godhead." Sentences like "the Godhead is attributed mainly with three functions of Creator (Brahma), Preserver (Visnu) and

Destroyer (Siva)" are heard frequently. What they neglect to tell after this statement, is that Brahma has no more than an walk-on part and that an extremely important person — the Goddess — is left out of this picture. While the notion of the trimurti is seen in Hindu scripture, the importance given to it in 19th and 20th century thinking is more than it warrants. The uninitiated western audience after listening to this is left to believe that Brahma the creator is very important and that the Destroyer could not be very good. In other words, it is my impression that statements about the trinity mislead more than they inform, obscure more than clarify about the Hindu tradition.

4. All rituals have an inner meaning and significance which frequently have to do with promoting good health and a safe environment. In other words, science and Hinduism are fully compatible. We have already discussed at length about the "inner meanings" of rituals; what I did not touch on then is the compatibility between science and religion, the perceived value of yoga, meditation and their impact on the human brain and body. Many discussion groups in this country focus on the merits of these activities or other religious rituals; they are seen as leading to better human health or safer environment. Such interpretations are seen in the "antiseptic" properties of turmeric or cowdung, and I have even heard that the reason why we break a coconut in a temple is to let the "ether" out of the coconut and thus replenish the ozone layer. The audience was suitably impressed with this explanation.

Conclusion

In this chapter, we have seen the continuity and innovations of some of the Hindu traditions as mirrored in the Penn Hills temple and other temples in this country. In building the temple, some participating communities have (a) a local place of worship with icons of the lord that have been formally consecrated and where formal prayers can be offered by the priests on behalf of individuals; (b) a place to conduct sacraments, and (c) a place where they can send their offerings of devotion either in gratitude or as a petition for particular favors and receive a token of the lord's grace (prasada) in return; (d) an institution that has self-consciously undertaken the role of educating the younger generation born here, through weekly language and religion classes, frequent discourses, sponsorship of classical music and dances (which have a broad religious base in India), through summer camps organized for Hindu children born in this country, and through an "outreach" bulletin that is mailed to anyone who wants it. New temples are rising up all over the American landscape; two new ones are being planned for in central Florida and active fund raising is going on for construction of shrines in Tampa and Orlando. In the Orlando temple, the community hall is being built even before the shrine. This is understandable in a situation where a community is trying to feel its strength and assert its identity in the midst of a larger society in which they feel marginalized culturally and linguistically. The community hall is a place where different groups can meet and have language, music, and dance classes. It is significant that the organizing groups have not yet made a decision on which deity is to be enshrined and according what mode worship is to take place; it is in this context that there is greatest fragmentation among the Hindu traditions. Devotees of Visnu, Siva, the Goddess, Ganesha, or those who worship Visnu as Rama or Krishna want the temple to be primarily dedicated to that deity; others who believe themselves to be "non-controversial" and "liberal" advocate a non-denominational, almost antiseptic room of meditation, with an abstract sacred syllable being the focal point and no deity enshrined. Animated discussions issue forth from these suggestions and a member present at the deliberations remarked wryly: "It is a pity that a temple that was meant to unite our Hindu community here becomes the focal point of division." The key word is "community"; because of the many communities and many traditions, a consensus is almost impossible. Lines are drawn on sectarian, caste, and regional lines, and the debates continue.

The Penn Hills temple, meanwhile, continues its leadership as one of the "premier" institutions in this country. Here, while sacred time is gently manipulated in this country to coincide with secular time — or at least make the word holiday mean literally that — Hindus, sometimes inadvertently, sometimes quite self consciously affirm the importance of sacred land in a very traditional way. In interpreting their religion and trying to make it more relevant and meaningful, some Hindus have favored the view that all religious phenomena is to be understood as symbols to an inner, hidden truth; and occasionally these symbolic interpretations have more in common with western dream analysis and popular psychology than they have with traditional Hindu exegesis. In the process of building a temple and explaining one's religion to one's children and to the community, several dominant motifs have arisen in the self-understanding of many Hindus here and in India; with enough repetition, they may become ratified.

Index of American Temples Mentioned in This Chapter

1. Sri Venkateswara Temple, South McCully Road, Penn Hills. Mailing address: P.O. Box 17280, Pittsburgh, PA 15235-0280. (412-373-3380)

2. Sri Venkateswara Swami (Balaji) Temple of Greater Chicago, 1145 West Sullivan Rd. Aurora, Il. 60507. (312-844-2252)

3. Lord Venkateswara (Balaji) Temple, Hindu Temple Society of Southern California, 1600 Las Virgenes Canyon Road, Calabasas, CA 91302. (818-880-5552)

4. The Hindu Temple of Atlanta [Lord Venkateswara (Balaji) Temple]. Box 298, Riverdale, Georgia 30274-0298

5. L.O.T.U.S.(Lord of the Universe Society), P.O. Box 61274, Honolulu, HI 96839. (for information call 808-395-7914 or 808-395-1181)

6. LOTUS (Light of Truth Universal shrine), Yogaville, Buckingham, VA . (804-971-7284)

7. Sri Meenakshi Temple Society of Houston, Rt. 5, Box 5725, Pearland, TX 77584.

8. Iraivan Temple, San Marga sanctury, P.O. Box 1030, Kapaa, Hawaii 96746. (The San Marga sanctuary is located 4 miles inland from the Coconut Coast, on the N.E. side — near Kapaa— of Kauai.)

8

Transmission and Transformation of Rituals[1]

K. K. A. Venkatachari

Rituals are powerful mechanisms for the preservation and adaptation of religious traditions. Both the written prescriptions for the observance and the practice of rituals are important in the process of transmission, and especially important in adaptation for people who have emigrated to new social and religious settings. When I left India in 1974 to spend four months at Harvard, I took four packets of darbha grass and seeds for the Vedic *tarpanam* ceremony on the new moon day of every month for my father, and I performed the ritual each month. When I traveled the next year to Utrecht and Harvard, I also carried the ritual packets, but did not perform the rituals because (1) the *sankalpa mantra* states that the son is performing the ritual in Bharata and (2) because the timing is incorrect if done in America because of the ten hour difference. I wondered if the rituals would be appropriate if not done according to the regulations. When my wife unpacked the packets upon my return home, she was distressed that I had done something very wrong by not performing the rituals. When I was in California in 1977, a Srivaisnava woman immigrant asked my opinion: Is it permitted for her to perform *puja* to Satya Sai Baba in California with her friends even though she is Srivaisnava? I did not have a clear answer. I told her that if the answer was "No!" there was no clear alternative to suggest, but if she performed those acts of worship, she could change to worship more appropriate for a Srivaisnava later. These two experiences illustrate difficult questions raised by Hindus in America as they attempt to transport their religious traditions and rituals to a new country.

Ritual patterns from their experience in India are taken by many immigrants as normative for their practice in their new homes even though it is virtually impossible to copy exactly the rituals either as they are described in the sacred texts or as regularly performed in India. Hence, the question debated by sincere Hindus: Is a basic error committed when changes are made in the rituals to make them conform to the requirements of the immigrants and their society? Some conservatives criticize what are interpreted as evidence of disregard for the tradition and for the purity of Hindu practices. Others make pragmatic arguments for changes that are necessary to make the tradition accessible to their children, and, perhaps, also to themselves. How much change is permitted? How can the tradition be adapted? These are serious questions for emigrants, both those who move socially or geographically in India and those who go abroad.

Historical analysis shows that Hindu rituals have been adapted throughout history to meet the needs of people in new contexts. Times of rapid social change provide impetus for adaptation of rituals because such adaptation preserves the vitality of ritual in new social settings and functions to preserve the tradition at the time it is being transformed. Such change is not a modern phenomenon, but has been present in Hinduism for centuries, and it provides a justification for some of the changes that are taking place as Hinduism is being transported to America by immigrants. This historical analysis will deal with examples from domestic rituals, annual rituals, and temple rituals.

Historical Analysis

According to the scriptures, three authorities are ranked in order: (1) *Sruti* or the Vedas, (2) the eighteen *Smrtis* of the *rishis*, such as

Manu, and (3) *acara* or custom. Custom is accepted as an authority only when it does not contradict either *Sruti* or *Smrti*. The eighteen *Smrtis* belong to different periods, and we find that the later authors sometimes reject the authority and teachings of the earlier texts. Yajnavalkya says, "To a sonless woman (widow) when in season, a younger brother or a cousin of the husband, commanded by the Guru and desirous of raising a son, should go, after applying clarified butter to his body."[2] Manu was aware that this custom had been practiced before his time and condemned it.[3] Hence, one author accepted the practice, another rejected it. Similar examples are present in the text, showing that ancient authors who had received a code of conduct from society were willing to take into account new circumstances and reject practices that were not suitable in their society. The 11th century Tamil grammarian, Pavanantimuni, author of *Nannul*, argued that there is nothing wrong in rejecting the old practices and accepting new ones to meet the needs of the time.[4]

Domestic Rituals

Adaptation to social circumstances is also allowed by the *Grhya sutras*, which are codified mantras taken from the Rig Vedas, Yajur Veda, Sama Veda, and Atharva Veda organized for use in life cycle rituals, starting from the conception (*garbhadhana*) to the last rites for the dead (*antyesti*). In the early period of the 4th to the 1st centuries B.C.E. people needed direction how to perform the various rituals, so different authors produced several works representing customary behavior in different regions. The sutras were both descriptive and prescriptive, but the authors were careful to allow the assimilation of local customs and practices, thereby implying some form of Vedic approval of such actions. Weddings were rituals that invited adaptation to local custom. Apastamba, the earliest author of a *Grhya sutra*, concludes his discussion of wedding rituals with the phrase "*avrtascastribhya pratiyeran*," which means, "learn from the women and others the *avrta*." The meaning of the word is obscure, but the phrase seems to permit the introduction of non-Vedic rituals that are widely practiced in a local region.[5] Asvalayana, another important author of a *Grhya sutra*, clearly says that different ritual elements and customs are permitted at different times and in different regions.[6] The writing of these two authors are accepted by many in South India.

The commentators belonging to the 11th and 13th centuries C.E., more than 1400 years later, try to interpret the meaning of the word, avrta, and suggest that it refers to rituals like the *raksabandhana* and the *palika*. Raksabandhana, an all-India ritual, is the tying of a thread soaked in tumeric power on the right wrists of men or the left wrists of women at the beginning of almost all rituals in South India, except last rites, and during many rituals in the North. It has been accepted in South Indian practice as an authentic ritual even though it is not prescribed in the Vedic tradition or mentioned in the *Grhya sutras*, and it is given a Vedic flavor by introducing during the tying of the thread a Sanskrit mantra that was originally associated with Vasuki. Palika is a ritual performed by women in conjunction with most of the life cycle rituals in South India. Five small clay pots filled with clay taken from an ant hill are placed on a small platter in a corner. Seeds of nine kinds of grains (*navadhanya*) are planted on the first day, and women provide light and water during the five days of the rituals. Those performing the ritual attend the pots following the Vedic ceremony each day. During the planting of the seeds, the priest recites a Vedic hymn connected with each variety of grain, which again gives a Vedic flavor to the ritual. These are performed for people of all castes, but among people of the farming caste, both raksabandhana and palika are given special importance, and their timings are mentioned on invitations. Both are tribal or indigenous customs of fertility cults that have been assimilated into Brahmanic rituals.

Srivaisnava Brahmins have changed the Vedic last rites for doctrinal reasons. According to Vedic tradition, the corpse is polluted and polluting, and, therefore, during the cremation the sons wear the sacred threads on the right shoulder, opposite the normal practice. Srivaisnavas hold the doctrine that the body of a person is not polluted or polluting even after death because it has provided the vehicle for the soul to attain the supreme abode (*paramapada*). Hence, the sons are permitted at the ceremony to continue to wear the thread on the left shoulder during the ritual immediately after the death when the body, either male or female, is being washed and the Srivaisnava marks are being applied. Hymns of the alvars are chanted during this ritual. This non-Vedic ritual is accepted by Brahmins without any hesitation, and is part of the introduction of Tamil doctrines and practices. Both Vedic and Tamil practices are present because in another part of the last rites the sons wear the threads on the left side.

The annual Vedic *sradha* ceremony for a father or mother contains a ritual in which the soul of the parent is invoked over the heads of Brahmins who then partake of the food. According to the Srivaisnavas, the soul of a parent cannot return because it has already attained the supreme abode, so the question is raised whether they should perform the ritual. Ramanuja in a different context raised the issue of observance of all Vedic rituals, and determined that they should be performed in order to fulfill social custom and expectation of their neighbors. Therefore, they perform the ritual, but after the invocation, they say, "By the feeding of these Srivaisnavas, let the Lord be pleased." Saiva texts of the 14th century, e.g., *Aghora sivacaryapaddhati*, instruct devotees to invoke the sons of Siva because the parents' souls have attained the feet of the Lord; nevertheless, the Saiva priests have now gone back to the Vedic tradition of invoking the souls of the parents, because of the influence of Smarta Brahmins.

Festivals

In one of the 5th century dramas, the statement is made, "The Bharatiyas are given to the enjoyment of festivals." Festivals have been part of Indian culture for centuries, and some have developed into all-India festivals. Dipavali is prescribed in puranic literature, but it has been adapted to the customs of various regions, religions and social classes of India. Various puranas reflect regional differences and contain references to four days of rituals that are still present in India, but with regional variations: (1) *Naraka caturdasi*, a day of celebration of the death of the demon, Narakasura; (2) Laksmi puja; (3) New Year's Day; (4) *Bali pratipat*, a day for blessing sisters, which is of special importance in Maharashtra. Jains adopt the Laksmi puja and the New Year's Day practice of blessing the financial records of businesses. The Laksmi puja is done primarily by the business community of the North, without discrimination of religion. In South India the non-brahmins feast on goat meat on the first day, if it is not on the new moon day, and on the second day they eat vegetarian food. These social and regional variations permit the observance of the "same" festival throughout India, albeit in diverse ways.

Navaratri is also prescribed only in the puranas as nine nights for worship of the mother goddess — puranas mention Durga, Laksmi, and Sarasvati. Later in the 13th and 14th century texts codify the earlier prescriptions by designating the first three days for Laksmi, the second group for Durga, and the final days for Sarasvati. In Bengal the entire nine days are an elaborate festival for Durga, while in South India Siva temples have all nine days for Parvati and Vaisnava temples have all nine days for Laksmi. The Sakta cults of Bengal have been a dominant influence on the observance of this festival. Because no temple to Sarasvati exists in South India, both Saiva and Vaisnava Brahmins reserve the ninth day for worship of Sarasvati in their homes, and part of the ritual is that children perform puja before their school books. The tenth day is observed all over India, but in the South it is considered an auspicious day to begin any undertaking, especially schooling. In South India the day is auspicious, but it is not a public holiday to observe the death day of Ravana as it is in the North. There is no uniform text for observance of Navaratri, hence, it has assimilated a number of local customs that result in regional variation. Universality demands diversity of practice.

Temple rituals

Festivals appear on temple calendars and even rituals like *raksa-bandhana* and *palika* that are part of domestic rituals are also observed in temples according to prescriptions in the *agamas*. The agamas, as compendia of instructions concerning temple construction and rituals from the 7th century, are valuable sources of information about changes that have taken place in society. Agamas prescribe the palika ritual for many rituals as *ankurarpana* or "sprouting ceremony." One of the agamas says that even though it is not prescribed as a ritual in Vedic material, performance of the ritual will please the

Lord. The raksabandhana is performed in the temple at the beginning of rituals, first on the image of the deity and then on the wrist of the priest, to indicate that the ritual will be completed without interruption. Thereafter, during the ritual the priest is separated from domestic rituals, even the last rites of the parents, which shows how non-Vedic rituals have been incorporated into temple rituals.

Vedas contain no references to image worship, but agamas from several traditions — Vaisnava, Saiva and Sakta — discuss in the first few pages the worship of images and associate such worship with Vedic material. Marici is responsible for one of the earliest Vaisnava texts for instructing temple priests, and, when asked by other rishis how to correctly worship, he responded: "Meditating on the benign supreme Narayana and prostrating before him, they will attain the supreme abode by chanting some mantras from the four Vedas acceptable to him."[7] He develops the idea that image worship is implied by the Vedas and concludes: "The worship of that One is in two forms: worship of the formless One by performing oblations to the fire, and worship of images in the temple. Image worship is considered to be superior to worship of the formless one because it can continue even when no patron is present for the fire sacrifice."[8] One of the earliest Saiva agamas, Ajitagama, says that both the Vedas and all twenty-eight of the Saiva agamas have come from Siva's mouth, and the supplements to the agamas (angas) appeared from an aspect of Siva (urdhvamukha).[9] The Mahanirvanatantra is a tantric text associated with the Sakta tradition that responds to rapid cultural and religious changes that are causing a breakdown of traditional customs and practices. Even though the text is in the style of traditional agamas and gives the impression of ancient authority, the work was probably written sometime in the 18th century in the form of a conversation between Parvati and Paramasiva.[10] The author implies that the new text supersedes the ancient texts. Paramasiva says: "I will tell you the essence of the Vedas, Agamas and Tantras. If a person masters this Tantra, what purpose will be served by studying the Vedas, Puranas and Sastras? All of those are for the welfare of the society, but that welfare can be achieved through this Tantra. Therefore, I am revealing this to you, Oh Devi."[11] Many of the regulations and much of the discipline of rituals are relaxed: "The Supreme is to be meditated upon through worship without strain or stress. No special efforts are to be made, no fasting, no ritualistic purity, nor considerations of timing or direction of worship."[12] Thus, it can be seen that throughout the centuries orthodox Hindus have not been isolated from the rapid changes in society, but have accommodated their rituals and prescriptions to the changed circumstances.

New festivals and rituals have been introduced in temple practices throughout the centuries. Inscriptions at Tirumala from the 11th century through the 14th century record the introduction and evolution of the twenty-one day festival of chanting the hymns of alvars and offerings to be presented during the chanting of each hymn (*adhyamana utsavam*), which are not mentioned in the *Vaikhanasa agama* that are the authoritative ritual text at Tirumala. This festival is still performed at Tirumala. Inscriptions also report the introduction during the 13th through the 15th centuries of new grand annual festivals (brahmotsavam) by the Vijayanagara kings. Similarly, the local princes at Trivandrum introduced into the temple monthly festivals in which thousands of lamps were lit on the day of the birth star of every ruler, and these rituals are still performed in the temple even after the abolition of the royal purses. Thus, new festivals and changes in rituals were permitted and were not considered to be antithetical to the existence of ancient regulations.

Aspects of Transformation of Tradition

Emigration in the modern period is raising significant questions as Hindus from many regions of India attempt to preserve aspects of their tradition in North America. They construct temples and follow some domestic rituals, but they question the validity of their activities. Some seek for scriptural sanction for adaptations they make in ritual practices; others say that the main thing is their sincerity in worship so the exact forms of worship are not important. The examples derived from the historical analysis illustrate five aspects to be considered in the transformation of the tradition: language, regionalism, sects, text / commentary, and text / performance.

Language

The question of what language is appropriate for worship troubles modern immigrants, but it is not uniquely a modern problem. In 1988, while I was staying with a Gujarati family in Vancouver, their teenage daughters asked me if we are permitted to use the English language in our prayers. Their parents were insisting that they use either Hindi or Sanskrit. I told them: "We know a few languages, but don't you think that God knows many languages better than we do. Language is only the vehicle for thought; the vehicle is not important, but the thought is important." My response is supported by an anecdote from the 12th century:

> Once Vankipurattunampi stood close to some women of the cowherd community while he was praying to Visnu. Mutaliyantan observed this and accosted Vankipurattunampi,"Why do you go and stand with these illiterate cowherd women while praying to the Lord, when you could very well stand among the Vaisnava bhaktas." To this Vankipurattunampi replied: "It is true that we have a little learning. These people may be illiterate, but the Lord's grace is on them like water which flows from a higher to a lower level." Then Mutaliyantan asked: "What did they pray? And what did you pray, sir?" Vankipurattunampi replied: "They prayed to the Lord (in pure Tamil): 'Please drink milk and eat these fruits. Please wear this golden sacred thread. Live a hundred years. Wear this silk upper-cloth.' My prayer was in Sanskrit: 'Be victorious, be victorious.'" Then Mutaliyantan said: "So you could not forget your rough sounding Sanskrit even at this place. It seems that we will continue to be the same wherever we are. Please come over here."[13]

This is a most interesting incident, for here Ramanuja's disciple Vankipurattunampi (also called "Andhrapurna") indicates that no language barrier exists in the worship of God. He joins those who do not know Sanskrit because they are the recipients of God's grace and because any language can be used by any person. This is the tradition supported by Ramanuja and his followers when they introduced Tamil hymns as part of the puja rituals and the tradition continued at Tirrumala when the singing of Annamacarya's songs were introduced and at Srirangam when Tyagaraja's music became part of the daily worship. Away from their mother land, where Indian languages are scarcely spoken, the future generations will have to use English for prayers and rituals, and this conforms to linguistic adaptation that has already taken place in times past in India.

Regionalism

Regionalism is closely associated with language difference, but other regional variations are present. A very minor difference among the regions will serve to illustrate this point. The common practice of priests in South India is to have the upper body uncovered when they perform puja as a sign of respect. Indeed, the sacred thread originated as a substitution for an upper cloth that would be dangerous during the fire sacrifice, and is therefore called *yajnopavita*. Because it is relatively cold in Melkote, the priests wear woolen shawls across the left shoulder for warmth in the same position over the thread. In North India, priests serve in the shrine while wearing shirts for the same reason. Also in North India, any Hindu can approach the images, but in South India only the pujaris are permitted into the shrine. These are meant only to illustrate many variations in Vedic rituals that have evolved over time.

Sects

The fact that sectarian differences exist is demonstrated by the codification of these differences in twenty-eight Saiva agamas and a hundred and eight Vaisnava agamas. Even among Vaisnava temples, some like those at Tirumala, Triplicane and Sriperumbudur follow the *Vaikhanasa agamas* and others like those at Srirangam, Kanchipuram, Kumbakonam and Melkote follow the *Pancaratra agamas*. Priests in Kerala (*nambudri*), unlike other priests in South India, perform rituals in temples to all three deities — Visnu, Siva and Devi — so they follow the *Tantra samuscaya*, which gives instructions for all three.

Sectarian differences also have a regional basis. Temples in North India did not develop agamas, even though the *Narada pancarata agama* governs ritual in some places. The codification of rituals resulted, rather, from the puranic tradition, and the *Agni purana* and the *Garuda purana* prescribe rituals that are performed in the temples. Modern sects adapt the earlier codifications for their own special deities, sites, and rituals. Great and sudden variation of practice always threatens division and the creation of new religious groups, many of which then try to arrest the process of transformation and change that brought them into existence.

Text/Commentary

The process of commentary on philosophical and theological texts in order to interpret and apply ancient texts to the commentator's time is well-known. Commentary on texts is the primary mechanism of intellectual development and adaptation to changing circumstance. The same is true in the development of rituals. The *Grhya sutras* and *Dharmasutras* have a number of commentaries from the 8th century to the 13th century. Among these commentaries, that by Mitaksara in the 10th century is considered to be an authoritative commentary on rituals and other rules. Commentaries are necessary because the sutras, like rituals themselves, are enigmatic with surplus of meanings. From the 14th to the 16th centuries a number of people wrote independent works discussing the intricacies of the sutras and rituals, the most important of which was *Vaidyanatha*. Even in this century a similar work, *Vratacandrodaya*, was composed and is widely used in Gujarat and Rajasthan. It contains mantras to be used in worship of many deities and instructions on how to perform the rituals. It is both a codification and adaptation of traditional rituals. The most important process of evolution is in the oral transmission of the ritual tradition from the priest who acts as guru to teach younger priests how and why to perform various rituals. If a devotee questions why a priest does a ritual in a certain way, the response is usually, "That is our practice (*acara*)," meaning, "That is the way my teacher told me to do it." That points to the power of both example and the oral tradition in the transmission and transformation of ritual.

Text/Performance

Performance is always different and richer than the written text, which is only a model for performance. Indeed, as mentioned above, if texts do not give details for a ritual or if an action is not prohibited in the Sruti or in the Smrti, the customary practice becomes authoritative. Ritual, understood as the communicative aspect of customary behavior, is a primary means of transmission of traditions and has its own power and authority. Anthropologists and textual scholars discuss the relative symbolic power of texts and performance and which is the "correct" form of a tradition. Performances are introduced that are not mentioned in texts. For example, it has become customary to keep ashes of a deceased person for many days and to transport the ashes to distant locations for disposal, as, for example, was done in the case of Rajiv Gandhi's death, so the performance has become a part of the tradition without textual support. Performance changes under the influence of contingencies caused by rapid social change before the texts or commentaries — or even the oral tradition — catches up. A study of the performance of rituals under constraints in North America would provide significant data about the manner in which the tradition has evolved and is evolving. In June of 1975 I was at Harvard when a Hindu scholar was married, and I was asked about the legitimacy of a ritual performed by a woman, who learned the texts and acted as the *purohit*. The day after the Hindu wedding, John Carman performed a Christian ceremony because the bride was a Chinese Christian. The act changes more quickly than texts, but rapidly becomes authoritative. Indian immigrants to Java came long ago as laborers, and because of difficulties of communication and because they were poor and could not bring priests from India, as has now become the custom among new immigrants to North America, they lost contact with the texts and oral tradition. Nevertheless, Hindus in Java still continue to perform the rituals. At a conference in 1985 at Pune, a Hindu from Java indicated an eagerness to know how to correctly perform the rituals and what texts they could follow. Performance plays a major role in preservation of religious traditions among immigrants who are separated from texts and religious scholars.

Application to the North American Scene

First, immigrants can engage in the process of transformation of rituals to meet the needs in their new circumstances with confidence, knowing that adaptation and transformation of rituals have been part of the Hindu tradition from ancient times. It is not possible for people living in North America to observe festivals as long as nine or ten days or to continue all of the prescribed life-cycle rituals, but it is consistent with the history of Hinduism in India for festivals and rituals to be adapted to local circumstance. Just as regional languages have become part of many rituals in India, so English is an acceptable medium for many of the mantras and explanatory elements of ritual in this country. New rituals and festivals will be created and adapted to the American calendar, just as Memorial Day, the Fourth of July, and Labor Day have become times of major Hindu gatherings. The ability of Hinduism to adapt to constant and even dramatic social change is a reason for its survival and success in such a diverse country as India. Now it is spreading with immigrants around the world, and can have similar success.

Second, Hindu scholars should consider the possibility of preparing a new codification of basic Hindu rituals, both domestic and temple, for the use by leaders of Hindu religious institutions in North America. Such a ritual text should not be rigid in application, but should include alterations that are already permitted in India and those that are necessary in this country. A new ritual calendar could be prepared. Rituals from all parts of India and from many sects should be included, which will require the participation of many scholars in its preparation. Mobility and rapid communication within India is already causing more uniformity of practice in India — witness the effects of the televising of the Ramayana and the Mahabharata — and that process is accelerated among immigrants who gather in North America from many regions and Hindu sects of India. Such guidance would be very valuable in helping Indians in North America from either losing their traditions or becoming irrelevant to future generations as they adapt to American society.

Conclusion

Ritual functions both to preserve religious tradition and in performance to transform the tradition to conform to aspects of the cultural setting. Ritual both stretches and takes new shapes in response to external pressures and springs back toward its original shape as the vehicle for preservation. This two-fold aspect of ritual is evident in the history of Indian religion and is becoming a part of experience of Hindu immigrants. It is not a new process that should be attacked as dangerous; indeed, it is essential to the vitality of any religion.

9

Swaminarayan Temples and Rituals: Views of Sadhus A Tale of Two Temples: London and Amdavad

Vivekjivandas Swami

Traditions are preserved and transmitted in stone and paintings, through the human word and letter, and through actions or ways of life. Through our talents and commitments we humans are master carriers of traditions. Throughout the stream of generations we have preserved and reshaped traditions for new generations, and we have employed many means for the transmission of traditions. The temple institution in Hinduism has nourished and transmitted the ideals of India's culture and religion through a living human experience of rituals and traditions. The focus of this chapter is on some aspects of the temple as an object of transmission of religious traditions as these have been a part of personal experience in the Bochasanwasi Swaminarayan Temples in London and Amdavad. Since I have been exposed to the temple in London as a member of the youth organization and to the temple in Amdavad in India as a sadhu for the past fifteen years, I shall describe and discuss the transmission of Hindu tradition in both.

I became a member of the Bochasanwasi Swaminarayan Sanstha during my early teen years. Before I joined the youth organization, I knew a lot more about Christianity than about Hinduism simply because I was taught about Christianity in the schools. Having had little knowledge of Hinduism and little faith prior to my initiation as a member, the London Swaminarayan temple played a significant role in inspiring me to commitment. In the early 1970s, I knew of no cultural or religious center for the immigrant community from India and East Africa other than the first Swaminarayan temple, which had been dedicated in 1971 as a converted Christian church in the Islington section of north London. Entering the temple, one entered a part of India by means of symbols found inside and the traditions honored there.

Major architectural differences exist between major temples in India, such as that in Amdavad, and those in England, East Africa, and the United States, represented by the London temple. In Swaminarayan Hinduism two types of temples exist: *shikhar-badhha mandir*, which is traditional in its architecture and ways of worship, and *hari mandir*, which is less impressive in appearance. Temples of the first type have three tall pinnacles, domes both large and small covered with a variety of sculptural figures and designs. Sadhus are essential for such temples to conduct the daily worship rituals and to provide services for the marble or metal images in the sanctum sanctorum. The sadhus administer programs of the temples, including the five periods of worship daily in the sanctum, the discourses following each ritual, and the regular festivals of the temples. No sadhus of the Bochasanwasi Swaminarayan Sanstha reside outside of India, so no temples of this type have yet been established in England or the United States. Temples of the second type do not have the large spires or domes, and the carvings and decorations are simple. The consecrated images are of a type of marble sculpting or painting on canvas that do not require the permanent, daily service of a sadhu. Such temples are managed by lay devotees between regular visits by sadhus. Worship and discourses are conducted by the lay devotees. These simple temples are found in India only where the Swaminarayan following is small, but all the temples in England and the United States are of this type. The Bochasanwasi Swaminarayan Sanstha currently has three hundred temples of the second type and nine of the larger temples in India and twenty of the second type in

England, the United States, and East Africa. In the early 1970s, by contrast, the temple in London was the only Swaminarayan temple in England or the United States.

The influence of the larger temples is more pronounced because of the presence of the sadhus. Indeed, the larger temples in India are the residence for scores of sadhus, and they play a significant role in the transmission of Swaminarayan Hinduism. A second major difference between the Amdavad temple and the London temple is the difference in environment and dominant culture. The transmission process is much more difficult in London because young people are caught in the experience of two cultures. I shall discuss these two temples by discussing my experience in both regarding the important aspects the transmission of symbols of faith, language, and moral duty.

Symbols of Faith in London

Since I had grown up in a British environment where school and friends contributed significantly to shaping my identity, my ignorance of Indian religious traditions was acute. I was an alien to my native culture and to the religious traditions of the Swaminarayan faith. What I saw and experienced in the London temple was new and strange because of my primary exposure to the traditions of my country of residence. The celebration of Christmas was normal to me, and the Indian festival of Diwali, to which I had not been fully introduced until I started going to the temple, was new and difficult to understand. I was more used to singing Christian hymns than Hindu devotional songs. The symbols of faith and culture that meant most to me were of English origin simply because they were celebrated all around me, whereas the Indian religious traditions were unfamiliar until the dedication of the temple in London. As an example of simple things: "A" meant "Adam" or "apple" and did not include "aarti" or "Akshar." So I viewed everything, including India and the Hindu way of life, through the symbols and experience of England to which I had been exposed. The temple in London, simple in architecture and program, provided nevertheless a new and original set of symbols and pictures through which to experience Indian life and traditions as they really are.

The London temple contributed to my gradual discovery of my identity and developing of faith in Swaminarayan Hinduism. This shift toward Hindu religious traditions, which was by no means an easy one, required exposure to the symbols, worship, and habits of Swaminarayan tradition. The temple provided both the site and the sights of that gradual shift in axis. The temple scene provided an initiation into new modes of religious activity, which meant that I became a strict vegetarian and an active participant in the worship and discipline of the temple. I started performing the daily acts of personal worship of the images (*puja*), placing the sect mark (*tilak*) on my forehead each morning at worship, and observed other parts of the religious discipline. The participation of other young members in these activities created a strong bond between us that made the understanding and acceptance of these new symbols possible. Entrance to the London temple began the long journey to appreciate the importance of these Hindu traditions.

The group of young people began to spend the weekends at the London temple to permit a greater exposure to and involvement with the symbols of Swaminarayan tradition. Every Saturday evening during the early 1970s youth meetings were held for prayers, singing, and discourses. I and some of my friends regularly served the temple by serving food to the devotees and by cleaning the utensils until late at night. Physical service gradually enhanced my faith and attachment to the temple and its programs. After our temple chores were completed, we gathered for a late-night discourse that explained elements of our faith. Even though I understood little of it at the beginning, I can say that I felt good about participating and was curious about the tradition. We slept on Saturday nights in the temple. The next morning, following our personal acts of worship and breakfast, we would clean and wash the temple premises. Personal worship of the Lord in the temple caused us to feel privileged to perform these acts of service, and this too helped consolidate my faith. Study of religion, reading of sacred texts, and discussions of problems were possible in the temple, whereas they were not at home. So, the exposure to service, worship, and listening to discourses in the temple contributed significantly to shaping and solidifying my faith.

The Akshar Purushottam Swaminarayan Temple in Amdavad, India

This growing commitment was reflected in the shaping of tangible differences between my school friends and myself. I stopped taking school dinners with them because I had become a vegetarian, norms of my behavior changed, and my weekend hours were spent at the temple, all of which diluted my friendships with those outside the temple. Obviously being different was not a comfortable feeling at first, but as my faith grew I found my new friendships at the temple more than compensated for the loss.

Language in London

Since English is my first language, I felt tremendously hand-
icapped in absorbing and understanding the traditions of the
Swaminarayan faith that were transmitted in the Gujarati language.
At first I had a distinct lack of interest in anything that was in
Gujarati, which left me ignorant and uncomfortable when prayers,
songs, and discourses were being conducted at the London temple.
Gradually, however, my friends helped me learn Gujarati, and the
free flow of questions and religious discussions in the temple moved
back and forth from English to Gujarati. The senior members of the
Swaminarayan group conducted the programs in Gujarati, and
regular exposure to Gujarati in the temple enabled me to learn the
language. Appreciation for the language enabled me to start singing
devotional songs, and this led to participation in dramas, folk dances,
and finally giving speeches in Gujarati. The two days of the week in
the temple provided the greatest exposure to the Gujarati language,
even though in my time there was no program for learning Gujarati.
I couldn't read or write Gujarati, but I was able to understand when
others read or spoke.

I realize today how weak the transmission process becomes in the
absence of the primary langauge. Because I know the language well
today, I may take some of its advantages for granted, but having gone
through the period of not knowing Gujarati, I realize and appreciate
the power of language as a vehicle for transmitting religious traditions.

When I went to India in 1976 to become a sadhu, I found that,
unlike England, India has many media for the transmission of
religious traditions: holy festivals, the spoken language of Gujarati,
educational institutions, pilgrimage shrines, temples, sacred rivers,
and the extended family. My leap as a young person from the temple
in London to settlement in India as a sadhu landed me in an
altogether different life, context, and people, something which I had
partially expected but had not experienced.

The leap was great because as a young person in England my
manner of life, besides the temple, included sports, study, family, and
considerable freedom. Initiation as a sadhu, however, removed me
from all those things, except the temple, which now occupies the

entire manner of my life. As a youth in London I had two homes, a material home with the family and a spiritual home at the temple; now as a sadhu I have only one home, the temple. The difference between the two settings and the power of transmission of traditions can be expressed by an analogy: the difference between being a part-time student and a full-time student. The total number of hours committed obviously produce a rapid pace and greater depth of learning. The transmission of religious traditions in the temple in Amdavad is more exhaustive and faster.

Symbols of Faith: Amdavad

In contrast to the first temple in London, the Amdavad temple is far more traditional in size and shape, and it is looked after by sadhus who administer a fuller program of religious activities. My role as a sadhu in that temple exposes me to the articles of faith at a much more profound level. As a sadhu, the observance of strict disciplines of absolute celibacy, poverty, humility, renunciation of desires represented by taste, and detachment from family and relatives governs my life. It is required that a sadhu attend at least three of the five periods of worship and discourses every day. Our saffron clothes and daily worship remind us of our total commitment. At least three fasts every month and fifteen fasts in one special month of the year form a part of the monastic discipline. Serving the Lord in the temple, which is in some cases a full-time service, is also a part of our faith. In every temple we have a senior saint who leads the group of sadhus, and obedience to his wishes is part of our faithfulness to the spiritual leader of the Bochasanwasi Swaminarayan Sanstha, H.H. Pramukh Swami Maharaj.

Language in Amdavad

As part of the monastic training course, I engaged in an intensive study of Gujarati, the primary language of communication in the temple. Since all conversations and discourses in the temple are in Gujarati, there was much more extensive exposure to the language than in London. The native environment also facilitated learning. Having learned the language in six months, I had access to books and teachings of the religious traditions through both words and actions in the temple. I also learned the epics, philosophies, religions, and traditions of Indian culture.

Devotees visiting the temple look to the sadhus for guidance, instruction, and answers to their questions. Since the Amdavad temple attracts a large number of people of all ages each day, conversations with devotees provided valuable experience in the use of the language. Gradually, I and other new sadhus became spokesmen for Swaminarayan Hinduism and ourselves transmitters of the religious traditions. Greater knowledge of teachings of the religion and regular participation in the rituals created changes in feelings, attitudes, and moral judgments.

Moral Duty

The result of exposure to both the symbols of faith and the language used in the temple is a change in attitudes and moral judgments from negative to positive. This means an erosion of ego and the manifestation of humility, the blunting of sheer logic and the development of faith, the erasing of ignorance and the functioning of discrimination, and a change from intolerance to tolerance. In short, the physical involvement with the symbols of faith and learning the language lead to a self-evaluation and a feeling of commitment within the individual.

Especially in the London temple, I was exposed to people of different natures, and working with them allowed the development of tolerance. As a sadhu in the Amdavad temple, where the exposure to people of different types is greater, tolerance was further strengthened. Tolerance requires an intrinsic change in sadhus brought about by the diminishing of the ego. After accepting the holy vows of a sadhu at the Amdavad temple, I experienced the storm triggered by ego clashes through the inescapable interactions with different types of people. I had to compromise and even surrender. Only later I came to realize the benefits. The task is difficult when one is required to work with people who love conflict and ignorance, but still remain cooperative and value that person.

Love also has a more profound and purer expression now as a sadhu in the Amdavad temple. At the London temple as a youth, my love for the Lord and Guru Hari Pramukh Swami Maharaj partly depended upon external conditions such as academic success or material happiness, whereas today as a sadhu I realize the futility of a love that bargains or demands.

My fellow sadhus and I have come to realize that the temple inspires us to look and search inward. The atmosphere is conducive to the promotion of introspection and to a greater stability of daily life. So, in the temple the transmission of traditions go deeper and deeper, from the physical to the mental plane and from the mental to the spiritual plane.

If Yogiji Maharaj, who was the master and predecessor of Pramukh Swami Maharaj, had not established a Swaminarayan temple in London, I am certain that many Indians like myself would not have had the opportunity to participate in Hindu religious traditions. For many of my colleagues, the London temple became the arena where they were introduced for the first time to our religious traditions. Transmission of these traditions in both temples took place gradually, and the process of change was difficult to go through. When there are things you do not understand and lifestyles to be transformed, the transmission becomes difficult. In spite of these difficulties and conflicts, the main reason why I kept going to the temple and remain in the temple is the wish of my guru, Pramukh Swami Maharaj. The temples owe their power of transmission not merely to the presence of the images of God but also to the faith inspired by holy sadhus.

The Evolution of Swaminarayan Festivals: Internal and External Transmission of Traditions

Brahmviharidas Swami

Sir Monier Monier Williams, a Sanskrit scholar and the former head of Oriental Studies at Oxford University, rightly observed, "No country upon earth rejoices in a longer list of holidays, festivals and seasons of rejoicing, qualified by fasts, vigils and seasons of mortification than India." In saying this, he recognized the fact that the Indian way of life is rooted in festivity. It would not be incorrect to state that India's cultural heritage lies not in the manuscripts of history but in her festivals, which continue to keep her traditions alive. Despite the fact that the basic cherished traditions have undergone little change, the festivals, which are the strongest media of transmitting these traditions, have evolved slowly under the influence of geographic and demographic demands to meet the changing needs of society.

This chapter introduces the broad categories of Indian festivals and examines the evolution of festivals in Swaminarayan Hinduism. The Cultural Festival of India held in Edison, New Jersey, in August, 1991, provides a model of both the internal and external transmission of religious traditions through a modern festival.

All major festivals of India, celebrated by either the whole country or in selected regions or by individual religious groups fall under four major categories: (1) Festivals are celebrated to mark different stages of life, such as birth, adulthood, and marriage. Such stages in development are considered sacred and are celebrated by the prescribed rituals and traditions. (2) Celebration of other festivals express gratitude for changes in seasons. Seasonal changes directly affect productivity of crops and both the fertility and migration of animals. The economy and the livelihood of India is focused on agriculture and is strongly dependent on the crops and animals; hence, festivals involve propitiation of the divine forces at changes of seasons. (3) Festivals celebrate the victory of good over evil, as one remembers in the destruction of the demon Ravana by Lord Rama and the killing of Narakasur by Lord Krishna, which are celebrated with great pomp and enthusiasm. (4) Other festivals commemorate events sacred to a particular religious, cultural, or social group. Such festivals acclaim the birth of important figures, commemorate special events, or celebrate specific beliefs and practices.

While the festivals of the first three types remain fairly common and uniform amongst all Hindus, the fourth type is unique and specialized. It continues to change as new additions of festival days and events are made to the calendar as the group develops and its history expands.

Thus, the Bochasanwasi Sri Akshar Purushottam Sanstha has added new festivals to the Indian calendar as part of Swaminarayan Hinduism. It is a socio-religious organization that is very much a part of mainstream Hinduism, while possessing features of an independent religious group that progresses on its own line and boldly reforms itself to satisfy the challenges of new trends. This dynamism provides the opportunity for an interesting study of the evolution of its festival activities.

Swaminarayan Hinduism originated in northern India at the birth of its founder, Lord Swaminarayan (1781-1830) in the small village of Chhapaiya. Throughout its two centuries of history Swaminarayan Hinduism has flourished, leading to the development of over 3000 centers and almost a million adherents. The faith has prospered under the auspices of a unique, unbroken line of gurus, a *guruparampara*, through the succession of spiritually enlightened masters who have guided and steered the fellowship. This growth from a humble beginning to its current widespread distribution of followers, with the resulting modifications in its activities, provides examples of how religious groups strive to preserve, promote and protect their traditions.

Festivals are a primary means of transmission of traditions among Swaminarayan Hindus. Their deity, Lord Swaminarayan, stressed festivals: "My disciples with means should celebrate festivals in temples with great pomp and enthusiasm" (*Sikshapatri*, 56). He also said, "I perform Vishnuyaag [a large festival of non-violent sacrifice] and hold large congregations on festivals like Janmasthami, Ekadashi, etc., and celebrate such festivals every year, and therein gather all brahmacharis, sadhus and satsangis with a purpose that if anyone who attends these festivals, even if he be a sinful man, would be redeemed of his sins and would attain the divine abode of God, if he remembers the brahmacharis, sadhus or satsangis at the time of his death." If we interpret these words, leaving aside the spiritual aspect of salvation, we find that Lord Swaminarayan advocated large festivals and through them managed to spread his traditions and messages in a manner unmatched by other contemporary religious groups. [See the charts of festival observance among Swaminarayan Hindus.] Lord Swaminarayan accepted all the major Hindu festivals, and he sparked off many reforms, which eliminated distorted features and revived the purity of essential traditions from the past. He waged war on distortions and injustices of festivals in his time, such as the killing of innocent animals for sacrifices and the singing of rude and vulgar festival songs. He introduced a system of separate seating arrangements for men and women to safeguard the chastity that was endangered by the promiscuous mixing of the sexes in large gatherings. Lord Swaminarayan also removed the barriers of caste and creed, and inspired festivals that reached out to all and created a strong cultural unity that had been lacking in earlier Hindu festivals.

The profound changes ushered in by Lord Swaminarayan were instrumental in amassing people of all background and beliefs, talents and traditions, intellect and interests. The festivals facilitated mass communication of ideas between people at a time when mass communication was very slow and difficult. The Swaminarayan festivals were regularly able to gather the entire group of followers on one site to permit the imparting of standard traditions at one set time, which strengthened the followers' faith in and commitment to the traditions and messages of their leader. This strength and uniformity of traditions, beliefs, and manner of life of Swaminarayan followers is praised by a Gujarati saying: "A Swaminarayan is a Swaminarayan wherever he is. He will never waver or falter from his vows." The credit for such strong uniformity despite the diverse geographical, financial, and intellectual differences among the devotees goes largely to the festivals that bind them into a close union.

Modern growth, mobility, and communication has brought about significant changes in the festivals observed by the Bochasanwasi Swaminarayan Sanstha. Until 1981, the festivals in the Swaminarayan faith continued in a slowly evolving path introduced by Lord Swaminarayan. Then, like a quantum leap, a surge of reform developed under the leadership of H.H. Pramukh Swami Maharaj, the current spiritual master. The five years prior to 1981 were spent in planning and organizing for a huge thirty-seven day festival to observe the bicentenary of the birth of Lord Swaminarayan. Plans were made to cater to the needs of those who were not followers of Swaminarayan as well as to the staunch devotees. Features never before found in a festival were included: conventions and conferences, anti-addiction drives and blood donation camps, music concerts and folk dances, exhibitions and landscapes, food stalls and amusement arcades. Although the outward appearance of the festival changed dramatically, the traditions it transmitted remained the same. The main adaptation in this "new age of festivals" was that it addressed the needs of non-believers as well. That was the first large, month-long festival held by the Swaminarayan group.

The Cultural Festival of India held in Edison, New Jersey, marks an additional step in the evolution of festivals which attempt to reach both believers and non-believers, of Indian and non-Indian origin in a foreign land and in a foreign language. This foreign environment lacks exposure to Indian traditions, so the structure of the festival was grounded in education. The festival grounds were like a mini-township, with forty acres of beautifully landscaped grounds on which were displayed five majestic archways, four temple monuments, twenty-two artistic displays, three exhibition halls, over thiry food stalls, two performance stages, and a large auditorium. Over 2600 volunteer workers from Swaminarayan centers across the country served in thirty-two departments. The festival was attended by tens of thousands each day and over seventy thousand on Sundays. Despite the fact that the festival was structured to meet the demands of the American context, breaking new ground, the main function of festivals in transmitting traditions was maintained.

The festival in the United States transmitted Indian culture to children whose parents are incapable of explaining the traditions them, even though they are excessively fearful about raising their children in isolation from the traditions. America is a multi-racial melting pot, requiring ethnic harmony, so the idea of universal fraternity was conveyed in the exhibitions of the Cultural Festival in a manner relevant to the new context. The festival was an attempt to meet the needs of the host culture while not straying from its basic purpose of promoting Indian traditions. The festival intentionally focused on two aspects: (1) internal transmission of traditions and (2) external transmission of traditions.

Internal transmission occurs to the Swaminarayan followers who were the direct participants in the festival. External transmission is to the visitors who came to observe the festival. In no way was its aim to convert or proselytize, but instead to inspire faith in whatever noble values the person held. The Cultural Festival of India marked the centenary of Yogiji Maharaj, the predecessor and guru of Pramukh Swami Maharaj. Therefore, the festival had great religious appeal to members as well as an intense cultural attraction for those outside. For the Swaminarayan followers participation was an emotional, spiritual experience due to their deep reverence and attachment to Yogiji Maharaj, whom most of the followers had known intimately. For the visitors, both Indians and Americans, the festival was an opportunity to experience India through the various displays and artifacts, elaborate exhibitions, performances of folk dances and classical music, spicy Indian food and impressive temples. The two distinct processes were continuously at work, the internal transmission and reaffirmation of traditions and the exposure of visitors to the true depth of Indian culture.

The festival was well-received by visitors, some of whom saw it as a first pilgrimage to India. Many were attracted by the symbolism in the works of arts, others by the forms of Lord Ganesh, Nataraj, or Laksmiji, spending time to copy the explanations given at each display. It is true that the festival may not have introduced Indian traditions into the lives of outsiders, but it did generate great interest and resulted in education. Respect for the Indian traditions was seen when non-Indians willingly took off their shoes before entering the temple shrine or stopping to bow down to the images therein. Guides at the temples and exhibitions responded to a large number of inquiries for information.

Aspects of nature worship as practiced in India were clarified through observing the artifacts of the Sun God, Moon God, and the Ganges. People practiced the *namaskar* greeting and pronounced the Indian greetings to carry the memory of India back to their homes. Visitors learned by watching Indian marriages performed on the site, carefully explained by commentators. They enjoyed Gujarati food and dances. Several conventions were held in conjunction with the festival to enhance an intellectual awareness of the values of Indian culture, including a Child Development Convention, a Youth Convention, a Women's Convention, a Cultural Unity Convention, an Anti-addiction Convention, and a Conference on the Transmission of Tradition. Parents brought children from distant cities to show them aspects of Indian culture. One parent remarked, "I feel I have regained a part of India long lost within me." Many other people learned about the festival through reports in the media — newspapers, television, radio, newspaper supplements and magazines — because a concentrated effort was made to extend the impact of the festival through modern media.

The other, more important, feature of the festival was the internal transmission, measured by the changes that occurred in the lives of the followers who were direct participants and volunteers for the festival. Smaller festivals are always a labor of love, but the Cultural Festival of India exemplified great devotion, dedication and sacrifice by more than 2600 people who temporarily renounced their jobs, homes, hobbies, holidays, and money to assist with the festival. It was an example of service through *tan, man, dhan* — physically, mentally and financially. The Guru Bhakti Celebration, held on one day of the festival, demonstrated the Vedic tradition of *Guru Aagna*, in obeying the commands of the guru. Some came to take their seats for the event as early as 4:30 am, and, despite the desire of every devotee to be present for the occasion, some of the Swaminarayan followers who had come from as far away as California and had spent three years preparing for the event nevertheless sacrificed the moment to serve at a different part of the festival grounds at the command of the guru.

One young boy came to the festival because his mother told him that there would be 180 sadhus at the event. He had never seen so many sadhus in saffron in one place. The tradition of seeing sadhus and talking with them to obtain guidance was revived at the festival, and many people reported significant changes in behavior. Some became vegetarians, and many vegetarians promised to avoid onions and garlic, foods not traditionally allowed in the Swaminarayan faith. Others reported that daily baths followed by morning worship, singing of devotional songs, chanting of mantras, memorization of scriptures, and regular attendance at religious discourses would be henceforth part of their discipline. Many took vows to daily show respect to their parents by touching their feet and to eat only after offering food to God. Teenagers, who would rather have key chains and fashion articles, were seen carrying the prayer beads, the *mala*, as a mark of faith.

The strongest tradition the Cultural Festival of India nourished was the tradition of festivals itself. Many regained faith in festivals and have realized that festivals are not wasteful expenditures of energy and money or displays of narrow-minded devotion, but rather that festivals provide a powerful means for the transmission of traditions. Three distinct reasons are given for why festivals like the Cultural Festival of India are the most effective medium for transmitting traditions: (1) They are dynamic in the sense that they continuously change and evolve to satisfy the needs of people in different contexts. (2) They create an exclusive environment over a long period of time — like a giant laboratory of traditions where people can see, hear, touch, experiment with and directly experience traditions. (3) They are a strong sensory experience for people of all social, economic and educational levels, and that in an instructive and entertaining manner.

Analysis from 1991-1992 A.D. Calendar
2048 Samvat Year Hindu Calendar

In the analysis, only the major festivals of Hindu calendar have been included. The objective of the analysis is not to display a detailed calendar of Hindu festivals, nor a complete list of its religious and political celebrations. It is to provide a reasonable comparison between major religious celebrations (not necessarily celebrated throughout India but by large regions) and a particular religious group. Here the Swaminarayan group tends to selectively accept major religious celebrations but has its own special festival days centered around its founder and the spiritual hierarchy. It is important to note how the festivals grow in number and shift in emphasis as the religious group grows and spreads world-wide. Also note that other festivals such as centenaries and bicentenaries or the special Cultural Festival of India celebrated by the group are special events not included in the analysis.

Charts of Festivals Observed by
Bochasanwasi Swaminarayan Hindus

These charts show the statistical relation between general Hindu festivals observed by many Hindus and those festivals that are observed by a single sampradaya — the Bochasanwasi Swaminarayan Sanstha. Moreover, the analysis identifies the portion of festivals shared by all Swaminarayan Hindu groups and that portion unique to Bochasanwasi Swaminarayan Hindus, many of whose festivals center on the founder and members of the spiritual hierarchy.

Religious Days Observed in a Year by Swaminarayan Hindus

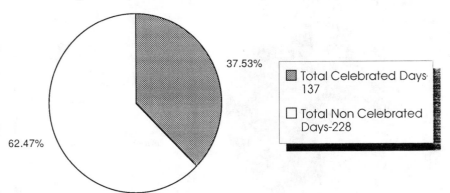

37.53%

Total Celebrated Days 137

Total Non Celebrated Days-228

62.47%

CHART 1: More than a third of the year for the Hindus is spent in some form of religious celebrations (excluding national and political festivals).

Types of Swaminarayan Festivals in Relation to General Hindu Festivals

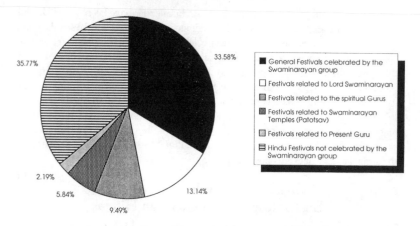

CHART 2: Bochasanwasi Swaminarayan Hindus selectively observe festivals of mainstream Hinduism as well as its own exclusive festivals.

Types of Festivals Observed by Bochasanwasi Swaminarayan Hindus

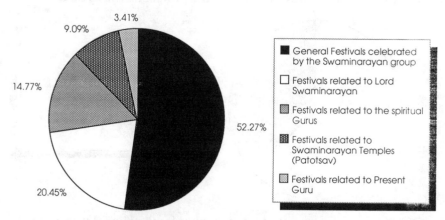

CHART 3: Nearly half of the festivals celebrated by this group are exclusive to the group and not observed by other Hindus.

10

Transmission of Sacred Scripture in the British East Midlands: The *Vachanamritam*

Douglas Brear

A wooden cot specially prepared and brought from Surat by Shree Jadavjibhai, was placed on the veranda near the hall facing north [at Kariyani on Wednesday, 19th September, 1820]. Velvet mattresses covered with white bedsheets were neatly spread over along with a round white pillow placed as a back rest. Red velvet cushions were also arranged on it. All the four sides of the cot were richly decorated with golden fabrics which were kept hanging. Shreeji Maharaj was seated on this cot facing north. He had put on a white turban woven with golden fabrics and had covered His body with a rich silken garment interwoven with golden fabrics. Over this garment, he had put on a cotton shawl having a black border. Munis and bhaktas from various places had assembled before him. All the devotees were looking at the lotus-like face of Shreeji Maharaj, just as the chakor bird looks amorously at the full moon.[1]

We see before us here Sahajanand, Lord Swaminarayan, the founder of the Swaminarayan Hinduism, at the height of his powers, and acknowledged by his followers to be divine.[2] The movement of which he is the founder and which takes its name from him now thrives not only in its native Gujarat, but also wherever Gujarati communities are found throughout the world; a branch of it was responsible for the organization of two substantial Cultural Festivals, the first in London and Amdavad in 1985, the second in New Jersey in 1991.[3]

Sahajanand's public ministry lasted in Gujarat from 1802 until his death in 1830, during which period the numbers of adherents grew steadily. He had to overcome much opposition at a time when not only was Gujarati society in a state of disorder, but also the traditional religious disciplines were widely ignored. At his instigation, his *sadhus* became directly involved in social welfare work and in manual labor for the good of the community, and his own ethical teaching was in part specifically directed against prevalent social evils of the day, a factor which ranged him alongside the contemporaneous British administration in Gujarat.

Major Doctrines of the *Vachanamritam*

The *Vachanamritam* comprises discourses given by Sahajanand over a ten year period, from November 1819 to July 1829, and it is arranged in numbered sections named after the locations in which the discourses took place. It is a voluminous text, almost seven hundred pages in the English translation from the Gujarati. Given its provenance and its form, it is inevitable that the text does not present a consistent and rigorous thread of philosophical argument from the beginning to the end. In what follows, attention will be directed only to those elements which are accepted by all branches of the Swaminarayan tradition. Broadly speaking, four major subjects from the core of the text's teaching may be isolated as being important: the nature of the individual; cosmology and cosmogony; the nature of the divine; and the dynamics of the spiritual life. The whole text is, of course, inspired scripture, but these four areas are undeniably central, and, taken together, provide a representative picture of the transmission of a sacred text in a particular tradition. These four areas are among the classic concerns of Indian philosophy, and no novelty should be sought in the teachings of Sahajanand. He is concerned above all to interpret *sruti* correctly — he repeatedly refers his hearers to certain classic texts, the absolute authority of which he unequivocally acknowledges — and his speech is replete with scriptural phraseology, imagery and references.[4]

Nature of the Individual

It is appropriate to deal first with the nature of the individual, since comprehensive knowledge of the *jiva* [essential self] is stated to be part of real knowledge (*Sikshapatri* 104). It can be seen only by careful introspection.[5]

The framework for the understanding of the phenomenon is the traditional Samkhya scheme of twenty-four evolutes (*tattvas*), and so important that "if [one] obtains the knowledge of these tattvas, he can be released from his ignorance."[6] The constellation of classic terms taken over by Sahajanand expresses the truth that the individual's psycho-physical make-up comprises a unity — within it are both material, solidly physical elements (the body with its motor and cognitive organs) and mental elements (that complex of factors which relate to thinking, deciding, desiring, and so on). The latter are characterized by the tradition in metaphors of lightness, brightness, or purity, and are called collectively the internal organ (*antahkarana*).[7]

As the tradition had always emphasized, the innermost self, the jiva, is not to be identified with any of these factors; the tattvas are non-sentient, whereas the jiva is the knower.[8] Moreover, the jiva is omnipresent, although it is felt progressively more strongly in those laments which are associated with the mental or psychic dimension of the personality;[9] all these "purer receptacles" serve as media for the self's activity.[10] Indeed, the fact of their doing so accounts in large part for the difficulties which stand in the way of realizing this essential ontological distinction. Practically, the ignorance which includes the confusion of these distinct entities, has its root in the contact between the sense-organs and the objects of sense. Once this contact is allowed to become attachment ("I am the gross body") the process of rebirth ensues inexorably.[11]

The terms used in the discussion of this subject and the teaching given on it are clearly consistent with the broader traditions of Hindu thought. The same applies to Sahajanand's treatment both of the three states of consciousness — waking, dreaming, and deep sleep — throughout all of which the jiva persists unchanged,[12] and of the three bodies — the gross, the subtle and the causal — the last of which comes to underlie all levels and dimensions of that ignorant and worldly understanding of life referred to in the previous paragraph, and to be, therefore, crucially involved in the karmic process.[13]

The frequency with which Sahajanand adverts to the subject attests the centrality of comprehending the workings of karma. All his discourses make use of the classical categories of the *gunas* and the three types of karma;[14] he provides particular examples of the types of life-factors which are conditioned either by karma in general or by specific karmas;[15] he specifies some of the areas which are emphatically not due to karmic influence;[16] and he gives insights into the mechanics of the process and into particular rebirth prospects.[17] Of course, given Sahajanand's expressed theological and philosophical stance, the underlying activity of God is emphasized: it is he who directs the karmic process throughout the three states of consciousness[18] and who both inspires and enlightens the jiva.[19]

Cosmology and Cosmogony

All this running beyond the confines of a single individual life in a single world, involving a series of existences in different locations, naturally leads Sahajanand to the second of our four topics, the development and structure of the cosmos. Although it is by no means an easy matter to piece together his comments, scattered through ten years of discourses, into a coherent, or even a consistent, whole, there is clearly much that echoes the tradition, and the basic "blueprint" is, once again, the Samkhya scheme.[20] Since the development of the tattvas proceeds according to a principle of progressively more gross and solid manifestation, it may, perhaps, be helpful to suggest an additional image to complement the traditional ones found in the *Vachanamritam* itself. The process may be envisaged in terms of a series of three concentric spheres, each progressively more solid. The initial stage of evolutionary manifestation (and the least solid and material) takes place, as it were, on the outermost edge of the outermost sphere; the process unfolds successively "inward," ultimately giving rise to the sensible cosmos, the innermost, grossest sphere, "furthest away," so to speak, from the source. Within this innermost sphere, to retain the image, there develops, or materializes the threefold universe, the triloka, in which souls transmigrate. This comprises the multiple world of nature and of human endeavor (the theater in which the order of dharma obtains and in which the individual must strive to draw closer to god), the dazzling but invisible worlds of the lesser deities, and the darker levels beneath, whose denizens are the demons, spirits of the night, and serpents.[21]

This state in which the cosmos is sustained is described as being a body of the cosmic God,[22] and the long age during which it exists as his waking day,[23] both images hallowed by ancient usage. In terms of the supplementary one here proffered, all three spheres are fully manifested, the innermost being further "solidified" into the triloka. The period during which the cosmos rests in a state of destruction is the night of the cosmic God when the triloka is destroyed and the earth reduced to an atom; the various deities die and the unreleased jivas return to *maya*[24] — the cosmic deity is in his deep sleep.[25] In terms of our image, only the outermost sphere is manifest, whilst the other two are latent or at rest, the triloka having disappeared completely. At the end of this period creation begins again; the two outer spheres are active and manifest, whilst the inner is in process of so becoming and of "crystallizing" into the triloka.

The cosmic process is thus seen as an immensely long alternation both of the expression or manifestation of potentiality, and of the return or lapsing back of that expression into potentiality. At the end of a period of such alternations (the length of which is calculated in the traditional manner)[26] the whole series of tattvas is withdrawn into the maya whence it came. Not only does the cosmos cease to exist, but the underlying, supporting potentiality is reabsorbed. The life of the cosmic deity himself ends,[27] as the Supreme Person, *Parabrahman*, God voluntarily withdraws maya back into himself.[28]

Nature of the Divine

If the reason for the importance of this whole subject be sought, it soon becomes clear that knowledge of the processes of cosmic life infallibly leads to a realization of God's greatness. The self is important to the worldly consciousness, yet it is truly insignificant in relation to the cosmos. The cosmos itself is undergoing a process of alternate manifestation and dissolution, the jiva being carried along, a mere chip on the face of the waters. There being innumerable macrocosms, millions of cosmic gods, our particular cosmic process is merely one of many, all functioning at different rates;[29] all these incalculably vast unfoldings are themselves part of an even greater one which is itself ultimately found to be rooted in god and solely his work.[30]

However it is not sufficient to know God simply as the supreme controller of this and of all other universes; knowledge of his human form is more important still, as befits a teaching which is solidly devotional in character.[31] Sahajanand and the tradition which follows him place great emphasis upon this matter of incarnation, upon God's motive for self-manifestation,[32] upon the manner in which it reveals his nature,[33] upon the way in which it takes place, and upon the apparent tension between god as incarnate and god as transcendent.[34]

Dynamics of Spiritual Life

Much of what the *Vachanamritam* says on this is standard bhakti theology within the tradition of Ramanuja; Swaminarayan bhakti is nevertheless distinctive, for its ideal exponent (the *ekantika bhakta*) fulfills ekantika dharma, and this consists of yoga, dharma, and *vairagya*, in addition to bhakti.[35] In the *Vachanamritam* the first of these is usually called *atmanishtha*. All four comprise a seamless robe the threads of which are variously isolated according to the exigencies of the occasion or the implication of a question.[36] Some summary indication of what is involved in each is necessary if the character of Swaminarayan spiritual life — at least of the four major subjects from the text's teaching to be here discussed — is to be appreciated.

First, atmanishtha or jnana (knowledge) is the capacity to distinguish between being (*sat*) and non-being (*asat*), between the essential self and all that is not the self.[37] This involves coming, through a process of introspection concentrated upon precisely those factors outlines earlier, to an awareness that in the words of the

Sikshapatri, "Jiva...resides in the heart,...indivisible and eternal...separate from the three bodies" (105, 116). Further, when pursued in combination with austerities, atmanishtha is an effective way of lessening the intensity of the instincts; indeed, although other beneficial effects result from it, the general statement holds good that atmanishtha is a paramount aid to detachment.[38]

Detachment being vairagya, the inter-relationship between the elements of ekantika dharma already become clear — certainly atmanishtha and vairagya are especially said to be closely-related.[39] Vairagya is the state of being "not attached to anyone but God," detached in affection, "unaffected by...bodily enjoyments."[40] This state is available to both the renouncer and the householder.[41] Each person should carry out the dharma of that state to which he or she has been called by god, in a spirit of disinterest, without (on the part of the householder) attachment to the relationships associated with the state,[42] and enjoying only those sense-pleasures which are related to god.[43]

To be attached to god, however, is to have bhakti. The emotional aspect of bhakti is frequently discussed[44] and is described precisely as it is in the tradition[45] — there is no other way for ultimate redemption than devotion.[46] It is not an easy matter because the human mind is so unstable that the purity of bhakti easily becomes sullied by base motives.[47] Further, although it should be emotionally warm, the affective dimension must be accompanied by knowledge of god, both in his human form and in his greatness and glory as cosmic ruler.[48]

The fourth and last component of the ekantika dharma, and one with which the *Sikshapatri* is most particularly concerned, is one's appropriate duty (*svadharma*).[49] This is closely connected with the other components, and, as usual, statements can be found which *prima facie* contradict one another, and which make sense only in terms of the ekantika dharma as a whole, taught over a considerable number of years.[50] The emphasis upon it is unequivocal: a devotee follows all injunctions without distinction, insofar as the routines of life allow[51], and those who do not do so — and such persons can be recognized[52] — are to be rejected from the community.[53] That which is presented in the *Sikshapatri* is assumed throughout the

Vachanamritam: the duties of the varnas, of sadhus and householders, of men and women, of wives and widows, are laid down with a scrupulous precision which stands directly in the tradition of the Dharmashastras.[54]

The teachings of Lord Swaminarayan as presented in the Vachanamritam, and as outlined above, are basic to the entire Swaminarayan community: they are understood and meditated upon by all spiritually mature satsangis. How are these teachings actually transmitted?

Transmission in the East Midlands

Swaminarayan Hinduism is divided into two main branches, and at one time there was mutual animosity, but harmony and a degree of mutual respect now reign, at least between the spiritual heads and among the virtuosi. The two original gadis (seats) of the acaryas are at Amdavad and Vadtal, from where the two incumbents, lineal descendants of the family of Sahajanand, preside. In 1906, a reform movement was instigated, partly in the face of laxity among certain Vadtal sadhus, and partly on account of doctrinal differences; from this has grown the Bochasanwasi Shree Akshar Purushottam Sanstha (hereinafter AP Sanstha), a separate organization having its own spiritual leader, sadhus, temples, shrines, and philosophy. In what follows, attention will be directed largely to this younger branch.[55]

It should not be inferred from this that the Vachanamritam is of merely minor significance for the original gadis and their members; this could not be the case, given the nature of the text. It is simply that the parent gadis do not have a tight and formal organization, and no directives are issued from either Vadtal or Amdavad which lay down study-programs. The Leicester satsangis who are affiliated to the old gadi at Amdavad do indeed read, study, and meditate upon the Vachanamritam, and ensure that its teachings are faithfully transmitted, but they do so in an informal fashion. A satsangi noted for his spiritual wisdom gives discourses on an ad hoc basis, or else a visiting sadhu will speaks at greater length. The teachings of the Lord Swaminarayan as enshrined in the Vachanamritam saturate the whole Swaminarayan community, but as far as the old gadis are concerned, there is no machinery available (in what is, moreover, in Leicester, a small body of devotees) for the kind of systematic meditation on those teachings which will be described in what follows. The situation is entirely different in the AP Sanstha.

Ultimately, the reason for this is that this is a sect, in the classic sociological sense, manifesting all the characteristic features which have come to be accepted as distinctive of sectarian movements.[56] Furthermore, the Sanstha's doctrinal emphasis involves guru-bhakti at an intense level,[57] so that "commitment of the sectarian [which] is always more total and more defined than that of the member of other religious organizations"[58] becomes even more focused. If the directives from the center are those which have the approval of the spiritual head, and if "one should worship him with the same intensity with which one offers worship to God,"[59] then it is inevitable that the following of the directives which express the guru's wishes will be unquestioning and enthusiastic.

A point worth making is that although an urgent need for religious nurture is recognized, the attitude is one of confidence that the need can indeed be met, that the generation-gap can indeed be bridged. This confidence comes precisely from the knowledge that the nurture-program is being carried out according to the wishes of the spiritual head; and it is this knowledge which gives "the power, self-assurance, and ability necessary to perform that tasks required," and which helps "to relieve them of anxieties."[60]

The AP Sanstha's program of nurture and spiritual development inevitably involves study and elucidation of the *Vachanamritam*. The manner in which this is done provides a clear example of the transmission of tradition at a time and in circumstances which are characterized by rapid change.

Formal classes and less formal groups cater for all ages. The initial idea for the organization of classes for young people was formed in India during the period of Yogiji Maharaj's leadership, and from there it spread to the communities in East Africa; although weekly *satsang* meetings at the temples had been encouraged earlier, 1952 saw the inception of regular Sunday gatherings of young male devotees in Bombay. On his visit to Africa in 1955, Yogiji Maharaj encouraged the devotees to start youth activities, and his flair, dynamism and concern led, within ten years, to the establishment of many *yuvuk mandals*, groups of dedicated young men, in Gujarat and East Africa.

These yuvuk mandals were the prototypes for the other groups which now exist, *bal mandals*, for younger devotees, also being set up during the same period. In Leicester, in English East Midlands, the Temple Committee was instructed in 1977 by the guru to establish classes for young people as soon as possible, and from this beginning the present efficient and comprehensive system evolved. Four classes exist for *balaks*,[61] run on Sunday mornings by a group of six teachers: this group monitors progress carefully and plans the content of classes at its monthly meetings. A *balika* class, for young girls under sixteen, runs simultaneously, but is less formally-organized, being taught by an older girl; it follows the same syllabus as the bal mandal.

The aim of the yuvuks who teach the young boys is twofold: to teach about religion and to relate this teaching to wider issues and to moral values. In the ordered prosecution of this aim they are assisted by the weekly sabha syllabus, prepared by the London temple in 1980: *inter alia* this sets out the basic devotional elements with which children are expected to become familiar, and lays down the principle that *Swami ni vats* — short, pithy sayings from the sermons of Gunatitanand Swami — should be learned. The booklet makes clear the extent of the "general knowledge" which a child is expected to have by the time he moves up to the yuvuk mandal, and within this broad vocabulary of religious life are found the three gunas, the four *purusartha*, and the five *visesh vartamaan*. In 1987, the Sanstha produced under the instruction of the guru a booklet entitled "What we should know" (*Janana Jevu*) and it is now used as a matter of course as an authoritative guide to instruction. Short essays are set from time to time, and to commemorate the thirtieth anniversary of the founding of the bal mandal, a collection of representative essays was printed in 1985, and these reveal the extent to which this broad vocabulary has been assimilated. Thus, for example, the concepts of *seva* and *Akshardham* (a theological crux for the Sanstha) are already part of the instruction.

The teachings of *Vachanamritam* naturally have no immediate place in this, since its philosophy is too complex and its form too discursive for the minds of the very young. It is clear, however, that the basic groundwork laid in the bal mandal prepares the children for their later exposure to the full glories of Lord Swaminarayan's extended discourses. Terminology which is basic to the *sanatan dharma* as a whole is introduced, together with that which is more particularly related to the *Vachanamritam's* modes of utterance. In particular, "balaks are taught *Swami ni Vato*...and these sermons are basically a layman's guide to the *Vachanamritam*,...in easy form for all to understand."[62]

This situation changes once a child has moved to the yuvuk mandal; this is not a class as such, but a sabha (meeting). It is organized by yuvuks themselves, although there are always older men present. The aims of the Youth Organization are set out in a leaflet produced by the Leicester temple: at what is seen implicitly as a time of profound and rapid social ferment, the aim is to save young people from "the degeneration of moral, cultural, and religious values in young people."[63]

An example of the prosecution of this aim, both in the preaching of the spiritual head and in the nurture of the young, is provided by the reading presented at the Leicester young women's group on Sunday, February 15, 1987. The fortnightly *Patrika*, issued from Amdavad on the twenty-seventh of the previous month, had included a report under the headline, "In today's colleges habits [bad habits] are increasing instead of decreasing," which instructed: "Swamishri calls the youths to attend the college of Brahma-knowledge.... If our faith, thoughts, food and company are good then we will become good too. Our habits are our good enemies. On top they look very good but are eventually harmful. Believing them to be our friends we will never be able to break away from them. We will never enjoy God's happiness until we have broken our habits.... We have found this satsang so we should try to improve our lives. What is the benefit of satsang? We develop good abilities. In the college of Brahma-knowledge, bad qualities/habits are discarded and good qualities are attained....If we have not rid ourselves of our bad habits, then it is difficult to develop love for someone else, to do service for them."[64]

The leaflet produced by the Leicester temple, referred to above, provides general information about the activities of the bal and yuvuk mandals. It may be remarked at this point that the nurture provided at the temple is not in fact mainly directed at the offspring of satsangis, and that many of the participants were not born into the satsang. What we see here, then, is consciously both the transmission of the teachings of the tradition itself and of the broader principles of the sanatan dharma of which it is a representative and which it sees as requiring proper teaching in the given circumstances of twentieth-century Britain, when many children of Indian extraction are totally ignorant of their religious heritage.[65]

In December 1986, the spiritual head of the AP Sanstha attended a children's assembly in Bombay, the report of which was discussed in the Leicester young women's group on February 15, 1987. In his address to the youth leaders, he included the following comments: "If the boys receive good education then the community will improve. Today's parents or elders are never free because everyone is busy trying to earn money. Therefore today, no one knows what the *Ramayana* or the *Mahabharata* are. With children you have to become like them. We should have their innocence. If there is fighting and bad language in the house then the children will do the same. If there are strange photographs kept then the children receive the same print. But if from childhood the seeds of devotion are sown, then when they grow up, they will still have them. Whatever effort we make for the children will be beneficial to us in the long run."[66]

In these words are encapsulated the concern to transmit the broader Hindu tradition as well as to inculcate sound values in the twentieth-century world. They are quoted from a fortnightly publication which is sent from India to all AP Sanstha temples. The headquarters of the Sanstha in Amdavad houses an active Publications Department, and among its production is a monthly newsletter, in Gujarati, *Nilkanth*. This sets out the specific syllabus to be covered in sabha, and among the contents of the syllabus are some fifty short sections (*vachanamrits*) of the *Vachanamritam* which are considered to be particularly appropriate for teaching purposes.[67]

Guidelines are provided as to their elucidation, and these are used in the Leicester sabha — used, rather than being slavishly followed — for interpretation.[68] All major elements of the teaching of the text, as summarized above, find their place in these recommended vachanamrits, and they are all taught in such a way as to emphasize the character of practical Swaminarayan religious life. The content of these texts may be summarized as follows: True happiness and fulfillment in this life, and the assurance of felicity after death, are hindered by the world's tempting show (maya); to take it at its face-value and to be seduced by its variety will involve an individual in attachments, fruitless desires, invidious distinctions, and choices based on selfishness. In this emotional and psychological soil will flourish all the passions of pride, egoism, greed, envy, and anger; and the resultant life will be at bottom fruitless and aimless, directed towards the merely transitory, and dominated by ultimately insatiable desires.

Detachment (vairagya) and introspection are a way towards the eradication of carnal desire: It is important to be aware of the internal structure of the psyche so as to be able to observe the workings of the wayward mind in the face of that which bewitches it. Once the internal organ is clearly observed and understood, control can be exercised; the habit of intolerance will weaken; non-attachment will emerge as the guiding principle of experience; and spiritual vigor will replace weakness and vacillation. A complementary change of perspective will take place if the creation and functioning of the cosmos as a whole be investigated and meditated upon — the individual jiva and its concerns will appear as truly insignificant in the face of these immense, millennial and divinely-governed processes.

The surest way, however, to reach this right view and right orientation and to see the truth of things is through devotion to God and dedicated service. Total and loving surrender will remove the veil so that God may be seen and met; the transcendent creator and supreme controller may be seen to be incarnated in human form; and the world and the self confronted, understood and controlled. The best context in which to undertake this quest (and the one which will insure that it be successful) is provided by the satsang, the fellowship of devotees — united in service and devotion to god, in hearing the scriptures which tell of him and of his doings, in absolute obedience to the guru, and in living disciplined and fruitful lives according to the prescription of dharma. Lord Swaminarayan's own divine nature exemplifies these profound ontological truths, and his own total non-attachment and dharmic life epitomizes what an ekantika bhakta should be.

The practical teachings summarized in the foregoing paragraph were graphically and tersely exemplified in comments made by the spiritual head of the AP Sanstha to a devotee who was going to the United States: "You are going to America, but keep your satsang. Many of our devotees live there and abide by the rules laid out by Lord Swaminarayan. Therefore, concentrate on leading a moral life whilst doing what you are going to do there. Never get involved in consuming liquor or flesh. Don't think we are inferior to the Americans; compared to them we are morally superior....Don't forget your dharma. You should never forget your background wherever you are living."[69]

In the preceding paragraphs a summary has been presented of what the sanstha considers to be salient teachings of Sahajanand, drawn from a set of *vachanamrits* recommended for study by yuvuks. In the sabhas this is presented in such a way as to meet the wider expressed aims of the Youth Organization as quoted above. Hence, the moral and spiritual implications for those living in late twentieth-century Britain are sedulously drawn. The tradition which this scripture exemplifies is presented as providing strength, stability, comfort, and certitude amid the shifting sands of social, spiritual, and ethical confusion. This faithfulness to the permanent values of the tradition is complemented by that creative openness in interpretation noted earlier.

Three examples will suffice to show the tone and content of this teaching in practice. The first is the discussion of Gadhada I, 74 which took place in the Leicester young men's group on Saturday, February 14, 1987, and on the following Saturday. The theme of the text is, "The true understanding/spiritual faith of a devotee is realized when he faces adverse circumstances." The discussion included the following comments: "When do we know that a devotee or a friend is sincere? In times of difficulty. For example: A *bawo* (a type of ascetic) was going past a village when he saw a man crying. When he asked why, it turned out that the man's son had just died. The bawo tried to comfort the man by saying that everyone must die one day, and so on, and after some time the man got over his son's death. The bawo started living in the same village, and kept a goat on whose milk he fed himself daily. One day the goat died, and the bawo started lamenting and crying. The man who had been comforted said, 'Just six months ago you explained to me about this false body and so on, and now your are crying.' The bawo replied, 'That was your son but this is my goat!' The man then realized what little understanding the bawo had. Gunatitanand Swami says in one of his talks, 'You cry for those who die yet those who cry will also die, so one day we will all die. Therefore cry for yourself and not for others! True devotees will find it a lot easier to overcome grief (although they may have true feelings for the relatives) when a close one dies. With this knowledge we can also overcome the fear of death.'"

"There are different types of understanding/knowledge. For example, we can read or hear that malaria is acquired by mosquito bites. You have some friends who come back from India and catch malaria; they go to hospital for treatment. Your knowledge that malaria is caught by mosquito bites is reinforced, reaffirmed, made more firm. You might go to India and get malaria yourself. Your knowledge has been experienced now and fully developed. So, for example, if you go to India or anyone else is going, you advise them to take tablets to prevent malaria, as you have full knowledge now. Similarly, the intensity of spiritual wisdom (*jnana*) differs. For example, Dadar Khachar, the prince of Gadhada, at whose place Lord Swaminarayan stayed for most of his ministry, was a great devotee, but he had a lot of problems. He lost a complete harvest, and he had a court case which he lost. But still he kept his faith in Shriji Maharaj. He never for a moment thought, 'If he is God, why couldn't he have done this and so on?' He took it all as though, 'God is testing my faith in him.'"[70]

A second case which also exemplifies faithfulness to the permanent values of the tradition complemented by openness of interpretation is the discussion which took place in the same men's group on February 14, 1987, on *Sikshapatri* 116 about "true understanding." The discussion included the following comments: "The final purpose of this human existence is to become truly realized and with this understanding to worship God. In any other body, this soul goes through what it has to go through. But in a human body it can choose, for example, to direct its course for future rebirths depending on its actions. If any other body, plant, or animal has one thousand pounds to spend, they will spend it, die, and enter the next body. But in the human body, one thousand pounds can be increased in value or decreased, depending on your deeds. In this way the future course of the soul is directed....We have the ability to advance our souls and redeem ourselves. We can gain salvation, ultimate redemption, and reach a further happiness. The *Bhagavad Gita* states that there are four *dukhs* or miseries, including birth and death. Who would now wish to enter their mother's womb? No one! But if we don't liberate ourselves, we will have to suffer that same misery in future births."

A final example is the brief discussion, on Saturday, March 7, 1987, in the young men's group. The text was Sarangpur 8 on the subject of jealousy. The following example was given: "A father left his money and estate to two sons. Later they fought over who has the money and who has the estate. After sharing it out, one son, who had the money, put fire to his brother's estate. This was an act of sheer jealousy. If you want to go forward in satsang and if you feel jealous of someone, for example, who might be a good drum-player or guitarist or well-versed in the scriptures, then approach that person to assist you in going forward. Learn from him."[71]

Examples given earlier have included material drawn from discussions held in the young women's group. In 1984 the *yuktis* (young women between the ages of sixteen and thirty-five) had received permission to hold their own sabha, separate from their elders.[72] They organize it themselves, but an older female devotee is always present, to facilitate and to explain the *Vachanamritam*. More discussion takes place than in yuvuk sabha, and "when the *Vachanamritam* is read, [the leader] tries to bring in examples [from] everyday life to make difficult concepts easier to understand; she encourages the yuktis to participate, to interrupt and ask questions, and to put forward examples of their own."[73]

This selective approach to the *Vachanamritam* within the context of an ordered group is abandoned only once a devotee has attained the age of thirty-five, and enters the *vadil mandal*: from now on, the whole of the *Vachanamritam* is read and explained. The fortnightly

Swaminarayan Satsang Patrika, received by all devotees, provides detailed guidelines for the particular *vachanamrit* which is to be studied as part of the weekly satsang. To use the Western term, an annual lectionary is produced, so that, in principle, all two hundred and sixty-two *vachanamrits* will be covered in generally chronological order.[74] This arrangement holds for all AP Sanstha groups in the East Midlands.

The formal religious life of the Sanstha does not consist solely of sabhas and classes held at the temple; conventions (*samaiya*) — organized originally by Sahajanand himself — and youth camps/conferences (*shibir*) are occasions for study, discourses, and lectures; specifically doctrinal matters from the *Vachanamritam* can be more extensively treated, particularly at the youth conferences.

The teachings of Sahajanand as set out in the *Vachanamritam* are not only studied and meditated upon, internalized and reverently interpreted by mature Swaminarayan devotees. Within the AP Sanstha they are also carefully and consistently taught to the young men (less consistently to the young women), who have all been prepared in the bal mandal for their reception. Within the AP Sanstha, a worldwide system of annual examinations, with questions set and marked by sadhus at Amdavad, provides a means of assessing the success with which this enterprise of spiritual education is being prosecuted: "they give an indication of the level of articulation which the youngsters have reached concerning their religious tradition, as the answers themselves reflect precise theological points within the Sanstha."[75]

The practical expression of the life of devotion within satsang is service (seva). This cardinal teaching — not only of the *Vachanamritam* but indeed of the whole bhakti tradition — is put into practice to an immediately visible extent in the satsang; so obvious is the point that little attention need be given to it. However, the practical means which have been developed within the AP Sanstha to organize seva insure that this core behavioral element of the *Vachanamritam*'s message is effectively enshrined in the life of the satsang, and is so to a particularly notable degree.

A booklet is produced by the temple, entitled *Seva descriptions*. This book contains a list of all the areas of temple life either in

which yuvuks are expected to be involved, or which they are
expected to run themselves. Thirty-eight areas are listed, comprising
all the jobs required for the efficient running of the temple. On
joining the yuvuk mandal, each youth is given a seva application
form, on which the choice of seva department(s) may be indicated:
kitchen, maintenance, subscriptions, sport, Gujarati teaching, and so
on.

Underpinning all devotional religion, however, is worship, and it
is this dimension to which attention may, finally and briefly, be
drawn. *Lex orandi lex credendi*, and the contents of Swaminarayan
liturgy, whether old gadi or AP Sanstha, express, in an immediate
and repeated form, one of the crucial teachings of the
Vachanamritam, namely that God is to be worshipped not only in his
transcendent fullness but also in his human form. In *Kirtan* and
above all in the long and impressive incantatory night-hymn, *Chesta*,
the sheer beauty of Lord Swaminarayan is lovingly and passionately
described: how he walked, what he wore, how he moved, how he
spoke.[76] It is at this point that "the doctrine of the human form of
God" is felt along the pulses, and an account of the transmission of
teachings would be inadequate without attention being drawn to the
dimension of which it is a part.

Conclusion

The *Vachanamritam* is the foundational scripture of a living and
active tradition, a thread of the Hindu tapestry. As the record of the
discourses of one who made no claim to diverge from the sanatan
dharma,[77] its truths are in no degree inconsistent with those of that
millennial wisdom. The transmission of these teachings continues,
then, as it has always done, to provide a framework of timeless truth,
stability, and certitude, such that the stresses and vagaries of social,
intellectual and moral ferment may be accepted, understood, and
transcended.[78]

The tradition in question, however, having a particular and
distinct identity, its scripture contains also those emphases and truths
on which this identity rests. Here again, and with all the enthusiastic

commitment of the classic sect, the teachings are transmitted faithfully, and — in the younger branch — energetically.

Yet, the intellectual world of late twentieth-century Britain — by which so many of the brightest young men and women have been formed, as doctors, accountants, nurses, dentists, and so on — is allowed to contribute its insights, just as the communication structures of an electronic age are utilized. In East Africa, "there was a weekly sabha just as there is here, but it was more academic.... Then, illustrations were given from the classical Indian sacred books such as *Ramayana*...but now we can't do that, they won't understand. They need illustrations of today, not of the ancient scriptures." In these words of a temple secretary,[79] is encapsulated the position of the Swaminarayan tradition in the East Midlands in the late twentieth century — the teachings of that tradition, as expressed in the *Vachanamritam*, are indeed transmitted, but the mode of this transmission has to be sensitive to the needs of the times.

In the case of the AP Sanstha, whose transmission is centrally organized, the sensitivity of its spiritual leaders to the need for appropriate change and development is clearly reflected. Acharya Maharaj Tejendraprasadji Pande of the Amdavad diocese and his heir Lalji Maharaj are also as aware as anyone of the changing circumstances of the world in which their followers live. It so happens that there are no organizational structures which would allow this awareness to be in some way expressed in actual binding decisions. The reasons for this lie, of course, in the status of an acharya. Over and above any such sensitivity, however, lies the scriptural status of the *Vachanamritam*. Its truths, which transcend social particularities and which provide a context for the successful negotiation of rapid social change, are never allowed to be compromised.

11

Sacred Threads of Several Textures

Raymond Brady Williams

Tradition is a series of shared, repeated, structured, communicative acts — verbal, gesture and physical — that form a heritage, binding generations together and forming social groups. A function of such communicative acts that form tradition is to shape and preserve personal and group identity, an especially important function among new immigrants. The threads that form tradition are individual and group memories, and the process by which the tradition is preserved, adapted and transmitted is incredibly complex, analogous to the function of DNA structures. DNA is semi-conservative replication because half of the strands is new material. The complexity of the biological structure of the gene code, which is the fundamental form of heritage transmission, is vast enough, quite apart from the social forces that influence the mating of parents. These are, however, relatively limited, concrete, and available when compared with the multiple threads of communication by which the cultural heritage of a people is passed on among immigrants to a new generation and in new locations.

The process of communication of tradition is compatible with almost any substantive content and includes all of what we think of as culture. An individual communicative act is sometimes called "a tradition," and the structured complex of related acts can be called "tradition. "Indeed, any shared culture of a group is constructed of (1) individual communicative acts, (2) subsets of traditional material — such as legal, economic, linguistic and political — and (3) a more or less coherent constellation of group-defining elements. Some confusion exists because all three are referred to as a "tradition." Tradition is that which provides a syntax of languages — verbal, ritual, and visual — enabling us to continue the conversation of culture and civilization and to maintain a creative thrust toward the future.

Religion is the sacred thread which serves as a very important subset of the structure of transmission because religion functions in part to provide a transcendent basis for personal and group identity, a natural outgrowth of human character as a symbol-bearing creature. Such transcendence is, potentially, a powerful force both in the conservative stabilizing of a social world and in the transformative challenge to elements of a received tradition, the latter because religious commitment permits an individual to stand within a tradition involving transcendence with the power to call into question all traditions, including ultimately aspects of itself. It provides ballast that enables immigrants to preserve their identities and adapt to new surroundings. Transmission of a tradition is always both a celebration and a quest. Religion is prominent at stages in the immigrant experience because in the midst of rapid social change it provides a transcendent anchor for memory that relates personal and group identity with the past. It validates those who are entrusted with transmitting and revising the sacred tradition and it provides both social and ritual occasions in which personal identity is merged with group identity.

Recent emigration from India to the United States is an example of rapid social change brought about by modern mobility and communication. Although many of these immigrants are part of the scientific and technical elite who had already made adjustments in their world-views to accommodate elements of Western tradition, immigration is potentially a disruptive event because it involves a loss of omnipresent plausibility structures for much of the cultural memory. Tradition is that about which one could say, "That's the way we have always done things or thought about them in my family or group." Traditioning is essentially a social act, and traditions are group possessions. Immigration causes dramatic change because the social group and context are changed: "That's the way we always used to do it, but can we here and now? How can we?" Active response to these questions results in new formulations of the traditions of immigrants in response to differing social contexts and needs in America.

The Asian-Indian community and their religious organizations are "made in the U. S. A." because the immigrant group is unique to the United States in its character and structure. Asian Indians of the same type do not exist as a social group in England, Canada, East Africa, and certainly not in India. A result is that the traditions of Asian-Indians are assembled in the United States from imported components by relatively unskilled labor (at least unskilled by traditional standards) and adapted to fit new designs to reach a new and growing market. Please forgive the analogy to television sets and automobiles, but the analogy illustrates the point that emigration has made traditions a major aspect of international communication. No individual tradition nor the structured relations of traditions can be moved from one social location to another without dramatic changes in a process of adaptation.

Such adaptation is not only demanded by the future and hope; it is also permitted by the past and memory. The reason is the heterogeneity in tradition. Any developed society or culture has many diverse strands of tradition available to persons and groups within the society, and hence, also, several identities are available. Even within a relatively homogeneous religious or ethnic tradition a freedom for selection exists that permits an individual or group to choose elements for application to specific situations. Indeed, in any temporal process a tradition is transformed by a process involving both selection and rejection of elements, and no tradition remains rigidly fixed through time. In times of rapid social change, such as that caused by emigration, the process of adaptation is accelerated, more pronounced, and highly visible. One is reminded of a motion of an early New England School Board:

Resolution:

We are going to build a new school;

We are going to build the new school on the site of the old school;

We are going to build the new school out of the materials of the old school;

We are going to carry on classes in the old school while the new school is being built.

Resolution:

We are going to create a new religious community;

We are going to create it in the new world;

We are going to build it out of materials from the old country;

We are going to carry on the religion in both worlds while the new community is being built.

The focus of this chapter is on the process and strategies of adaptation that are characteristic of Asian-Indian religious groups in the United States, and the goal is a typology of adaptive strategies. It is therefore necessary to deal with the structured character of the traditions as repeated, communicative acts shared by members of newly formed social and religious groups, and also with both the memory and the reality of the continuing traditions in India. Each of the adaptive strategies is implicit in the traditions in India and is acceptable and recognized in the new American setting. Both continuity and discontinuity are aspects of the adaptation of religious traditions in the United States — imported components assembled into new configurations in the United States.

Strategies of Adaptation

Five trajectories, models, or ideal types of adaptive strategies can be discerned among Asian-Indian religious groups, and indeed among secular organizations as well. They could be called "ideal types" because they are rarely observed unmixed, but they nevertheless illustrate ways in which religious groups attempt to reformulate and transmit religious traditions and hence are valuable for the analysis of and predictions about processes of adaptation. The negotiation of adaptive strategies is a long, involved process in which the religious groups function differently in the sacralization of personal and group identity. These differences are due to elements of theology, peculiar group histories, and the social and political contexts in new settings, and these in turn determine how religions are reappropriated by immigrants. Differences among strategies are evident in the characteristics of religious leadership, creation of sacred spaces, observance of sacred times, and use of language and arts in the transmission of tradition. Five strategies of adaptation in evidence among Asian-Indian religious groups are: individual, national, ecumenical, ethnic and hierarchical.

Individual

Most early Asian-Indian immigrants came as solitary individuals and located where few Asian-Indians lived. Hence, one strategy of adaptation was preservation of religious identity through acts in private or its opposite in the private disregard for any religious heritage. Such individualism allowed students and young professionals to experience what Gandhi recalled from his student days in London as "the Sahara of atheism," during which many ignored both the rituals and discipline of their caste and religion. Some who are now prominent in religious organizations refer to that experience as a "period of shame" as a warning to their children to flee assimilation. An undetermined number of Asian Indians avoid participation in religion, and a few are critical of "temple building" and the preservation in the United States of Indian religions, but no overtly anti-religious Asian-Indian groups are prominent. Some Hindus and Jains maintained puja articles or small home shrines that were used for private worship. Some Muslims observed daily prayers privately upon arrival. Followers of various religious traditions engaged in private study of sacred texts or in acts of prayer, meditation, and devotion. In these ways the coals of religious devotion and individual identity were gently fanned and kept alight.

In most cases it was an amateur activity because the immigrants were not trained as religious specialists, nor did they occupy traditional religious occupations. Indeed, most of them were part of the technical-scientific elite, who occupied themselves with religious rituals, texts and philosophy as a new avocation. A few Brahmins,

A home shrine containing images of deities and ritual
paraphernalia.

some Parsis from priestly families, and a few women had been trained
by parents and possessed expertise in the performance of the daily
and annual ritual cycles. Otherwise, they relied on randomly
available "handbooks." The only Asian-Indian religious group that
brought their own religious specialists with them were the Christians,
who had graduate students in some American seminaries and whose
pastors were husbands of nurses who had gained access to "green
cards." In the early days of settlement, even these persons were
engaged in study or secular occupations and were not religious specialists for groups. Lay people of various religions preserved the

religious traditions in private acts in the earliest days, and gradually these lay people began to establish and exercise leadership in religious groups. The first forms of adaptation of Indian religions to the United States were created in this individual creativity, and it is impossible to overestimate the importance of this stage in the adaptation process even though it is further removed than other forms from observation.

An important extension of the individual forms of worship and discipline is found in the nuclear families as they were formed in the United States. Personal shrines or ritual objects were expanded to include objects from the spouse's religious tradition, and dietary practices and other forms of personal discipline were changed in families to conform more closely with traditional patterns, as diverse as the traditions from which they were imported. Home shrines and family rituals are important in Hinduism and other Indian religions, and it is out of these that nascent religious groups began to form when couples invited other Asian Indians to their homes for social-religious gatherings. One branch of Swaminarayan Hindus has formalized a religious duty to have a period of family worship each evening. An in-depth study remains to be done of home shrines and family rituals among Asian-Indian families.

National

National strategies of adaptation result from the creation of a fragile national unity during the colonial period and the period of independence in India. National identity is reformulated in the immigrant setting in the United States. Several factors reinforce the national identity. The very process of emigration is determined by quotas, and designation is determined by national origin; other aspects of identity — ethnic or religious — are omitted from immigration records. Designation of groups for political and social purposes in the United States is by national identification, so that "Asian -Indian" becomes the official national designation of a group. That comports with both the ability of most Americans to identify and respond in socially defined ways to people identified with a nation-state and a corollary discomfort with some other forms of ethnic or religious identification. It also comports with strategies for building a national identity in India that will undergird the unity and security of the Indian democracy, and in the United States it also provides a political and social identity with potential in size and coherence to be an effective social group to support immigrants through the process of adaptation and an increasingly effective force in American politics. Immigrants do not join groups, even religious groups, in order to separate themselves from the rest of society, but as one aspect of establishing the means for adapting to and integrating themselves into the larger society. A national group is a time-honored agency for immigrants in negotiating a place for themselves in America; hence, it becomes a powerful aspect of personal and group identity, potentially more powerful and effective abroad than within India.

The national strategy of adaptation results in numerous organizations with an all-India ethos that are primarily secular in nature. India Cultural Centers and/or Associations and professional organizations of Asian-Indian physicians, engineers, and those engaged in business developed early in most cities. These organizations sponsor cultural performances in film, dance, theater, and music, honor politicians and bureaucrats from India, observe all-India political and cultural holidays, and unify the community for some forms of political action. They cooperate with other national groups in International Centers and in educational projects for the larger community. Such Indian Cultural Associations are important religiously because they are not rigidly secular, but rather tend to incorporate religious aspects in their programs. It is difficult to excise religious aspects from Indian culture and the arts, with the result that Hinduism becomes the unofficial religion of many of these associations — but not without tension and dissent. Members of minority groups complain about Hindu religious rituals and ethos that pervades some of these associations. Pakistan Cultural Associations performs a similar function for Pakistani immigrants, and it is ironic that many Indian Muslims find their primary social and religious affiliation with the Pakistani association rather than with the Indian association. The close association of civic and religious affiliation is demonstrated by the role of these associations.

National identification is a central aspect of some primarily religious organizations. The Vishwa Hindu Parishad attempts to be inclusive of all religious traditions that had their origin in India, as they say, "in Bharat." Its constitution refers to "the purpose of prop-agating dynamic Hindu Dharma representing the fundamental values of life comprehended by various sects and denominations including Buddhists, Jains, Sikhs, Lingayats, etc.," and defines "Hindu" as "a person, natural or legal, or one believing in, following or respecting the values of life, ethical and spiritual, which have been developed in Bharat and including a person calling himself a Hindu." Notice that this designation of "national" differs from that of the modern secular nation-state, both because it excludes minorities from religions with origins outside of India — Muslims, Christians, and Parsis — and includes converts of other nationalities. Recent tensions within India have made more difficult the preservation of a national religious unity, and the challenges in America have made a national religious identity difficult for Asian-Indians.

The conflict regarding the Rama temple in Ayodhya has caused the Vishwa Hindu Parishad to stress its dominant Hindu character in order to support the building of the Rama temple, to condemn the Muslim minority, and to engage in political activity and fund-raising in order to support Hindu fundamentalism in India. The parallel organization of Muslims is the Consultative Committee of Indian Muslims, but it makes no claims to represent the religions of Bharat. Tensions between Sikhs and Hindus resulting from the Blue Star occupation of the Golden Temple in Amritsar caused a decline in participation by Sikhs in Parishad activities resulting in a more exclusive emphasis on Hinduism. The strategy has resulted in growth in both numbers and financial support for an organization that had previously been very small and insignificant among Asian-Indians. The Ayodhya crisis has brought new opportunities to the Parishad, but it is in the process of fundamentally changing its character and focus.

Religion has become a most potent symbol of the powers threatening both national unity of heterogeneous populations of modern, secular nations — even one like India, where 82 percent of the population is Hindu — and national identity of immigrants. Thus, the Vishwa Hindu Parishad is caught between emphasizing a form of civic unity through the observance of traditional all-India holidays and festivals, honoring important officials of the Indian government, and stressing religious harmony, or, on the other hand, of stressing religious particularity through criticisms of some religious minorities, attacks on policies of the Indian government, and support of Hindu fundamentalism in India. Civic loyalties and identities are in tension with religious ones and influence the strategies of adaptation in the United States. Thus, many Asian-Indians participate in all-India social, professional, and political organizations, and in religious organizations that aspire to national identity with increasing difficulty.

The Vishwa Hindu Parishad has a national organization with officers and organizations in major American cities, but it serves primarily as an umbrella group that maintains informal associations among Hindu groups, temples, and religious leaders. Those religious leaders from India most prominent in Vishwa Hindu Parishad activities have become identified as the leading sadhu-saints of neo-Hinduism. Other than national and international conferences, a publication, and fund-raising for activities in India, the organization has few programs. It does not sponsor its own temples or religious programs; rather, it tends to lend support to the programs of approved religious and political groups. An unmixed national religious strategy for Asian Indians has been very difficult to implement in the United States even though some national ceremonies take on a religious flavor distinctly Hindu in character.

Two national identities are involved in the development of any immigrant group: the nation of origin and the nation of residence. Citizenship, legal or emotional, could be in either. Tension between the two identities is often experienced as a generational gap between Indian parents and their American children, but the situation is more complex because elements of both national identities are found in every generation. Thus, religious organizations have the option of stressing, for example, either Indian national and religious holidays or American ones, or of elevating their estimation of the national administrative structures and leaders of America above the traditional ones of India. The amalgam is demonstrated in the observance of most religious festivals on the long weekends of

American national holidays — Fourth of July, Memorial Day, Labor Day. The national aspects of religious identification continues to exercise influence on immigrant organizations.

Ecumenical

The ecumenical strategy of adaptation incorporates Asian-Indians in religious organizations under the banner of an inclusive definition of religion that transcends ethnic, denominational, or sectarian identification. Religion is an acceptable marker of identity, informal but, not official, in the United States, so the question, "What are you?" is appropriate, and it is legitimate to answer, "I am a Muslim, a Christian, a Jew, or a...." The terminology may imply a concrete homogeneity that does not exist in any of the religions. Moreover, it is characteristic that a member of the majority responds with a more narrowly bounded identification: "I am a Baptist...or Catholic." Members of minorities tend to respond, however, with an ecumenical term: "I am a Hindu, a Muslim, or a Christian."

Several paths to an ecumenical strategy exist. Islam makes explicit universal claims, and an ecumenical strategy is the official policy as Muslim immigrants from many cultures unite in mosques that proclaim a universality that rules out overt exclusiveness. Arabic is the language for prayers, and English for everything else in ecumenical mosques. Although it is possible to determine which mosques in large cities serve primarily "Asian Muslims" — those with roots in India and Pakistan — by attending to the origin and training of the imam, the names of persons on the board of directors and the language used in social intercourse, no mosque is officially designated for a particular group. Emigration from India and Iran brings together Parsis and Zoroastrians from different cultural settings into an ecumenical Zoroastrian group in America that exhibits elements of an ecumenical strategy of adaptation. Christians from India join Christian community churches without denominational affiliation as well as denominational churches. The ecumenical strategy is joined with the national in the formation of Indian Christian Fellowships that include persons from groups that are quite separate — theologically, structurally, linguistically, and socially — in India.

An ecumenical Hinduism is developing in the United States that unites deities, rituals, sacred texts, and people in temples and programs in ways that would not be found together in India. In temples and centers created on an ecumenical model, emphasis is placed upon all-India Hindu "great tradition," on devotion to major deities, and upon some elements of the Sanskrit tradition in an adapted "Sanskritization." Major temple complexes, such as the one planned in north Dallas, includes shrines for a diverse set of deities, including many regional and sectarian forms that would not be placed in the same temple in India. The American temples become meeting places of the deities that immigrants bring with them from India. Study and devotional groups use universally accepted Hindu texts, such as the *Bhagavad Gita* and the *Ramayana*. Languages used are Sanskrit for rituals and English for instruction, commentary, and business. It is difficult to import religious specialists from India who are sufficiently ecumenical in their expertise and adept in communicating the tradition in English to American children; hence, Sanskrit rituals, including the life-cycle and home rituals, are often performed in Sanskrit by traditionally trained specialists from India, but instruction and administration continues to be the preserve of the lay leaders. Sectarian leaders on tour from India are incorporated as guests during their annual calendar of events, but primary leaders are developed from within the immigrant group. The sacred festivals observed are those from the calendar observed throughout India. Time and space are made available for the rituals, guests, and festivals of the larger regional and sectarian groups among the local immigrants in order to attract their participation. In general, those groups and temples that adopt an ecumenical strategy are most open to the adoption of forms characteristic of other religious groups in America. Some examples of this adaptation are (1) the piano playing to accompany the singing from hymnbooks of transliterated Sanskrit texts by children in Sunday Schools, (2) administrative structures as well as personnel that are distinctly American in style, and (3) forms of congregational worship. Indeed, what is termed here as "ecumenical" may be viewed from another angle as the creation of American Hinduism, American Islam, or American Zoroastrianism analogous to the creation of American Catholicism or American

Judaism by earlier immigrants. Nevertheless, in an ecumenical strategy Hinduism is packaged differently in the United States than it appears in India. The fusion of many cultural and religious aspects in the Cultural Festival of India held in Edison, New Jersey, in August 1991 exhibited elements of ecumenical Hinduism, although the religious group that sponsored the festival has successfully followed an ethnic strategy of adaptation in the development of the religious group in the United States.

Ethnic

An ethnic group is a minority population within a larger society, recognized as a distinct group by others in the society, whose members claim a common background, real or fictional, and who participate in shared activities — including speaking the same language — in which the common origin and culture are significant. Among Asian-Indians the primary ethnic groups are those based on the regional-linguistic divisions in India. The Gujaratis, Punjabis, Telugu, Bengalis, and Malayalee seem to be the more prominent, but other ethnic groups are in evidence in major population centers. "Asian-Indian" may become a clear ethnic label used by members of the second generation in the future, but the operative ethnic designations among Asian Indians now are regional-linguistic ones — Gujarati, Punjabi, Malayalee. Some Asian-Indian religious groups actively recreate ethnic boundaries and follow strategies of adaptation on an ethnic trajectory.

Swaminarayan Hinduism has grown among Gujarati immigrants because of the effectiveness of an ethnic strategy. Language is for Indians the main symbol of regional and ethnic identity. Gujarati, as the medium of all the rituals and communication of the Swaminarayan groups, creates a major boundary that excludes meaningful participation by most non-Gujaratis. Thus, the Swaminarayan group, the primary social group outside the family that requires and supports the use of Gujarati, maintains close ties with all aspects of Gujarati ethnicity. A requirement for significant leadership is good oratorical ability in the Gujarati language, and other symbols of ethnic identity are evident at the meetings of this group: Gujarati dress, cuisine, iconography, music, and dance. The primary ties are to religious leaders and sacred sites in Gujarat. This union of ethnic and religious elements in personal and group identity has a powerful attraction for first-generation immigrants, more powerful than that of the union of Indian national elements with either secular elements or with an ecumenical Hinduism.

A similar union of Sikh religion and Punjabi ethnicity is evident in gurdwaras in the United States, and some differences of interpretation and practice between the immigrant Sikhs and the converts — the so-called "white Sikhs" — relate to the role of Punjabi ethnicity in defining Sikh religion. The potent mixture of religion and ethnicity is evident in the conflict about attempts to establish an independent state, Khalistan, in the Punjab and the occupation of the Golden Temple by the Indian army. In some American cities one can attend Islamic prayers in Hyderabadi mosques where, following the prayers in Arabic, one can observe all the elements of an ethnic strategy of adaptation. Tamil Christian Fellowships and Gujarati Christian Churches create similar boundaries in order to maintain the localized traditions from India. In each of these cases, ethnicity reinforces the religious identity of individuals and the group and inspires in many immigrants a profound emotion resulting from the perception of the continuity of their personal identity across the traumatic divide of emigration and, they hope, across an equally broad chasm separating the generations.

Hierarchical

The chief characteristic of organizations adopting this strategy is loyalty to a living religious leader who provides a unity for the group beyond ethnic or national loyalties. The group preserves a specific tradition and set of rituals transmitted and authenticated by a hierarchy, and the current religious leader is the living symbol of the hierarchy who attracts personal loyalty and marshals resources for institutional development. Institutional adaptation and growth is facilitated by the centralization of guidance and decision-making in the hands of a single person who can direct the energies and resources towards clearly defined goals validated by religious authority. These authoritative religious leaders are often the mediators between past and present, between parents and children, between the forms of religion in India and their emerging counterparts in the United States.

The most successful example of this strategy of adaptation is the Nizari Ismaili Muslims, who are followers of Prince Karim Aga Khan, identified as the 49th Imam in direct descent from the Prophet's family. Although the majority of all Ismailis in North America trace their origins back to parts of the Indian subcontinent — primarily Sind, Punjab, Gujarat, and Kutch — Nizari Ismailis deemphasize ethnic aspects in their rituals or programs. Three reasons exist for muting ethnic identifying marks:(1) Nizari Ismailis are small minorities in many countries and come from several ethnic groups, so an institutional claim to transcend ethnic identification is necessary to preserve inclusiveness and unity. (2) In recent years the Imam has guided the community to emphasize harmony with aspects of Sunni Islam, such as using Arabic in prayers and down-playing some theological and ritual accretions from the Indian context. (3)The current Imam and his grandfather have guided their followers in a rapid process of modernization, evidenced by both their educational and professional success and their migration in large numbers from Third World countries to the West. Much of the guidance of the Imams has been directed at accomplishing this transition, which includes the specific instruction to assimilate as much as possible the social and political culture of the countries of migration, rejecting the host culture only when it makes difficult the observance of religious duties.

Hence, the primary unifying fact is loyalty to the Imam and obedience to his guidance. Religion is thereby separated from ethnicity, at least officially. A result is that tensions between the generations regarding use of ethnic language, observances, marriage customs and other areas of dispute are removed from the religious realm and institution and confined largely to family decisions. English is a preferred medium of communication, except for ritual prayers and hymns. Programs of the religious community are directed toward helping members assimilate as quickly and as smoothly as possible into the economic, social, and political arenas in the countries of their residence. The direct guidance and institutional leadership of the Imam has resulted in significant growth of the community in the United States, even though this growth is largely concealed from public view. The community of some 40,000 people meet in more than 75 *jamat khanas* located in most American cities and is administered by a centralized organization through regional and national councils, with final authority issuing from the Imam's secretariat in France.

Attachments to a guru in Hinduism enhances the attractiveness of a hierarchical strategy of adaptation, especially among those groups that attempt to make converts from several national and ethnic groups. The small Sai Baba groups in the United States focus on devotion to the guru, and loyalty to him maintains unity among immigrants from several countries. The primary group boundary is established by personal devotion to the guru. A similar strategy, though more complex, has been followed by the International Society for Krishna Consciousness in its devotion to A.C. Bhaktivedanta Swami Prabhupada, which for a time united immigrants from India with converts from other countries. Rancor and division following the death of the guru illustrate a weakness of this strategy, the weakness that division takes place in the institution at times of transition from one leader to another or due to dissatisfaction of part of the membership. Loyalty to the guru can be very volatile. By itself, a hierarchical strategy leads eventually to schism of the religious community. Perhaps that is the reason this strategy is most successfully followed when joined with elements of other strategies.

Strategies of adaptation are malleable because immigrants are able to stress several overlapping identities, depending upon the context. Among family and friends the individual identity is named; in the political sphere, the national; socially among Asian-Indians, the ethnic or even sub-ethnic caste; in religious gatherings the ecumenical or hierarchical affiliation is stressed. Thus a person can name herself or be named as "Sangita," — perhaps even "Chicago Sangita" — "Asian Indian," "Gujarati," "Patel," "Hindu," or "Swaminarayan," depending on the context of the conversation. Strategies of adaptation appear in unique combinations in various religious organizations. The ethnic and hierarchical strategies are neatly joined in the Bochasanwasi Swaminarayan Sanstha, which combines a distinctly Gujarati cultural garb with loyalty to Pramukh Swami as the perfect abode of god. The ethnic and ecumenical are fused in the development of Sikhism in the United States. Mosques in the United States that serve primarily Hyderabadi Muslims follow an ethnic strategy *de facto* and an ecumenical strategy *de jure*. The Vishwa Hindu Parishad vacillates between forms of national and ecumenical strategies of adaptation. The strategies may change within a given organization as the immigrant group develops through time, and the strategies may differ in separate locations in the country. All of the immigrant religious groups are adjusting to the demands of American society in ways that will eventually lead to a new national form of the various religions — American Hinduism, Islam, Sikhism, Jainism — that incorporate elements of these strategies, and American religion itself is being dramatically changed.

Selection of Adaptive Strategies

Evolution and adaptation of religious organizations for survival in a new cultural ecosystem is analogous to the process geneticists envision in integrated theories of adaptation. Within the pool of characteristics of various religious traditions are wide arrays of specific characteristics from which are selected certain constellations, which could be called strategies, that promote the viability of the religious organization through time. A major question concerns the various factors that make it more likely that a religious group will exhibit elements of one strategy more than another. Why did a Hindu group in Dallas develop an ecumenical strategy in the early 1980s, while Mar Thoma Christians developed an ethnic strategy in Chicago about the same time? Coincidence, perhaps, but elements creating a coincidence can be suggested. Various models of adaptive strategies suggested here and the ways selection takes place are analogous to processes and theories of adaptation in genetics.

Sewall Wright, an important figure in the field of population genetics, developed a shifting-balance theory of evolution in which he combined for the first time the random effects of genetic drift and the environmentally directed effects of selection into an overall synthesis. He focused on relatively small localized populations that evolved independently by adjusting to their local environment. He visualized the process as a kind of topographical map on which adaptive successes were projected on a vertical dimension as adaptive peaks or valleys. A common way to visualize the process is to imagine marbles rolling around on a gently vibrating, indented table. The vibration represents the random effects of genetic drift and very local environmental effects. The depression into which it rolls represents favorable combinations of characteristics, and the depression is deeper the more advantageous the characteristic for adaptation, with the result that it is more difficult for the marble to be jostled up out of the depression by random action.

Migration is always a powerful force in upsetting both the genetic stability of natural populations and the cultural stability of social groups. In models of organizational adaptive strategies, preferences of individual immigrants for characteristics from their religious tradition may function randomly, analogous to genetic drift. Variables of social location are similar to environmentally directed effects in Sewall's model. Thus, the social process of adaptation is both intentional and directed. Variables of social location are crucial in selection from the sets of individual preferences the structures of characteristics that are favorable for success in adapting in a new social setting and for incorporating elements from a more diverse population brought together by emigration. A good predictive model would encompass more exhaustively a full range of variables; the following variables are suggestive: length of residence, population density, generational transition, and majority-minority status.

Length of residence

The length of residence for the Asian-Indian community as a whole is circumscribed by the change in the immigration law in 1965, which opened the United States to emigrants from India and other countries that had previously been effectively barred. Except for part of the Sikh community in California and some students who were in the United States prior to 1965, the length of residence of most Asian Indians is less than a quarter of this century. Individual transformation of new immigrants from the moment of arrival to become well-settled citizens is dramatic, and equally dramatic is the development of groups from a handful of friends meeting as the primary Asian-Indian organization outside the family to large institutions with well-developed programs. At sequential stages throughout this period the community as a whole has developed the several strategies of adaptation mentioned above. It is important to note, however, that length of residence for any specific group of Asian Indians may not conform to the general pattern. For example, Asian Indians moved to some cities and towns of the United States much later than others — to Indianapolis later than New York, to Edison, New Jersey, later than Flushing, New York, and to Atlanta later than Houston or Chicago — and length of settled residence in a given location is more important to strategies of adaptation than the length of time since entry to the country. Moreover, new immigrants arrive regularly and begin the process of adapting to the new social and religious setting. The experience and adaptive strategies of those who arrive and seek out already existing religious organizations differ greatly from those who arrived in the first years of Asian Indian immigration and were forced to create organizations and new religious identities. Hence, the length of residence cannot be charted on one twenty-five year graph; nevertheless, a typical process of adaptation can be proposed.

The first months or years of residence form a period when the individual strategy is dominant because others who share the same or similar traditions are not present or because networks of communication have not been established. A leader of a large Asian-Indian religious organization in Houston remembers once during the early period when he stopped his car on a busy street and ran back to talk to a person who appeared to him to be from India, an effort undertaken because he was so lonely and eager for companionship. Others tell stories of trying to engage in private acts of worship and preserve their discipline — usually stories about avoiding alcoholic drinks, drugs, and remaining vegetarian, and less often about struggles to preserve chastity — and recount their failures. Personal correspondence with religious leaders in India provided some assistance and solace during this period.

The next period involved the creation of organizations with the widest possible boundaries using a national strategy. Secular organizations, such as Indian Cultural Associations or Centers, were established to observe holidays, provide social occasions, teach children aspects of Indian culture, and, prior to the introduction of video cassette recorders, to view movies from India. Meeting rooms of universities to which students had access were early meeting places. Tolerance of caste, ethnic, and religious differences was a characteristic of these organizations. Increasingly as time passed they involved also aspects of religious ritual and teaching. Cultural classics and artifacts of India are closely associated with religion, so meetings of these secular organizations began to take on a religious character. For example, they sponsored prominent Hindu or Jain religious teachers for lectures or recitations under the auspices of the ostensibly secular organizations.

Minorities quickly adopted ecumenical strategies because they became suspicious and uncomfortable with many of the religious aspects of these meetings. Thus, they sought Christian, Muslim, and even Sikh groups that would both unite people from India and provide a social location for negotiation with co-religionists from other countries. The ecumenical strategy became attractive to Hindus and Jains as well when religious organizations were developed, often under the umbrella of India Cultural Centers. Many of the early immigrants, who were part of the technological "brain drain," had not been active, certainly not leaders, in specific religious groups in India. They came as graduate students and young professionals, at the stage in life that generally involves the least religious activity. Thus, most were not very devout in terms of loyalty to specific religious traditions, and they were not traditionally trained in religious lore. One woman told about asking her mother to send a book containing a transliteration of an old family ritual text she could use for meetings. General manuals for use in death rituals became necessary early, with transliteration of the Sanskrit to enable traditionally unlettered persons to lead the rituals. Thus, a general, ecumenical Hinduism or Jainism — perhaps some melding of both — that would make the least demands on the lay leaders for knowledge of ritual and theology was attractive. During this period, regional and sectarian differences among participants were largely muted.

After a period of residence, when sufficient immigration had taken place and networks had been established, religious organizations that adopted ethnic strategies were formed in most cities. Gujaratis were prominent among the early immigrants, so it was common to see on bulletin boards of Indian food stores — the primary mode of broadcast along with word-of-mouth before the advent of Indian newspapers or shows on radio and television — inviting Gujaratis to attend Gujarati Christian Fellowships, Gujarati Bhajan Singing Groups, or Gujarati Gita Study Groups. As soon as length of residence and growth in numbers permitted, such ethnic groups were formed. People outside urban areas often traveled great distances on week-ends in order to participate in such ethnic groupings.

Religious organizations emphasizing a hierarchical strategy developed in large numbers after a long period of residence. Those organizations are drawn from populations much smaller than ethnic or national, so it generally takes a longer period of immigration and residence for a sufficient number to be gathered. Some groups are developed from members who previously had no contact or loyalty to the religious leader, so more time is needed to attract a membership and create loyalty to the hierarchy. One characteristic of hierarchically organized groups that permits some to organize early is that the process may be initiated by the leader at any stage of the immigration process. The example of the Bochasanwasi Swaminarayan Sanstha is that the guru of the group, Yogiji Maharaj, instructed a young chemistry instructor in New York to start an organization in the United States in 1971, when only twenty-eight followers were known to be in the United States and prior to the visit of any Swaminarayan religious specialist. The first temple was dedicated in the basement of a house on Bowne Street in Flushing in 1976. That early initiative provided the foundation for the remarkable growth that has resulted in eight temples and over fifty centers in the United States.

It is difficult to project how religious institutions will develop during the next quarter of century. That development will be more directly affected by the other variables than by the simple passage of time. The shape of continuing emigration of Asian Indians from various religions will be a significant factor. The first part of the next century will, however, be a period of significant adjustment both for Asian-Indians and other Americans as new religious groups take their place in the fabric of American religion.

Population Density

Closely allied with but not identical to length of residence is increase in population density of Asian Indians in most urban centers. Hence, the stages of development of religious organizations representing the various strategies can be traced in those areas that were primary locations for early immigrants — Queens in New York, northwest Chicago suburbs, western Houston. Population density cannot be placed on a time-line for several reasons. The urban areas did not experience growth of the Asian-Indian population at the same time, and the size of the community is relatively small in some urban areas and always volatile. Moreover, the population in most areas has grown rapidly so that it appears to be a stable, growing community, but the community is very unstable because new immigrants experience very high rates of mobility as they move from place to place to find an economically and socially secure home. The Asian-Indian community is in constant flux. For example, a survey taken in 1990 of people in attendance at the Swaminarayan Hindu Temple in Glen Ellyn, Illinois showed that over 40 percent had been in the Chicago area for less than five years. Even within a large urban area, such as the New York/New Jersey metropolitan area, Asian Indians move into new residential areas and establish religious organizations. Asian Indians have not occupied ghettos in American cities, but the move of many Asian Indians in the past decade from Queens to Central New Jersey results in many new religious organizations. The pattern of development and strategies of adaptation are changed because some of the organizations are satellites of organizations in the previous area of residence.

As population density increases, the adaptive strategies develop through the pattern developed above, individual, national, ecumenical, ethnic and hierarchical. At one stage in the development a bifurcation takes place through the development of regional or national centers that attract the allegiance and participation of Asian Indians from a wide geographical area. Asian Indians living in relatively isolated locations continue individual practice of their religion or participate in organizations following national or ecumenical strategies on the local level, but also travel to centers that become almost traditional pilgrimage sites for special occasions, either for family rituals or events in the Hindu annual cycle. Dedication of these national centers are occasions for celebration for large segments of the Asian-Indian community. Thus, different strategies were adopted at the local and national levels. The first and most successful Hindu temple in gaining a national clientele is the Venkateswara Temple in Penn Hills near Pittsburgh, dedicated in 1976. Increasingly, a sacred geography is developing in the United States marked by many Hindu temples that constitute a kind of pilgrimage cycle, analogous to pilgrimage sites in India. One couple visiting the Venkateswara Temple in Aurora, Illinois indicated that they spent their vacation as a pilgrimage to visit most of the Hindu temples as they crossed the country. Many of these temples are in the South Indian style and exhibit only very tentative ecumenical forms for two reasons: South Indians are known as the "temple-builders" in India, and the program established by the Tirumala Tirupati Devasthanam gave impetus and direction to the establishment of temples with traditional South-Indian architecture and rituals. Jains have a much smaller population density in the United States, so it is not surprising that the first Jain pilgrimage temple in the United States, advertized as the first Jain pilgrimage temple outside India, was just dedicated on August 4-11, 1991, in Blairstown, New Jersey. It provides a national center for Jain families from locations where only a handful of Jain families live. Such pilgrimage centers are creating a new sacred geography of the United States, similar to that created by Catholic monasteries and shrines for earlier immigrants.

Increase of the general population density of Asian Indians both in major urban areas and across the country, even though not uniform, provides the base for development of hundreds of religious organizations that serve various needs of the community by providing an array of adaptive strategies. Some organizations are formed and disappear because they do not exhibit the array of variables that lead to selection for survival. Others come into being and gradually are transformed to conform to the needs of a developing community, while some are very successful in defining a strategy of adaptation that is successful for immigrants in various stages of adjustment to their new surroundings.

Transition of Generations

The most obvious of the stages of development of the immigrant community is through the generations, and the aspirations and fears that immigrants have regarding their children and the tensions that develop between the generations shape a major dynamic among Asian Indians as well as other immigrant groups. Religious organizations are a primary forum in which this dynamic is expressed and encountered.

First generation immigrants are torn between the utility of strategies of adaptation that are individual, national, and ecumenical in character and the emotional attraction of strategies that stress ethnic and hierarchical loyalties. The absence of a critical mass and of readily available networks of communication for the first immigrants forces them to adopt strategies that first demand individual and private devotion and then establish the most inclusive boundaries possible so as to include the largest number of people. They feel most "at home," however, when they are able to share the same ethnic language, food, dress, and customs, or when they create a new group united by the intense emotion of loyalty to a specific religious leader. Ethnic religious gatherings are often the only social location outside the family where the ethnic language, dress, cuisine, arts and customs are welcomed, valued, and expressed. As soon as immigrants are empowered by growth in numbers and financial stability, such groups are formed in most cities.

Ethnic and hierarchical strategies are reinforced by what could be called the "late first generation immigrants," those who arrive years later than the establishment of the Asian-Indian community. Immigration continues at a rapid pace, so the community is constantly absorbing new people from India with significant effects. A survey of 192 persons at an Asian-Indian religious gathering in 1990 indicated that 39 percent had been in the United States less than five years and another 19 percent less than ten years. Most of these new immigrants in the 1980s came under provisions in the immigration laws permitting family reunification, so many do not have the same educational or professional accomplishments demanded of the early immigrants. As a group they do not come from the educated, scientifically trained, professional elite, which are among the most alienated from religious traditions, but move directly from families in India to families, social groups, and religious organizations already established in the United States. They provide a renewable continuity with religious organizations and traditions in India. They are a relatively conservative force among the immigrant community to preserve ethnic characteristics and sectarian loyalties. Recent revisions of immigration policy again emphasize professional and technical skills. It is difficult to predict what group will be selected for immigration under future policies, but undoubtedly growth will continue.

Some immigrants come with their small children. One of my students identifies himself as a member of the "first and a half generation" because he emigrated from India as a young boy with his parents. He feels that he and his peers share a special burden and unique perspective because they were under intense pressure both to preserve the ethnic language and cultural ties and to excel in American educational and social arenas. They are expected to preserve Indian ethnic identity when few resources were available outside the family. Ecumenical religious groups and secular national groups provide new identifications, but family pressures are first for ethnic identity and then for some forms of sectarian identity. Only when the second generation began to reach school age were programs for children much in evidence, and some from the "first and a half generation" missed early affiliation with any religious group.

Indeed, the major stimulus for the development of Asian-Indian religious organizations of all types was the appearance of the second generation at school-age. When children of immigrants reached the age when their most influential peer pressures were outside the home, their parents turned to religious organizations to counter what many considered to be pernicious influences of American youth culture. The character of these organizations is defined by the tensions between the needs of parents, met most directly through

ethnically defined groups, and the needs of the children, which ecumenical and national groups satisfy. One Muslim group in
Indianapolis almost split in a controversy about the study of the
Koran in English, so the children could understand, or in Urdu, so
the women could understand and the men enjoy. It may be easier for
loyalty to a religious leader to be transmitted to children of the
second generation than for all the rudiments of ethnic affiliation,
including language, to be transmitted. Personal devotion to the Aga
Khan by Nizari Ismaili Muslims or to Pramukh Swami by some
Swaminarayan Hindus is possible apart from a detailed knowledge of
language, ritual, or theology and is equally available to members of
different generations. Indeed, parents may have primary emotional
attachment to the previous leader, while the children become
attached to the current one. A combination of strategies is possible,
one that meets the needs of both generations, as, for example, the
union of Gujarati ethnic identification and devotion to the guru as
the manifestation of god in Swaminarayan Hinduism. It is a union
that has resulted in great success in adaptation, one celebrated in the
Cultural Festival of India in New Jersey.

The third generation of Asian Indians is not yet formed, so it is
only possible to speculate about the strategies of adaption for the
future. Will Herberg in *Protestant, Catholic, Jew* argued that the third
generation from earlier immigrants was crucial in defining American
religion in the second half of this century. He referred to Hanson's
Law: what the son of immigrants rejects, the grandson rediscovers
and adopts. The form of the religious identification of the third generation from earlier immigrants was under an ecumenical guise in the
creation of American Catholicism and American Judaism, so one
may speculate that other forms of American Hinduism and
American Islam will also develop under the influence of the third
generation of Asian Indians. The fourth generation may continue
some ethnic and religious identification, but it is different. Ethnicity
is not completely lost, since many continue to identify themselves
with various ethnic groups, but the form is a kind of "symbolic
ethnicity" made up of holidays, ethnic festivals, ethnic foods, with
little of the whole structure of ethnic identity remembered by persons
of the first generation. Symbolic ethnicity may be a half-way house

on the way to full assimilation and some form of secularization. It is risky, however, to predict the future experience of Asian Indians based on that of earlier immigrants because the religious and ethnic context into which immigration occurs is so different from that of the late 19th and early 20th centuries. Affirmation of "pluralism" has become a politically correct posture, and ethnicity is now supported by government programs and reinforced by some public antipathy toward assimilation. Asian Indians are relatively minor players in the negotiation of ethnic groups in the future shaping of American religion and culture, but that negotiation will determine how ethnicity and new religious groups are integrated.

Majority-Minority Status

This is the most complicated variable because majority or minority status is always relative in degree, and every distinct religious group is an operative minority in some contexts, especially in a heterogeneous society. Both India and the United States are heterogeneous, and due to regional variation, immigrants from India cannot be considered as each leaving the same place regarding religious variations in the population. The relation that exists among the various religious groups, particularly in matters related to relative dominance and numerical superiority, depends on the area from which the immigrants come. What does it mean, then, that new immigrants establish themselves in the United States as Muslim, Hindu, Christian, or Sikh? It certainly means a dramatic change. A Gujarati Hindu from an area where nine out of ten people are Hindus is suddenly in a situation where Hindus are a tiny minority. Punjabi-speaking Christians from Pakistan or Malayalee Christians from Kerala, on the other hand, are suddenly part of a nominal religious majority, one in which they must make a place for themselves, perhaps even as a new denomination. Muslims from India find much in common with Muslims from Pakistan as they worship in mosques with immigrants from many other countries, claiming to be part of the second largest religious group in the country. For all of these groups migration causes tremendous disruption of religious location.

It is difficult to project effects on the topography of adaptive strategies caused by changes in relative majority or minority status. The tendency is for small minorities to join ecumenical groups for worship and fellowship. Shia Muslims participate in Sunni mosques, and Asian Indian Christians join in community churches or Indian Christian fellowships in order to have larger groups for support. Christians from Kerala join on Christmas and Easter in ecumenical Malayalee services that unite Protestant, Catholic, and Syrian Orthodox Christians.

The formation of religious groups by immigrants, even those with the most narrowly conceived ethnic or hierarchical boundaries, do not function primarily to separate persons from the rest of the population, but rather to provide the necessary basis on which the individual and group can negotiate effective relations with the majority population as variously defined. Thus, that negotiation can be viewed as reaching out in concentric circles to form less stable, but more inclusive, social networks. The negotiation moves in general from individual to hierarchical to ethnic, to national, to ecumenical and finally to the American national community. A Swaminarayan Hindu joins with other followers of Pramukh Swami, then she affiliates with other Gujaratis, and then negotiates with other Hindus, joins in Asian-Indian organizations, and with all these supports negotiates from a position of strength with other groups in American society. The concentric circles of negotiation are in evidence all around us, creating a variety of religious organizations that are increasingly visible and active in shaping American religion for the 21st century.

Conclusion

The Asian-Indian community is dynamic, and the strategies of adaptation are malleable to meet the diverse needs of a growing population. None of the five strategies mentioned above exists in an unmixed state. Which strategy or elements are dominant in a particular group depends on many things: on the tradition, history, and theology of the religion, on vagaries of the current situation in the United States, and on the conscious decision of members and leaders of the group regarding both their own future and that of their children. One should not underestimate the role of individual initiative, creativity and leadership in this process. Groups adopt elements of more than one strategy, and any individual immigrant is a member of several groups stressing different strategies, which result from the need to preserve several identities within one unity and the desire to be able to choose from several overlapping identities according to the context.

Pluralism in American religion is far more complex than a listing of major ethnic or religious groups because within each group so designated great variation exists in types of adaptive strategies employed and in resulting religious structures. The result is a kaleidoscope of elements in constant movement that is brilliant with vital colors and complex in its moving structures. It is not the result of the processes that led to the model of "melting pot" or even of the "triple melting pot" that characterized earlier analyses. Those patterns were discernible in part because of two transitory aspects of earlier immigration experience: (1) until 1965 emigration was predominantly from Europe, and for much of the previous century people from Asia were systematically excluded, which meant that most immigrants were Christians or Jews, and (2) during the depression of the 1930s and World War II immigration virtually ceased and in some periods there was a reverse migration, so the resident population was relatively stable, uninfluenced for almost a quarter of this century by new immigration. Neither of those aspects is likely to be operative in the near future. Energy and elements already present will move the kaleidoscope at speeds sometimes threatening disorientation, and new elements and energy will be interjected through new immigration. The challenge will be to develop strategies that will permit effective and peaceful negotiation among diverse groups that will enhance a civic unity. Religious groups will have a significant role in those negotiations.

Americans are more religious that citizens of other industrialized countries as measured by belief in god, membership in religious groups, attendance at religious services, and financial support of religious activities. This relative vitality of religion in the United States is due in large measure to the fact that in a country of immigrants each immigrant group has had to establish new identities in order to establish a place for itself among the rest. Religion has been an important element in the identities created because it both establishes a continuity with the past for individuals from each immigrant group and provides a transcendent basis for identity that provides a secure bridge across the chasm between the past abroad and the present here and between the present generation and those to come. That is a major function of religion in the process of transmission of tradition. Americans are religious because either their ancestors or they themselves have reestablished and preserved personal and group identities in a new setting by forming religious groups of various types. Religions will not remain the same in the United States into the next century, but the new immigration represented by Asian Indians insures that religion will continue to occupy a significant place in American culture.

Academic Study of Religions and Asian Indian-American College Students

John Y. Fenton

Asian Indian-American Students in American Colleges

The Student Population

The college-age Asian Indian-American population has grown rapidly in the past eight to ten years. According to the 1980 U.S. Census eleven percent of all Asian Indians were between fifteen and twenty-four years of age, while twenty-eight percent were below fifteen years of age.[1] Figures from the 1990 U.S. Census are not yet available, but it is nevertheless clear that most of the twenty-eight percent have now reached college age, probably doubling the college-age group. Added to this pool are all of the new immigrants of college age who have arrived since 1980.

The increased Asian Indian college-age population is swelling enrollments in Indian religion courses across the United States. Annual enrollment of students of South Asian origin in the college of Emory University in Atlanta, where I teach, was quite small until it abruptly increased to approximately one hundred students about eight years ago. Parallel with this change, enrollments of South Asian students in my courses in Hinduism, Buddhism, and in surveys of Asian religions rose until they are now regularly more than fifty percent of the class. This is for me a dramatic shift. Prior to 1983 I was teaching Americans of European descent who were interested in religions that were native to cultures other than their own. Now the majority of my students are immigrants or children of immigrants from South Asia. (Another ten percent of my recent students have been of Chinese, Japanese, or Korean origin). The marked increase I have experienced is paralleled by similar changes in enrollments in college courses dealing with Asian religious traditions in urban colleges and universities across the United States.[2]

These demographic changes in the student-age population are part of the still evolving post-colonial era in the study and teaching of religious traditions. In particular, the new multicultural actuality of American academia adds urgency to the need to move beyond merely Eurocentric interpretation and presentation of non-European cultures and religious traditions. The shift for me confronts other teachers as well. This is not only a different classroom audience, the changed identity of our students raises questions about what we are teaching, how we are teaching it, and who we, the teachers, are.

The religious situations of India and of America are quite different. Asian Indian young people need to know the American situation accurately. The academic study of religious traditions can and should play a vital role in their acculturation into American culture, and it can assist them in the creation of American forms of Indian religious traditions.

First and Second Generation Asian Indian Immigrants

The students are, for the most part, Indian-Americans whose enculturation and maturation are taking place in this country through American public and private educational systems as well as through popular culture. The parents of these students are Asian Indians in America who immigrated as adults. The parents are bicultural; the second generation children are Americans of Indian heritage.[3]

This second Asian Indian generation is in some respects very different from previous second generation immigrants from Europe. They are children of the "new immigrants" or the "new ethnics." Their parents are middle and upper class and they were already highly educated at the time of immigration. This second generation is also not subject to any pronounced discrimination by reason of national origin or race, and, in the arena of American higher education, they have been quite successful.

Second generation European immigrants tried to divest themselves of "old country" culture and language so as to Americanize as rapidly as possible. But second generation Asian Indian-Americans appear to have a strong interest in maintaining their Indian identity and looking within their own communities for cultural support. One reason for this difference is that the insularity and self-sufficiency of communities or communalities within India is continued in many respects overseas. The scope of communities is sometimes broadened overseas, for example, from particular groups of Patels to all Gujaratis, but it seldom includes all Asian Indians, or even all Hindus. Another reason for the insularity lies in the overseas Indian experience of the class/race system throughout the former British Empire. In eastern and southern Africa, for example, Indians were sandwiched between native Black Africans and Europeans with fairly rigid social barriers separating the three groups. In addition, American society is relatively open to pluralistic cultural orientations and currently tolerates "Indianness" to a greater degree than it did in earlier periods. A final factor in the greater retention of Indian identity is that South Asian immigrants already enjoy a higher social status than the pre-1965 first and second generation European immigrants.

Asian Indian-Americans as College Students

Due to family pressure and the example of financial success provided by the first generation, almost all Asian Indian-American college students are highly motivated. Contemporary immigrant psychology also emphasizes education as the means to success in America. Only a few are poor students. There is little indication that drugs are a problem, although I have been told by young Asian

Indians from several urban areas that student consumption of alcohol is increasing.

Like so many other students at this time, Asian Indian-Americans sometimes place too much emphasis upon the practical and the pragmatic aspects of education. They are very good at taking tests and they usually make good grades, but only a few are exciting or stimulating students. A few have been brilliant. Their curiosity and creativity may surface more often in the scientific areas in which they generally specialize. The overwhelming first choice career of Asian Indian-American college students is medicine, followed by other technologically advantageous and well-paid specializations. Some major in the social sciences or business, but very few Asian Indian students consider "impractical" careers in the humanities.

Why Asian Indian-American Hindus Take Religion Courses

Asian Indian-American Hindu students, like other Americans in their age group, participate in and know popular American culture. But those who enroll at Emory University have not learned much about their religion either at home or from religious institutions. I have now taught about one hundred fifty college students of South Asian extraction, and like young Hindus across the United States and Canada they have been exposed to localized Hindu tradition by being present at family and voluntary group worship, but they understand little about Hindu worship. Before taking courses in religion hardly any Hindu student could give a meaningful inter-pretation of what occurs in *puja* — except for the "important" events such as *arati* (the offering of fire) which signal to them that the puja is almost over and that *prasad* (food) will soon be served.

Of course, most students in America enter college with inadequate knowledge about their own religious traditions and the religious traditions of other people. In this regard, Asian Indian students are no more poorly informed than most native-born American Christian students. But the religious situation in America is completely different from that of India. Except for Christians, second generation Asian Indians in America are a religious minority, as Hindu-Americans, (some are Sikhs, Jains, or Muslims and a very few are Parsi or Jewish) in a Christian dominated society. Asian

Indian-American Hindus, our main concern in this paper, are also greatly outnumbered by two other much larger minorities in American society — Muslims and Jews.

Asian Indian-American Hindus study religion to fulfill personal needs rather than professional goals. They take courses in religion to learn something about their religious heritage, to understand the other religious traditions around them in America (especially the culturally dominant Christian tradition), and to construct their lives as minority immigrant Hindus in religiously plural America. Because they are Asian Indian-Americans they have a special need to know about their own religious traditions, about other traditions, and to cope with their own religious identities. While they begin initially with religion courses which satisfy bachelor's degree distribution requirements, they continue with additional elective courses in religion. A handful at Emory University choose religion as a second major or a minor, but none, so far, has chosen a vocation related to religion. At a few other universities Asian Indian-American students are just beginning to take up graduate studies of South Asian religious traditions. However, they will no doubt be a significant minority at the graduate level in the academic study of religion after another decade.

Coping Religiously in American Society

As far as their relationship to Hindu religious traditions is concerned, Asian Indian-American Hindu students may be grouped into three basic categories which are parallel to those of their first generation parents.

Traditional Hindus

There is a clear-cut disparity between the generations that spans the ethnic and religious divisions of the immigrant Hindu population. The first generation immigrants are fairly religious (at least as religious as the average American) and roughly a quarter of them are actively involved in Hindu religious institutions. But despite the very visible temple-building activities which occupy long-term first generation immigrants and new, recent immigrants in urban centers across the United States and Canada, temple-oriented worship (puja) has little resonance with second generation college students except for a few young women. Student participation in rituals has been perfunctory for most of their lives, and major changes will have to occur before they will have much loyalty to Hindu temples. If better Hindu education programs become available by the time this age group begins to have children, it is possible that second generation attitudes toward temples will change. New, growing immigrant Hindu movements such as Swaminarayan also seem to be enjoying some success in holding second generation student interest despite their inclusion of temple puja in their programs of worship.

Cultural Hindus

About one third of the students are what might be called "Cultural Hindus."[4] Hinduism, in so far as it pertains to them, is equivalent to the customs of the ethnic group accompanied by broadly Hindu or Indian moral principles. Hindu ritual survives for them as a second-hand celebration of ethnic heritage and as festival (fun and games). In the future, Asian Indian community festivals might also become tourist attractions. In crisis situations some kind of individual or temple puja sometimes serves these students as an extraordinary coping device.[5]

Neo-Hindus

Some form of modernized Hindu religion, which I will dub "Neo-Hinduism"[6] (also called "Renaissance Hinduism" and "Ecumenical Hinduism"), is the most popular option for students looking for a religious identity in American society. "Neo-Hinduism" refers to modernizing Hindu reform and renewal movements which began to originate in India as early as the eighteenth century. Most Neo-Hindu movements share a cluster of ideas — such as their claim to have recaptured the original thrust of Hindu spirituality while avoiding the corruptions and degenerations which have accrued to Hindu tradition over the centuries.[7] They now proclaim the spirit of Hinduism in a universal form. They regard the message of Hinduism as eternal and as the essence of all true spirituality. True spirituality, in turn, is transcendent to all specific religious traditions and sects, and it is in essence the same in all religions. The authority for the spiritual renewal of many contemporary Neo-Hindu religious movements resides in a modern guru or his successors who re-present the ancient spiritual truth in a form adapted to the modern situation.

Hindu religion for the second immigrant generation is more general and abstract than the first generation because they have not lived in India. In fact, college students' religiosity bears resemblance to Western Enlightenment morality, and their spirituality tends to be neither very specific nor very deep. They have internalized basic Neo-Hindu ideas and this orientation constitutes the basic stance from which they participate in classroom discussions. Many students who have no interest in religious organizations, puja, or meditation are nevertheless attracted to a view of the world rooted in contemporary interpretations of the Vedanta systems of theology and of the *Bhagavad Gita*.

Students pick up the Neo-Hindu attitude of toleration toward the variant strands in the Hindu tradition and also toward other religious traditions. People are exhorted not to convert, but to find the true spirituality in their own religious traditions. But the officially proclaimed "toleration" of Neo-Hindu ideology is in fact rather limited. While, on the one hand, the founders of all religious traditions are regarded as true *avatars* of God (differences being due merely to different historical and cultural circumstances), on the other hand, this recognition is withdrawn because almost all of the traditions which grew up after the founders are declared to have been corrupted and falsified by the followers of the founders. Hindus in America have often told me, for example, that Jesus was a true prophet or avatar, but that the Christian religious tradition is corrupt. Neo-Hindu ideology thus tends to regard the religious traditions of others as true in principle, but degenerate in fact.

The Neo-Hindu explanation of religious differences is a hindrance to Hindu students who want a realistic appraisal of their situation in America. This assessment of religious traditions is a projection that fits other religious traditions into a predetermined Hindu template. While it may not put majority Hindus at a disadvantage in India, it prompts the Hindu minority in America to believe that the Christian majority believes that Hindu and Christian faith share a common spirituality and recognize that the Christian traditions are corrupted. There is no evidence that this is the case. Christians, of course, also make similar baseless judgments about other religious traditions. When British Christian missionaries in India presented Christian faith to Hindus as, for example, "The Crown of Hinduism"[8], they offered a parallel preliminary acceptance followed by ultimate rejection. In this reading, Christian faith was regarded by the missionaries as completing what Hindu religiosity is unable to attain and can only long for. Christian missionaries projected value judgments upon Hindu religion which prevented them from an accurate assessment of Hindu spirituality. When Indians countered Christian paternalism with their own projections of acceptance in principle but rejection in fact, the result was mutual and very deep misunderstanding. It would be tragic for Christians and Hindus (and Muslims) to perpetuate such basic ignorance of each other in America.

One legacy of this impasse which is still of concern is the adoption by Indian Hindus of the English Christian word "idol" to translate *murti, pratima, arca,* and other Sanskrit words which would be more accurately rendered in English as "image" or "icon." "Idol" is not a neutral, descriptive term. Any English or American dictionary states the meaning of the word clearly: An "idol" is "a false or non-existent god," "an object of heathen worship," "a false or misleading idea; a fallacy."[9] English Christian missionaries called murti "idols" because they were sure they knew what Hindu worship using images meant because Christian theology already dictated what they should think of them, namely: "Hindus worship sticks and stones."

Neo-Hindu movements will probably chart the major lines of development for Hindu religious traditions in America because they hold promise for the American context of Hinduism. Neo-Hindu ideas undergird, for example, the consolidation of some previously separate ethnic and sectarian religious groups in several American cities. The resulting "Ecumenical Hinduism"[10] is a new American religious development with no exact counterpart in India. But Neo-Hindu ideas about other religious traditions will impede the ability of Asian Indian-American college students to deal realistically with the American religious situation. Simply put, Neo-Hindu claims for the spiritual or moral superiority of Hindu religion will almost inevitably present them with a false picture of both the Hindu and the other American religious traditions.

It is my belief that it is a part of a religion teacher's task to help Asian Indian-American college students (and other students as well) learn to *take other people seriously in their differences*, not just in their assumed similarities. It is relatively easy for us to accept other people who seem *not* to be other because we project them to be like ourselves. It is far more difficult to recognize the "otherness" of the other. Once real differences have been seen as they are, it still demands a great deal from us to accept people who are in important respects not like us at all. Tolerance based upon projected similarity that really does not exist provides a flimsy foundation for interreligious relations. The misinformation that results on both sides is worse than no information because people think they know other people when they do not. Christian, Jewish, and Hindu students seldom have much reliable information about Islam, but they nevertheless have rather strong opinions about the value of Islam which they have picked up from parents, religious organizations, the news media, and popular American culture. Christian students often have strong preconceived ideas about Hindus.

There is a great educational need for Asian Indian-American students to become reliably informed about both their own and about other religious traditions in America. The need is even greater for the children of immigrants who have traded their dominant religious position in India for minority status in America. What Asian Indian-American students need to cope religiously in America can at least be assisted by the academic study of religion. The academic study of religions is not inimical to religious faith. It is essential to an informed faith. Even if some Hindu parochial schools or *gurukulas* are eventually established for the education of Asian Indian-American Hindu students, they also should incorporate interpretive approaches to religions which are basic to the academic study of religion.

The Academic College Study of Religion and Religions

Academic study of religions in American colleges and universities can provide support at several levels for Asian Indian-American students who are developing their religious options. It is part of the pedagogical intent of the academic study of religions that all students, not just Asian Indian-American students, acquire an informed, humanistic, adult appreciation both of their own religious tradition, and of at least one other religious tradition.

Cross-cultural and Critical Analysis

The history of religions as a discipline is concerned with the study of religion and religions in human history and the interpretation of an important aspect of human beings through the study of religions. The study of religions is part of the continuing process of Americanization for Asian Indian-American students. Academic study of religions introduces students to critical methods of analysis and to cross-cultural, cross-traditional interpretations of human religious traditions. Academic study situates Hindu religious tradition, for example, in the context of the other major religious traditions, showing comparable structures and systemic disparities — not by means of theological or philosophical projection, but as part of the much more difficult, demanding, and hazardous endeavor to describe other traditions accurately, and to interpret them both in their own terms and in cross-cultural perspective.

It would be absurd to claim that American historians of religion achieve complete objectivity either about their own or other religious traditions. But it is a fundamental goal of research in religion that the infrastructure for description and interpretation become as broad as possible and that evidence and interpretation, and outsider and insider points of view, be juxtaposed so that they can continually correct each other. It is of utmost importance, for example, for the religion scholar to listen to, to dialogue with, and to be corrected by people whom she or he attempts to understand.

Confronting the religious traditions of other people is basically similar to confronting other people. Successful understanding of other people never consists merely of the concepts we construct about them, or of the emotional dispositions we develop toward them. No matter how closely we relate to other persons, they always remain other than, and more than, the relationship we have with them. Thus also when a scholar interprets a religious tradition, the people of that tradition are brought into a relationship and remain "other" at the same time. There can be relationship and appropriate, critical, analytical understanding even when this understanding is never exactly the same as the otherness of the other. True understanding of the other entails recognition that the other is never completely understood. This limitation becomes a problem, it seems to me, only when we forget that the otherness of the other, either interpersonally or inter-traditionally is intrinsic to understanding people. When otherness seems to vanish, it is a clear signal that we have misunderstood. Academic interpretation is a continuing two-way exchange: first, between scholars and the people they are interpreting, and, second, among scholars themselves in critical, analytical conversation with each other.

There cannot be ethnic and religious identity qualifications for teacher-researchers in free and open academic study of religion. The basic question for both teaching and research in religion is training, ability, and creativity, not personal or group identity. I do not mean to claim that insider's and outsider's points of view are equivalent or irrelevant, but rather to state the obvious fact that the outsider frequently can have fresh insights into a religious tradition which the insider could not provide without the outsider's stimulation, and that most aspects of a religious tradition are as accessible to outsiders as they are to insiders. The qualified outsider has a different perspective from the insider, but not an inferior perspective — unless the outsider neglects to receive and absorb correction from insiders. For example, the only major studies of Indian immigrant religions in America to date have been done by non-Indians.[11] New research on Asian Indian religions in America carried out by Asian Indian immigrants will be forthcoming, however. And immigrants will be researching their own stories with greater frequency — as has already been done by members of the Association for Asian American Studies (primarily by Japanese and Chinese immigrants and their descendants).

But, as the recent controversy over appointments to the new India Studies chair in the South Asian Studies Department at Berkeley has shown,[12] the ethnic and religious identity of the teacher/researcher population is both a political and an epistemological issue. There are not yet enough scholars from India and Asian Indian scholars teaching and carrying out academic research about Indian religions in America. The field is dominated by Americans of European descent with Christian, Jewish, or secular religious orientations. Academic, cross-cultural, and critical study of religions requires full and equal participation by all parties, both religiously and ethnically inside and outside, lest the mutual exchange of interpretation and correction which is essential to the academic study of religions be truncated. The conversation between "outsider" academicians and "insiders" will not really be epistemologically adequate unless the "insider" is a "member of the club," an equal partner in academia.

Appreciating the Dynamics of Hindu Tradition

The history of religions approaches which we employ in the teaching of Hindu religious tradition often enable students to appreciate Hindu ritual processes as meaningful forms of worship for the first time. Meditation disciplines can also be made accessible as physiological, psychological, and symbolic processes. Systematic study of sacred oral and written tradition (both shruti and smriti) can acquaint students with particular parts of the tradition, and initiate them into the process of reading and interpreting texts for themselves. In similar fashion the whole range of the tradition's dynamic processes can, in principle, be illumined as fully valid ways human beings are religious. Currently, both Asian Indian and non-Asian Indian students enter courses with a high interest in the conceptual structure of Hindu tradition, and, it appears that this dimension of the tradition is most likely to be of continuing interest to Asian Indian-American students in later years.

Addressing the Whole Hindu Tradition

Hindu college students often have inaccurate notions about forms of Hindu tradition other than the one to which they have been exposed. The project of formulating what the whole Hindu religious tradition means for them is part of the task of constructing Hindu tradition for their situation in America. It is, in fact, part of the Americanization of Hindu religion for second generation college students. An obvious contribution which academic courses concerned with the Hindu tradition can make is the presentation to students of a sense of the *whole* Hindu tradition in its historical context — in all of India, among overseas Indians, and over the last three thousand years.

Self-Discovery by Comparison

Asian Indian-Americans need to understand American religions accurately. Hindus and Christians in America are poorly informed about each other. Hindus are not more prone to false ideas about Christian tradition than Christians are about Hindu tradition. But Christians in America have such dominant cultural influence that they have little motivation to correct misinformation or prejudice concerning religious minorities. Minority traditions, however, have very good reasons to be better informed and, in America, this includes Hindus. Classes concerned with non-Hindu religions can help Asian Indian-Americans gain reliable interpretations of the other religious traditions in America, not only of Christianity but also of the significant minority traditions of Judaism and Islam. Accurately depicting the other religious tradition also helps students, by comparison, to assess their own religious identity.

There are structural similarities, I believe, which are shared by all or most religious traditions. At the same time, however, religious traditions are systemically very disparate. To explain these statements, I will compare religion in the singular to language and particular religious traditions (plural) to particular languages. It is arguable, and perhaps probable, that there is a single underlying structure to all human languages. But there is no single language (and there never will be one) that enables a person to understand all of the other languages. Even when languages are closely related to each other (e.g., Spanish and Italian), the very similarity can lead to misunderstanding because words function as part of linguistic and cultural systems rather than as autonomous fragments. Languages (plural), like the religions (plural), form different systems. Moving from one to another requires translation. Even translated parts cannot be interchanged because the valence of parts changes according to the system in which they function.

For example, no Christians I know of "do puja for Jesus" as an avatar. Despite the fact that there are structural similarities, both between the Christian eucharist ritual (especially in its Roman Catholic forms) and puja, and between the Christian concept of incarnation and the Hindu concept of avatar, eucharist and incarnation are not systemically equivalent to puja and avatar and the one pair cannot simply be substituted for the other. Many Hindus in America have told me that they perform puja for Jesus at Christmas time. While the openness and inclusivity displayed in this worship are remarkable, it should be realized that the puja for Jesus is an act of *Hindu worship*, a sort of Jesus *Jayanti* (birthday). It is not Christian worship and would not be recognized as a legitimate form of *Christian worship* by Christians. Eucharist-incarnation and puja-avatar are structurally similar, but systematically disparate.

Hindu Principles Valuable to American Religious Culture

Course work in Hindu religion can assist students to appreciate the positive religious and cultural contributions Hindus can offer for the enhancement of American religious culture. Following genuine comparison, it is possible to ask realistically: What have Hindus to offer *religiously* to the religious life of America? Asian Indian-American Hindu students must wrestle with this question individually and collectively as they develop a sense of their uniqueness and self-worth as Hindus in American culture.

One obvious example of a Hindu religious contribution to American culture is the Yoga traditions of meditation. However, Yoga does not appear to be very important in the daily lives either of Hindu immigrants to America or of their children. Another example which has been important to me personally is the Vedanta Hindu depiction of the process of theological argument as *darshan* (seeing). The traditional six (or three pairs of) darshana, or schools of theology, in Hindu tradition are not so much "viewpoints" as different "methods by which one can learn to see." What is important about traditions such as Advaita Vedanta is not their conceptions — either of the obviously visible world or of the ostensibly less visible Truth or Reality (*sat*), but what these methods make it possible to see beyond their conceptions by using these conceptions as a means to see the Real (sat). Vedanta, for example, has a peculiar method of argumentation that illustrates this process of theologizing. Truth is never produced by argument nor is it the result of inference. Unless Truth is discovered or uncovered it is not to be found. Accordingly, Vedanta theological argument takes the form of disproving false views (*purvapaksha*), but it does not argue about the Truth directly. Removing the false views removes asat (non-Truth); it defeats misconceptions that obscure truth (sat). When all false views have been discarded (when the veil of *maya* has been removed) — self-luminous or self-established Truth shines forth of itself. Theological arguments are successful, in this view, when they create opportunities for insight (darshan) by removing misinterpretations. Insight may or may not occur, but it cannot be produced by argument.

The Hindu notion of darshan (to see, seeing) has many facets and ramifications which are, I believe, commensurate with this theological method. Murti (images), for example, can be construed as sensible opportunities to discern Reality (sat). The notion of darshan may be at least partially unique to Hindu tradition (as Diana Eck has argued)[13], but it could be religiously very suggestive to Christians and it may have structural similarity to the ideal of "seeing God" in Christian theology.

Self-Image Issues[14]

Research assignments provide occasions for students to tackle individual problems intrinsic to their lives as Hindus in America. Grappling systematically with religious issues raises questions which may eventually feed into their own developing personal form of the Hindu tradition for the American context. The underlying questions for many students seem to be: "Do I want to be a Hindu?" and, "How can I be that in America?"[15]

Some of the term paper topics the students choose appear to be of more technical than existential import. Such papers assess the physiological effects of Yoga meditation or of Transcendental Meditation; or they might ask whether moral and religious aspects of traditional *Ayurveda* have any practical application for contemporary medical practice in America. Women students with training in *Bharat Natyam* are often interested in the religious symbolism of dance; and, occasionally, they explore what connection there might be between dance and spirituality.

But other Asian Indian-American students choose to write about problems with which they are personally concerned and which they must eventually resolve for themselves. Paper topics cluster around issues related to students' images of themselves, especially questions related to family. Both men and women students write about marriage — whether it should be arranged or free choice or some combination of the two; whether they should marry only within their *jati* (caste), whether they could marry partners who are not Hindus, or whether they could pick spouses who are not even Indians. Papers also examine parent-child relations; questions of the religious meaning of sexuality, abstinence, and asceticism; and the relationship between sex and bhakti (devotion) in Hindu religion, especially in the Krishna tradition. And they explore issues of personal morality, as exemplified, for example, by the stories of *Mahabharata* characters such as Abhimanyu or Karna.

Asian Indian-American women who write about the subordination of Hindu women, feminine symbolism, *sati*, suicides by women, and the murder and abuse of women both in India and in America are the students most obviously concerned with developing new images of themselves. These young women struggle to develop a Hindu self-image that is not demeaning.

For many second generation women, the conflicts between women's liberation, Indian tradition, and American culture is symbolized and embodied concretely in the first generation woman physician who works full-time at the office and also works full-time in the home as wife, housekeeper, and mother, but with little or no help from husband and sons. Second generation women pre-medical students are very aware of the difficulty of combining these roles successfully. Many are dissatisfied with the tradition of *pativrata* (subordination and devotion of the wife to her husband) and, like Christian, Jewish, and Muslim women in similar circumstances, they are searching for a re-created religious symbolism of women. They want a new model for what it means to be a woman, but they do not want to break with the past or with their families. They search through the tradition for a new religious identity that will accord both with the professions for which they are training and with their roles in their home families, as wives, and as mothers. The imagery of the Goddess (*Devi*) and the promise of improved status in some of the Neo-Hindu reform movements are two of the popular subject areas for their explorations.

The Role of the Teacher

It is not the argument of this paper that second generation Asian Indian-American Hindu students need to be taught by professors who are not Hindus. The subject is the educational value of the academic study of religion. Academic study of religion offers a cross-cultural critical perspective, an appreciation of the dynamics of the whole Hindu tradition, a realistic approach to differences and similarities among religious traditions in the United States, a background for developing a sense of religious identity, and a positive appreciation of the worth of Hindu tradition in American religious life. The academic study of religion is not a substitute for, nor a rival of, spirituality; and it is not intended that it should be. Moreover, college courses in religion are not meant to replace instruction in religion by religious institutions nor to supplant relationships between gurus and their disciples. The *academic* study of religions provides an understanding of religion that is of a different quality of interpretation, one that can enhance the religious education of Asian Indian-American Hindu students and enrich their Americanization as Hindus. Academic study of religions is not a threat to Hindu or any other spirituality. It is an avenue to knowledge without which second generation Hindus in America will be less prepared to confront the tasks of their adult lives.

Professors of religion now in their fifties have spent most of their careers teaching about foreign religious traditions to native-born Americans. But now a large segment of our students come from Asia and from religious traditions native to Asia, and formerly Asian religious traditions have become American religious traditions. The scholarly dialogue that is so essential to the process of interpreting other religious traditions has now become much more immediate and routine than the dialogues with texts and the excursions to foreign cultures for field trips that characterized earlier decades. The non-

Hindu teacher of Hindu religious traditions is now challenged by her or his own students and by the local communities to which they belong to an extent that surely will improve our mutual understanding.

The academic study of religion is not possible without the critical apparatus of humanistic and social scientific scholarship. I do not believe that American academic teachers of religions should play the role of gurus or that American students should play *sishya*, the devoted intellectual and spiritual children of the teacher. Unlike the guru/sishya model, what is transmitted by academic teaching when it works best is not a traditional mold, but a questioning and constructing attitude and method. The dark side of religion must also be appreciated. Sometimes religion is dangerous and detrimental, but at other times it lifts the human spirit toward its highest aspirations. It is not the purpose of the academic study of religion to enlighten or to "save" students. It is the purpose of academic interpretation of religion to illumine the role of religions in human life, and for that reason enlightenment, insight, darshan, and salvation are included in the material of religious life that scholars, both students and professors, attempt to interpret. The "insight" sought by the student of academic religion is grasping, for example, the role that "seeing the Real" (darshan) plays in Hindu religious life.

The teaching and the study of religion are not uninvolved or lacking passion or empathy, and the discipline of religious study does not dissect or destroy its subject matter in order to interpret it. There is a double dynamic involved in teaching Hindu tradition (and probably in teaching any religious tradition): One major part of teaching is what can be made explicit and what is generally the primary content of test questions and the examinations students write. This side of teaching is concerned with such palpable materials as information, artifacts, documents, responses to questions, reports of observations of behavior, symbols, designs, ideas, facts, theories, interpretations, and opinions of texts, informants, or teachers. The other major part of the teaching of Hindu religion has to do with insights to which the student may arrive during the process of study. Evidence of such insight becomes manifest in examinations and papers students write or in class discussions — even though the examination questions or research assignments usually do not (and possibly can not) explicitly or directly ask for them. The creativity (rather than accumulation of information) which teachers invite from students lies in another dimension of the teaching event — alongside, but not within, the confines of grading structures, and outside the more or less objective measures of academic performance which are usually employed to determine grades. Unfortunately, it is possible for a student (or a professor) to memorize and to say all of the right things about religion and still not be able to see the point.

The real subject matter of a course in Hindu religion is not even touched by the question too many students ask professors these days: "What do you want me to learn?" The teacher does not even know what he wants the student to see beforehand. It can be recognized, but it cannot even be asked for directly. What creative scholarship is can only be indicated indirectly. Direct statement approximates, but ultimately misleads. This aspect of the teaching of Hindu religion involves, parallel to the Hindu idea of darshan, developing an opportunity for students to see by helping them remove whatever obscures their vision. The academic teaching of religion mimics, in this respect, a ritual or theological process even though it is neither a ritual nor a theology. Academic "insight" is much less a deductive process from premises, or generalizing about evidence, or of constructing conceptual models than it is a process of receiving sight and giving it expression. Genuine academic teaching that takes place about Hindu religious tradition makes it possible for this process to occur. Genuine academic teaching is a sort of invitation that, when most successful, is mutually exchanged between teacher and student.

The student's insight is her or his own. The student's vision is his or her discovery; it is not the teacher's, and it is not just old or timeless truths newly transmitted or newly acquired by yet another human being in a line of succession. The dis-covery or un-covering is not just the re-covery of eternal truth. Academic study of Hindu religion calls for critical, analytic insight. It is renewable, not once for all time, and remains alive only as it is renewed. It is probable, not certain. It is convincing, and enticing, but not overwhelming. It is embracing, not closed. It is to be shared rather than hoarded or protected. Finally, the academic study of religion is conversational and open-ended, not dictatorial and final.

Asian Indian Hindu students and their parents should therefore embrace the academic study of religions as a valuable asset in their college (and graduate level) educational development. Academic study of religions can assist the students' acculturation and it can be an indispensable tool for the nurturing of new varieties of Hindu religious tradition on American soil.

13

A New International Religion: Radhasoami

Mark Juergensmeyer

Americans have always been drawn to the mysteries of India's religious ideas. Emerson and the Transcendentalists were fascinated with them, as were a good number of other nineteenth-century authors.[1] It was not until the end of that century, however, when Swami Vivekenanda came to Chicago in 1893 and dazzled the World Parliament of Religions with his presentation of an intellectually respectable Hinduism that Americans in large numbers began to take seriously the possibility of adopting India's religious concepts as their own.

Yet Hinduism is not an easy faith for foreigners to adopt. It is closely tied to a cultural and social system that is specific to the Indian subcontinent, and only by divorcing its ideas and teachings from this context could it effectively be transported to Western soil. Vivekananda's Vedanta Society, which offered selections from Hindu philosophy taught in a church-like worship setting, was one attempt to make that transition possible. Other attempts included syncretic movements — such as Theosophy — that brought Hindu ideas and images into a rich intercultural mix.[2] Many of the ideas that

Theosophy appropriated from India came from new forms of Hinduism, and one of them would itself become in this century an international religion: Radhasoami.

The Origins of a New International Religion

Writing at the turn of the century in a book entitled *Voice of the Silence*, the founder of Theosophy, Madame Blavatsky, describes certain ethereal sounds that are linked with transcendent spiritual regions to which the transcendent soul has access. Her descriptions of the sounds and the regions are strikingly similar to the ones given by the nineteenth-century founder of Radhasoami, Swami Shiv Dayal.[3] Hervey deWitt Griswold, the first outsider to study Radhasoami teachings and those of another early leader of Theosophy, Annie Besant, described them as "practically identical."[4]

The teachings that the Radhasoami teachers propounded, and that Madame Blavatsky and Annie Besant found so interesting, are rooted in Indian tradition and yet accessible to followers from a wide range of cultural backgrounds. They were first formulated by Swami Shiv Dayal Singh in Agra in 1861.[5] They showed a mix of influences — Kabirpanthi, Sikh, Nath yogi, Vaisnava — and they focussed on the efficacy of sacred words and the saving power of a spiritual master in transforming the self and achieving access to other-worldly realms beyond. Swami Shiv Dayal advocated a form of yoga that was appropriate for householders as well as sadhus, and his following, largely members of his own urban merchant-caste community, continued to be a lively if increasingly fragmented group after his death. He was succeeded by other spiritual masters, and presently there are at least twenty lineages in the Radhasoami family tree. Some of the branches have prospered. During the 1930s the residential community at Dayalbagh, near Agra, developed an enormous complex of industries, shops, and model farms and dairies; at the same time the colony at Beas, in the Punjab, created something of a utopian city of its own. In the last thirty years Beas has greatly expanded its membership throughout North India, and it and one of its offshoots — the Ruhani Satsang in Delhi — have developed large multicultural networks that are in many ways prototypes for a new kind of international religious organization. Today the Radhasoami movement has become the largest of the new religious communities in North India. All told, in its various branches and under the several names by which it is known, the Radhasoami community can claim over a million initiates in South Asia, and tens of thousands more in other parts of the world.[6]

Many of the first foreigners to be attracted to the new religion came from the Theosophists' fold. The first reference to Radhasoami by a writer outside the movement came from a Theosophist,[7] and one of Swami Shiv Dayal Singh's successors, Rai Saligram, was a subscriber to the *Theosophist* magazine.[8] Further connections between Radhasoami and Theosophy were established by members of Theosophy who crossed over to Radhasoami membership, and are listed in Radhasoami records as some of their earliest foreign initiates: Myron Phelps, a man named Hurst, and someone identified by Radhasoami historians only as "a German Theosophist."[9]

One of the reasons such people gave for switching from Theosophy to Radhasoami was their desire to join a movement that seemed to them more authentically Hindu. Even though the leaders of Theosophy borrowed their ideas from Hinduism, and perhaps even from Radhasoami, their movement was essentially Western in its form and interests. The Vedanta Societies also had a strong Western impetus; though their teachings had Hindu roots, they were presented in such a way as to answer to Western philosophic concerns, and a Christian style of worship was adopted. Radhasoami was different: it maintained the same ideas and practices whether in India or the United States. And it was open to all. In fact, Radhasoami was the first religious movement of Hindu ancestry where foreigners had direct and easy access to an original, un-Westernized form of religion. So when the Radhasoami organizations opened their doors to foreigners early in this century they were inaugurating something new: a universal Hinduism.

The Global Expansion of the Radhasoami Tradition

At about the same time that the German Theosophist traveling in India became the first foreign initiate of a Radhasoami master in the last decade of the nineteenth century, an American woman sent her son to India to inquire about visions she had received in her yoga practices. He too found his way to the Radhasoami master, Rai Saligram.[10] Saligram had occupied the high position of Postmaster General of Uttar Pradesh, and some of his other foreign followers were his British colleagues in the postal service. An American lawyer from Philadelphia became a resident of the Radhasoami colony of Soamibagh, near Agra, from 1913 to 1914.[11]

Beginning in the 1930s the records of both the largest Radhasoami communities — Dayalbagh and Beas — give evidence of a growing number of Westerners coming to settle among them. The successors of the Great Master at Beas, Sawan Singh, have been the most active in internationalizing the faith. One of them, Kirpal Singh, established a new organization in Delhi, the Ruhani Satsang ("Spiritual Fellowship"),[12] and started the practice of going on tours abroad. The number of his foreign initiates increased rapidly in the 1960s and early 1970s. Eventually there were over 13,000, comprising some ten percent of the movement's population.[13] At Beas the leadership passed to Jagat Singh, who helped propagate the idea that Radhasoami was a universal faith. He pointed out that the idea of sacred sound is found in many religious traditions, and that concepts found in Radhasoami and its sant precursors are parallel to gnostic philosophy, Taoism, and the *logos* theology of the New Testament. Charan Singh devoted an entire book to the Gospel of St. John, and another to that of St. Matthew, comparing "the word made flesh" in the New Testament with *shabd*, the sacred word in Radhasoami.[14]

The medium for many of Charan Singh's writings, and the language into which almost all most Radhasoami publications are translated, is English, and it is the medium for the conduct of Beas's and Dayalbagh's organizational affairs. Although the liturgical language in the Agra branches has always been Hindi, and in Beas, Punjabi, the language used to communicate with the outside world has been English, an important choice in internationalizing the faith. At Agra, the preference for English began with the second guru, Rai Saligram; English was the medium in which he and his compeers were intellectually and organizationally most comfortable.[15] The publication program of most branches has expanded enormously in recent years. Almost all volumes are available in at least one of India's regional languages, but most are also available in English and in a great variety of other international languages as well. At the Ruhani Satsang, for example, the masters' writings have been translated into 42 languages, including Czech, Hebrew, Swahili and Indonesian.

The Radhasoami organization has made it possible that those who hear its message abroad need not come to India to be initiated into its mysteries. The concept that makes this possible is proxy initiation, which seems to have been established as a policy of the Beas branch as early as 1911. In that year Dr. H. M. Brock, a dentist from Port Angeles, Washington, asked for initiation for himself and Mrs. Brock, and a Punjabi immigrant who was a Radhasoami initiate was given the power to initiate them on the guru's behalf.[16] After that the American expansion began. Since the actual initiation takes place in the initiate's own country, where the channel of spiritual authority flows through the master's representatives, the status of some of those local Radhasoami leaders is considerable.

The offices at Beas have become the headquarters of an international organization that boasts more than 300 centers in India and over 200 others elsewhere in the world. Over 50,000 persons have been initiated outside India, and in recent years the rate of new initiations abroad has been several thousand per year, with the largest numbers occurring in the United Kingdom, South Africa, and the United States.[17] The percentage of their financial contribution is even greater than their proportion of the community's membership.[18] More important still is their symbolic contribution. They accord to the movement the prestige of reversing the direction of missionary conquest, and they confirm with their physical presence the conceptual claim that Radhasoami transcends the cultural limitations suggested by its home on Indian soil.

The Most Recent Phase of International Expansion

For years the mainstay of the Radhasoami network overseas was that same small community of mystics and seekers who supplied the clientele for Theosophy. During the first half of this century there were never more than a few hundred of them. The American initiates of the Beas master, Sawan Singh and Jagat Singh, together amounted to only 245.[19] The enormous growth in Radhasoami membership abroad has been recent, and has come from quite different directions.

One period of foreign expansion accompanied the Western interest in Asian religion and in "new religious movements" in the 1960s and 1970s. The masters made triumphant world journeys, and local satsang organizations blossomed throughout North and South America, England and continental Europe, Southeast Asia, and Africa — especially South Africa. Some foreign satsangis established communes, reversing the spiritual individualism that marked the earlier generations of foreign devotees. For others, their Radhasoami faith was a matter of private practice that was appealing in part because it seemed to be primarily a matter of technique and knowledge rather than piety and dogma, and because Radhasoami teachers were exotic yet accessible. The kind of Hinduism that fascinated Westerners in the sixties as one of meditation practices and communal spirituality, and Hindu yoga was of special interest to those who wished to experiment in world spirituality. Radhasoami's *surat sabd yoga* was seen as one style among several that Hinduism offered.

Radhasoami teachings were also introduced to Westerners indirectly, through groups that utilized Radhasoami ideas but presented them under their own banner. The Eckankar movement, for example, borrowed directly from the writings of Radhasoami teachers, and its founder, Paul Twitchell, was an initiate of Kirpal Singh.[20] Kirpal Singh had followed his own master, Sawan Singh, in linking the first phrase in Guru Nanak's morning prayer, "eckankar," to the highest level of spiritual consciousness;[21] Twitchell followed suit and made it the name of his movement. The teachings of the Divine Light Mission, led by the boy guru Maharaj-ji, are essentially those of Radhasoami as well,[22] and other spiritual leaders of the time were also influenced by Radhasoami teachings.[23]

The groundswell of Western interest in Asian religion began to subside in the 1980s, and so did the expansion of Radhasoami membership in Western countries in all branches except those associated with Kirpal Singh. The slack in overseas membership in the Beas branch was soon taken up, however, by a new group of Westerners: members of Indian immigrant families that had settled in the United States, England, and elsewhere abroad. There have been Indian immigrants in the West for most of this century, and some of them, like Kehr Singh Sasmas, the man who brought the Brocks to the faith in 1910, and Bhagat Singh Thind, a teacher of spirituality in Southern California who published twenty books on Radhasoami-related themes in the 1950s,[24] were longtime admirers of Radhasoami thought. The great wave of Indian immigration to the West is relatively recent, however, beginning in Britain with India's independence in 1947, and in the United States when changes were made in American immigration regulations in 1965.

Among the recent immigrants were some who had been initiated in India before coming to the West. One of these was T. S. Khanna, the American representative of the Ruhani Satsang who has done much to spread the teachings of Kirpal Singh and Darshan Singh. Khanna was a government administrator who has been assigned to the Indian embassy in Washington, and who stayed on after his tour of duty had been completed to work for the U. S. government and to help with the American branches of the Ruhani Satsang organization. Unlike Khanna, however, most recent immigrants who have embraced Radhasoami have done so after arriving in the U.K. or the United States, finding in Radhasoami a form of religious community and a kind of spiritual teaching that is congenial to their changed circumstances. Among them is Salina Mansukhani, one of the many Sindhi satsangis abroad, who was chosen Miss India-USA in 1986. She claims that coming to the Beas Dera, where she stays in the foreigners' guest house, gives her a bit of America in India; and when she is back in the United States, her association with Radhasoami gives her a bit of India in America.[25] These dual characteristics of Radhasoami culture, in fact appeal to all three groups of Westerners that have been attracted to its membership — the old seekers of a spiritual science, the new followers of gurus, and members of the new immigrant communities from India. In each case Radhasoami provides a community that is both Indian and

Western, and a set of teachings that transcends nationality and is easily adapted to any cultural setting.

Julian Johnson and the Spiritual Quest

The story of a Westerner's spiritual quest that is best known in Beas and Ruhani Satsang circles is the one told by Julian Johnson in his published letters, *With a Great Master in India*. This book and his *Path of the Masters* have been bestsellers among English-reading satsangis in India ever since they were issued in the mid-1930s, and they retain their status in the Beas branch's bookstores even in the 1980s.[26] Johnson's story is idiosyncratic, but it describes a certain kind of Radhasoami seeker from America: fiercely individualistic and skeptical of much of the spirituality of his age, yet overwhelmingly committed and articulately defensive of his new faith.

"I was born with an irrepressible desire for knowledge," Johnson claimed.[27] After graduating from college in Bolivar, Missouri, and receiving theological training at the University of Chicago and a medical degree from Iowa State, Johnson was still unsatisfied with the promise of Western knowledge. After several careers — as a Baptist minister, a missionary to India, a medical practitioner in the U.S. Navy, and a doctor in private practice in California — he remained personally unfulfilled. He began a spiritual search that led him to "New Thought" in Christian Science and in "Spiritualism" but "none of these seemed to get at the root of the matter."[28] Johnson came to much the same conclusion after turning to Theosophy and Rosicrucianism. He finally came to "the darkest hour" of his life while visiting southern California's Imperial Valley in the winter of 1928-29 when "nothing but blank darkness, bitterness of soul and despair settle on me." The only hints that things were to become radically better was a sensation Johnson experienced one morning on waking. He felt he was "floating on an ocean of love."[29]

It was then that he chanced to visit an old friend of his in Ashland, Oregon, an elderly woman who was an initiate of Sawan Singh, and who shared with Johnson her copy of Rai Saligram's *Radhasoami Mat Prakash*. Rai Saligram's use of the phrase "Ocean of love" immediately struck a resonant chord with Johnson. He

accepted the woman's offer to put him in touch with Dr. H. M.
Brock in Port Angeles, Washington, who arranged for his initiation.
In 1932 he set sail for India, and upon arriving at the railway station
at Jalandhar, an hour or so away from the Beas Dera, he found that
the Great Master had come to welcome him. In a letter to the
Brocks, Johnson reported that he "would have known he was the
Master" even if they had not been introduced. He was rendered
speechless, and "a great sense of peace" came into his soul.[30]

Johnson settled down in India, where he became the American in
residences at Beas. He did some medical work, but his writing and
Dera activities where his real occupations, and they amounted to
virtually a full-time job. While in India he came to meet Elizabeth
Bruce, a devotee who had previously charmed the Dayalbagh master,
Anand Swarup.[31] In time he brought her to Sawan Singh and to
Beas, and they were married. As a sort of wedding present, Johnson
wrote a biography of her life, entitled *The Unquenchable Flame*.[32] At
the same time, he continued to travel with the Great Master
throughout India, recording his own thoughts and his master's
utterances. Johnson described the land on which is master trod as
being a special place: not India or America, but a different world
altogether:

> And now what shall I say? Am I still on earth, or am I in some
> weird border land? And how shall I estimate the values or describe
> the situation? It is all so strange, so unlike anything in the
> homeland.... We think of ancient religious teachers who have visited
> this land and probably stood upon this very spot, including Krishna
> and Buddha and even Jesus himself. For it is known that he visited
> here. We try to recall some of the doctrines of the ancient sages,
> prophets and Mahatmas; and all the while we are conscious of the
> fact that the greatest of them all sits on a bench here by us at this
> moment, calmly reading a book.... [His] powers far transcend those of
> the greatest prophets of old; aye, even of the beloved Master of
> Nazareth and Galilee.[33]

Johnson's story is peculiarly his own, and yet many aspects of it
parallel the stories of other seekers from America, England and
Europe. Most Westerners who have found the Radhasoami path
came across it after an active search; most found it as an answer to

questions that had been troubling them long before. A young man from Texas, who reported having had experiences of leaving his body, hearing remarkable sounds, and seeing dazzling blue and white light at the time he had suffered a terrifying automobile accident, felt he needed assistance in interpreting his experience.[34] A clairvoyant in England also had out-of-body experiences that, from her point of view, needed proper direction. A student in southern California had no such experiences, but felt a deep spiritual emptiness that he knew would be fulfilled by a remarkable person; he formulated a set of expectations regarding the perfect teacher and the perfect teachings, and had gone to meetings in the late 1970s to hear touring Indian religious masters.[35] He was determined to find one that would meet his measure, but each seemed limited and unsatisfying. One day while talking to a friend in a restaurant, a passing waiter said, "just remember 'Radhasoami'." The next day, in a different restaurant, he heard the phrase again, and when he asked the owner what it signified, the owner produced a picture of Charan Singh. As soon as he saw it, the Californian instantly recognized him as the one for whom he had been longing.

The restaurant setting and the mysterious waiter are characteristic of two motifs in stories of this sort: a public location and a chance meeting with an unusual stranger. Another satsangi from California told about his discovery of the faith while walking on the beach. He was confronted by a strange person who seemed to know his inner desires and who suggested that he read books on Radhasoami. The stranger disappeared, but the Californian's interest was piqued, and soon he had the opportunity of meeting a Radhasoami master who was visiting the United States on tour. Like other seekers, he reported experiencing a great sense of relief at being saved from his desultory searchings.

A Special Knowledge

At least some of the initial fascination with Radhasoami derives from the fact that it was spawned in a land with a deep and intriguing religious past: a "strange" land, as Johnson put it, "hoary with age and rich in history."[36] The remote and romantic quality of India's landscape evokes biblical images, and the mysteriousness of things Indian is one of the things that make Radhasoami seem special. At the same time, the ideas are quite accessible. In one of his first letters home, Johnson exclaimed that Radhasoami teachings were "so obviously true" and "so clearly rational." The logic of the faith, he felt, met "all demands of both reason and intuition."[37]

Even today, Westerners at the Dera come less as pilgrims than as students enrolled in an intensive course in Radhasoami theory and practice. On many evenings Charan Singh holds question-and-answer sessions solely for his Western guests. New initiates are encouraged to be serious in their study of Radhasoami theology, to "enter the laboratory of the masters" and "sit down before the facts, as a little child, and enquire of them."[38] John Leeming, a scientist from Arizona, claimed in his introduction to an abridge version of the Radhasoami textbook, *Philosophy of the Masters*, that its contents constitute "the key to the laboratory of mind and spirit," and are "no less scientific that the introduction of new tools and references given the scholar as he progresses from general science to physics."[39]

Those Westerners in Radhasoami trained in the physical sciences include doctors, dentists, and chiropractors. The general level of academic attainment among American satsangis in Johnson's time was sufficiently high that he could enumerate the college professors among his colleagues in the Great Master's circle. There continue to be a large number of scientists and academics among the foreign satsangis of the Beas, Ruhani, and Sawan-Kirpal branches, including professors at Claremont, Harvard, Hawaii, Rhode Island, Texas, California State University at San Diego, and Lancaster in England. Johnson's other profession, that of a clergyman, is also represented among present-day satsangis. Roland deVries, the current representative of Beas in America, was formerly a Presbyterian minister, and several missionaries to India became themselves converts to Radhasoami. It would seem that those who have some knowledge about Western science and religion are among the most skeptical of their claims to truth, finding replacements for them in Radhasoami's religious science.

Radhasoami knowledge is seen as more than a bridge between religion and science: it fulfills both. "Most religions are built on the experience or 'revelations' of some bygone teacher," John Leeming explained, stating that, unlike Radhasoami, these older religions "offer no scientific way for us to advance in our understanding."[40] Leeming feels that Radhasoami unifies these seemingly irreconcilable approaches to life, and offers an alternative to the "two-culture" dilemma of modern civilization. Paul Brunton began his search in "secret India" determined that it would be scientific:

> I searched through a welter of crass superstitions, incredible impostures and ancient pretensions for those things which are true, which will stand the acid test of thorough investigation. I flatter myself that I could never have done this did I not contain within my complex nature the two elements of scientific skepticism and spiritual sensitivity, elements which usually range themselves in sharp conflict and flagrant opposition.[41]

What Brunton found that so impressed him were forms of spirituality that seemed to be based on knowledge similar — or even superior — to modern science. In a similar vein, Julian Johnson claimed that "religions, or spirituality, as taught and practiced by the Masters...is a free and exact science," because it is "subject to the same analysis and demonstration as any other science." Since Radhasoami relates to "laws of Nature," it has developed methods "as exact, and its results as uniform as in any science known."[42]

This way of thinking betrays a great deal of faith not only in Radhasoami but also in science: it implies that scientific investigation is the major means of authenticating what is true. But there are other moments in which Johnson expresses a certain fatigue with Western rationality, suggesting that Radhasoami's truth is beyond science's grasp. Johnson claimed to have been led astray by science and "modern achievements" in his youth, finding the wisdom of his master far superior.[43] Katherine Wason concurred, saying that Radhasoami ideas came from a "higher consciousness."[44]

This notion that beyond the more accessible, scientific teachings of Radhasoami is a more rarified truth might explain why there is an air of secrecy about some aspects of Radhasoami teachings and practices. One of the first descriptions of Radhasoami by an outsider, a Christian missionary in India, called it "a semi-secret sect."[45] Some say the reference to Radhasoami teachings as the "secret of secrets" suggests only the intimacy of the truth that is conveyed from master to disciple, not its exclusivity.[46] Even so, the Soamibagh branch has stamped on a manual of meditation practices that "under no circumstances" is it to be shown "to anyone who is not a follower of the Radhasoami Faith."[47] Similarly, the Beas and Ruhani Satsang branches keep their initiatory mantra a secret: they forbid satsangis' divulging the words whispered to them at the time of their initiation.

The fact that a certain amount of secrecy surrounds Radhasoami teachings and practices means that the Radhasoami knowledge is special, something meant only for the few. "It is an amazing thing," a woman from South Africa remarked to me at the Beas Dera, "to think that this treasury of information is held in the hands of such a small circle as ours. What the world wouldn't give to know what we know!"[48] Knowing what others do not know is indeed an exciting aspect of faith, and this feeling of rare privilege is enhanced, for Western satsangis, by the fact that the truths are to be found in an unusual and distant land. The "strangeness" of India that impressed Johnson at Beas has impressed many seekers of India's spirituality, including Paul Brunton at Dayalbagh. "I feel quite humbly," he wrote, "that I have been privileged to see a remote aspect of India seldom seen and less understood by ordinary travelers."[49] By identifying with Radhasoami's esoteric knowledge the Westerner forms a personal link with an enduring culture, a fact that is not only aesthetically pleasing but personally reassuring, for an esoteric knowledge ultimately transcends time itself. In the final section of *With a Great Master in India*, Johnson creates a parable of an elegant dance in which the dancers, representing all of humanity, fritter away their time in the illusion that the dance will continue forever; meanwhile a fortunate few listen to the exhortations they hear from a bearded man who urges them to escape from their sham while time remains.[50]

Knowing Someone Important

Those who do escape and embrace the Radhasoami faith, are linked not only to a special knowledge but also to a special person. For Westerners, such reverence requires a leap of faith. It is not surprising, then, that the words of Western satsangis often take on a biblical luster when they ponder the master's glories. "I sit at the feet of one whose powers are not limited by time or space," Julian Johnson wrote, "whose very glance has in it the power of death or of eternal life; aye, whose commands even the waves of this ancient sea must obey."[51] Another Western satsangi, a Black American from Chicago whose three brothers are all Baptist preachers, said that his interest in Radhasoami stemmed from his interest in the Bible: "I had always wanted to live in biblical times," he said.[52]

Gandhi's Christ-like attraction for Westerners owed much to his strange combination of familiar and foreign features,[53] and in describing their attraction to the Radhasoami faith, some Westerners have also dwelled on the masters' distinctive physical characteristics. Brunton, for example, described Anand Swarup as "an alert American mind encased in a brown Hindu body."[54] Johnson, who had a strong antisemitic streak, was also fascinated by his master's skin color: he claimed he belonged to "the Aryan, the pure white race," and that the color of his skin "is about that of the average American with a good coat of sun tan."[55] Although today there is much less emphasis on the peculiarity of Indian features, still the marvelous beards and turbans of the Beas and Ruhani Satsang masters have a striking appeal to the Western eye.

Even more impressive, of course, is the conviction that behind this physical appearance is an accessible form of God. At the end of the evening sessions that Master Charan Singh holds for his Western followers on the second floor of the Beas guest house, all rise and hold their hands prayerfully as he walks down the aisle and down the stairs. As soon as he leaves the hall, the crowd scrambles to the balcony for one last glimpse of his presence as he crosses through the garden and returns to his own residence. On one of these occasions an American man softly said, "there goes God."[56]

For people with Christian and Jewish backgrounds, he must be God, or at least have sufficient spiritual weight to bear the role played by scripture and revelation in biblical traditions. One American satsangi from Georgia said that he was attracted to Radhasoami because Christian religious teachers lacked a voice of authority and could not give him "straight answers," whereas the

Beas masters could.[57] Others are inspired by what appears to them to be the manifestation of Christ in the present day.[58] For those Western satsangis who are more secular, the master's teachings replace older forms of philosophy, explaining "the origin and purpose of life."[59]

In addition to the religious and philosophical reasons for thinking of the master in ultimate terms, there are psychological motivations. Sudhir Kakar points out that the exaggeration of the master's qualities goes hand in hand with the magnification of one's own pride in knowing such a person. These "psychological mechanisms of idealization and identification," he says, "give a newfound centrality to the self."[60] According to Kakar, "the uncritical eulogizing of the guru" is linked to "the disciple's desparate need for the idealization and identification with the Master."[61] By enlarging their master's role in the cosmos, some disciples may be magnifying their own, and they see in their master's features the ideal characteristics they hope for in themselves.

An American devotee, Katherine Wason, describes her initial attraction to the "kind, beautiful face" of the master as one characterized by power and love.[62] Julian Johnson also used the language of love in describing his master, whose heart "holds only loving kindness to all"[63] and whose voice "is vibrant with love."[64] These words signal what is perhaps the most personal motivation drawing Johnson and other devotees into the master-disciple relationship, the longing for an intimate union. This desire often finds expression in poetry, as in this bit of doggerel composed on the occasion of Charan Singh's visit to the United States:

> It's Master's love that brings Him here —
> to help American bloom,
> To purify the atmosphere
> as Love, for love, makes room.[65]

A Network of Spiritual Associates

When Julian Johnson first arrived at the Beas Dera in 1932 he was impressed with the conviviality of its residents: "Their love appears to know no bounds. They treat me as if I were truly their own brother returning from abroad."[66] His description of the Radhasoami community as "a real brotherhood" is echoed by many who come to the Dera and regard it as an Indian home.

Still, satsangis from America and Europe are much more ambivalent about home and family than their Indian counterparts, and this ambivalence is displayed in their attitude toward the Radhasoami fellowship. In fact, many of them disdain what they regard as the "country club" atmosphere of the Dera. They regard the relationship with the master as the only one that has any significance, and avoid Radhasoami events. One prominent American satsangi refuses to attend bhandaras at Beas because they are too frenetic. "I wouldn't go across the street to attend one of them," he says.[67] When someone as individualistic as Julian Johnson speaks of the Radhasoami "brotherhood," therefore, he is more likely to be embracing a set of associates than a set of relatives. Neither he nor other Westerners of his generation has had any interest in creating separate residential communities modeled after Beas or Dayalbagh.

Most Westerners feel that the only purpose of a separate colony is to live near the master, and that is rarely allowed. Long-term residence by Westerners is discourage at most Radhasoami centers. The leaders of those centers do not want their communities to be swamped by foreigners, and the Indian government's restriction on extending visas to foreigners for lengthy periods of time is an obstacle as well.[68] Only a few Westerners have lived at Radhasoami centers more than a year or so. Among the better known Western satsangis in residence in India in recent years have been the British novelist, Kate Christy, and her musician husband, Malcolm Tillis, at Sawan Ashram; Paul Hogguel from the Netherlands, who lives near his master, A. P. Mathur, at Peepalmandi in Agra; and Dr. Randolph Stone, the Chicago chiropractor who created "polarity therapy," who was allowed to set up a house with his niece, Louise Hilger, at Beas.

For Western satsangis, the Radhasoami fellowship provides a network of spiritual comrades throughout the world. When Kate Christy and Malcolm Tillis travel abroad they move from one set of satsangi contacts to another, just as Christian missionaries used to do when they traveled from place to place in foreign lands. Even satsangis who do not travel can come in contact with a far-flung fellowship at Radhasoami rallies and through newsletters and correspondence. The Radhasoami networks in each country have their own activities, and local leaders achieve a certain prominence within them. In the Beas branch, for instance, the four representatives in the United States who have power to administer proxy initiation also superintend the local centers. At present these are H. F. Weekley of Washington, D.C., who is in charge of the Eastern seaboard; Roy Ricks of Chicago and Gene Ivash, a professor of physics at the University of Texas, who have jurisdiction over two sections of the Midwest; and Roland deVries, the former Presbyterian minister who is in many ways dean of the American representatives, who supervises the Western regions from his home near Nevada City, California.[69]

Such relationships remind one less of a kinship network than a corporate one, but those who take on the roles often profess a great disdain for the spiritual emptiness of most modern organizations, especially those of religion. Julian Johnson was almost vitriolic on the point: "As soon as any religion is settled upon a people in organized form," he claimed, "religion becomes a dead letter, and the priests grow fat."[70] Westerners who despise religious community and those who yearn for it can both be satisfied by the Radhasoami style of organization, in part because it contains an inner contradiction: it is both communal and individualistic. It is similar in this way to a modern bureaucracy, which also contains this tension between individualism and social compliance. Some Western members of Radhasoami have reconciled the contradiction, however, by taking an individualistic approach to their home cultures but adopting a more communal attitude toward their participation in the transnational community of Radhasoami.

The double identities of such satsangis — an allegiance to the cultures of their birth and to the transnational culture of Radhasoami — is the outward manifestation of an even more important dichotomy in their lives: a split between two levels of reality. At one level is the world perceived by the senses and through conventional reason, and at another the worlds beyond. The Radhasoami setting permits the soul to begin what Johnson calls "its triumphal journey to distant worlds."[71] It therefore offers more than what Weber called the "instrumental rationality" of modern bureaucratic, industrialized society. It offers an instrumental rationality of its own, with suprarational dimensions; and it offers a universal message framed in distinctly Indian terms. The Radhasoami fellowship is geographically centered and wears India's distinctive cultural garb, but what it ultimately offers to searching, modern Westerners is much more profound than a change of cultural scene.

Social Transformation of a Global Society

The global fellowships of Radhasoami from one point of view may be seen as spiritual meritocracies: places where, the master willing, people are healed and find salvation on account of their own individual efforts and their own personal relationships with the master. Modern Indian followers find in Radhasoami's individualism an antidote to what is sometimes perceived as the oppressively communal character of traditional Hindu social organization. Modern Western followers, however, are attracted to what is often lacking in urban European and American societies, except occasionally in religious gatherings — a sense of community. In their critique of American individualism, Robert Bellah and the other authors of *Habits of the Heart* find churches and other religious associations to be among the few vestiges of community in a lonely and alienating society, and even they are often permeated with the acquisitive values of the culture around them.[72] In an earlier work, Bellah argued that those who joined new religious movements in the 1960s and 70s did so in part as a "repudiation of the tradition of utilitarian individualism."[73]

Those who come to the Radhasoami communities expecting a similar repudiation are not wholly disappointed, for the utilitarian aspects of individualism in the Radhasoami communities are softened by bhakti and blended with communalism. This mix is sufficiently interesting to lead observers such as Sudhir Kakar to regard it as one of the Radhasoami communities' more remarkable accomplishments,[74] for it defies the common observation that the social world is divided between communities (such as families and ethnic groups) that cohere because of emotional ties, and organizations (typically of an economic or political character) that are held together because they serve to satisfy a plurality of individualistic goals.[75] Radhasoami is both, and would seem to provide the prototype for a new social option.

What holds these two seemingly opposing elements together is a form of leadership that is peculiarly premodern: personal authority. An authority with whom one has an intimate relationship — a father, a spiritual master, or a divinely granted king — is capable of doing much more than adjudicate between the competing interests of individuals: he or she can awaken conscience, command sacrifice, and engender loyalty and love. In premodern societies the institution of kingship served both individual interests and the cause of communal identity by providing a single figure to whom a large group of people could relate, and through the monarch be in touch with one another as well. What made kingship work was a relationship of trust that, as Reinhard Bendix has observed, was virtually always buttressed by religion.[76] The democracies that replaced kingships relied upon a different sort of trust for their authority: a trust in reason, due process, and the good will of civic-minded citizens. It is not surprising that when trust in these elements has been eroded, people embrace an earlier form of public authority, such as the spiritual kings of Radhasoami. The personal relationships that Radhasoami followers form with their leaders allow them to restore their faith in social organization, at least in the protected settings of the Radhasoami communities.

Harbinger of a New Kind of Global Religion

The characteristics of Radhasoami thought — an appropriation of a truth greater than science, a therapeutic approach to the self, and the reestablishment of personal authority in the social realm — appeal to those who for various reasons have tired of the modern world, but are unsatisfied with what the more traditional forms of faith offer as alternatives. They constitute a form of faith that is modern in a distinctively Indian way, for it is hard to imagine another culture that would have as easy access to notions of the truth as an active agent, the self as a fluid, malleable entity, and authority as an element of intimate relationships. Yet despite the fact that Radhasoami's modernity is distinctively Indian, there are aspects of the Radhasoami tradition that are similar to modern forms of religion throughout the world.

Among these global forms of religious modernity are the use of high technology, sophisticated organization and effective publications. Perhaps more important, however, are several modern characteristics of the religious message itself. One of these is the univerality of the Radhasoami message and its claim to transcend the particularities of any one cultural tradition. Like the new religious movements in Japan, the Radhasoami teachings relate to dilemmas that are of obvious importance to busy urban lives everywhere: the loss of a sense of personal authority, the insecurity that besets individuals loosed from traditional social moorings, the need for a moral and personal integrity grounded in rational principles, and the desire for a community that conduces to the fulfillment of each individual's potential.

A second feature that the Radhasoami message shares with other forms of modern religion is its orientation toward the future. Like the charismatic preachers of Christian revivalism, the authoritative voice in Radhasoami's tradition come from masters who live in the present but speak on behalf of an even greater authority whose nature is yet to be revealed. The word *Radhasoami* designates a divine terminus of time: the final stage or region towards which all souls seek to travel, the arena in which all existence will finally be fulfilled. What may appear at first to be a Radhasoami form of millenarianism is different from many Christian futurist movements, however, in that it conceives of the future as a process of evolving transformation. Since it does not expect a radical break in human history, it is more like some forms of Christian socialism in attempting to form ideal societies even in the present day.

The integrative logic of Radhasoami is the third feature that it shares with other forms of modern religion. This integrative way of thinking contrasts sharply with the fragmentation of knowledge that has characterized the modern age. Jurgen Habermas, echoing Max Weber, has said that what he calls the "enlightenment project" of modern thinkers was intent on separating traditional religious thought into three distinctive modes of reasoning: cognitive-instrumental, moral-practical, and aesthetic-expressive.[77] In reuniting these ways of thinking, Radhasoami and movements like it may be considered not just modern but postmodern, for in repudiating the schisms characteristic of modern thought they revive important aspects of premodern thinking: the tendency to regard experience and objective reality as related, as in the Sanskrit philosophical systems, or to see all knowledge as part of a single, coherent framework, as in medieval Christian theology.

In both these premodern views, as in Radhasoami's, personal experience was central.[78] In academic circles this latter notion has been discredited until recently, when a few scholars have revived the idea that all knowledge is in some sense "personal knowledge," to use Michael Polanyi's words, or "local knowledge," as Clifford Geertz has said — knowledge informed by the way that human subjects perceive what they know.[79] The religious point of view has often been in disagreement with the Enlightenment "project," and although the Reformation was compatible with the Enlightenment in its humanistic attitudes and its detachment from traditional authority, in another sense the Reformation served as its counterpoint. It provided an antidote to the Enlightenment's harsh objectivity by offering a religious view of truth that was personal, intimate and integrative. Modern religious movements throughout the world rejuvenate this Reformation spirit, although their own religious past, rather than Europe's. In India this is not difficult to do, for an affirmation of personal knowledge similar to the Reformation's occurred in medieval India in the radical bhakti movement associated with the medieval sants. This Reformation is continued by Radhasoami in the present day.

Many of those who defend the old religious traditions see these new forms of religion as a threat. In India, they see the signs of Radhasoami's vitality — the religious socialism of Dayalbagh, the marble cathedral at Soamibagh, the massive crowds at Beas, the visionary plans of Ruhani Satsang — and fear that the successes of the Radhasoami tradition will spell the end of popular forms of Hinduism and Sikhism. Writing in 1908, Hervey deWitt Griswold despaired that Radhasoami was a "disintegrating and dissolving force" in Indian culture, "continually gnawing at the vitals of old

Hinduism."[80] More recently, however, L. A. Babb has placed Radhasoami alongside two other new communities in the Hindu tradition, the Brahmakumaris and the followers of Sathya Sai Baba, and concluded that rather than gnawing at Hinduism's vitals, these modern forms of religion have helped the tradition to survive. They allow Hinduism to adapt to new conditions in some ways while retaining other, more essential aspects of the Hindu spirit.[81] Raymond Williams makes much the same argument in describing the Swami Narayanan movement in Gujarat as a "new face of Hinduism."[82]

It is obviously true that Radhasoami is in a certain sense a new expression of Hinduism, but it is also a genuinely new religion, a modern religion, a tradition in the making. Its central notions — that truth and authority can be embodied in a person, that transformation of the self occurs through the purification of perception and energy, that love and community can be experienced in dispersion, that social service is based on personal commitment, and that time and place have ultimate centers — each contain features of modern and in some cases even postmodern religion. As such, the Radhasoami faith may be a harbinger of the religion of the future, not only in India but elsewhere in the world where modernity is received with a certain amount of suspicion. Many in these areas now seek what the adherents of the Radhasoami communities have found: a global pattern of religious expression and experience that allows them to identify with their cultural past without accepting what they see as its superstitious and gaudy excesses, and to embrace modern ways of living without becoming captive to what they perceive as alienating forms of society and sterile forms of thought.

GLOSSARY

Ācārya   religious teacher; spiritual preceptor; heads of Swaminarayan dioceses of Amdavad and Vadtal.

Advaita   "non-dualism;" school of vedanta founded by the teacher Sankara in the eight century C.E.

Āgama   ritual and sectarian texts different from the Vedic and Puranic tradition.

Akṣara   the abode of the supreme person; an eternal state; thought to have an impersonal form as a state of being and a personal form as an abode of god.

Akṣardhām   the heavenly abode of state of the supreme person; equivalent to aksara in the impersonal form.

Āḷvār   "one who is immersed," title given by Srivaisnavas to one of twelve poet-saints of the 7th-10th centuries C.E whose 4000 Tamil verses they acknowledge as the vernacular veda.

Āmnāya Maṭhas   four mathas, one in each of the four cardinal directions of the Indian subcontinent, said to have been established by Adi Sankara who installed his four principal disciples as their heads: Sringeri (south), Dwaraka (west), Badrinath (north), Puri (east).

Anavatāra   manifestation of a deity in an image.

Andal Āṇṭāl   a female poet-saint who lived around the eighth or ninth century C.E. and who composed hymns in honor of Visnu; considered to be a paradigmatic devotee by Srivaishnavas, she is enshrined in almost all Srivaishnava temples.

Ārati   ritual of waving a lamp in front of the deity.

Arcā   image of the deity; when consecrated, the image is believed to be transformed so that the deity is really present both spiritually and materially within the image.

Asat   non-being.

Āśrama   a religious community; residence of a religious community.

Atmaniṣṭha   spiritual realization.

Avatāra   descent form of the god (often Visnu) in an earthy form such as Krishna or Rama.

Avidyā   ignorance.

Ayurveda   a traditional form of Hindu medical diagnosis and treatment which is still employed in India and, among some Asian Indian immigrants, in the United States.

Bāl Māndal   childrens' association.

Bālak   male child.

Bālikā   female child.

Bhajan   devotional song in communal context.

Bhakti   the path of devotion as a religious discipline; the development of love as a means of spiritual liberation. A bhakta is one devoted to the Lord.

Brahmacārī   a celibate student; often used for the vow or state of celibacy.

Caturmāsya   the four-month period of retreat during the rainy season when sannyasis of some orders refrain from wandering/travel.

Darśana   seeing; the sight of the deity or the blessing received from a holy person or a deity.

Dharma   moral and/or social duty and law; divine and/or eternal law.

Dīkṣā   the initiation of a disciple by his guru; initiation into a sampradaya.

Dīpārādana   waving lighted oil lamps in front of an object being worshiped.

Divya Deśa   "A sacred place." Refers to any one of 108 sacred temples sung about by the alvars.

Eka-Daṇḍa   the tall walking stick of the guru as sign of authority and jurisdiction.

Gādī   the seat of a religious leader; headquarters of an acarya. See pitha.

Ganeśa   "lord of a group of demi-gods;" name of Siva's son. He is worshiped before undertaking any important task and is considered to be a remover of obstacles.

Garuḍa   name of the "king of birds," the sacred bird on whom Visnu rides.

Gopuram   the main entrance into a temple complex, usually four entrances from the four directions, one of which is major.

Gotra   the clan name used by high caste Hindus to indicate blood kinship.

Gurukula   a "guru school," a religious school under a guru's supervision which intends to transmits the tradition, especially religious tradition, to young people.

Guruparampara   a lineage of teachers, each of whom after the first is a disciple in the lineage immediately prior to him; a list of the lineage of one's teachers.

Homa   ritual of sacrificial offering in which various items are placed in the fire.

Indriyas   sense-organs.

Ista-Devata   one's personal deity to whom worship is directed.

Jadadguru   a world teacher, one with universality to teach a broad spectrum of people; major gurus of the various sampradaya.

Japa   repetitive prayer, sometimes on beads, reciting the names of god.

Jati   literally "birth"; often translated "caste"; the hereditary social group within which most Hindus seek their marriage partners; each such group typically has a more or less definite ascribed rank within a social hierarchy of such intramarriage groups.

Jayanti   "birthday," the annual celebration of the birthday of some Hindu deities such as Krishna (usually in August).

Jiva   the essential self.

Jñana   knowledge; the path of knowledge as a religious discipline; the search for wisdom that brings spiritual liberation.

Kalasa   a metal ritual pot.

Krishna Krsna   the ninth incarnation of Visnu.

Kumbabhiseka   ritual of dedication of a temple.

Lakshmi Laksmi   "fortune, prosperity," name of Sri, the consort of Visnu.

Lingam   the phallic symbol representing the divine energy of Siva.

Mahila   woman.

Mala   a rosary, sometimes worn around the neck.

Mantra   a revered word or syllable recited for its effect in meditation, sometimes given esoteric meaning.

Matha Mutt   the complex of buildings housing an ascetic or group of ascetics with their disciples.

Mathadipatis   heads of monastic foundations (mathas).

Murti   "image," embodiment, manifestation, appearance of a deity in the form of an icon used in worship.

Nammalvar   the most important alvar; author of four poems, including the Tiruvaymoli.

Nārayāṇa one of the most frequently used names of Visnu.

Pāduka the guru's sandals.

Paramparā a line of spiritual descent.

Pāthaśālā a school in which the Vedas are taught, principally for Brahmin boys.

Paṭṭābhiṣeka a coronation, involving sprinkling (abhiseka) with consecrated liquids, especially water.

Pīṭha a "seat," here the seat of the guru and of a deity; also called a gadi.

Pradakśina circumambulation in a clockwise direction, keeping the object being circumabulated on the right.

Prākāram a temple courtyard, sometimes covered so as to form a corridor or hallway.

Prasāda "favor, clarity," refers to the symbols of favor distributed by a priest or religious teacher; food from that offered to the deity or to the guru.

Pūjā worship; ritual and prayer offered in home, temple, or matha.

Pundit Paṇḍita teacher of the oral tradition who transmits the Veda and other religious and secular literature.

Purohit a Brahmin priest, especially one who performs domestic rituals, as contrasted with the rituals performed for the deity in a temple.

Puruṣārtha the four letigimate goals of life (dharma, artha, kama, moksha).

Rāma seventh incarnation of Visnu.

Rāmānuja eleventh century theologian, considered to be the most important teacher of the Srivaisnava community; author of commentaries on the Brahma Sutra, the Bhagavad Gita, three hymns and several other works.

Sabhā society; gathering; meeting.

Sādhana the undertaking of a particular religious practice in the context of a spiritual path.

Sādhu a holy man; ascetic; world-renouncer.

Sahasrakalasabhiṣekam libations with 1008 pots of water to sanctify a site.

Śāligrāma a symbol of Visnu, an image of a disc on a black stone.

Samādhi the grave of a holy person or location of the cremation of a famous person; a meditative trance in which the highest truth is experienced.

Sampradāya a teaching lineage passing from generation to generation through transmission by teachers.

Samsāra the cycle of birth and death; transmigration.

Sanātana Dharma "the eternal dharma," the term for the Hindu tradition; used of "ecumenical Hinduism" in the United States.

Sangha an assembly of Buddhist monks, probably the oldest such monastic institution.

Sankara a ninth century (788-820) theologian who taught the philosophy of advaita (non-dualism); he is said to have established monastic orders in various parts of India; those teachers (acaryas) in this lineage are Sankaracaryas; also called "Adi Sankara" — original Sankara.

Sanmata six alternate ways of worship, attributed to Sankara, corresponding to Siva, Visnu, Sakti, Surya, Ganpati, Kumara.

Sannyāsī an ascetic or renunciant following the fourth stage of Hindu life.

Sanstha fellowship; a religious community; a Hindu sect.

Sarada a form of the goddess Sarasvati, the goddess of learning.

Śāstra revered books expanding the sutra literature; the Dharma Sastras are the law books.

Satsang a religious gathering or group; "satsangi" is a member of the group.

Śeṣa name of the serpent on whom Visnu reclines in the ocean of milk; the paradigmatic servant.

Sevā service; volunteer service to the religious group or to the guru.

Shamiana a temporary cloth-covered canopy, resembles a tent.

Śisya a student or disciple of a master teacher or guru.

Śiva "pure, auspicious," one of the main gods worshiped by Hindus.

Śrī a term connoting auspiciousness; a name of Visnu's consort; a title used much like the English "Mr."

Śrīcakra in yoga; a cakra is one of the seven centers (literally, wheels) of psycho-physical energy within the body; in establishing a temple or seat of learning as a sacred center is to consecrate it as a meeting ground of human and divine energies.

Śrīvaiṣṇava a community that worships Visnu and his consort Sri; accepts the Tamil songs of the alvars as equivalent to the vedas and reveres Ramanuja as its most important acarya.

Śruti heard; the sacred Vedas heard by the ancients and transmitted through the generations; the most sacred religious texts; to be distinguished from smrti.

Swami   a holy man, a god, literally "lord."

Tampiran   monk.

Tīrtha   a ford or crossing of a river; a sacred place, typically on a river or body of water, where it is claimed pilgrims can more easily cross over to liberation.

Tiruvāymoḷi   "sacred word of mouth, sacred veda;" a poem of Nammalvar considered as revealed literature by the Srivaisnavas.

Tiru Vēṅkaṭam   name of a hill in the modern state of Andhra Pradesh, South India; one of the most important pilgrimage centers for Hindus today; mentioned in Tamil literature going back to at least the fifth century C.E.

Triloka   the cosmos.

Upanāyana   the initiation ceremony for twice-born boys in which they are invested with the sacred thread, the sacred thread that gives this book its title.

Utsavamūrti   "festival icon;" a movable metal image carried through the streets in processions during festivals.

Vairāgya   detachment.

Vaisnava   "relating to Visnu;" a devotee of Visnu.

Vedānta   "end of the Vedas;" school of theological interpretation principally based on the Upanisads, the Bhagavad Gita and the Brahma Sutra.

Vēṅkateśwara   Lord of the Venkata Hill; name by which Visnu is known in his manifestation in Tiru Venkatam or the Venkata Hill.

Vidyāpīṭh   a seat of learning, a major center of religious education.

Viśeṣa Vartamān   the five elements of the Swaminarayan code of conduct (non-covetousness, selflessness, abandonment of indulgence in the sense of taste, desirelessness, and non-attachment).

Visnu   "all pervasive;" the most important deity for the Srivaisnava community.

Yuktī   young female.

Yuvuk   young male.

Notes

Chapter 1 Handing Down and Reaching Across: Stability and Movement in Indian Religious Traditions

John B. Carman

1. Basavanna, *vacana* 820, as translated by A.K. Ramanujan, *Speaking of Siva* (Baltimore: Penguin Books, 1973), p.19.
2. *Ibid*, pp. 19-22.

Chapter 2 Winning Souls for Siva: Arumuga Navalar's Transmission of the Saiva Religion

Dennis Hudson

1. *Hinduism Today* was founded by His Holiness, Gurudeva, Sivaya Subramuniyaswami on January 5, 1979 in Hanamaulu, Hawaii, for these stated purposes: "1. To foster *Hindu solidarity* as a 'unity in diversity' among all sects and lineages; 2. To inform and inspire Hindus worldwide and people interested in Hinduism; 3. To dispel myths, illusions and misinformation about Hinduism; 4. To protect, preserve and promote the Hindu religion, especially the Saiva Dharma; 5. To nurture a truly spiritual Hindu renaissance." (*Hinduism Today*: International edition [October, 1990], 2). It is published monthly by Himalayan Academy, 1819 Second Street, Concord, California USA 94519.

Sivaya Subramuniyaswami (b. 1927) through his guru Siva Yogaswami (1872-1964) descends within a siddha (*Natha*) lineage within Saiva Siddhanta known in Jaffna as the Siva Yogaswami Guru Paramparai of the Natha Sampradaya. Its first *sat guru* was a risi from the Himalayas who initiated Kadaitswami who traveled to Sri Lanka. Kadaitswami initiated Chellappaswami, who initiated Siva Yogaswami in 1910. Siva Yogaswami initiated Subramuniya at his Columbuthurai ashram in 1949. Sivaya Subramuniya Swami began actively teaching in the West in 1957.

This siddha or natha lineage differs from the Meykantatevar theology that Arumuga Navalar followed by giving prominent place to Tirumular's "Sri Mantra" (*Tirumantiram*) interpreted according to a theology of "monistic theism" that denies the ultimate "pluralism" of eternally distinct Lord (*pati*), soul (*pasu*), and matter (*pasa*). See *Saiva Dharma: A Catechism for Saivite Hinduism: Lesson I*, 8th ed. (Kapaa, Hawaii: Saiva Siddhanta Church, 1981), 2 and 23; and "Insight: A Four-Page Section on Monistic Theism, the Non-Dual Philosophy of Saivism," a special reprint from *The New Saivite World*, Autumn, 1984.

2. See "Arumuga Navalar and Hindu Renaissance Among the Tamils," *Vernacular Religious Polemics and Social Change in 19th Century India*, ed. Kenneth W. Jones

(Albany, New York: SUNY Press, forthcoming); and "Tamil Hindu Responses to Protestants: Among Nineteenth Century Literati in Jaffna and Tinnevelly," *Indigenous Responses to Western Christianity*, ed. Steven Kaplan (forthcoming). I follow here the detailed outline of the chronology of his work, "Navalar valkkaiyil mukkiya campavankal," in *Arumuka Navalar Nurrantu Malar, 1979* (Columbo: Sri La Sri Arumuka Navalar Capai, 1979), 299-304. My continuing study of Arumuga Navalar is based on research conducted as a Fulbright fellow in Madras, 1983-1984, and has been supported generously by Smith College.

3. Muttucumaraswamy, *Sri La Sri Arumuga Navalar, The Champion Reformer of the Hindus (1822-1879): A Biographical Study*, new rev. ed. (Colombo, 1965), 49-51.

4. The *Pala Patam* was originally three books written in 1850 and later made into four (*Pala Patam* 1-4 [Madras: Sri Arumukanavalar Vittiyanupalana Accakam, 1: 1978, 2, 1977; 3, 1955; 4, 1969]).

5. Arumukanavalar, *Civalayataricanaviti*, 5th ed. (Madras, 1881). I have translated and discussed it for the forthcoming *Sourcebook on Asian Religions*, ed. Donald L. Lopez, Jr. (Princeton University Press).

6. I have used a copy of the 1852 original (without title page) in the U. V. Swaminatha Aiyar Library (No. 8233a) and a copy of the 15th printing of 1933 in the Tirumaraimalai Adigal Library, *Tiruttontar Periyapuranam... Arumukanavalaravarkalal kattiya rupamakac ceytu* (Madras: Vittiyanupalanayantiracalai, Ankiraca Varusam, Pankuni Macam [1933]). B. Ratna Nayakar Sons reprinted it in 1967 with slight modifications and with drawings, but no indication that it was rendered into prose by Arumuga Navalar as *Periyapuranam vacana kaviyam* (Madras: B. Irattinanayakar Sons, Tirumakalvilacam Press, no date).

7. *Caivatusanaparikaram* (Madras, 1956). I have discussed it in "A Hindu Response to the Written Torah," *Between Jerusalem and Benares: Comparative Studies in Judaism and Hinduism*, ed. Hananya Goodman (Albany, New York: SUNY Press, forthcoming).

8. It appeared in two versions: *Caivavinavitai*, Book One, 16th ed. (Madras, 1919), consists of 135 questions and answers; Book Two, 16th ed. (Madras, 1968), consists of 418.

9. T. P. Meenakshisundaram Pillai noted in "Ceylon Tamil Poets" (in V. Muttucumaraswamy's translation), "On the one hand there was prose known as High Senthamil, and on the other hand Kochchai-Thamil — an ascent and a descent — (a crest and trough). Navalar levelled these, applied plaster to it; he made it a shining white wall. Yes! In this levelling process, many beautiful paintings on the peaks have disappeared. In his prose style, we cannot discern 'prose paintings' as we glimpse the anger of Sivagnana Yogi. In Navalar's prose, it creeps with obedience gently. In Navalar's prose style, there is nothing that betrays any emotion. From the first to the last, there is one style...Therefore Arumuga Navalar was the father of modern Tamil prose, and laid its foundations firm and secure" (Muttucumaraswamy, *Sri La Sri Arumuga Navalar*, 28-29).

10. As stated by the *Oxford English Dictionary*, religion is "a state of life bound by monastic vows" or "action or conduct indicating a belief in, reverence for, and desire to please, a divine ruling power; the exercise or practice of rites or

observances implying this." See *The Compact Edition of the Oxford English Dictionary* II (Oxford University Press, 1971), "religion," definitions 1 and 3, page 2481.

If we take that statement out of the monastic context it fits Navalar's use of the Sanskrit word "samayam" nicely. According to Monier-Williams in *A Sanskrit-English Dictionary*, "samaya" means a "coming to a mutual understanding, agreement, compact, convenant, treaty, contract, arrangement..." It also means a "convention...established custom, law, rule, practice, observance," or sometimes means an "order, direction, precept, doctrine..." See Monier Monier-Williams, *A Sanskrit-English Dictionary* (Oxford, 1964 [1899]), 1164a.

11. Thirty-three crores; a "crore" is ten million. See "Caiva camayam" reprinted in *Arumukanavalar Pirapantattirattu* I, ed. by T. Kailacapillai, 3rd ed. (Madras, 1954), 86-88.

12. *Kolaimaruttal: Tirutturaiyur Cantalinkasuvamikal arulcceytatu. Itu Tirupporur Citamparacuvamikal arulcceyta uraiyutan* (Madras, 1924).

13. He named Katan, Matan, Cutalaimatan, Katteri, Maturaiviran, Karuppan, Patinettampatik-karuppan, Cankilik-karuppan, Periyatampiran, Muni, Kannaki, and Peycci.

14. For example, the contemporary Bengali Theravada teacher, Anagarika Munindra, who is associated with the sadhana of the Burmese teacher, Goenka.

15. See the first page of "Caiva virotam" in *Pirapantattiruttu* I, 17-24.

16. The following discussion of Ramalingaswamy is based on M. Po. Civajnanam, *Vallalar kanta orumaippatu*, 5th ed. (Madras, 1974); S. P. Annamalai, *The Life and Teachings of Saint Ramalingar* (Bombay, 1973); S. R. V. Arasu, *Voice of Vallalar (A Modern Critique on the Tiruarutpa)* (Madras, 1974); and "Iramalinkacuvamikal carittiraccurukkam," in *Iramalinkacuvamikal arulcceyta Tiruvarutpat Tirumurai* (Madras, 1928), 1-22. For Cidambaram Diksitars as followers of Sankara, see Arumuka Navalar, *Pirapantattirattu* I, 105.

17. See Dennis Hudson, "Violent and Fanatical Devotion Among the Nayanars: A study in the *Periya Puranam* of Cekkilar," in *Criminal Gods and Demon Devotees*, ed. Alf Hiltebeitel (Albany, New York: SUNY, 1989), 373-404.

18. *Tiruvarutpat Tirumurai*, 6; Annamalai, *Saint Ramalingar*, 14.

19. Which, I think, now houses the Tirumaraimalai Adigal Library.

20. Arumuka Navalar, *Pirapantattirattu* I, 108-109.

21. Arumuka Navalar, *Pirpantatttirattu*, 106.

22. Arumuka Navalar, *Pirpantattirattu*, 93.

23. Annamalai, *Saint Ramalingar*, 19.

24. Civajnanam, *Vallalar*, 185.

25. Annamalai, *Saint Ramalingar*, 136-137.

26. I follow the exposition of Annamalai, *Saint Ramalingar*, 106-138.

27. Annamalai, *Saint Ramalingar*, 18; Civajnanam, *Vallalar*, 186-196. The day was of the *Uttaradarsana* in the month of Ani.

28. The following description is that of Civajnanam, *Vallalar*, 186-188.

29. Civajnanam, *Vallalar*, 188.

30. Muttucumaraswamy, *Sri La Sri*, 44.

31. Reprinted in Arumuka Navalar, *Pirpantattirattu* I, 89-121. He published under the name of Mamantur Tyagesa Mudaliyar.

32. Arumuka Navalar, *Pirapantattirattu* I, 109.

33. I have explored this transmission in "Renaissance in the Life of Saminata Aiyar, a Tamil Scholar," *Comparative Civilizations Review*, No. 7 (Fall, 1981), 54-71.

34. See Hemendra Kumar Sircar, "Books in the Indian Languages," in *Early Indian Imprints* by Katharine Smith Diehl (New York and London: The Scarecrow Press, Inc., 1964), 63-75. I have discussed the scholarly study of Tamil literature in "The Responses of Tamils to the Study by Westerners 1600-1908," in *As Others See Us: Mutual Perceptions, East and West*, ed. Bernard Lewis, Edmund Leites, Margaret Case (New York, 1985), 180-200.

35. John Murdoch, *Classified Catalogue of Tamil Printed Books with Introductory Notices (Re-printed with a number of Appendices and Supplement)*, 1865 edition reprinted and ed. by M. Shanmukham (Madras, 1968), lx-lxi.

36. *Tiru Vi. Ka. Valkkaik kurippukkal* I (Madras, 1969), 160.

37. Sri La Sri Arumuka Navalar Caivappirakaca Vittiyacalai Arakkattalai, 24, Malaikattit Teru, Citamparam — 608001. A deed of 1910 noted that the "Saiva Prakasa Vidyalaya" at Vannarpannai in Jaffna and the "Saivaprakasa Vidyalaya" at Cidambaram both belong to Arumuga Navalar and are to be considered as parts of one establishment and are to share funds when necessary, but that the head of the Trust resides in Jaffna. The leadership is to be Saiva Velala, as article one makes clear: "The Board of trustees of the Vidyalaya, should consist of members who belong to the generation of the disciples of Arumuga Navalar. They should be well-educated Vellalas, who practised the Saiva Religion devotedly." The deed is translated and discussed in V. Muttucumaraswamy, *Sri La Sri*, 94-101.

38. The following story is related in a long footnote in *Sri La Sri Nallur Arumukanavalar Carittiram* by Ke. Kanakarattina [1882] (Jaffna, 1968), 1-5.

39. For a nineteenth century Saiva Velala exposition of that status, see *Cattiya Cuttiram* 7 by Tantapani Cuvamikal (1839-1898) in *Cattiya Cuttiram and Cattiya Vacakam* (Tiruvamattur, 1972), 19-22.

40. Muttucumaraswamy, *Sri La Sri*, 3; Kanakarattina, *Sri La Sri...Carittiram*, 1. According to the "Kailaya Malai," Pandimalavar brought to Jaffna a Pandya prince who built the town of Nallur and whose sons were called Arya Cakravarti (see Mudaliyar C. Rasanayagam, *Ancient Jaffna: Being a Research into the History of Jaffna from Very Early Times to the Portugese Period* (New Delhi, 1984 [reprint of 1926]), 272-273.

41. Tikiri Abeyasinghe, *Portuguese Rule in Ceylon 1594-1612*, Colombo, 1966), 39.

42. He wrote *Bauskaragama-vrtti* and *Sivajnanabodha-vrtti*. He translated *Cittantacikamani*, *Piramanatipikai*, *Piracatatipikai*, *Ajjnana Vivecanam*, *Civayokacaram*, *Civayokaratnam*, and *Civakamatimakanmiya Cankitrakam*. See Arumuka Navalar, *Pirapantat-tirattu* I, 125-126.

43. Mu. Arunacalam, *Tamil ilakkiya varalaru: Pannirantam nurrantu* I (Mayuram, 1973), 105.

44. Or at least those that were not Nayanars. Among the Nayanars, thirteen were Velalas and eleven at least were ranked below them, some "untouchable," but I do not know if any of them had been enshrined for worship inside the Cidambaram Temple by the nineteenth century. Navalar listed them according to varna in "Tiruttontar varunam," *Tiruttontar Periyapuranam...Nallur Arumukanavalaravarkalal kattiya rupamakac ceytu,* 15th ed. (Madras, 1933), 38.

45. Mu. Arunacalam, *Tamil ilakkiya varalaru: Patinankam nurrantu* (Mayuram, 1969), 88.

46. Article nine of the 1910 deed in Muttucumaraswamy, *Sri La Sri,* 96.

47. Arumuka Navalar, *Pirapantattirattu* I, 126-127.

48. *Palapatam* 4 (Madras, 1969), 75-83.

49. The five sacrifices are described in *Pala Patam* 4, 88.

50. *Caivacamayaneri* 1.3, in *Caivacamayaneri. Citamparam Maraijnanacampantanayanar arulcceyttatu. Yalppanattu Nallur Arumukunavalaravarkal ceyta putturaiyutan,* 3rd ed. (Madras, 1912), 13.

51. Arumuga Navalar summarized the social distinctions among those who participate in the Saiva religion in a speech he delivered to the inaugural meeting of an association to rehabilitate the sacred places in the ancient Pallava realm (the Tiruttontai Nattup Patipunniya Paripalana Capai) in January, 1868. The six divisions among Saivas are: 1) the Adisaivas, who are Siva Brahmans descending from the gotras of the five risis who had been illuminated by all five faces of the Sadasiva murti; 2) the Mahasaivas, who are Vaidika Brahmins who have received Siva diksa; 3) the Anusaivas, who are Ksatriyas and Vaisyas who have received Siva diksa; 4) the Avantara Saivas, who are Sudras who have received Siva diksa; 5) the Pravara Saivas, who are those among the six kinds of *anuloma* jatis who have received Siva diksa; and 6) Antya Saivas, who are those among all others castes who follow Siva. See Kanakarattina, *Arumukanavalar carittiram,* 74-75.

52. See Ram. Sharan Sharma, *Sudras in Ancient India: A social history of the lower order down to circa A.D. 600,* 2nd rev. ed. (Delhi, 1980), chapters 6-8.

53. George M. Marsden, "Evangelical and Fundamental Christianity," *The Encyclopaedia of Religion,* vol. 5, ed. Mircea Eliade (1987), 190-197.

54. See for example, "Yalppanac camaya nilai," "Caivacamayi," "Anacaram," "Tirukkoyiliun tiruvitiyilun ceyyat takata currankal," and "Caiva camayam," in *Pirapantattirattru* I, 33-88.

55. "Yalppanac camayanilai." See page 77 in *Pirapantattirattu* I.

56. *Periya Puranam* 6.1 (*Periyapuranam vacana kaviyam* (Madras: B. Rattina Nayakar Sons, [1967], 368-370.

57. *Pirapantattirattu* I, 77.

Chapter 3 The Sankaracarya of Kanci and the Kamaksi Temple as Ritual Center

William Cenkner

1. V. A. Devasenapathi. *Kamakottam, Nayanmars, and Adi Sankara* (Madras: The Institute of Traditional Cultures, 1975), p. 1. The translation is by the author who cites both a Tamil and Sanskrit text. It is significant to note that Vedantadesika is a towering figure in Visistadvaita.

2. *Ibid.*, p. 2, line 410-411. Again, Tamil and Sanskrit texts are cited.

3. *Ibid.* 4-43-8.

4. *Ibid.*.

5. *Ibid.*, p. 4. *Kancimahatmyam,* 31-70; *Kamaksivilasam,* 11, 6; *Kamaksivilasam,* 13-73.

6. *Ibid.*, *Virattahasappatalam* 31.

7. Mircea Eliade. *Shamanism: Archaic Techniques of Ecstacy,* trans., Willard R. Trask (Princeton, NJ: Princeton University Press, 1964), p. 268.

8. The *Cidvilasiya-sankara-vijaya* states that Sankara visited Kanchi and consecrated the sricakra with his own hand; the *Andandagiriya-Sankara-vijaya,* the most authentic biography of Sankara, also repeats this tradition and adds that Sankara attained *siddhi* there. See, *Sri Sankara-Vijaya of Anantanandagiri* (Madras: University of Madras Centre of Advanced Study of Philosophy, 1971). The *Jagadguru-paramparya-stuti* and the *Guruparampara-stotra* state that Sankara attained siddhi at Kanchi (*The Search for Sanskrit Manuscripts in South India,* ed., Dr. Hultzch [Madras: Government Press, 1905], Part III, no. 2146). Also see, N. Ramesan, "Sri Kamakoti Pitha of Sri Sankaracharya," in *Preceptors of Advaita* (Secunderabad: Sri Kanchi Kamakoti Sankara Mandir, 1969), pp. 429-467.

9. One tradition has Sankara placing himself as the head of the Kanchi Vidyapith. See R. Krishnaswami Aiyer and K. B. Venkataraman, *The Truth about Kumbhakonam Mutt* (Madurai: Sri Ramakrishna Press, 1977); also N. Ramesan, "Sri Kamakoti Pitha of Sri Sankaracharya, "in Preceptors of Advaita (Secunderabad: Sri Kanchi Kamakoti Sankara Mandir, 1968), pp. 429-467. Also see, William Cenkner, A *Tradition of Teachers: Sankara and the Jagadgurus Today* (Delhi: Motilal Banarsidass/Columbia, MO: SouthAsia Books, 1983), pp. 84ff.

10. Cenkner, A *Tradition of Teachers,* pp. 109ff.

11. See "Kanchi Paramachariya's Newest Syncretic Hindu Temple Complete After 18 Years," in *Hinduism Today* (May/June, 1986).

12. I will develop the principle of diffusion and circulation throughout this paper. See Surinder Mohan Bhardwaj, *Hindu Places of Pilgrimage in India: A Study of Cultural Geography* (Berkeley: University of California Press, 1973).

13. Cenkner, A *Tradition of Teachers,* pp. 123ff.

14. This is stated by Glenn Yocum in "A Non-Brahmin Tamil Saiva Mutt: A Field Study of the Thiruvavaduthurai Adheenam." A paper given at a conference on "Monastic Life in the Christian and Hindu Traditions: A Comparative Study" at the University of Florida, February 16-19, 1985.

15. William Cenkner, "The Sankaracaryas and Tradition in Contemporary Perspective," in *Third Annual Asian Studies Symbosium* (Hong Kong: 1981).

16. Devasenapathi, *Kamakottam, Nayanmars*, and Adi Sankara, p. 52.

17. *Ibid.*, p. 54.

18. Bhardwaj, *Hindu Places of Pilgrimage*, pp. 1ff.

19. Mircea Eliade. *Patterns in Comparative Religion* (New York and Cleveland: Meridian Books and World Publishing), pp. 3ff, 111, 231, 378; also Eliade, *Shamanism*, p. 259.

20. Jonathan Z. Smith. *To Take Place, Toward Theory in Ritual* (Chicago: The University of Chicago Press, 1987). p. 17. See also, Kees W. Bolle, "Imagining Ritual: Review Article" in *History of Religions* Vol. 30, no. 2 (November, 1990), pp. 203-212, which is a comprehensive review of Smith's work.

21. *Ibid.*, p. 46; also see p. 17.

22. *Ibid.*, p. 45.

23. Sri Jayendra Sarasvati, *Heritage of Bharata Varsha and Sanatana Dharma* (Madras: Oriental Cultural Educational Society, n.d.), pp. 7, 137, 215-249. These are discourses of the Sankaracarya of Kanchi in Delhi.

24. *Ibid.*, pp. 34, 75, 119.

25. *Ibid.*, p. 130.

26. See K. S. Ramaswami Sastri. *His Holiness in Madras, 1957-1960* (Madras: The Liberty Press, 1960).

27. Ramkrishna Aiyer, Comp. *The Archarya's Call, His Holiness Jagadguru's Madras Discourses, 1957-1960* (Madras: B. G. Paul and Co., end edit., 1971, Pt. I, pp. 41, 50.

28. *Hinduism Today*, April 1986, p. 1.

29. *Hinduism Today*, October 1987, Vol. 9, no. 7, p. 1.

30. *India Today*, June 1988, pp. 83-84.

31. This concept was discussed by Wade Daxey, "Tradition and Modernization in the Organization of the Dasanami Samnyasins." A paper given before the Mid-Atlantic Region of the Association for Asian Studies, Washington, D.C., March 1985.

32. Cenkner, *A Tradition of Teachers*, pp. 154ff.

33. The guru-sisya relationship exists in its most classical form between Sri Candrasekharendra, the elder acarya, and Sri Jayendra. As a youth the latter was educated by pandits in the Kanchi *pathasala* and later in the matha. Upon his selection as sisya, he was initiated into samnyasa by Sri Candrasekharendra and for the next twenty-five years was his personal student, always by his side whether in the mutt or on tour, receiving personal instruction. He was able to perceive and grasp the wider teaching and broader institutional role of his guru. On the other hand, Sri Candrasekharendra who assumed the Vidyapith at the age of thirteen seemingly never entered into a guru-sisya relationship in the classical sense. He was educated through the pandit system of the Kanchi Vidyapith. Yet he professes a strong devotion to the 66th Sankaracarya who expressed to his attendants the desire to install Sri Candrasekharendra as his successor but who died before he could call him a true sisya. Yet a spiritual relationship exists between him and his guru who in fact never taught him.

34. Paul Brunton, "With the Spiritual Head of South India," in *Sankara and Shanmata*, edited by N. Ramaratnam (Madras: M. L. J. Press, n.d.).

35. The late Indian philosopher T. M. P. Mahadevan and the late exiled Queen of Greece, Fredericka, can be numbered here.

36. Bhardwaj, *Hindu Places of Pilgrimage*, p. 213.

37. See David N. Lorenzon, "The Life of Sankaracarya," in *The Biographical Process*, edited by Frank E. Reynolds and Donald Capps (The Hague: Mouon, 1976), pp. 87-108.

38. "Kanchi Shankarachariya Tells U.S. Hindus: 'No More New Temples'," *Hinduism Today*, July and August, 1986, p. 17. This was reported by N. Janakiraman of Chicago.

39. Yoshitsugu Sawai. *The Faith of Ascetics and Lay Smartas: A Study of the Sankaran Tradition of Sringeri* (Ann Arbor, MI: University Microfilms International, 1984), pp. 236ff.

40. Bhardwaj, *Hindu Places of Pilgrimage*, pp. 225ff, 213; also Philip Singer, "Hindu Holy Men: A Study in Charisma," in *When a Great Tradition Modernizes: An Anthropological Approach to Indian Civilization* (London: Pall Mall Press, 1972), pp. 127-128.

41. Bolle, "Imagining Ritual," p. 201. Also Smith, *To Take Place*, p. 109.

42. *Ibid.*, p. 207; Smith, pp. 40-42.

Chapter 4 The Coronation of a Guru: Charisma, Politics, and Philosophy in Contemporary India

Glenn Yocum

1. Primary research for this paper was made possible by a Senior Research Fellowship from the American Institute of Indian Studies, 1989-90. I gratefully acknowledge the kind assistance of Mr. V. R. Gowrishankar, Administrator of the Sringeri matha, who facilitated my visit to Sringeri during the pattabhisheka of Shri Bharati Tirtha. I am also indebted to numerous devotees of the Sringeri swami who were generous with their time and help, most of whom must remain unnamed, though I can here record my thanks to Mr. Prakash Bhatt of Sringeri and Dr. K. Thiagarajan Iyer of Mysore. Mr. C. P. V. Narasimhan of Mysore offered invaluable advice during my stay in Sringeri, for which I am grateful. I much appreciate comments I recieved on an earlier draft of this paper from Vasudha Narayanan, William Cenkner, and Andrew Fort.

2. Basic information about the Sringeri mutt and the current pontiff are derived from matha publications (Sri Sharada Trust, n.d.; Ramalingeswara Rao, 1988), a popular chapbook pilgrim's guide sold in Sringeri (Sastry, *Sringiri*, 2nd, 1987), and a newspaper article (Vaidyanthan, *The Times of India*, October 15, 1989). I have confirmed details, where possible, by consulting William Cenkner's study of the Sankaracaryas (1983). Only quotations or information derived from sources other than these are noted below.

3. *The Hindu*, October 18, 1989.

4. T. Ramalingesvara Rao. "Sri Sannidhanam." Pamphlet published by the Sringeri Matha, 1988.

5. Ramalingeswara Rao, p. iii.

6. Ramalingeswara Rao, pp. ii, vi-vii.

7. Ramalingeswara Rao, p. vi.

8. The following is based on several lengthy conversations in Sringeri on October 18-20, 1989.

9. Ramalingeswara Rao, pp. ii, vii.

10. Navaratri is the major annual festival at Sringeri, appropriately so given the mutt's close connection with the goddess Sharada (a form of Sarasvati).

11. *Deccan Herald*, October 20, 1989, p. 3; *The Hindu* [Bangalore ed.], October 20, 1989, p. 4; *India Today*, November 15, 1989, p. 92.

12. *Deccan Herald*, October 20, 1989, p.3.

13. *Ibid.*

14. *Deccan Herald*, October 23, 1989, p. 3.

15. *Ibid.*

16. See Glenn Yocum. "Wisdom Made Visible (The Divine Teacher in Tamil Saiva Temple and Monastic Ritual" in Mariasusai Dhavamony, ed. *Spiritual Masters: Christianity and Other Religions* (Rome: Gregorian University Press, 1987), pp. 175-193 and "A Non-Brahman Tamil Saiva Mutt: A Field Study of the Thiruvavaduthurai Adheenam" in *Monastic Life in the Christian and Hindu Traditions: A Comparative Study*. Austin B. Creel and Vasudha Narayanan, eds.(Lewiston, NY: Edwin Mellen Press, 1990), pp. 245-279.

17. *The Hindu* [Bangalore ed.], October 21, 1989, p. 4.

18. See Louis Dumont. *Homo Hierarchicus: An Essay on the Caste System* (Chicago: University of Chicago Press, 1970) and *Religion/Politics and History in India: Collected Papers in Indian Sociology* (Paris: Mouton, 1970).

19. Sharada is in important respects a unique form of Sarasvati who at Sringeri incorporates characteristics more commonly associated with Laksmi. In prayers addressed to her she is called *mangala*, a common attribute of Laksmi that otherwise is not applied to Sarasvati (Vasudha Narayanan, personal communication, February 6, 1991).

20. There are Sanskrit prayers to Sharada in which the guru is said to share the *svarupa* of Sharada (*deshikendra svarupena*). Again I am indebted to Vasudha Narayanan for this information (personal communication, February 6, 1991).

21. "*Tirtha*" is one of the ten lineage names of ascetics in the Dashanami ("ten name") order, all of whom claim descent from Adi Sankara. "Tirtha" is thus given as a kind of monastic surname to renouncers in that lineage. The Sringeri pitha claims to represent all ten lineages and its jagadgurus have born names of various of the ten lineages (Dazey, 1990, 284-86).

22. Lawrence A. Babb. *Redemptive Encounters: Three Modern Styles in the Hindu Tradition* (Berkeley: University of California Press, 1987).

23. E.g., Babb, pp. 69-70, 183-84, 185, 212, 214.

24. Candrashekhara Bharati, the thirty-fourth pontiff of Sringeri, also emphasized

performance of traditional caste duties; see Cenkner, 1983, 104. Mutt publications typically view Sanskrit learning and the Sankaracaraya mutts as contributing to national integration in independent India, e.g., Sri Sharada Trust, n.d., 80-82.

25. *The Times of India* [Bangalore ed.], October 15, 1989, p.12.

26. Besides imputing immorality to the gurus of the Saiva Siddhanta mutts in Thanjavur District, several highly educated Brahmin acquaintances from Madras have told me that these non-Brahmin mathadhipati-s are also ignorant. This opinion was expressed very directly by a friend of mine. When I showed him some pictures I had taken of the guru of one of the Saiva Siddhanta mutts at the annual Guru Puja, an occasion on which the head of the mutt appears as a *mauna guru* ("a silent teacher" or "teacher observing silence"), my Brahmin friend said, "Of course he's silent. He doesn't know anything." A usually unstated but implicit corollary of this charge is that the Brahmin gurus of the South Indian Sankaracarya mathas (Sringeri, Kanchi) clearly do know something, indeed know a great deal that ordinary folk, including their lay Brahmin followers, do not know.

27. Apparently the Congress-I's close relations with the Sringeri matha stem from the time of Indira Gandhi's premiership. According to a personal communication from Shrivatsa Goswami, the two Sankaracaryas in north India (Puri and Dwarka) "blessed [Mrs. Gandhi's] opponents." She therefore managed to establish friendly relations with the Sringeri pontiff, which had the additional advantage of not compromising her secular image in the North while simultaneously showing her to be a friend of established Hindu piety in the more traditional South (Shrivatsa Goswami, personal communication, October 3, 1990).

28. Vasudha Narayanan, personal communication, February 6, 1991.

29. Gerald J. Larson. "'Conceptual Resources' in South Asia for 'Environmental Ethics'" in *Nature in Asian Traditions of Thought: Essays in Environmental Philosophy,* J. Baird Callicott and Roger T. Ames, eds. (Albany, NY: State University of New York Press, 1989), p. 271.

Chapter 5 The Divine-Human Figure in the Transmission of Religious Tradition

Brian Hutchinson

1. C.D. McMullen. *The Nature of Discipleship* (Delhi: I.S.P.C.K., 1976), p. 2.

2. Ramesh Dave. *The Bhakta and Bhagavan Relationship* (Amdavad: Swaminarayan Aksharpith, 1988), p. iv.

3. C. G. Jung. *Aion: Collected Works of C.G. Jung* (London: Routledge & Kegan Paul, 1959), vol. 9, part II, p. 182.

4. See B. Hutchinson. *The Guru in the Akshar Purushottam Swaminarayan Sect,* unpublished M.A. thesis at the University of South Africa, 1985 and *The Guru-devotee Relationship in the Experience of Members of the Akshar Purushottam Swaminarayan Sampradaya,* unpublished doctoral thesis at the University of South Africa, 1988.

5. E. Stanley Jones. *The Christ of the Indian Road* (London: Hodder and Stoughton, 1929), p. 200.

6. *Ibid.*, p. 33.

7. *Ibid.*, p. 23.

8. *Ibid.*, p. 39.

9. *Ibid.*, p. 16.

10. *Ibid.*, p. 86.

11. *Ibid.*, p. 77.

12. *Ibid.*, p. 16.

13. *Ibid.*, p. 39.

14. *Ibid.*, p. 50.

15. *Ibid.*, p. 69.

16. Dave, p. iv.

17. Dave, p. iv.

18. A. Jaffe. *The Myth of Meaning* (London: Hodder & Stroughton, 1970), p. 42.

19. Jung, quoted in W. B. Clift. *Jung and Christianity* (New York: Crossroad, 1982), p. 22.

20. J. Jacobi. *Complex, Archetype, Symbol* (New York: Princeton University Press, 1959), p. 60.

21. A. R. Fullar. *Psychology and Religion: Eight Points of View* (Washington, DC: University Press of America, 1977), p. 22.

22. *Ibid.*.

23. C. G. Jung. *The Integration of the Personality* (London: Routledge & Kegan Paul, 1950), p. 53.

24. Jung, quoted in Clift, p. 19.

25. Jacobi, p. 44.

26. Fullar, p. 23.

27. Jacobi, p. 119.

28. E. C. Dourley. *The Psyche as Sacrament* (Toronto: Inner City Books, 1981), p. 33.

29. Jacobi, p. 43.

30. E. C. Whitmont. *The Symbolic Quest* (Princeton, NJ: Princeton University Press, 1969), p. 28.

31. Clift, p. 70.

32. C. S. J. White. "The Sai Baba Movement: Approaches to the Study of Indian Saints" in *Journal of Asian Studies* Vol 31, no. 4, p. 864.

33. Jung, *Aion*, p. 69.

34. C. Bryant. *Jung and the Christian Way* (London: Darton, Longman & Todd, 1983), p. 90.

35. Jung, *Aion*, p. 40.

36. Jaffe, p. 43.

37. C. G. Jung. *Collected Works of C. G. Jung vol. 11* (London: Routledge & Kegan Paul, 1969), p. 469.

38. R. Hostie. *Religion and the Psychology of Jung* (London: Sheed & Ward, 1957), p. 123.

39. Abhishiktananda. *Guru and Disciple* (London: S. P. C. K., 1974), p. 29.

40. Jacobi, pp. 113ff.

41. *Ibid.*, p. 75.

42. Fullar, p. 25.

43. Jacobi, p. 88.

44. E. Bertine. *Jung's Contribution to Our Time* (New York: Putnams, 1967), p. 39.

45. R. C. Zaehner. *Mysticism, Sacred and Profane* (New York: Oxford University Press, 1978), p. 110.

46. Jung, *Collected Works*, vol. 11, p. 582.

47. Fullar, p. 30.

48. Jung, *Aion*, p. 3.

49. Fullar, p. 30.

50. Jaffe, p. 42.

51. Jung, *Collected Works*, vol. 11, p. 581.

52. Jaffe, p. 79.

53. Dourley, p. 68.

54. Hostie, p. 37.

55. D. Cox. *Jung and St. Paul* (London: Longmans Green, 1959), p. 250.

56. Cox, p. 252.

57. Whitmont, p. 63.

58. Peter Brent. *Godmen of India* (London: Allen Lane, 1972), p. 290.

59. Hutchinson, *The Guru in the Akshar Purushottam Swaminarayan Sect*, p. 250.

60. Jung, *Collected Works*, vol. 11, pp. 155ff.

61. Hutchinson, *The Guru-disciple relationship*.

62. F. Edinger. "Christ as Paradigm of the Individuating Ego" in *Spring* (1966), p. 6.

63. Jung, *Collected Works*, vol. 11, p. 256.

64. A. McGrath. "Justification and Christology, the Axiomatic Correlation between the Historical Jesus and the Proclaimed Christ" in *Modern Theology*, vol. 1, no. 1, pp. 45, 49.

65. Jung, *Collected Works*, vol. 11, p. 152.

66. Brent, p. 292.

67. Jung, *The Integration of Personality*, p. 3.

68. Clift, p. 5.

69. Jaffe, p. 85.

70. *Ibid.*, p. 84.

71. Jung, *Aion*, p. 175.

72. Hutchinson, *loc. cit.*.

Chapter 6 Rituals and Reinterpretation: South Indians in Southeast Asia
Fred W. Clothey

1. I have discussd this more extensively in the introductory chapter of Fred Clothey, *Rhythm and Intent: Ritual Studies from South India* (Madras: Blackie and Son, 1983).

2. *Ibid.*, Introduction.

3. For further discussion, see the concluding remarks to "Yakam": A Fire Ritual in South India" in *ibid.*, pp. 158-161.

4. From a conversation with Mr. Athisdam, Secretary of the Hindu Endowment Board, Singapore, in June, 1991.

5. From conversations and observations on April 9, 1991.

6. Milton Singer. *Traditional India: Structure and Change* (Philadelphia: American Folklore Society, 1959), pp. xii-xiii.

7. This estimate was made in a report released in July, 1991 by a special committee examining the needs of Indian youths in Singapore.

8. Vineeta Sinha, "Hinduism in Singapore: A Sociological and Ethnographic Perspective" (Unpublished M.A. Thesis, Department of Sociology, Singapore National Universtiy, 1987), p. 164.

9. For more extended discussion, see Fred W. Clothey, *Quiescence and Passion: The Vision of Arunakiri, Tamil Mystic* (forthcoming).

10. *Singapore Hindu Religious and Cultural Seminar, 1969-71* (The Organizing Committee, Third Singapore Hindus Religious and Cultural Seminar, 1971), pp. 14-15.

11. *Ibid.*, p. 15.

12. *Ibid.*, pp. 132-133.

13. *Ibid.*, p. 15.

14. The Hindu Centre, *Omkara* Vol. 10 (1983), pp. 15-18.

15. Reconstructed from conversations in June, 1991.

Chapter 7 Creating South Indian Hindu Experience in the United States
Vasudha Narayanan

1. Pamphlet published in spring of 1977, after April 14 when the sculptors arrived from India and just before the *Mahakumbhabiseka* ceremonies on June 8, 1977, pp. 2-3. The pamphlet is simply called "Sri Venkateswara Temple" and contains photographs of the early stages of temple construction.

2. "Annual Progress Report," *Saptagiri Vani*, vol. 15, November 1990, p. 2.

3. Along with this familiar derivation, a lesser known etymology is also given by Sri K.V. Santhanagopalachari in his discourse entitled "Shri Shreenivasa Kalyanam." He says that *vem* is sometimes interpreted as the ambrosia that gives

salvation, and *kata* is *aisvarya* or earthly good fortune. Thus *ven-kata* suggests that the hill gives earthly and other-worldly auspiciousness.

4. *Sri Venkateswara Temple*, vol. 6, no. 3, (1981 Third quarter), p. 14.

5. The Tirupati Devasthanam at Tiru Venkatam has also helped the temple at Aurora Il.(outside Chicago). They loaned the Aurora temple one million rupees (Rs. 10 lakhs) in 1985 and this was used for the making of the deities and transportation. Later it gave another million rupees in 1987 to be used towards the salaries of the traditional Indian sculptors.

6. T.K.T. Viraraghavacharya, *History of Tirupati (The Thiruvengadam Temple)*, vol. 1, pp. 95-98. It is important to note that this silver replica of the main deity was not the traditional *utsava murti* or processional image. Rather, the silver replica, called Manavala perumal or the Lord-Bridegroom received all the honors that were meant for the *mulabera* or the primary, immovable deity; thus regular *abhisekam* and food offerings were done to this smaller image. Frequently, this icon, Manavala perumal, is attached by a cord to the main deity to show his connection with him.

7. Viraraghavacharya, *History of Tirupati*, vol. 1, p. 102.

8. The pamphlet issued by Sri Venkateswara Temple during the dedication ceremonies on Oct. 22, 1978 spoke about the "granite statue." It is interesting to note in this context that one of the principal points made by the thirteenth century Srivaisnava theologian, Pillai Lokacarya, is that one should not think of the material with which the lord's form is composed. I have discussed this in my article "Arcavatara: On earth, as He is in heaven." However, it may be argued that prior to the consecration, it is permissable to talk of Ganesa as a "granite statue."

9. For a while in 1984 the temple added a resident astrologer, because major decisions in India are often taken only after consultation with an astrologer. The resident astrologer also matched horoscopes for weddings for a small donation. The Penn Hills astrologer said in the advertisement in the bulletin that her readings are "not legally binding"— a prudent disclaimer and concession to the times and place where she was working.

10. From a pamphlet called "Sri Venkateswara Temple" published in spring of 1977, after April 14 when the sculptors arrived from India and just before the Mahakumbhabiseka ceremonies on June 8, 1977, p. 2.

11. According to some local myths given in the *mahatmayams* and in oral tradition, Sri Padmavathi is not Laksmi, but a manifestation of Vedavati, a person who is said to have taken the place of Sita in the Ramayana, when she was abducted by Ravana. According to this version, Vedavati was imprisoned by Ravana, and later, when "Sita" walks into fire to prove her chastity, the real Sita is said to have returned to Rama. As a reward for enduring the suffering, Vedavati was promised that the Lord would marry her in kali yuga. This story is not widely known, and Padmavati is identified with Laksmi in literature and ritual.

12. However, it must be noted that Srivaisnava theology is ambiguous about identifying Antal with Bhumi (Bhooma) Devi, sometimes calling her an incarnation of Earth, and sometimes as the manifestation of Nila, a third consort of Visnu, worshiped by the Srivaisnava community.

13. From the pamphlet "The Historic Healing Stone — L.O.T.U.S. (Lord of the Universe Society) by Dipankar Sengupta, president of LOTUS. No volume or issue number; it was given to me in May 1991.

14. Viraraghavacharya, *History of Tirupati*, vol. 3, p. 51. N. Ramesan, in *The Triumala Temple*, says ten brahmotsavams were celebrated by the 16th century.

15. Before Samavai, there may have been one brahmotsavam celebrated at Tiru Venkatam; it was this queen who established the tradition of the festival at this important center.

16. While in 1988, the Penn Hills temple did not have a lavish Brahmotsavam during the Navarathri festival, it has celebrated it at other times.

17. The brahmotsavam in Tiru Venkatam was filled with rituals over ten days. The processions in various *vahanas* included a large Sesa vahana, a small Sesa, a hamsa (gander), wish-fulfilling tree (*kalpa vriksa*), Garuda, an ivory palanquin, Hanuman, an elephant, the "Sunlight" and "Moonlight" vehicles, a canopy of pearls, silver chariot, horse-mount, etc. The special outfits and decoration of the lord included his suit of flowers, and his impersonation of a woman (*nacciar tirukkolam*), where the lord appears as an entrancing woman (*mohini avataram*).

18. *Saptagiri Vani*, vol. 13, nos. 2 and 3, Second quarter and Third quarter 1988, pp. 2-3.

19. *Saptagiri Vani*, vol. 13, no. 4, p. 3. From p. 2 of that issue we learn that a special "kalasa" puja was performed for the Labor Day weekend.

20. On January 1, 1990 alone, the income of the Tiru Venkatam temple was reported to be Rs. 3,155,000. "The gold haul" in *The Week*, March 25, 1990, p. 19.

21. An interesting passage in Kamban's Tamil Ramayana makes this point very well. The monkeys who are ready to embark on a journey to search for Sita are exhorted *not* to go near Tiru Venkatam, or anywhere near it. The reason, we are told, is that Tiru Venkatam grants moksa immediately; the monkeys may get liberation and stay there, and therefore, not continue to search for Sita!

22. Pamphlet issued circa May 1977, just prior to the mahakumbha abhiseka on June 8, 1977, p. 2.

23. From a pamphlet called "Kavachas for the Deities," issued towards the end of 1986.

24. Bolle, "Speaking of a Place," in *Myths and Symbols: Essays in Honor of Mircea Eliade*. Edited by J. M. Kitagawa and C. M. Long (Chicago: The University of Chicago Press, 1969), p. 128-129.

25. *The New York Review of Books*, October 25th, 1984, p. 5.

26. On this issue, see Joanne Waghorne's "Introduction" in her book, *Gods of Flesh, Gods of Stone* (Chambrsburg, PA: Anima Publications, 1985).

27. Hindu Temple Society of Southern California, Sanctification of the Rajagopuram, Lord Venkateswara Temple, Oct. 1987, Los Angeles, no page number.

28. "Worship of the Lord and Its Significance — 'Tiru Aradhana'" by Brahmacharini Pavitra. *Saptagiri Vani*, vol. 7, no. 1, (May 1982), pp. 2-3.

29. For a more complete discussion on this subject, see my article "Arcavatara: On

Earth as He is in Heaven" in Waghorne and Cutler, *Gods of Flesh, Gods of Stone.*

30. *Saptagiri Vani*, vol. 15, no. 2, pp. 16-17.

31. "Significance of Maha Sivaratri" by Bri. Pavitraji in *Saptagiri Vani*, vol. 10, no. 1, p. 7. Alternate etymologies and meanings are not noted; for example, "telugu" is sometimes traced to *tene* and *agu*, meaning "sweet like honey," or sometimes translated to "language of the south." See Jackson *Thyagaraja — life and lyrics*, introduction, Oxford University Press, forthcoming.

32. From the pamphlet "Kavachas for the Deities" issued in 1986.

33. For example, see "Symbolism in Hindu Culture" by Swami Sukhabodhananda, vol. 15, no. 2; "Significance of Maha Sivaratri" by Bri. Pavitra, vol. 10, no. 1; "Shri Ganapati-Vinayaka" by Swami Chinmayananda, vol. 6, no. 2, vol. 8, no 2, and vol. 10, no. 3; "Brahma" by A. Parthasarathy, vol. 10, no. 4; "Deepavali Festival" by Chinmayananda, vol. 12, no. 3; "Temple and its significance" by Brahmacharini Pavitra, vol. 13, no. 4.

34. The Srivaisnava temple at Tillai, (Chidambaram) is located within the same compound as the famous Nataraja temple and poses a dilemma for orthoprax Srivaisnavas who will not bow to any god but Visnu. Here it is impossible to circumambulate Visnu (Govindaraja)'s shrine without including Siva in the *pradaksina*. Presumably, such strong sentiments of staunch Srivaisnavas are not found in this country. Some Visnu shrines — numbered within the sacred 108 *divya desas* — in Kanchipuram are now included within the *prakaras* of Siva temples.

35. The Thyagaraja Utsavam, though relatively late in origin and inception (going back only fifty years in India) has become a big event in this country. It honors the singer-saint Thyagaraja by singing his songs, and any one who wants to sing can do so that day. In the Illinois- Wisconsin area, it began in a modest way in basements of houses in Chicago, Madison or Milwaukee around 1976; by 1979, it was held in large halls of the Ramakrishna mission, and in a few years it had become a major enterprise. It is celebrated almost any place where there are more than a few South Indian families. Although celebrated on the fifth day of the waxing moon in the month of Margasirsa in India, in this country, it is celebrated whenever people are in the mood for a songfest. In 1990, people of North Central Florida had it on Thanksgiving day in a Jacksonville day care center; Gainesville celebrated it on the actual day in January, at the Catholic student center; Tampa and Miami had it within a few months. The Penn Hills temple has the public singing, but in line with its status, hosts well known singers from India for the occassion. This festival is seen by many South Indians as the main event by which they maintain, preserve and transmit their culture; the reasons for its almost *wild* popularity are complex and I hope to examine it in a separate paper.

36. There is close cooperation between the Education Committee of the Penn Hills temple and the Hindu-Jain Temple, and the two distribute achievement awards to graduating high school students.

37. "Temple News Briefs" in *Saptagiri Vani*, vol. 15, p. 4.

38. "Varamahalakshmi Vratam" by Bri. Pavitraji, *Saptagiri Vani*, Vol. 10, no. 2, p.7.

39. *Saptagiri Vani*, vol. 10, no. 4, Fourth quarter 1985, p. 3.

40. "Visitor's Guide" issued by Sri Venkateswara Temple, Penn Hills.

Chapter 8   Transmission and Transformation of Rituals

K. K. A. Venkatachari

1. I record my sincere thanks to my colleagues, Dr. N. B. Patil and Sri K. K. C. Lakshmi Narasimhan, for valuable suggestions and help. I am grateful to Professor Raymond B. Williams for his editorial assistance with this paper.

2. Yajnavalkyasmrti, Acaradhyaya, Vivahaprakarana, 67.

3. Manusmrti, Adhyaya 9, st. 64.

4. Nannul, Sutra 462.

5. Apastamba Grhyasutra, Patala 1, Sutra 15.

6. Asvalayana Grhyasutra, Adhyaya 1, Khanda 5, Sutra 1.

7. Mariciuvaca, Vimanarcanakalpa, Patala 1, page 2.

8. Mariciruvaca, Vimanarcanakalpa, Patala 1, page 5.

9. Ajitagama, Patala 1, 107b-114.

10. N.N. Bhattacharya, *History of the Tantric Religion* (New Delhi: Manohar Publications, 1982) and Chintaharan Chakravarty, *Tantra Studies in their Religion and Literature* (Calcutta: Punthi Pustak, 1972).

11. Mahanirvanatantra, Ullasa 2, stanza 27-32. Edited by Raghunatha Chakravrti and Setu Madhavacharya in Madras, 1926.

12. Mahanivanatantra, Ullasa 2, stanzas 52ff.

13. Bhagavadvisayam, Irupattunalayirappati, Book IX, p. 63.

Chapter 10   Transmission of a Swaminarayan Hindu Scripture in the British East Midlands

Douglas Brear

1. Kariyani 1, p. 210. References to the *Vachanamritam* (*Shree Swaminarayan's Vachanamritam* [trans. H.T. Dave, Bombay 1977]) are given by the name of the place where the discourse was delivered, followed by the number of the discourse, and the page number in the translation.

2. Gad. I.18, p.25-6; I.39, p. 67; I.73, p. 147; Loya 15, p. 299; Panchala 6, p. 339; Gad. II.9, p. 368; II.13, pp. 379-80, 383-4; II.22, p. 405; II.35, p. 431; II.55, p. 462; Vadtal 18, p. 528; Gad. III.10, p. 561; III.31, p. 611.

3. See the author's, "A Unique Hindu Festival in England and India 1985: A Phenomenological Analysis," *Temenos*, 22, 1986, 21-39.

4. See infra, n. 77.

5. Gad. I.49, p. 86; I.32, p. 52; I.60, p. 106; I.78, p. 161; Sarangpur 18, p. 208; Gad. II.26, p. 411; Gad. III.30, p. 608; III.35, p. 618.

6. Gad. I.12, p. 14. The teachings of Samkhya are conveniently found summarized in the first chapter of M. Eliade, *Yoga: Immortality and Freedom* (London: Routledge & Kegan Paul, 2nd ed., 1969).

7. A composite picture of Sahajanand's Samkhya-based teaching can be drawn

from the following texts: Gad.I.12; II.45, p. 446 and Kariyani I, p. 210. External circumstances can affect it for good or ill: physical circumstances (Gad. II.45, p. 445), or verbal and conceptual (Gad. I.70, p. 130; for the particularly dangerous criticism of God, see Gad. I.75, p. 151, Gad. II.53, p. 458). It is the locus of the gross and evil notions which involve one in sinful activity (Gad. III.22, p. 586). It can be polluted (Gad. I.56, p. 95; Kariyani 2, p. 216-7), across rebirths (Gad. I.35, p. 57-8); conversely, it can be stabilized, especially by knowledge of god and god's power (Gad. II.17, p. 393) but also by enjoyment of those sense-objects which bear on god (Loya 6, p. 261). See the contrast drawn at Kariyani 2, p. 217. Desire for Brahman is related to a buddhi unclouded by ignorance (Gad. I.50, p. 87). The process of distinguishing the workings of the internal organ forms part of atmanishtha, and is not for the early stages of spiritual endeavor (Sarangpur 12, p. 192). On the mind (citta), which reflects or imprints things, see Kariyani I, p. 211; Gad. II.6, p. 359;p II.63, p. 479.

8. Gad. II.34, p. 429; Kariyani I, p. 211; Loya 7, p. 264, n. 1; Gad. II.2, p. 348; II.66, p. 486; III.22, p. 586.

9. Felt, though not actually visible, in a manner similar to the preception of the wind (Kariyani I, p. 210-211).

10. Kariyani I, pp. 210-212, 221; Gad. II.20, p. 399; II.34, p. 429; Loya 15, p. 297-8. See also Sikshapatri 105.

11. Gad. II.66, p. 486; II.2, pp. 348-350; Loya 10, p. 276; Sarangpur 14, p. 199f. In general, it is vairagya and svadharma which can lead to control of the indriyas (Gad. III.8, p. 557), on the method of control, see Loya 5, p. 255; 8, p. 271; 10, p. 278; Panchala 3, p. 328.

12. On the waking state, Sarangpur 6, p. 180; Gad. I.65, p. 12; Kariyani 12, p. 238; on the dream state, Sarangpur 6, 180-1; Kariyani 12, 239; Gad. II.21, p. 402-3; Gad. III. 18, p. 578. Further, if all four aspects of the antahkarana function in tune with the thought-consciousness that the jiva is separate from the body, the dream-state "becomes purified and no undesirable dreams ever appear" (Gad. II.63, p. 479); tormented dreams are one result of culumny of god or of his saint (Gad. II.33, p. 425); disturbed deep sleep is due to the influence of the rajas and tamas (Gad. II.51, p. 455); on the state of deep sleep, Sarangpur 6, p. 181, and Gad. I.65, p. 121.

13. Sikshapatri, 116; Kariyani 112, p. 238; Sarangpur 14, p. 198-9; Gad. I.62, p. 111; Vadtal 7, p. 507; Gad. III.14, p. 570-1; III.20, p. 581.

14. Gad. II.34, p. 428. See the references to Bharatji at Gad. I.29, p. 45; III.17, p. 576-7, and to Ajamil at Sarangpur 9, p. 186.

15. Birth in India in the first place (Sarangpur 17, p. 186 and see Appendix C, p. 667); degrees of intensity of affection for loved ones or for god (Loya 10, p. 267); an unusual degree of maturity in a young person, the ability to withstand any deleterious influence of the eight influences upon the life of bhakti and of dharma (Gad. I.55, p. 95); the failure to worship god even in favorable circumstances (loc. cit.); the ability to maintain the thought-consciousness which, transcending the gunas, can drive out the evil instincts (Gad. II.27, p. 412 and Gad. III.14, p. 570-1, cited at n. 41); the addictions to which various individuals are subject are not due to karma (Loya 8, p. 270). The workings of all this should be understood (Gad. III.26, p. 596).

16. The eight factors (place, time, actions, company, meditation, mantra, initiation and scripture) are independent of karma. If they too were influenced, the whole edifice of do's and don'ts would collapse in the face of determinism (Gad. II.27, p. 413, and see Sahajanand's spirited rejection of such a Jain position at Gad. I.78, p. 155-7).

17. Gad. I.38, p. 63; Ahmedabad 3, p. 57-8; Sarangpur 14, p. 200; Sarangpur 4, p. 176-7; Gad. II.49, p. 453; Gad. I.77, p. 153; Vadtal 12, p. 515.

18. Gad. I.65, p. 122.

19. Karayani I, p. 213-4; Gad. I.41, p. 69. In the words of *Sikshapatri* 107, God "is independent and is the giver of benefits and consequences to all according to their karmas."

20. Gad. I.12; I.41; I.51: Kariyana 8; Vadtal 5. Knowledge of the evolution of the cosmos aids the development of vairagya (Gad. I.12, p. 15; II.1, p. 346).

21. Gad. II.9, p. 368; II.44, p. 444-5; Vadtal 12, p. 515; Gad. I.60, p. 107. The fullest discourse by Sahajanand on the universe of fourteen lokas was given on November 1806 and thereafter incorporated in a letter; it is printed as an appendix to the translation at pages 667-71.

22. It is not possible to harmonize all the terms used. Sometimes the cosmic deity is named virat or virat purush: he has days and nights of cosmic manifestation and dissolution (Gad. I.12, p. 14-15), and his body comprises the twenty-four tattvas (Gad. I.63, p. 114). At other times this deity is named vairaja purush or isvara, and is said to have three bodies: [virat (corresponding to creation), sutratma (sustenance) and avyakrut (dissolution)]. Cf. Gad. II.31, p. 420-1.

23. Sarangpur 6, p. 180. The notion of the cosmos as being the waking state of the cosmic god, as well as that of this god having three bodies reveals clearly the persistence of the age-old microcosm. For the states of consiousness of the cosmic god, see Sarangpur 6, p. 180-1, Gad. II.21, p. 402-3; for the bodies, Kariyani 12, p. 238; on the indriyas of the cosmic god, Gad. II.10, p. 369; for the cosmic body, Gad. I.73, p. 146; for the differences between the jiva and the cosmic god, Panchala 2, 320; for the body as the miniature form of the universe, Gad. I.65, p. 120; for the worship-pattern of isvara, paralleled with that of the jiva, Gad. II.31, p. 420-1.

24. Gad. I.12, p. 14-15; II. p. 482; Loya 9, p. 274; Vadtal 6, p. 504-5; Ahmedabad 2, p. 536.

25. Sarangpur 6, p. 180, cf. n. 27.

26. Gad. I.12, p. 14; Loya 9, p. 275.

27. Gad. I. 12, p. 15; I.51, p. 89; II.31, p. 420; Ahmedabad 1, p. 536.

28. Sarangpur 11, p. 196; Loya 13, p. 291; Gad. II.31, p. 420-1; III.13, p. 567. In contrast, the cosmic god is bound by maya and has his life-pattern governed by kala (time).

29. "Though such innumerable Pradhan Purushas originated from maya, an infinite number of Vairaj Purushas in the forms of various macrocosms were created" (Gad. II.31, p. 421). See also Gad. I.56, p. 99; Loya 4, p. 251; Ahmedabad 1, p. 534; the whole business is so insignificant that god takes no cognisance of what is going on (Gad. II.64, p. 481-2).

30. Gad. I.63; I.34, p. 55; I.51, p. 89; I.63, p. 114; II.39, p. 438. God is the soul of

macrocosms (Gad. II.17, p. 392, I.34, p. 54; Kariyani 8, p. 228-9). He inspires each element in the process (Gad. I.73, p. 147; Kaiyani 1, p. 214) and is the inner witness within everything (Kariyani 4, p. 222; Gad. II.20, p. 399). He orders the karmic process (Panchala 1, p. 316; Gad. I.65, p. 122. He allows time to function (Gad. II.50, p. 454; Gadtal 6, p. 505; Gad. III.37, p. 623). He creates the various heavens occupied by Brahma, Siva and the rest (Panchala 1, p. 316).

31. Vadtal 12, p. 515; Gad. III.82, p. 545.

32. Gad. I.63, p. 116; Kariyani 5, p. 222; Loya 4, p. 251.

33. Kariyani I.1, p. 215; Gad. I.51, p. 90; III.35, p. 619; Gad. I.78, p. 159-160; Gad. I.63, p. 115; I.71, p. 136-7; I.78, p. 162; Panchala 4, pp. 335, 343.

34. This is a delicate matter: cf. Gad. I.24, p. 34-5; I.56, p. 96; I.71, p. 136; Loya 4, p. 252; Loya 1, p. 291; Panchala 7, p. 343; Gad. II.9, p. 368.

35. For the four necessary characteristics of the ekantika bhakta, see Gad. I.47; Loya 6, p. 256; Gad II.49, p. 452; Vadtal 3, p. 497-8; Gad. II.38, p. 436; Panchala 3, p. 327-8; Gad. II.38, p. 436. Three characteristics are listed at Sarangpur 12, p. 191. The ekantika bhakta is further described as the one who has "no vasana except that of God and is brahmanised and offers worship to God" (Gad. I.11, p. 11), as the "one who carries on spiritual endeavors to contemplate on [sic] God in meditational worship" (Gad. I.15, p. 20; cf. Gad. II.55, p. 461), as the one who has realization of God in human form (Panchala 7, p. 343).

36. For example, the question concerning the method for ridding oneself of anger, described as a terrible thing in the satsang (Loya 1, p. 241), worse than adultery (Loya 14, p. 296), and passions is variously answered: atmanishtha, eightfold celibacy, and realization of god's glory (Loya 1, p. 241; Gad. I.78, p. 164). See also, Loya 1, p. 243; Kariyani 3, p. 220; Gad. II.7, p. 360; Gad. II.16, p. 387; Gad. III.11, p. 562; Gad. II.65, p. 484; Gad. II.1, p. 346; Ahmedabad 3, p. 538.

37. Gad. I.6, p. 6-7; I.16, p. 20-21; I.23, p. 32-3; Sarangpur 4, p. 175; Sarangpur 11 passim; Gad. II.62, p. 475-6; Vadtal 20, p. 531.

38. It leads to the removal of that guna-influence which is due to attachment to the body (Gad. I.58, p. 102). See also, Gad. I.33, p. 52; Gad I.61, p. 108; Loya 6, p. 261; Gad. III.21, p. 584; Gad. II.17, p. 393. It "consolidates the convictions as to the deleterious nature of mundane joys and miseries" (Gad. III.1, p. 540); without it, there will be attachment to the body and bodily relations (Gad. III.21, p. 585). It, together with devotion, allows a detached enjoyment of sense-objects, so that no further karma is built up (Ahmedabad 3, p. 537-8).

39. Atmanishtha leads to vairagya (Gad. III.24, p. 591-2). Vairagya develops out of atmanishtha (Vadtal 20, p. 231; Loya 10, p. 278-9); these two together allow detachment in affection (Gad. III.3, p. 546); they are essential attributes (Gad. III.1, p. 540; Sarangpur 15, p. 203), which the gopis had perfected (Sarangpur 15, p. 201). Both are said to be encouraged by sermons and discourses (Kariyani 7, p. 227; Gad. III.24, p. 592; Gad. I.56, p. 98; Gad. II.1`7, p. 393; Vadtal 20, p. 531; Gad. III.3, p. 546.

40. Gad I.21, p. 29; Loya 10, p. 279. Also on Janaka, see Vadtal 20, p. 531; for Bharatju, Gad. I.38, p. 63; Gad. III.3, p. 546; the gopis also had this (Sarangpur 15, p. 201); Vairagya is defined also as the awareness that "one has to leave this body any moment. During the phases of happiness or misery or under feelings of

pleasure or displeasure, this fundamental fact should not be lost sight of" (Gad. III.31, p. 607-8). For its development, see Gad. III.3, p. 547-8.

41. Vadtal 20, p. 531.

42. Kariyani 7, p. 226; cf. Gad. II.7, p. 360. It is better to be an unfrustrated householder than a frustrated sadhu. The state of the householder, after all, is according to god's will, and the householder is such according to god's will (Gad. I.14, p. 16-17); for an example, see Gad. III.29, p. 604-5.

43. Gad. I.32, p. 50-1; see, for the enjoyment of god-related sense-objects, Gad. I.26, p. 40-1; Loya 6, p. 261; Panchala 3, p. 329-30; Gad. II.48, p. 452.

44. Gad. I.73, p. 149. For similar questions and comments, see Gad. I.14, p. 19; Gad. I.72, p. 140-1; Gad. I.75, p. 152; Gad. I.78, p. 157; Sarangpur 3, p. 173; Gad. II.60, p. 470-1; Gad. II.66, p. 485; Gad. II.5, p. 53. On the distinction between levels of devotion, see Gad. I.72, p. 141; Loya 1, p. 242; Loya 2, p. 246-7; the gopis are distinguished similarly, Sarangpur 15, p. 202.

45. Loya 11, p. 284-5; Sarangpur 5, p. 179; Karayani 11, p. 236; Gad. III.7, p. 556; Loya 4, p. 252-3; Gad. II.11, p. 376; III.25, p. 593.

46. Devotional love is powerful (Gad. I.59, p. 104; II.62, p. 474; II.16, p. 388); it gives one confidence in adverse circumstances (Gad. I.72, p. 137: III.11, p. 563); it enables one to accept criticism (Gad. II.26, p. 411; cf. II.15, p. 386); it transforms a person's nature (Gad. I.62, p. 110; Sarangpur 11, p. 191; Gad. III.27, p. 598); it enables one to make up for dharmic failures (Vadtal 14, p. 518-9) and brings salvation even in the midst of worldly duties (Gad. II, 62, p. 474).

47. Gad. II.1, p. 347; II.41, p. 441; III.26, p. 596. Further it is exclusive: there must be no desire for mukti (Gad. I.43, p. 73-4; Gad. III.33, p. 614); no desire to attain atmanishtha (Gad. III.5, p. 553-4); no desire for heavens or heavenly rewards (Gad. I.9, p. 9; Gad. I.49, p. 86; Gad. I.71, p. 135-6; Vadtal 1, p. 492). The last-named can be sent as temptations (Gad. I.61, p. 108).

48. Vadtal 3, p. 497-8; the distinction between levels of bhakti is made at Gad. I.25, p. 37; Loya 16, p. 303; Panchala 3, p. 326; Ahmedabad 3, p. 539; Gad. III.33, p. 613. Worship alone can leave room for egoism (Gad. I.25, p. 37; Panchala 3, p. 326; Gad. II.41, p. 441) and emotion can be an unreliable guide for decision-making (Kariyani 7, p. 227). Rational thought can go a long way towards developing an awareness of god's greatness (Gad. I.63, pp. 112-4; Sarangpur 17, p. 204-205) and once gained it will infallibly dispel all vices (Gad. I.15, p. 20; II.4, p. 356) egoism (Loya 16, p. 304; Gad. II.53, p. 458; III.27, p. 599; III.28, p. 603) anger (Gad. II.27, p. 412; III.28, p. 603) attachment (Loya 9, p. 275: Gad. II.1, p. 346; I.60, p. 106-7; Sarangpur 1. p. 166; Gad. II.57, p. 465) and carnal desire (Loya 1, p. 241).

49. Dharma is crucial (Gad. II.51, p. 456), and observance of it brings redemption (Gad. II.6, p. 358-9); even if the Lord himself were to urge its rejection, he should be ignored (Loya 6, p. 260); yet it must not be overdone, or it may frustrate others (Gad. II.51, p. 456; Loya 6, p. 261). The same point is made concerning bhakti at Gad. III.13, p. 567. It may be remarked that it is precisely the antinomian character of certain spiritual positions to which Sahajanand draws attention (Gad. I.42, p. 71-2; Gad. I.77, p. 153; Gad. II.18, p. 394-5).

50. Svadharma can develop love for god (Gad. III.34, p. 616); it is, nevertheless,

possible to obey moral canons and yet not be attached to god (Gad. III.14, p. 569). Dharma is crucial (Gad. I.34, p. 56), yet it will not by itself lead to knowledge of god (Gad. II.16, p. 387, cf. Gad. I.14, p. 17-18). A true devotee follows bhakti and dharma (Gad. III.25, p. 594).

51. Gad. I.15, p. 20.

52. Gad. I.54, p. 94; Loya 5, p. 253-4, 6, p. 257, 17, p. 306; Gad. II.16, p. 389.

53. Gad. I.18, p. 25; Gad. II.13, p. 383; II.27, p. 412; II.28, p. 415.

54. The tone of the *Sikshapatri* is immediately seen from the repeated words "my disciples shall/shall not" and the text is Dharmasastra in miniature, with phrases and injunctions often very close to those found in Yajnavalkya Smriti: e.g. SP 20, Manu 4.138, Yajnavalkya 1.132; SP 162, Yajnavalkya 1.84; SP 126, Yajnavalkya 2.178ff.

55. For the detailed information on all this I am indebted to the work of J. Dwyer, *The formal religious nurture in two Hindu temples in Leicester* (Unpublished Ph.D. Thesis, Univ. of Leicester, 1988).

56. The AP Sanstha shares at least six of the general characteristics of sects: members are in voluntary association and have personally gained their own faith (M. Weber, *The Protestant Ethic and the Spirit of Capitalism* [London: Unwin University Books, 1974] p. 145 and B.R. Wilson, an analysis of sect development, *American Sociological Review* 24:1, 1959, p. 4); a strong commitment exists to maintain a strict moral discipline which is part of a general 'separateness' (Wilson, pp. 4,13; H.H. Gerth & C.W. Mills (eds) *From Max Weber: Essays in Sociology* [London: Kegan Paul, 1947], p. 316); it has a professional and centralized organization, based on personal charisma (Wilson, pp. 7,10; M.Weber, *Economy and Society* Vol.III [New York: Bedminster Press, 1968],p. 1204); lay members play a prominent role (Gerth & Mills, p. 317; Wilson p. 4); the community of believers is sovereign (Weber 1974, p. 145; Gerth & Mills, p. 316; Wilson, p. 4); sect members practice brotherly love towards each other in all affairs (Gerth & Mills, p. 321f.)

57. R.B.Williams, Holy Man as Religious Specialist: Acharya tradition in Vaishnavism, *Encounter*, 43:1,1982,p. 95.

58. Wilson (see n. 159), p. 4.

59. Williams, (1982), p. 95.

60. *Idem*, The Guru as Pastoral Counselor, *The Journal of Pastoral Care*, XL:4, p. 355.

61. Classes are divided according to the age groups five to nine, nine to thirteen, and thirteen to fifteen; a fourth class caters for those who have been attending for several years.

62. Personal communication from Dr. Dinesh Patel. In this connection the procedure of the New York branch of the Sanstha may be noted: it produces a comprehensive set of notes and questions which functions as a syllabus of religious instruction. It includes "Satsang Questions" (e.g., When was Lord Swaminarayan born? What were the names of his parents? What great works did Shreeji Maharaj accomplish on earth?), "Questions of Behavior" (e.g., What are the five things one should not forget?), and information sheets on the need of a guru, success and tolerance. In relation to the present point, the first set of questions concludes with a set which presupposes a knowledge of the terms

"Akshardham", "atman" and "darshan" and of the concepts of salvation, hell and rebirth.

63. Temple booklet, *Our Aims* (Leicester, n.d.), quoted Dwyer, p. 143.

64. Dwyer, *loc. cit.*, pp. 294-5.

65. Knott has drawn attention to a highly significant development which has occurred during the process of the presentation of the Hindu tradition to a non-Hindu public: increased self-awareness and 'standardization' have become apparent. A two-fold levelling process results in Hinduism being presented to non-Hindus as theistically similar to other world religions, and, to all, as the religion of the sruti texts and the major deities. See K. Knott, Hindu Temple Rituals in Britain: The Reinterpretation of Tradition, in R. Burghart (ed) *Hinduism in Great Britain* (London: Tavistock Publications, 1987) pp. 157-179; idem, *Hinduism in England: The Hindu Population in Leeds* (Unpub. paper; Religious Research Paper 4; Dept. of Sociology, University of Leeds [England]).

66. Dwyer, *loc. cit.*, p. 295.

67. These are: Gad. I. 20, 21,27, 34, 37, 54, 56, 58, 60, 71, 76, 77; Gad. II. 3, 7, 9, 13, 21, 22, 24, 25, 26, 27, 28, 33, 35, 37,51,54,59,63; Gad III.2,7,8,26,36,38; Loya 3,7,12; Panchala 3,7; Vad. 5,11,19; Kariyani 12. A booklet entitled Yuva Satsang Sabha was produced for the purposes of the Youth Festival held in Vidyanagar in May 1990; it contains short paragraphs from the above vachanamrits. (I am indebted to Dr. Dinesh Patel for this information).

68. Personal communication from Dr. Dinesh Patel. The Leicester temple has itself produced a booklet for its yuvuk sabha, compromising short explanations of what may here be described as the basic philosophical and theological vocabulary of the *Vachanamritam*; cf. Dwyer, p. 166-7.

69. Discussed in the young men's group on February 21, 1987, and in the young women's on the following day. See Dwyer, pp. 299f. and 333.

70. This faith attitude was strikingly revealed at a crucial stage in the preparations for the 1991 Cultural Festival of India in New Jersey. Only a short time before the date of opening, and when hundreds of thousands of pounds worth of equipment was already en route from India, the arrangements for the proposed site fell through. What could well have turned out to be a disaster was received by all concerned with total equanimity: "He is testing our faith." Shortly afterwards an alternative site was found. (Information provided by Professor Raymond Williams.)

71. Dwyer, pp. 326-7, 344f., 351.

72. This development reflects the capacity for flexibility which characterizes the A.P Sanstha in matters relating to organization. The imaginative innovations of Yogiji Maharaj have been adverted to, and his spirit lives on in Pramukh Swami Maharaj. In 1985 the balikas themselves — bored with many of the activities of the yukti sabha (yukti comprising women between the ages of sixteen and thirty-five) — requested Pramukh Swami Maharaj to allow them to meet separately: to this he agreed, and the Leicester balika mandal was the first of its kind in Britain. New developments are taking place in India, catering for young married women the presence of whose children disrupts the activities of the yukti sabha.

73. Dwyer, p. 175. In this regard, Pocock's comments on the education of girls are no longer relevant (D.F. Pocock, Preservation of the religious life: Hindu immigrants in England, *Contributions to Indian Sociology*, N.S., 10:2, 1976, p. 355.)

74. Not invariably because ekadashi days (of fasting) may demand discussion of an appropriate vachanamrit.

75. Dwyer, p. 267.

76. For example, a hymn which forms part of the standard pattern of worship at the sabhas contains the following: "O, Shriji Maharaj,You are wearing golden clothes. On your head is a golden crown. On your ears are golden ear-rings. Round your neck are beautiful garlands of roses. On your feet are lovely anklets. In your right hand is a colorful handkerchief and a golden scepter." See Dwyer, pp . 291-2.

77. The *Sikshapatri* claims to do no more than to comprise the rules of the disciplined life of dharma as expounded in all the authoritative texts and lists eight specifically accepted scriptures: Vedas, Vedanta Sutra, Srimad Bhagavat, Visnu Sahasra Nama, Bhagavad Gita, Vidurniti, part of the Skanda Purana, and Yajnavalka Smrti (93ff); observance of the prescriptions of the *Sikshapatri* will bring attainment of dharma, artha, kama and moksha (206). Sahajanand inherits both the traditions of dharma and the teachings on bhakti: the combination of these two, so clear a characteristic of the whole Swaminarayan orientation, is reflected in the names of Sahajanand's parents, Dharmadev and Bhaktidevi.　　　Sahajanand had fully mastered the philosophical traditions of India (Gad. I.41, pp. 68-70 (Chandogya Upanishad); Gad. I.52, pp. 90-92 (Samkhya, Yoga, Pancaratra); Loya 15, pp. 300-302, Panchala 2, pp. 318-324 (Samkhya and Yoga); Gad. II.31, p. 420-421 (Pancaratra); Gad. II.43, p. 444 (Madhva, Nivambarka, Vallabha); Vartal 2, p. 494-495 (Samkhya, Yoga, Vedanta, Pancaratra); Vartal 6, p. 504-505 (Jains); Gad. III.10, *passim*, (Madhva). He asks testing questions at e.g., Gad. I.56, p. 95-96, Gad. I.64, p. 117, Gad. I.65, p. 119, Gad. II.34, p. 428. (Cf. N.98 on Advaita Vedanta). This mastery is clearly revealed, first, in the manner in which he expounds his own position on jiva, maya, isvara, brahman, and parabrahman, the five 'eternal entities' (Gad. III.10, p. 561; these are dealt with *passim*, but cf. *Sikshapatri* 104,107,108); second, in the way in which he constantly makes reference to passages and persons in the authoritative scriptures (*passim*, but e.g. Gad. I.61, p. 108-109 (Vamana); Gad. II.26, p. 411 (Radha and Krsna); Gad. II.61, p. 473 (Daksa's sacrifice); Amdavad 1, p. 533-534 (Mokshadharma); *ibid.*, p. 534 (Markandeya Purana); Gad. III.11, p. 563 (Ramayana); there are also references to Surdas, Narsimetha, Tukaram, and Kabir; and third, in is use of modes of expression which bear the stamp of Vedic antiquity (Loya 6, p. 261; cf. Gad. II.15, p. 385, but *passim*). *Sikshapatri* sums this matter up: "I have compiled this Epistle and have incorporated therein the quintessence of all the scriptures"(204).

78. With the proviso noted above, n. 65.

79. Quoted Dwyer, p. 137.

Chapter 12   Academic Study of Religion and
Asian Indian-American College Students

John Y. Fenton

1. Gardner, Robert W., Bryant Robey, and Peter C. Smith. *Asian Americans: Growth, Change and Diversity*, "Population Bulletin, Vol. 40, Num. 4;" Washington, D.C.: Population Reference Bureau, 1985, p. 15.

2. Clothey, see pp. 127-146, above.

3. Williams, see pp. 249-250, above.

4. Fenton, John Y. *Transplanting Religious Traditions: Asian Indians in America.* New York: Praeger, 1988, 53-72.

5. "Cultural Hinduism" is also the religious orientation of a large fraction of first generation Hindus in Atlanta. *Ibid.*, pp. 52-54.

6. *Ibid.*, 56-59.

7. See the discussion of a "generic Hindu" outlook by Vasudha Narayanan in her chapter of this book, pp. 147-176.

8. Farquhar, John N. *The Crown of Hinduism*, second edition. New Delhi: Oriental Books Reprinting Corporation, 1971 (originally 1913).

9. *The Reader's Digest Great Encyclopedic Dictionary Including Funk and Wagnall's Standard College Dictionary.* Pleasantville, New York: The Reader's Digest Association, 1966, p. 666.

10. Williams, Raymond Brady. *Religions of Immigrants From India and Pakistan: New Threads in the American Tapestry.* New York and Cambridge: Cambridge University Press, 1988, pp. 51-54.

11. Fenton, John Y. and Raymond Brady Williams in books already cited.

12. Assisi, Francis C., "The India Chair at UC Berkeley", *India Currents*, June 1991, PP. 20-23, 33.

13. Eck, Diana L. *Darsan: Seeing the Divine Image in India.* Chambersburg, Pennsylvania: Anima Press, 1985.

14. See the discussion of "self-perception" by Vasudha Naryanan, pp. 164 ff, above.

15. Williams see pp. 230-231, above and Clothey , see p. 139 above.

Chapter 13   A New International Religion: Radhasoami

Mark Juergensmeyer

1. See my "Hinduism in America" in Robert Crim, et al., eds, *Abingdon Dictionary of Living Religions*, pp. 318-21; J. P. Rao Rayapati, *Early American Interest in Vedanta*, 1973; and Robert S. Ellwood, Jr., *Religious and Spiritual Groups in Modern America*, 1973.

2. Founded in 1875 by a Russian expatriate, Madame Blavatsky, and Colonel Olcott, an American, the teachings of Theosophy embraced Hindu notions of

karma and reincarnation. In 1882 the headquarters of the movement were moved to South India. Annie Besant, who had become the major figure in the world Theosophical movement, established her home there as well, and in 1917, after becoming increasingly involved in India's nationalist movement, she became president of the Indian National Congress. Given their interests in Indian culture it is not surprising that leaders of Theosophy would become aware of new currents in Hinduism.

3. Blavatsky's description is quoted in Kirpal Singh, *The Jap Ji: The Message of Guru Nanak*, 2nd edition, Delhi: Ruhani Satsang, Sawan Ashram, 1964, p. 24. The characterizations of the higher regions that Radhasoami teachings appropriate are based on ideas propounded by Nath Yogis, and it is possible that Blavatsky found these references to the sounds of the higher regions in Nath Yoga writings rather in Radhasoami sources. Since the Radhasoami writings were often in English and in the hands of middle class Indians, however, they would have been more accessible to foreigners such as Blavatsky.

4. Hervey dewitt Griswold, "Radha Swami Sect," 1908, p. 193.

5. Most of my information on the movement comes from its historical records and voluminous publications, especially those produced at the two Radhasoami centers in Agra (Dayabagh and Soamibagh), the Beas center in Punjab, and the Ruhani Satsang and Sawan-Kirpal centers at Delhi. In addition, I have conducted many interviews with leaders of the movement. The major secondary works on Radhasoami are J.N. Farquhar, *Modern Religious Movements in India*, New York: Macmillan, 1924; Agam Prasad Mathur, *The Radhasoami Faith: A Historical Study*, Delhi: Vikas Publishing House, 1974; Philip Ashby, *Modern Trends in Hinduism*, New York: Columbia University Press, 1969; and L.A.Babb, *Redemptive Encounters: Three Styles in the Hindu Tradition*, Berkeley: University of California Press, 1986. My writings on Radhasoami include "Radhasoami as a Trans-National Movement," in Jacob Needleman and George Bake, eds., *Understanding the New Religions*, New York: Seabury, 1979; "The Radhasoami Revival of the Sant Tradition," in Karine Schomer and W.H. McLeod, eds. *The Sants: A Devotional Tradition of India*, Berkeley Religious Studies Series, 1982; Chap. 19, "Radhasoami and the Return of Religion," in my book, *Religion as Social Vision: The Movement Against Untouchability in 20th Century Punjab*, Berkeley: University of California Press, 1982; and *Radhasoami Reality: The Logic of a Modern Faith* (Princeton: Princeton University Press, 1991). This article is largely adapted from that book.

6. See my *Radhasoami Reality*, Appendix C, for the sources on which I have based this figure.

7. A. P. Sinnett, *The Occult World*, London: Truebner and Co., 1884, p. 151.

8. The name of Rai Saligram was included in a list of new subscribers to the *Theosophist*, vol. 2, January 2, 1882. I am grateful to Daniel Caldwell, Librarian of the Tucson, Arizona Public Library for locating this reference, and to David Lane for bringing it to my attention.

9. *Souvenir of the Centenary of the Radhasoami Satsang*, Agra: Radhasoami Satsang Sabha, Dayalbagh, 1962 p. 60. A more recent connection between Radhasoami and Theosophy is the publication by the Theosophical Society of a book by I. C.

Sharma on Edgar Cayce. Sharma, who taught for some years in American colleges, was a devotee of a Radhasoami guru, Faqir Chand, and in the 1980s returned to India and became one of his Faqir's successors.

10. *Souvenir*, p. 60.

11. Myron H. Phelps, *Notes of Discourses on Radhasoami Faith Delivered by Babujj Maharaj*, Agra: Radhasoami Satsang, Soami Bagh, 1947.

12. For biographical information about Kirpal Singh, see Russell Perkins' introduction to Kirpal Singh, *The Night is a Jungle and Other Discourses*, Sanbornton, New Hampshire: Sant Bani Ashram, 1974; and *Portrait of Perfection: A Pictorial Biography of Kirpal Singh*, with text compiled from Kirpal Singh's written and recorded words and introduced by Darshan Singh, Bowling Green, Virginia and Delhi: Sawan Kirpal Publications, 1981.

13. Information on Ruhani Satsang and Sawan-Kirpal Ruhani Mission membership has been supplied in letters to me from J. M. Sethi, Secretary, Sawan Kirpal Ruhani Mission, October 1, 1985; May 7, 1988; May 22, 1988; and November 15, 1988.

14. Charan Singh (Maharaj), *St. John, The Great Mystic*, Beas: Radhasoami Satsang, Beas, 1970; Charan Singh (Maharaj), *Light on St. Matthew*, Beas: Radhasoami Satsang, Beas, 1978.

15. An example of Rai Saligram's penmanship in English may be seen in a photograph of one of his letters in *Holy Epistles and Other Sacred Writings*, Part 1, p. 36. Photocopies of letters written in English by Misra and Sinha are to be found in the same volume (pp. 153, 155, 220-21, 230-31, 263). At one time the Dayalbagh leaders encouraged their followers to write to the master only in English, according to a notice in their journal, *Prem Pracharak*, Sept 19, 1960, quoted in S. D. Maheshwari, *Truth Unvarnished*, part 1, p. 177. Present-day leaders assure me that today letters written in Hindi and the major regional languages are welcome (interview with G. D. Sahgal, President, Satsang Sabha, Radhasoami, Dayalbagh, August 6, 1985).

16. The Brocks were initiated by Kehr Sing Sasmas, an initiate of Sawan Singh's who emigrated from India in 1904, eventually settling in Oregon and the state of Washington. His own report of his early years in the United States and his attempts to spread the Radhasoami faith is printed as "The Dawn of Spirituality in the West," trans. and introduced by Bhadra Sena, *Sat Sandesh* (the English language magazine of Sawan Kirpal Ashram), April, 1977, pp. 23-31. See also Sawan Singh, *The Dawn of Light: Excerpts from Letters, 1911 to 1934*, Beas: Radha Soami Satsang, Beas, 1985.

17. My source for these statistics is *Radhasoami Satsang*, Beas: Annual Report, Beas: Radhasoami Satsang, Beas, 1975-84.

18. Although only 3% of the membership at Beas is foreign, 17% of the income in recent years has come from foreign sources (*Radhasoami Satsang, Beas: Annual Report, 1963-84*).

19. The American initiates of Sawan Sing from 1933 to his death totaled 175, and the initiates of his successor, Jagat Singh, totalled 70 during his three-year reign. From 1951 to 1974 the number of initiates grew dramatically to 5,000 (personal letter from Roland G. deVries, American representative of Charan Sing, November 13, 1974). Since then the number has tripled.

20. See David Christopher Lane, *The Making of a Spiritual Movement: The Untold Story of Paul Twitchell and Eckankar*, Del Mar, Ca: Del Mar Press, 1983.

21. Sawan Sing, *Philosophy of the Masters*, vol. IV, p. 26-29. The term *eckankar ek omkar)* is a central symbol of Sikhism, and literally means "1-Om," although Sikhs themselves often translate it more freely, such as "God is unity," or "divine oneness." See John Stratton Hawley and Mark Juergensmeyer, *Songs of the Saints of India*, New York: Oxford University Press, 1989, p. 65.

22. For a summary of Maharaj-ji's teachings, see Jeanna Messer, "Guru Maharaj Ji and the Divine Light Mission" in Robert Bellah and Charles Glock, eds, *The New Religious Consciousness*, Berkeley: University of California Press, 1976, pp. 54-55.

23. Harbhajan Sing Puri, known as Yogi Bhagan, who came from India to found the 3-Ho movement of American Sikhs, is said by some followers of Kirpal Singh to have been an admirer of their religious fellowship after leaving the Eckankar movement, utilizes the teachings of the Radhasoami tradition, and refers to Sawan Singh as one of his masters. See Bob Sipchen and David Johnston, "John-Roger," *Los Angeles Times*, August 14, 1988 and August 15, 1988.

24. See, for example, Bhagat Singh Thind, *The Pearl of Greatest Price, or Nam-Rattan*, Hollywood, Calif: privately published 1958. Thind describes his form of spiritual practice as "the Living Word, the Holy Nam or Surt-Shabad" (*The Pearl of Greatest Price*, p. vii). Much of his book, *The Radiant Road to Reality*, is borrowed from Julian Johnson's *With a Great Master in India* without acknowledgement. See David Lane, "The Radiant Road to Deception: A Case Study of Dr. Bhagat Singh Thing's Plagiarism," *Understanding Cults and Spiritual Movements*, vol 2, no. 2-3, 1987, pp. 20-23. Thind, who had come to the University of California, Berkeley, as a student in 1913, married an American woman and settled down in southern California, joining the American army in World War I. His name is well known in the history of the South Asian immigrant community in the United States because of his attempt to challenge the American government's restrictive immigration laws. He argued that the rules prohibiting non-Caucasians did not apply to people from India because they were of Aryan descent, and were thereby as Caucasian as White Europeans. Thind's appeal was denied and that was a major setback for the liberalization of immigration rules. For a discussion of Thind and the Thind decision, see Joan M. Jensen, *Passage from India: Asian Indian Immigrants in North America*, New Haven: Yale University Press, 1988, pp. 256-58.

25. Interview with Salina Mansukhani, Beas, November 12, 1986.

26. Interview with Dalat Ram, Bookstore Manager, Radhasoami-Beas Satsang Hall, Delhi, August 15, 1985.

27. Johnson, *With a Great Master*, p. 5.

28. *Ibid*, p. 7.

29. *Ibid*, p. 11.

30. *Ibid*, p. 23.

31. *Ibid*, p. 63.

32. Julian Johnson, *The Unquenchable Flame: Biographical Sketches of Elizabeth Rose Bruce, Sometimes Called "The Woman of Destiny"*. Beas: The Five Rivers Manufacturing Company, 1935.

33. Johnson, *With a Great Master*, p. 37-38.

34. Interview with Phoenix Salisbury, Beas, November 11, 1980.

35. Among the more mundane requirements exacted of this ideal master was that he would be vegetarian, not charge fees for his services, and wear his hair and beard uncut (interview with David Lane, San Clemente, California, August 14, 1988).

36. Johnson, *With a Great Master*, p. 37.

37. *Ibid*, p. 40.

38. John H. Leeming, Jr., "Foreword" to Sawan Singh, *Philosophy of the Masters (Abridged)*, p. xiv.

39. Leeming, "Foreword" to *Philosophy of the Masters*, p. xii.

40. Leeming, "Foreword" to *Philosophy of the Masters*, p. xii.

41. Brunton, *Secret India*, p. 15.

42. *Ibid*, p. 138.

43. Johnson, *With a Great Master*, p. 38.

44. Wason, *The Living Master*, p. 12.

45. Griswold, *Insights*, p. 139.

46. Darshan Singh, *The Secret of Secrets: Spiritual Talks*, Bowling Green, Virginia, and Delhi, India: Sawan Kirpal Publications, 1978.

47. Rai Saligram, *Jugat Prakash Radhasoami*, title page.

48. Interview with Emily Sandhurst, Beas, November 12, 1980.

49. Brunton, *Secret India*, p. 14.

50. Johnson, *With a Great Master*, pp. 113-118.

51. Johnson, *With a Great Master*, p. 38-39.

52. Interview with John Price, Beas, November 12, 1980.

53. C. F. Andrews, quoted in E. Stanley Jones, "The Soul of Mahatma Gandhi," in *The World Tomorrow*, December 1924; reprinted in the Charles Chatfield, ed., *The Americanization of Gandhi: Images of the Mahatma*, New York and London: Garland Publishing, 1976, p. 652. See also my article in J.S. Hawley, ed., *Saints and Virtue*, Berkeley: University of California Press, 1987, pp. 187-203.

54. Brunton, *Secret India*, p. 238.

55. Johnson, *With a Great Master*, pp. 24-26. Regarding Johnson's antisemitism, see also pp. 95-96, 147-148, 168. Johnson claimed that although Jesus' mother was "a Jewess," his father was "a man of pure Aryan blood" (p. 96). This antisemitic language is not common to Western Satsangis, however, and some estimate that half of the Beas branch's leaders in the United States have been Jewish (interview with Roland deVries, Nevada City, California, January 17, 1986).

56. This was overheard on a visit to the Dera on November 14,1980.

57. Interview with Frank Smith, Beas, November 12, 1980.

58. Interview with Roland deVries, Nevada City, California, January 17, 1986.

59. Leeming, "Foreword" to *Philosophy of the Masters*, p. xi.

60. Kakar, *Shamans, Mystics*, p. 145.

61. *Ibid*, p. 149.

62. Wason, The Living Master, p. 20.

63. Johnson, *With a Great Master*, p. 25.

64. *Ibid*, p. 25.

65. Ross Lionel Williams, "Master's Love Brings Him Here" in R. S. Greetings: North American Sangat, June, 1970, p. 40.

66. Johnson, *With a Great Master*, p. 26.

67. Interview with Roland deVries, January 17, 1986.

68. Charan Singh, *Spiritual Heritage*, p. 131. Visa restrictions apply to American visitors, but not to holders of British or commonwealth passports. In their cases, presumably, it is Dera rather than government policy that prohibits them from establishing long-term residence at Beas.

69. Interview with Roland deVries, Nevada City, California, January 17, 1986. For many years, prior to Prof. Ivash, the Midwest representative was Col E. R. Berg, a retired U. S. Air Force Colonel from Minneapolis.

70. Johnson, *With a Great Master*, p. 137.

71. *Ibid*, p. 185.

72. Robert Bellah et al., *Habits of the Heart: Individualism and Commitment in American Life*, Berkeley: University of California Press, 1985, pp. 219-49.

73. Bellah, "The New Religious Consciousness and the Crisis in Modernity," in Robert N. Bellah and Charles Y. Glock, eds., *The New Religious Consciousness*, Berkeley: University of California Press, 1976, pp. 333-352; reprinted in Paul Rabinow and William Sullivan, *Interpretive Social Science: A Reader*, p. 346.

74. Kakar, *Shamans, Mystics*, p. 138.

75. Toennies, *Gemeinschaft and Gesellschaft*.

76. In Bendix's massive study of kingship and the origins of modern democracy in five European and Asian societies, the first generalization made about kings is that their authority "depended on religious sanction" (Reinhard Bendix, *Kings or People: Power and the Mandate to Rule*, Berkeley: The University of California Press, 1978, p. 4). In a different vein, Clifford Geertz has remarked that "rulers and gods share certain properties" ("Centers, Kings, and Charisma: Reflections on the Symbolics of Power," in Joseph Ben-David and Terry Nichols Clark, *Culture and its Creators: Essays in Honor of Edward Shils*, Chicago: University of Chicago Press, 1977, p. 152).

77. Jurgen Habermas, "Modernity — An Incomplete Project," reprinted in Paul Rabinow and William M. Sullivan, eds., *Interpretative Social Science: A Second Look*, Berkeley: University of California Press, 1987, pp. 148-149.

78. In medieval physics, for instance, "the entire world of nature was held not only to exist for man's sake, but to be ...fully intelligible to his mind" (E.A. Burtt, *The Metaphysical Foundations of Modern Science*, Garden City: Doubleday Anchor, 1954, p. 18).

79. Michael Polanyi, *Personal Knowledge: Towards a Post-Critical Philosophy*, Chicago: University of Chicago Press, 1958; and Clifford Geertz, *Local Knowledge: Further Essays in Interpretive Anthropology*, New York: Basic Books, 1983.

80. Griswold, p. 194. Griswold a Christian missionary, saw Radhasoami as

Hinduism's form of the gnostic heresy, calling it "an old foe in a new dress" (p. 192).

81. Babb, Redemptive Encounters.

82. Raymond Williams, *A New Face of Hinduism: The Swaminarayan Religion*, Cambridge: Cambridge University Press, 1984.